Phil Jarratt has written more than thirty books, including award-winning surfing histories and bestselling biographies, such as *Home: The Evonne Goolagong Story* (Simon & Schuster) and *Mr Sunset* (General Publishing Group). His history of the surf-wear industry, *Salts and Suits*, was short-listed for the Blake Dawson Prize for business literature in 2010. He also writes regularly on travel for a variety of publications, and has been a frequent visitor to Bali over the past forty years. He lives in Noosa Heads, Queensland.

BALI
HEAVEN AND HELL

PHIL JARRATT
BALI
HEAVEN AND HELL

BLOODSHED, CHAOS AND CORRUPTION, FREE LOVE,
GREAT SURF AND HIGH TIMES UNDER THE BANYAN TREES

hardie grant books
MELBOURNE · LONDON

*To Jackie, who has shared the adventure of Bali,
and in memory of Rennie Ellis,
who was our spiritual barometer.*

First published in 2014 by Hardie Grant Books, 2nd edition published in 2015
Hardie Grant Books (Australia)
Ground Floor, Building 1
658 Church Street
Richmond, Victoria 3121
www.hardiegrant.com.au

Hardie Grant Books (UK)
5th & 6th Floor
52–54 Southwark Street
London SE1 1RU
www.hardiegrant.co.uk

All rights reserved. No part of this publication may be reproduced, stored in a retrieval system or transmitted in any form by any means, electronic, mechanical, photocopying, recording or otherwise, without the prior written permission of the publishers and copyright holders.

The moral rights of the author have been asserted.
Copyright text © Phil Jarratt 2015

A Cataloguing-in-Publication entry is available from the catalogue of the National Library of Australia at www.nla.gov.au
Bali: Heaven and Hell
ISBN 978 1 74379 092 2

Cover design by Nada Backovic
Text design by Loupe Studio
Typeset in 11/14 pt Granjon by Cannon Typesetting

Front cover image: Heading for the surf, Jalan Legian, 1974; photo Dick Hoole. Back cover images: Jalan Pantai Kuta, sarong seller Wati in foreground, 1972; photo Chris Hazzard (main image). Coast patrol during the battle for independence, 1946; photo P.L. Dronkers (KITLV; top left). Wayne Lynch, Uluwatu, 1973; photo Dick Hoole (top middle). Dancing lesson, 1930s, courtesy of Foto Wanita Bali Tempo Doeloe (top right).

Printed by McPherson's Printing Group, Maryborough, Victoria

The paper this book is printed on is certified against the Forest Stewardship Council® Standards. FSC promotes environmentally responsible, socially beneficial and economically viable management of the world's forests..

FSC
www.fsc.org
MIX
Paper from
responsible sources
FSC® C001695

Contents

Introduction: My Personal Bali Odyssey (1974–2015)		xi
Chapter 1	*Kali Yuga*: Being	1
Chapter 2	Blood on the Bamboo	10
Chapter 3	The *Bule* Raja of Kuta	22
Chapter 4	*Puputan*	33
Chapter 5	'Bali Is Ruined'	42
Chapter 6	The Golden Age	57
Chapter 7	Our Hotels in Kuta	73
Chapter 8	*Merdeka!*	84
Chapter 9	Our Mission in Bali	97
Chapter 10	The Year of Living Dangerously	108
Chapter 11	Bali Style	117
Chapter 12	*Morning of the Earth*	131
Chapter 13	The Hippie Highway	146
Chapter 14	Bukit and Beyond	159
Chapter 15	The Traders	174
Chapter 16	*Balinese Surfer*	190
Chapter 17	Rhonda and Ketut	203
Chapter 18	Into the Mystic	216
Chapter 19	Expatria	228
Chapter 20	The Day After	243
Chapter 21	Tipping Point	255
Chapter 22	*Kertha Yuga*: Hope	265
Chapter 23	Be Here Now	278
Epilogue: The Guns of Midnight		285
A final word about some of the major characters in this history		295
Endnotes		298
Acknowledgements		322
Index		324

Introduction
My Personal Bali Odyssey (1974–2015)

The distractions of Western capitalism have reached critical mass. We need to pull in the reins and heal Bali's wounded, overcrowded, over-developed, over-polluted soul. It's up to the surfers. It always has been. There is no place on earth where surfers are more powerful within the overall community than Bali. We must come together and start throwing punches at the problems. Now that is a powerful dream.

Stephen Palmer, surfer

Despite its many layers of crowded confusion, its mysterious worlds within worlds, its dog-shit-spattered footpaths, clogged streets and odious drains, Bali has always had a therapeutic effect on my soul, right from the beginning when most of the above did not yet apply, to the present day, when all this and much more is sadly true.

It started like this.

In early 1974 I came home from London nursing a broken heart. Although the special girl had said she'd wait for me while I had the mandatory year's working holiday in Europe, she hadn't. Her dad, who liked me better than the other guy, fronted the cash for the flight home so that I could try to win her back, but it ended in tears when I caught her in bed with my rival. In a rage, I took a pair of scissors from the kitchen and cut into neat bits the Carnaby Street dresses I'd bought her with my last week's wages in London, then stormed out of the flat and never saw her again.

I took a job on a Sydney newspaper, but then Albert Falzon, the seriously cool filmmaker of *Morning of the Earth* and the publisher of *Tracks*—in other words, an absolute god in the surfing world to which I aspired—phoned

Introduction: My Personal Bali Odyssey (1974–2015)

and asked if he could buy me lunch. At some fancy city bistro Falzon offered me the editorship of *Tracks*, then the most exciting youth publication in Australia. I was over the moon. Within a few weeks I'd quit the city job, thrown away my tie and moved into a rented house overlooking Whale Beach, just a hop, step and jump away from the magazine's office.

Then Albe dropped a clanger. Yes, he still wanted me to edit *Tracks*, but next year, not this year. He'd forgotten that in 1972 at the world surfing championships in San Diego, he'd offered the job to a *Rolling Stone* writer named John Grissim, and now Grissim was on his way to take him up on it. He'd pay me a retainer to hang around and write the odd article, but I'd have to find other work.

I was hanging gloomily around the *Tracks* office one day when 'other work' walked through the door in the form of a loud, jovial, chain-smoking fellow who was introduced to me as 'the Mexican'. David 'Mexican' Sumpter had just made a surf movie called *On Any Morning* and he wanted me to go on the road with him to promote it. He said: 'You can write a funny story and my whole life is one big funny story, so it shouldn't be too difficult.' He was delighted when I used my contacts at the newspaper I had so recently departed to get them to run a feature article titled, 'Surfie filmmaker lives on dog food and yoghurt to finance new movie.'

The Mex and I hit the road up and down the coast, with him gluing posters all over towns while I chatted up the local papers and radio stations. His personal hygiene was highly questionable, but he was a funny man with a good heart and we did good business. After the Melbourne premiere he handed me $250 in cash and advised me to give it all to a photographer named Rennie Ellis, who was a partner in a company called Bali Easyrider Travel Service. 'You need to go to Bali,' the Mex said. 'Clear your head of all that girlie nonsense and get some perfect waves all to yourself.'

I visited Ellis at his Prahran office, thus beginning a friendship for life, and he said he could squeeze me onto a Rip Curl trip, leaving in a few days. With the return airline ticket, three weeks' bed and breakfast and a motorbike thrown in, it cost $49 more than Mexican had paid me, but I was in.

I knew a little—very little—about Bali. In our last year of school, a surf-chick girlfriend had told me she was going there as soon as we'd finished our final exams, probably to live. I was dumbstruck. She gave me an impossibly exotic address where I could write to her: Poste Restante, Denpasar, Bali. A few years later we hooked up again in London and she told me about

Introduction: My Personal Bali Odyssey (1974–2015)

the huts in the jungle next to the perfect waves, the gorgeous, friendly people and the fragrant aroma of frangipanis, satay sauce and clove cigarettes. Albe Falzon had also told me stories about the mystical aura of the place and the incredible waves that he had found on the lonely Bukit Peninsula, and Mexican Sumpter had filmed around Kuta Beach with Nat Young and Wayne Lynch, and he, too, had some wonderful tales.

I still vividly recall the excitement as the plane broke through the clouds on descent and we saw glistening waves breaking along the coastal cliffs to the south and to either side of the runway. And then smelling that intoxicating mix I'd heard about as soon as we disembarked and hit the tarmac, followed by the craziness of the tiny terminal, and waiting forever for our surfboards to appear, and the pandemonium outside as the porters and *bemo* drivers hustled for our buck. I loved it immediately. My ex, my now-you-see-it-now-you-don't editor's job and my whole shitty year in Sydney dissolved into ancient history. This was now; this was Bali.

We sat in the back of a three-wheeled *bemo*, facing each other on benches on either side, our boards and bags stacked down the middle. I peered through the small barred window at the driver in the cabin, surrounded by garish ornaments hung from the rear-vision mirror and roof, jabbering away to his offsider in the passenger seat, one eye occasionally on the narrow sealed section of road, his hand never far away from the horn.

Our unofficial tour leader was Brian Singer, the co-founder of Rip Curl Surfboards and Wetsuits, a new company running out of Torquay, Victoria, near the famous Bells Beach. Brian had been to Bali for the first time the previous year, so he knew the ropes, and this year he'd brought along some of his employees and some of Torquay's better young surfers. When we arrived at Kodja Inn, not far from the beach on Jalan Pantai, the first thing the Torquay surfers did was unpack their boards and start waxing the decks and fastening cords to fibreglass loops on the tail that they would then attach to their legs by means of an adhesive strip.

By contrast, no unpacking of my single board was necessary. It had travelled naked, a solitary 'FRAGILE' sticker pasted to its bottom. The previous year, in my first international travels, I had surfed all over France, Spain, Portugal and Cornwall, but I had never seen a board bag or a leg rope. After we had all enjoyed a warm-up surf in the friendly beach-break waves at the end of the track, Brian Singer took me aside and suggested that since the swell appeared to be rising and we might surf the sensational new

Introduction: My Personal Bali Odyssey (1974–2015)

reef-break discovery, Uluwatu, in the morning, it would be advisable for me to use a leash so that I wouldn't smash my only board on the reef.

'But I haven't got one of those thingies,' I protested.

'A rovings loop,' he supplied. 'After dinner I'll take you over the way to meet a guy who should be able to fix that for you.'

We watched the sun set over Kuta Beach, drinking the local Bintang beer purchased from a pretty girl in a sarong who seemed to glide along the sand with an ice bucket balanced on her head, then we walked up the dusty beach track to the night fish markets where we sat on benches and ate whole fish with our fingers, washing it down with more Bintang. The entire meal cost less than a dollar. Everything cost less than a dollar!

Having settled his young family for the night, Brian came across the garden to the bungalow I was sharing with Bob Pearson, a schoolteacher from Santa Cruz, California. 'Grab your board,' he said. 'We'll go see Boyum.'

On the other side of the track, perhaps 30 metres closer to the beach, we turned into a dark laneway and then right into a candle-lit courtyard, from which point we could gaze into a house where a mixed group of Western and Balinese men were sitting around a table. A muscular blond with a slightly protruding jaw got up and shone a flashlight in our direction. He smiled and said: 'Sing Ding! *Apa kabar?*'

Brian introduced me to Mike Boyum and explained my predicament. In an instant Boyum had issued some instructions in Indonesian or Balinese—I had no idea which—and two young men grabbed my board and took it away to be modified. 'Take about half an hour,' Boyum said to Brian. 'We're just having some soup. Join us?'

I was rather pointedly excluded from the conversation, which was mainly about the great Hawaiian surfer Gerry Lopez, who was either about to arrive or had just left, I can't remember, but I was handed a small, chipped bowl of murky mushroom soup that I neither needed nor wanted after our seafood binge. Noting Brian's enthusiastic slurping, I joined in and put away perhaps half before pushing it aside. It was enough.

I can remember laughing madly about nothing as we danced back to our *losmen* (bungalow) in the dark, me carrying my surfboard fitted with its sexy new leggie loop, Brian Singer loping along in front, saying, 'Jesus, what a first night!' I slept fitfully and uneasily, and at one point, fearful of waking Bob in the next bunk, I sat outside on the porch and smelled the night air, alternately counting my blessings and imagining large animals in the garden.

Introduction: My Personal Bali Odyssey (1974–2015)

I wasn't right for days thanks to the mushroom soup, but we surfed Uluwatu the next morning, my new leash kept my board from danger, I caught a few waves that tested me, and between sessions I had time to ponder what this adventure would mean to my life.

Like so many people in those days, I had experienced a psychedelic mushroom trip upon arrival, but I had few negatives to report, other than that I would have preferred to know what I was getting myself into. Although I had messed around with LSD prior to this, tripping on psilocybin was not to become part of my long-term Bali experience. On the other hand, sharing my first night in Bali with Brian Singer and Mike Boyum profoundly influenced my perceptions, not about Bali itself but about *bule*s (Westerners) in Bali and the freedoms and opportunities this island seemed to offer. I had just turned twenty-three and this was such a cool new world. I couldn't believe how so many things—getting ditched by my girl, meeting Albe, getting the editor's job, not getting the editor's job, meeting the Mex, meeting Rennie—had fallen into place and allowed me to be here, at this point in time. Of course I knew virtually nothing about Bali's incredible history prior to my arrival, nor even the much shorter history of the *bule*. All I knew was that for me the planets had suddenly aligned.

Brian Singer, who is still my friend, would go on, with partner Doug Warbrick, to become a multimillionaire surf-industry mogul. Mike Boyum would become lifestyle instructor to surfing's superstars while bungling dope deals for the Brotherhood of Eternal Love and other drug cartels, before dying mysteriously in the Philippines in his early forties. Practically everyone I met on that first trip was doing something interesting, on one side of the law or the other.

On my third day in Bali in 1974, someone advised me to cycle across the cow paddock to a place called Arena Bungalows to see Dick Hoole, who could organise a fake student pass for me so that I could buy airline tickets at a discount. I did as I was told and went to visit Dick, whom I'd met once or twice on the Gold Coast. A genial guy who loved a chat, Dick distractedly told me to come in when I arrived at his door. I was somewhat shocked to find him stretched out on the floor of his room stuffing Thai marijuana sticks into the hollowed-out balsawood stringer of his surfboard. 'Won't be a sec,' he said. 'There's a thermos of tea on the porch, help yourself.'

At the time, Dick was a struggling surf photographer who needed to subsidise his lifestyle in whatever ways he could. Back then we were all into

Introduction: My Personal Bali Odyssey (1974–2015)

that, even Brian Singer. During that Bali trip, Brian and I and a couple of other Torquay lads travelled overland to Yogyakarta, Java—a horrendous bus and train journey in those days—to buy batik print shirts to smuggle back into Australia. I had no idea, and barely made my money back on the hideous shirts I bought, but if it was good enough for the boss of Rip Curl, it was good enough for me.

In 1975, now the editor of *Tracks* at last, I came back to Bali with my new girlfriend, hung out with Miki Dora, Gerry Lopez, Rory Russell and other star surfers of the day, had coffees and cakes at the cool new joint at Bemo Corner called Made's Warung, got stoned at full-moon parties at the abandoned Kayu Aya Hotel (later the Oberoi) at the far end of the road, got to know the Windro family at Uluwatu, sat in the cave out of the noonday heat with Aussie mates Fly and Hocky, drank Foster's beer with the rising tide of ocker tourists at places like Norm's Bar, and pigged out on the buffet breakfast at the new Bali Hyatt in Sanur.

In 1977 I came back with another new girlfriend, now my wife, and as we hiked along the track past Windro's village, heading for another day of perfect Uluwatu surf, the village kids began to chorus: 'Pillip's got new darling, Pillip's got new darling …' That was when I knew I'd made it. Despite some embarrassment, I felt a surge of pride, a kind of belonging. I felt like I was a Bali guy, an old hand, a Bukit pioneer. I was deluded of course, but I was also enchanted by the sense of belonging, no matter how fleeting, and that has never left me.

Since those halcyon days I've ridden many perfect waves and nearly choked on the brown effluent-filled water of the monsoon surf, tried to start an English-language magazine in Bali, produced, with Rennie Ellis, a guide for travelling in Bali with kids (publisher reneged, too soon), covered royal cremations and US presidential visits as a journalist, holed up in bungalows and villas and written books, taught my kids to love Bali, taught my grandkids to love Bali, leased some land, lost it, fallen out of love with Bali, fallen back in, seen friends prosper in Bali and others fail and die. As much as we love to travel to new places, as much as we lament change, as all old people do, my wife and I feel that we are joined at the hip to Bali, and we will come here until we can no longer, for whichever reason.

So this is not a dispassionate account of Bali's recent and not-so-recent history. The first part, dealing with Bali before my time, a mysterious and frequently scary place where black magic and head-lopping accompanied

Introduction: My Personal Bali Odyssey (1974–2015)

the rise of an extraordinarily rich and enriching culture, is a history drawn from the many excellent resources available and credited at the end of the book, but also it is drawn from a sense of connectivity, that the Bali found by the first *bule* intruders who washed onto the Bukit reefs from a shipwreck in the sixteenth century and were offered food, shelter and women, was not so different from the Bali that became the world's first centre of cultural tourism in the early part of the twentieth century, largely on the back of a bare-breasted marketing campaign, if you will forgive the anatomical impossibility of that metaphor.

The second part closely parallels my personal experience of Bali's development from the 1970s to the present, but it is a much broader canvas than that. I've always been intrigued by the idea that just a few years before the international airport opened and the modern tourist boom began, Bali's village streets were awash with the blood of their own, for the third time in little more than half a century, and who could count how many times previously, in the millennium it took for Bali's warring rajas to develop some semblance of unity. I wanted to know more about those years of living dangerously that immediately preceded the mythology of the *Morning of the Earth*—the surf movie rather than Nehru's original 1950 'morning of the world' description—and fortunately I was able to find people who would talk about those sad and difficult times.

From 1970 on, like so many other long-term Bali tragics, I knew the names of the players—some of them were friends, some still are—and I knew at least part of many of the stories. Books and magazine articles had been written, but I had never seen a thorough depiction of this vital era in Bali's history, a period during which the karmic balance of this Hindu island has been tested by unprecedented growth, fuelled by inconceivable greed.

I decided to write a Bali book that joined the dots, from the Portuguese and Dutch sailors who fell upon her shores and never wanted to leave, through the slave trading and opium years of Mads Lange to the colonial era when fey Europeans and Americans like Walter Spies and Colin McPhee discovered, nurtured and exported the culture, to the barren early years of independence that followed Japanese occupation and yet another bloody war, and the eventual discovery of this 'peaceful paradise' by baby-boomer hippies and escapees from the war in Vietnam.

I wanted to tell all the stories—or as many as the protagonists would allow—and place them in a historical context that would perhaps make all of

Introduction: My Personal Bali Odyssey (1974–2015)

us who were around for part of this realise how lucky we were, and for those who weren't but now love Bali, realise what went before, and what went right and what went wrong, and maybe consider more carefully their roles in what comes next.

This book has no agenda other than that. I genuinely love Bali and have for some forty-plus years with no hope of change. Good and bad shit has happened here and it is all part of the story. For me it has possibly been the most adventurous part of a fairly adventurous life (so far), and my purpose in this book is to document the grand journey of how we, in our lifetimes, helped make Bali what it is, for better or worse, and how those who came before us weren't always so fucking smart either.

In 1936 Charlie Chaplin declared: 'Bali is ruined.' He was only half wrong. But there is always hope. Bali exudes that.

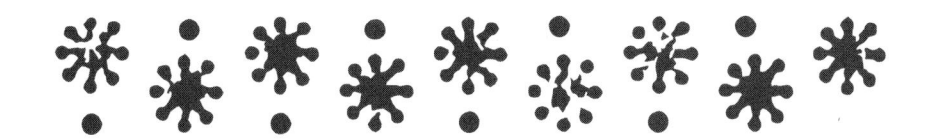

Chapter 1 *Kali Yuga*: Being

If we hate our brothers and sisters we are lost in Kali Yuga. *If we can love all of our brothers and sisters, we have already begun to move into* Kertha Yuga. *We have already won The War against Terrorism.*

Asana Viebeke L

Saturday 12 October 2002

Wayan Agus Parwita, twenty-three, a recent graduate of Bali Polytechnic's diploma course in tourism and hotel management, had a spring in his step as he walked the short distance from his sparse rented room behind a tourist *losmen* on a *gang* (lane) off Poppies Lane II, to the Coral Reef restaurant to begin his afternoon shift at 3 pm.

It was a warm afternoon but the intense humidity of the approaching wet season had not yet fully kicked in, and, considering he was deep in the concrete jungle of modern Kuta and could not see much of the sky, Wayan only imagined that the day looked bright and full of promise. Although it wasn't really what he'd studied for, he liked his job at the Coral Reef, which was why he'd been there for almost a year now, since he'd been given a major role in preparing the place for its grand opening, and now oversaw the whole front-of-house operation. A year back he'd merely been filling in time waiting for his results, but he'd come to like the team at the Coral Reef, he had a good relationship with his Japanese boss and he was learning a lot.

Wayan was also looking forward to the family reunions and religious celebrations of *Galungan*, coming up in just a couple of weeks. Although the family compound was only half an hour away in the village of Cepaka, just inland from the beaches of Canggu, working long shifts at the Coral Reef meant he didn't get to see his parents and younger brother, Made, as often as he liked. And frankly, the tiny rented room, hemmed in by noisy

Bali: Heaven and Hell

nightclubs, didn't have a lot of appeal. Tonight, however, there was a private function at the Coral Reef—a Japanese wedding—and chances were he'd finish early, grab some sleep and be able to head home to Cepaka first thing in the morning.

When he got to the restaurant and started laying tables, his workmate, Kadek, had an even better idea. 'There's a *wayang kulit* puppet show at Pererenan late tonight. Why don't we ride down there after work?' Cepaka was no more than a five-minute motorbike ride from Pererenan. Wayan could sleep in his own bed. It was agreed.

The wedding party arrived from the Ritz-Carlton Hotel on time and the guests were rowdy and ready to move out to somewhere more exciting by 10 pm. At 10.30 pm the restaurant was empty, the last of the guests weaving in the direction of the Sari Club, a couple of hundred metres up the lane. Although he'd never been inside it, Wayan knew it was way too early for that place, but you couldn't give a drunken Japanese any advice, he knew that, too. He and Kadek rallied their troops and had the place ready for lockup by 10.45 pm. He contemplated going back to his room and grabbing a few things, but what the hell, he'd be back in Kuta the next afternoon.

The two young Balinese men walked to their motorcycles parked in the small bay around the back, revved their engines and took off northbound for Pererenan. As he negotiated the bike around the Saturday-night revellers on busy Jalan Legian, Wayan thought what a lucky break the Japanese wedding had been. Normally, he wouldn't be finishing up and walking home past the Sari until well after 11 pm.

It was just after 11.05 pm when Wayan and Kadek pulled up alongside each other at the traffic lights at Lio Square, Kerobokan. At this rate, they'd easily be in Pererenan for the start of the show at 11.30 pm. Suddenly, Wayan heard a loud bang, like a clap of thunder. (His helmet was one of the things he hadn't gone back to the room to collect. Kadek, who was wearing one, apparently hadn't heard.) 'Thunder,' shouted Wayan. 'We'd better go fast or we'll get wet!' They looked up at the sky and saw nothing but stars. Wayan shrugged at his friend, the light changed to green and they roared into the night.

✳ ✳ ✳ ✥ ✳ ✳

On the Sayan Ridge, high above the Ayung River, approximately 30 kilometres from Kuta as the crow flies, Richard Flax accepted a glass of red

Chapter 1 *Kali Yuga*: Being

wine from a waiter and stepped outside the sumptuous villa onto the terrace, where guests had gathered for an after-dinner cigarette. Despite the billowing cloud of second-hand smoke—this was Bali, you could never escape it—it was a spectacularly beautiful night, a three-quarter moon and a sky full of stars illuminating the cascading rice fields that stepped down to the river.

Although Flax and his wife, Judy, and their two children still chose to live in Legian, where their spacious and stylish compound had now been thoroughly hemmed in on all sides by concrete-box development, they loved to get away an hour or so from the coastal strip, to the places in Bali where you could still breathe, and stare into a dark night and remember what the light of fireflies was like, all those years ago.

An urbane, balding man in his fifties, Flax was a Londoner who had once worked at Christie's, but since 1975 Bali had been his home. He was a man of action and, although he had a propensity for calling a spade a shovel, he was widely respected for his ability to build businesses and cut through red tape to help people in trouble. For many expats he had become the island's 'Mr Fix-it', the go-to guy when a friend with no health insurance had come off a bike and needed the kind of attention the local hospitals could not provide.

Flax and Judy circulated amongst friends on the terrace, each watching the other's alcohol consumption—they had the drive home to face and didn't want to be organising their own medivac. Flax swirled his glass and was about to respond to something ludicrous that a leading photojournalist had just said, when his ears pressure-popped, like they do as a plane descends when you have a head cold. Forgetting his counterpoint, he asked the journalist: 'Did you feel that?'

The guests fell silent and looked at each other, slightly puzzled, then glanced around reassuringly at the serenity of their surroundings, before slowly resuming their conversations. And then the phones started ringing, purring, buzzing. Flax dug into his pocket to answer his. It was a diplomatic contact in Denpasar, dead drunk.

'I fucking told you man, your security is shit!'

Flax knew immediately that the caller was referring to a heated conversation they'd had recently over an article in the *Jakarta Post* that had claimed Bali had no security problems, but he said: 'What on earth are you talking about?'

'Where the fuck are you? Bombs going off all over the place. We just had an explosion here in Renon ...'

Bali: Heaven and Hell

The line went dead. Flax looked up and saw people cursing into their phones all over the terrace. He knew enough about emergency procedures to realise that mobile communications networks had been shut down. Whatever this was, it was big. No one spoke much; they just gathered their bags and their children and started to move off into the night, anxious to get to the sanctuary of their homes.

✳ ✳ ✳ ✳ ✳ ✳

Charter-boat skipper Tony 'Doris' Eltherington had had a huge Friday night, celebrating some Mexican sailor's birthday. Six boats had rafted up together in the Benoa yacht harbour and it had gone on all night. He didn't want to go anywhere, but the new girlfriend twisted his arm and they drove into the Kuta Markets for dinner. Afterwards he sat morose in the passenger seat while his girlfriend drove the obligatory Saturday-night lap around the hotspots.

They parked illegally and briefly caught up with some friends, drinking beers at a roadside bar. It was on at the Sari Club later, the friends were saying, everyone would be there. Doris knew that was true; half the surfers in town were at the opening of the Mambo store just down the road, and the Sari would be their afterparty. So that would be another reason to avoid it. Doris drained his Bintang and coaxed his girlfriend back into the car. They edged their way through the traffic and headed for Benoa.

Doris had barely closed his eyes when a massive impact to the side of the boat knocked him out of bed. *Fucking Daniel!* he thought. Mad Pommie bastard couldn't anchor properly and he'd whacked them again, and this time there had to be some damage.

The veteran surf explorer and skipper wrapped a sarong around his waist and stormed up on deck, his girlfriend following. *Holy fucking hell!* He mouthed the curse in silent disbelief as he surveyed the bright-red sky above Kuta, just 4 kilometres away across the mangroves. His girlfriend clutched his arm and buried her face in his shoulder.

'My God, what is it?'

Doris bent low and plucked a cigarette and lighter from one of his on-deck stashes. He lit it and inhaled deeply. 'It's Hiroshima, babe, that's what it fucking is.'

✳ ✳ ✳ ✳ ✳ ✳

Chapter 1 *Kali Yuga*: Being

Rag trader Alison Chester was having a ball, as women do when they have a rare hens' night out. She was finishing up a long dinner with a small group of girlfriends at the home of her Australian friend, Natalia, wife of Bali's sharpest young entrepreneur, Made 'Kadek' Wiranatha, owner of a string of nightclubs and hotels, including Double Six on the beach at Seminyak and The Bounty, along Poppies Lane II from the Sari Club. Kadek had threatened to show up to join them for a late drink, after he'd done the rounds of his establishments, but as the girls had joked, like that was going to happen!

Suddenly, the Batu Belig mansion shuddered with the force of a distant explosion. Mouths fell open around the table. Everyone sobered up instantly. Natalia said: 'It sounds like the Pertamina's blown up.' There was a Pertamina gas station on the main road at Kerobokan, not far away. They went outside to scan the night sky, but saw nothing unusual.

Natalia's mobile rang. It was Kadek. He didn't say where he was. There had been an explosion in Kuta ... The phone went dead.

Alison suddenly turned white as a sheet. Her daughters, Rachel and Emma, had gone off to a huge party in Kuta, the opening of a surf shop or something. Everyone was going. She borrowed the house phone to call them.

'Mobiles are dead,' one of the women called out. She nodded and started to dial Rachel's home number. Someone there might know. Anxiety was rising through her body. She couldn't remember Rachel's home number.

'I have to go,' she whispered to Natalia. 'I'm sorry.'

She was sobbing as she drove to the security gate. The guard leaned into the window and whispered: 'Big bomb, *ibu*.' He shook his head sadly.

Alison felt herself collapse into the driver's seat. She forced herself out of the car and staggered back into Natalia's house. Miraculously, she remembered Emma's home number. Rachel answered.

'Yes, Mum,' she said. 'We're both here. We're okay.'

✳ ✳ ✳ ✳ ✳ ✳

The Sari Club was just starting to warm up when Melbourne gaming attendants Shelley Campbell, twenty-six, Amber O'Donnell, twenty-seven, and Belinda Allen, twenty-three, strolled in just before 11 pm. The 'old hand' of the trio, having visited Bali a few times now, Shelley was in control of the evening. She took a quick look around the half-full club and told Belinda they were heading across the street to Paddy's Pub. Shelley had heard from a friend that AFL stars Mick Martyn and Jason McCartney had just arrived in town and were drinking in one place or the other. She had met the handsome McCartney before and was determined to find the footballers. Amber had her own plans.

On their way out of the Sari, Belinda had to make a toilet stop. Slightly impatient with her friend, Shelley paced up and down outside the cubicles. An explosion shook the building and flung Shelley and another girl against a concrete wall. The Sari Club continued to shake.

'What the fuck was that?' said the second girl.

'It must be an earthquake,' Shelley whispered, choking with concrete dust.

As they lay on the bathroom floor, trying to pick themselves up, a second blast blew out a concrete wall, releasing a searing hot wind. From the rubble, Shelley could make out flames behind it; they stood out in the chaotic darkness. A girl staggered out of a cubicle. It wasn't Belinda. Shelley craned her neck around. She could make out Belinda's distinctive white sandals beneath a pile of rubble. She wasn't moving.

Summoning all her strength, Shelley crawled across the floor and tried to lift the toilet door off her friend. She couldn't do it. She started screaming Belinda's name and was still screaming when two young men shook her and told her: 'You have to get out.'

※ ※ ※ ※ ※ ※

Teammates Mick Martyn and Jason McCartney had arrived in Bali that afternoon for an end-of-season holiday, enjoyed a few beers by the pool at the Hard Rock Hotel, grabbed some dinner and headed for Paddy's to start the serious end of the party program. They had been at the bar for two rounds when a small Javanese man walked through the pub and stopped at the DJ stand, not far from the end of the bar the footballers were using. He paused momentarily, then reached across his chest and pulled a lever to ignite the vest bomb he was wearing.

The impact knocked McCartney to the ground and when he tried to open his eyes he had no sight. Next to him on the ground, Martyn was quicker to pick himself up, but the first thing he saw was a fireball hurtling towards him. With fire burning most of his upper body, he had no time to

Chapter 1 *Kali Yuga*: Being

notice that McCartney was also on fire. By the time he had his own situation under control, McCartney lay seriously burnt, his eyelids fused together.

Somehow, Martyn pulled his friend's burning shirt off him and got him to his feet. They started to move towards the exit but became separated in the chaos. Martyn found McCartney stumbling on the road outside Paddy's.

'Jas, it's me. We've gotta get out of here.'

'How do I look, mate?'

'You've got a few burns.' McCartney had started to swell from internal burns and Martyn feared for his life. 'Mate, I've got to get you back to the hotel.'

McCartney nodded. Inside a minute Martyn, a big, forceful man, had commandeered a motorbike and driver for McCartney. 'Hang on, Jas, you'll be right,' he reassured his mate. And to the driver: 'Hard Rock Hotel. Now!'

Mick Martyn felt his head spinning. He looked around in the weird fiery light for someone to drive him to the hotel. The party was over and it had only just begun.

✳ ✳ ✳ ✳ ✳ ✳

In his apartment at the Aromas complex off Jalan Legian, surf-industry pioneer Stephen Palmer was cleaning his teeth before going to bed. His girlfriend, Hanni, was already asleep and he was ready to join her. His hand gripped the toothpaste tube and involuntarily sprayed the bathroom mirror white as an explosion suddenly rocked the apartment. Windows smashed and the building shuddered. Palmer felt like he'd been punched in the solar plexus.

When he had gathered his senses, he went outside to survey the damage, his first thought being that a gas bottle had exploded at the *warung* (eatery) next door. But down at street level everyone was shouting and pointing south, in the direction of Kuta. Palmer looked towards the line of screaming signs and jerry-built shopfronts that was Jalan Legian and saw what looked like a miniature nuclear explosion, a mushroom cloud rising up from the buildings and spreading.

Palmer went back inside to focus himself. Hanni was up, he told her everything was okay, they were safe. The mushroom cloud was rising from a place very near one of his Surfer Girl shops, and the horrible thought occurred to him that perhaps his generator had blown up. He had a 200-litre drum of diesel out the back. Holy shit! He could be the cause of this. Quickly putting on some shoes and telling Hanni he would be back soon, Stephen Palmer ran out and started making his way towards the disaster.

As he walked in the direction of the light, with every step Palmer became more concerned. Bruised and bloodied people were rushing towards him as fast as their shock and injuries would allow. Soon he could see that beyond the onrush of survivors, there was a wall of flame. He turned back to Aromas, grabbed his bicycle from the basement and pedalled frantically down to the beach, then south along the beach road and up Poppies Lane I, hoping to approach the disaster, whatever it was, from the southern side.

Its windows had been blown out, its roof shifted a metre, but Surfer Girl was still there. Palmer parked his bike inside and hurried towards the eye of the storm. He recalls:

> It was like a football riot, masses of people trying to get away. Straw thatched roofs were going up in flames all over, so I decided to get back to the shop where we had a maintenance team working that night. We got buckets and went down the street putting out the small fires that were breaking out everywhere. You did what you could, but there was fear and confusion everywhere.

※ ※ ※ ※ ※ ※

The immediate effects of the terrorist attacks on two Kuta nightspots and the symbolic bombing outside the United States Consulate in Renon were devastating and paralysing. Understandably, in the long hours of night that immediately followed, with communications systems shut down and shocked tourists wandering the narrow, corpse-strewn lanes and alleys in search of loved ones, the overwhelming sentiment felt by everyone whose life had been touched by the horror—and in Bali, that black night, anyone who had a heart was touched, if not heartbroken, by what had occurred—was this: how could this happen to Bali? How could this happen to our Bali, where only good things are meant to happen, where people are beautiful and peaceful and kind? How? Why?

By Saturday night in the United States, Sunday morning in Europe, the news cycle had caught up. A year, a month and a day since the horror

Chapter 1 *Kali Yuga*: Being

of 9/11, the cable networks chorused, the evil forces of Islamic extremism had punished the innocents again. More than 200 dead, they were saying, in an act of such savage brutality that it had left the peaceful Balinese Hindus dumbstruck and emotionally shattered. Never before, earnest on-the-spot reporters in sweaty flak jackets told their viewers, had this island paradise been subjected to such horrors. The world could only look on in sorrow, the reporters chorused, and wonder, why Bali?

'Bali's darkest hour' quickly became a tagline for all kinds of media coverage, and in public relations terms it certainly was. No cheap airline tickets or beer-included, all-you-can-eat buffet special deals were going to quickly bring back the tourist dollars and heal the financial wounds, and for many who lost family or friends, paradise, too, had been forever lost.

But the reality was that in historical terms, 'Bali's darkest hour' was barely even a twilight. Just four years before the opening of Bali's Ngurah Rai International Airport ushered in the jet era of tourism in 1969, as many as 100,000 Balinese had been slaughtered in the towns and villages as part of the bloody transition from Indonesia's first dictator to its second.

Twenty years before that, thousands more Balinese had killed or been killed in the vicious guerilla warfare that was the struggle for independence from the Dutch. Forty years before that, the raja of Badung had led a thousand of his followers in ritual and bloody suicide to protest the Dutch invasion of South Bali. For a hundred years before that, Balinese tribesmen had slaughtered the Dutch whenever they attempted to cross the central mountains. For a thousand years before that, the Balinese kingdoms had settled their differences, however petty, with hefty doses of black magic and liberal use of the *kris* sword.

As shocked and saddened as they were by the events of 12 October 2002, the Balinese had a strategy in place for dealing with such bloodletting. It was called acceptance, and it led to survival.

They knew this way of being, it was within their culture, whereas the expatriates who had claimed their land had much to learn.

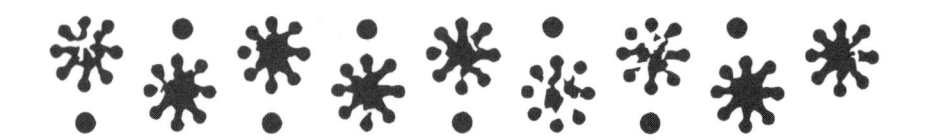

Chapter 2 Blood on the Bamboo

The King of Bali sends the King of Holland his greetings ... I grant permission for all whom You send to trade as freely as my own people may when they visit Holland and for Bali and Holland to be one.

Letter allegedly written by the Dewa Agung of Klungkung, 1601

In the rain shadow of Bali's remote north-east coast (if indeed anywhere can be considered remote on an island that covers a mere 150 kilometres east to west and 80 north to south) is an unremarkable-looking village named Sembiran.

What *is* remarkable about Sembiran, however, is that to get to it you drive virtually straight up a mountain from the coast, through featureless, overgrown, uncultivated land that, at the end of the dry season, is a tinderbox waiting to ignite when that inevitable kretek cigarette butt is hurled from the back of a motorbike. Above this potential disaster zone, on the first plateau as you begin the climb of more than 2 kilometres to the heights of the Batur caldera, nestles a Bali Aga village of neglected statuary, heavy wooden houses, some 5000 people and a handful of clues as to who made the first contact that the Balinese tribesmen had with the outside world.

Bali Aga villages are so designated because they represent the pre-history of Bali, meaning the largely undocumented millennium before the arrival of the Majapahit refugees from Java from the twelfth and thirteenth centuries. The name comes from the legend of the Indian yogi Maharishi Markandeya, who was said to have walked from India to Bali via Java. A blue light led him to the East Java village of Aga, where hundreds of villagers followed him across the strait to Bali and built their homes in the hills. Generally inaccessible, and thus more easily defended, these Aga villages

Chapter 2 Blood on the Bamboo

managed to hold back tribal invaders and retain their cultures and animist beliefs while the greater part of the island adopted (and adapted) a polyglot form of Hinduism that became known as Hindu Dharma.

Sembiran, however, provides some of the very few known clues about Bali's even more distant past, around 2000 years ago. In the 1960s archaeologists discovered more than sixty ancient stone-and-metal tools during digs around the hilltop village. In the 1990s finds by Balinese archaeologist I Wayan Ardika revealed a 2000-year-old stone stamp, thought to have been part of a casting mould for a bronze drum. Pottery shards from pieces made in India between 250 BC and 200 AD, found at Pacung on the adjacent coast, add credence to the theory that the Sembiran area was an important trading post perhaps as long as 2300 years ago, and the starting point for the gradual infusion of Indian culture and religion throughout Bali. But the Indian traders were working the spice routes. They'd take gold and silk wherever they could, but they had no interest in conquering this arid coast.

This was the first time, but by no means the last, that Bali would be spared invasion through misconceptions about its coastline. What the Indian traders saw at Sembiran was the very edge of what would later become known as the Wallace Line, a theoretical boundary postulated in 1869 by the great naturalist and explorer Alfred Russel Wallace, that runs along the Lombok Strait, then north between Sulawesi and Kalimantan, dividing the lush flora and fauna of Asia from the barren landscapes of greater Australia. Had the Indians put ashore at Buleleng, 30 kilometres to the west, they would have been greeted by fields of green stretching up to the foothills of lush, tropical mountains. Likewise, many centuries later, when the Portuguese voyagers were forced to abandon Bali landings by the power of the swells breaking on treacherous southern reefs, they had no idea that a day's sail along the coast would have taken them to protected waters.

After the Indians came the Chinese, then the Japanese, then the Bugis pirates of the Banda Islands to the north, and who knows who else may have visited and departed without leaving a trace. Despite their apparently short stays, the influence of the traders spread through the tribal villages, particularly in the north, where their schooners could anchor more easily, but no one invaded the island and the Balinese were able to absorb the bits and pieces of Hinduism and Buddhism that they were attracted to, without forfeiting what there was of a Balinese identity. (And it must be said that, based on the little we know of those times, a tribesman of the southern coast may have had little in common, other than ancient Mongol bloodlines, with one from the high villages of Kintamani.)

The artist and Bali scholar Miguel Covarrubias noted back in the 1930s:

> ... the population of the islands [of what was then known as the Malay Archipelago] ranges from such forms of primitive humanity as the Negritos, the Papuans, the Kubus, who seem only a few steps away in the evolutionary scale from the orangutan, to the supercivilized Hindu-Javanese, who over 600 years ago built monuments like Borobudur and Prambanan, jewels of Eastern art.

Covarrubias was operating in a time before political correctness might have subdued his simian slur, but despite his terminology, he was captivated by the diversity of the Malays:

> Through the centuries, civilization upon civilization from all directions has settled on the islands over the ancient megalithic cultures of the aborigines, until each island has developed an individual character, with a colourful culture, according to whether Chinese, Hindu, Malay, Polynesian, Mohammedan, or European influence has prevailed.

From as early as 700 AD, Hinduism began to spread across Bali until the peculiarly Balinese Hindu Dharma became the predominant culture. This was a slow process, but because the influences came from Hindu East Java rather than from India, just across a 2-kilometre strait, they were constant, and by the end of the first millennium, the Indian concept of the God-King was entrenched across Bali.

Although the God-Kings of Bali were pretty much left to their own devices for a few centuries, in 1343 the aggressive general of Java's Hindu Majapahit Empire, Gadjah Mada, imposed his rule over Bali, meeting only minor resistance. The island became a province under the rule of a Majapahit governor, who soon promoted himself to the title of Dewa Agung (Great Deity), becoming the first in a long line of hereditary rulers. This rule by divine right was flung into confusion, however, when in 1515 the Majapahit Empire was overthrown by the Islamic Mataram Empire. The influence

Chapter 2 Blood on the Bamboo

of Islam had been growing in Java since the twelfth century, they had the numbers and the support of the common people, and the surviving Majapahit leaders, warriors, priests and scholars were forced across the strait into exile in Bali.

Although they differ on exactly who did what and when, Bali scholars generally agree that this exile of Majapahit's 'best and brightest' ushered in a 'Golden Age', a period in which Bali was united and its Hindu religion and culture flourished. At the centre of Bali's unification was the notion that the Dewa Agung, now installed in his court at Gelgel, was not only the sole rightful ruler of Bali, but of the world. This was not as extravagant a claim as it sounds, since the Balinese knew of other worlds, such as Java and Makassar, but did not consider them part of their own. The concept of a world ruled from Gelgel was the foundation stone of a united Bali, and it worked just fine as long as the World Ruler was a reasonable man, which he often was not.

Gelgel, in the verdant foothills of the east-coast hinterland, had been developed into Bali's centre of government, culture and commerce, and at its heart was a spectacular palace whose architecture, gardens and animal menagerie were designed to symbolise the entire world over which the incumbent held sway. Equally symbolic were the cells and courtyards that housed the royal slaves and concubines, while other quarters held misshapen albino dwarves who were periodically put on display to demonstrate the frightening diversity of humankind in the places that lay beyond Bali's civilised world. A simple agrarian and artisan society, with no mineral wealth it was aware of nor treasures to be traded, Bali's incredible trappings of courtly riches had been imported and could only be maintained by keeping the vast majority of people in servitude while the tiny minority lived it up in the royal court. At this time it has been estimated that only about 1000 Balinese enjoyed the favours of the court, while some 300,000 struggled through the Golden Age with barely enough to eat.

Although the Majapahit influences had sown the seeds of contemporary Balinese culture, the Gelgel freak show of the World Ruler was not destined to last. At the apex of the Golden Age, Bali controlled Blambangan (now Banyuwangi) in East Java, and the islands of Sumbawa and Lombok on its other flank, but the expansionist Dewa Agung, Raja Bekung, waged war on East Java and lost, then his heir forfeited Sumbawa and Lombok, and Bali's regency princes rebelled against Gelgel rule. In a last-ditch attempt to restore order, Gusti Sideman, last man in for the Dewa Agung team, built a new palace in Klungkung to symbolise a fresh start, but it was not far enough away in distance or in concept to save the dynasty.

The World Ruler of Bali became the World Ruler of Klungkung, specialising in pomp and ceremony, much like modern monarchs, but ceding control of the island to about a dozen rajadoms, or regencies, of which eight survive today. This transformation of Bali to a more representative form of feudalism coincided with the beginnings of the age of exploration, and the arrival of the European colonists and fortune hunters.

※ ※ ※ ※ ※ ※

The spice trade had become one of the most important and lucrative in the world, with magical, mystical and miraculous properties claimed for such everyday commodities as nutmeg (said to both cure the plague and sustain an erection), black pepper, cinnamon, ginger and the like, but most importantly in those times before cold storage, spices could make bad food bearable. However, the Eastern spice trade had been controlled by Arab traders since the rise of Islam in the seventh century, and it wasn't until Portuguese navigator Vasco da Gama in 1498 established the route to the East via the Cape of Good Hope that Europe began to dominate Eastern trade and colonisation. The Iberians led the way, but England and Holland were not far behind, and when Sir Francis Drake sailed through the Spice Islands in 1579, it is possible he became the first European to set foot on Bali. The Magellan expedition (1519–22) had identified an island that may well have been Bali as 'Java Minor', and the mid-century Spanish mariners actually put it on their charts as 'Bale' and 'Boly', but no one was tempted onto its perilous coast when their mission was to head further north to the Moluccas group and load their ships with precious spices.

The Portuguese made the first attempt to establish a fort and trading post on Bali. In 1585 the colonial government in the capital, Malacca, sent an armed ship laden with men, building materials and goods to trade, south to the small island, where it foundered on the reefs of the Bukit Peninsula, Bali's most southerly point, presumably while looking for a safe landing on the southern coast. Most of the ship's company perished, but five seamen made it to shore on the unforgiving plateau and, in a second miracle in quick succession, they were discovered and taken to the court of the Dewa Agung,

Chapter 2 Blood on the Bamboo

who put them under house arrest but in comfortable houses of their own, furnished with everything they needed, including wives.

If these five survivors can be regarded as the first Western or *bule* residents of Bali, then the treatment they apparently received established a pattern of acceptance and hospitality that continues, in most aspects, to this day. But there is only one report as to how they fared in Bali. Twelve years later, when the Dutch expeditionary fleet, under the dubious command of Cornelis de Houtman, landed off Padangbai on the east coast, not far from Gelgel and Klungkung, their reports included an encounter with a Portuguese survivor, one Pedro de Noronha, who told them that while he had first yearned to return to Malacca, he had grown accustomed to his life on Bali, where he had the comfort of a wife and two children.

Houtman, by all accounts, was a piece of work. He did not start out as commander of the fleet, but after a two-year eastward voyage—during which time haggling over price saw no trading completed and more than one hundred Spice Islanders slaughtered, and all of Houtman's superiors had mysteriously disappeared, along with three-quarters of the fleet's company and one of its ships—he arrived in Bali light on men but full of bravado. Despite his questionable report card, Houtman was a tourist at heart and immediately fell in love with Bali, or at least the majestic view of it from his anchorage, and he renamed it 'Young Holland'.

But Houtman was not one of the four-man party sent ashore to negotiate a trading agreement, presumably regarding his safety as more important than matters of commerce. Indeed, the Dutch took the precaution of holding the same number of Balinese hostage, to guarantee the safe return of their men, and over the duration of their stay, Houtman stepped ashore only once, for a matter of hours. Baturenggong, the Dewa Agung, was temporarily in residence in the port of Kuta, where he was preparing an expeditionary force to sail to Java and regain Blambangan, captured by the Mataram, when the *Hollandia* dropped anchor inside the reef and the shore party rowed in. As busy as he undoubtedly was, the World Ruler made time for the Dutchmen, providing temporary wives, sustenance and hunting trips. One of the party later reported that they 'drank from vessels of gold'; an illustration in the phenomenally successful published journal of the Houtman expedition showed the World Ruler riding in an ox-cart, under the shade of an umbrella held by a slave, while spear-carrying royal guards formed a protective outrider. Thus the other world's first detailed account of Bali's 'heathen kingdom' was a positive one, particularly when contrasted with Houtman's bloody encounters in the Islamic sultanates of the East.

When the Houtman fleet left Bali for the return voyage to 'Old' Holland (with 245 bags of pepper, 45 tonnes of nutmeg and thirty bales of mace in the hold—just enough to allow the expedition to break even), it did so minus three members of the shore party, who elected to stay in the service of the Dewa Agung and make their lives in Bali, where they learned the language, took permanent wives and became accepted in the ruler's court. When the Heemskerck expedition arrived in 1601, two of these men were employed as translators and advisers. Nothing is known of the fate of the third. Already the idea of the *bule* getting happily lost in Bali was established.

These Dutch adventures signalled the beginning of the era of the Dutch East India Company, or Vereenigde Oostindische Compagnie (VOC), in 1602 given a twenty-one-year licence by the Dutch Government to monopolise the spice trade and basically do as it saw fit in order to achieve that goal, reporting on its activities every ten years. The VOC was the world's first public company, with some 1800 shareholders taking up its initial offering, but only about 200 major shareholders exerting any control over its vast operations. VOC's giant shipyards made Amsterdam the key commercial hub of Europe, and in Asia the company built up a vast network of bases and warehouses, controlled from 1619 by the VOC headquarters and fortress in the Javanese city of Jakarta.

Part of the brief of the VOC was to wipe out Portuguese and English interests in the region, resulting in more than a decade of bloody warfare on the high seas, culminating in the sacking of Jakarta and the creation of the Dutch-style city of Batavia in its place, and the virtual genocide of the Bandanese islanders in order to take the tiny British-held outposts of Run and Ai at the edges of their group of islands.

This bloodthirsty takeover of the Spice Islands was achieved thanks in large part to the brutal command of Jan Pieterszoon Coen, who became governor-general of Batavia and built a huge fort with workshops, warehouses and residences for company staff. Around this a city grew which was, in turn, surrounded by a perimeter wall. As governor-general, Coen was the highest VOC official in the East Indies. He chaired the Council of the Indies, the executive committee that made all regional decisions.

While the board of the VOC in Holland had mixed opinions about genocide (Coen himself dismissed the slaughter of 15,000 Bandanese with,

Chapter 2 Blood on the Bamboo

'They are an indolent people of whom little good can be expected'), slavery (Coen bragged that the remaining British in Banda were so impoverished by his raids that they 'had to sell their whores' for food), and the desecration of cultures, they were very much in favour of Coen's strategy of building a trade network within Asia itself that would generate enough profit to pay for the ongoing purchase and shipment of spices to Europe. Since an exchange of letters between Batavia and Amsterdam took almost two years, the primary product base of Coen's Asian trade network—slaves and opium—was well established (and hugely profitable) before the board was shown the fine detail. When it did finally become aware of the legal but morally questionable business in which it was engaged, the VOC ordered Coen to disengage immediately, which is to say within a handful of years, by which time Coen had such enormous personal wealth that he gladly handed off the business to favoured independent traders outside Batavia Castle.

As it happened, the best source of slaves was Bali and the Balinese courts had developed a taste for opium. Here there was business to be done. What little was known of Bali in Europe, most of it from the publication of the journal of the Houtman expedition, was hypnotically exotic. It seemed to be a wealthy land where food was plentiful and beautiful, naked women existed for little else than pleasuring their menfolk. The European fascination with the Hindu practice of *suttee*, or the burning of widows, which had already been observed in India, became imbued with more sexual overtones after the Houtman journal reported on the sacrifice of twenty-two female slaves, who teased onlookers by slashing themselves with a ceremonial *kris* sword and smearing blood on their lips and foreheads before handing back the sword to the executioner for the fatal piercing of the heart. Of course it was understood that they were slaves, but surely women who so playfully submitted to such sacrifice would deny a man nothing in bed. Compared with their strict Protestant morality at home, the Dutch found their idea of Bali, however misguided it may have been, totally intoxicating.

The Balinese had been slave trading since the tenth century, but the VOC turned it into an industry. A slave could be traded overseas for as much as ten times his or her value at home, and there was no shortage of stock because the rajas had the traditional right to enslave and sell any person who was 'an encumbrance or an embarrassment to the state', a description that covered criminals, orphans, debtors and the families of men who had died without leaving sufficient support. This was seen as a policy of tough love, ensuring no one was a burden on the state and each paid his own way.

Batavia became the principal market, but Balinese slaves, both men and women, were highly valued throughout the East, with as many as 500 of them filling cargo holds bound for French Mauritius and Bourbon (Reunion). By the middle of the seventeenth century, Balinese slaves constituted more than half of Batavia's slave population of 15,000, and the Balinese export market was around 2000 a year. While the VOC had effectively bypassed the island on its spice-trade routes, the alternative human-trade route between Bali and Batavia became extremely lucrative for both sides.

At the same time, the Dutch began to see Hindu Bali as an important ally in the eastern archipelago, because both hated the Islamic kingdoms with equal venom. But this did not mean that the merchant-funded Dutch forces were going to answer the Dewa Agung's appeals for military help. They were too busy shipping opium and slaves and protecting their trade routes from the rampant piracy that grew as tales of Spice Islands wealth circulated around the known world. The English, on the other hand, who had little to thank the Dutch for in the Indies, were happy to supply the rajas with weapons to fight the Islamic Javanese, and the northern port of Buleleng became the centre of Anglo–Balinese plotting against the Dutch and, more particularly, the VOC.

Balinese male slaves began to get a bad reputation amongst the Dutch for quite reasonably 'running *amuk*' (a Malay word for dangerous and violent behaviour that soon got currency in Europe) during the long, cramped ocean voyages to their new places of enslavement. Jan Troet, one of the cruellest and best-known slavers in the archipelago, protested bitterly to the VOC after a boatload of slaves had run *amuk* and taken his ship, leaving him stranded in Sumatra. While it is difficult now to feel any sympathy for a brutal slaver, Troet's reports horrified Dutch officials and added substance to the growing view in Holland that Bali was a dangerous place that should be avoided.

By the end of the eighteenth century, Dutch colonialism was well established throughout the East Indies (although not on Bali) and the VOC had outlived its usefulness and become something of an international embarrassment. The world economy was changing rapidly, and the Company was on the verge of bankruptcy, so the Dutch government formally dissolved it in 1800 and took over the running of the Dutch East Indies itself, but only until the Netherlands fell to Napoleon in 1808, when a representative of

Chapter 2 Blood on the Bamboo

the emperor was sent to take command. One of the first acts of the French governor-general was to send an agent to Bali to negotiate a contract with the raja of Badung for the supply of slaves to help defend Batavia.

Meanwhile, however, the British and the Dutch had resolved their differences in the face of their joint concern about Napoleonic expansion, and in 1811 the Dutch government in exile in London sent a representative of the Calcutta-based English East India Company to take over as lieutenant governor. Thomas Stamford Raffles was just thirty, but he already had an impressive record as a thinking man's colonialist, and energetically set about creating a prosperous free-market economy throughout the Indies, including Bali, for which he developed a special affection.

Raffles was only in the East Indies for five years before the Dutch reclaimed it, but he made an indelible mark in Bali, establishing its importance as a museum of ancient Javanese culture, 'its laws, ideas and worship', and giving recognition to the solid community structure of the villages that remained strong despite the despotic rule of the rajas. In his 1817 magnum opus, *History of Java*, Raffles wrote of the 800,000 Balinese:

> Neither degraded by oppression nor enervated by habits of indolence or luxury, they perhaps promise fairer for a progress in civilisation than any of their neighbours. They are strangers to the vices of drunkenness, libertinism and conjugal infidelity: their predominant passions are gaming and cock fighting. In these amusements, when at peace with the neighbouring states, all the vehemence and energy of their character and spirit is called forth and exhausted. Their energy, their modes of life, and their love of independence, render them formidable to the weaker states in their neighbourhood, and secure them against all attacks from any native power in the Indian archipelago.

Elsewhere, Raffles noted that while Bali was way behind Java in the field of the arts, its agriculture was highly efficient, with the rice fields, fed by clever irrigation systems from streams and rivers, yielding two crops a year and maize in the dry season.

> Though the island produces cotton of the most excellent quality, the natives have not generally learned the art of

Bali: Heaven and Hell

painting or printing the cloth … Their principal manufacture
is in *kris*es and warlike instruments; they make fire-arms
and ornament the barrels, but purchase European locks.

Balinese exports included rice, cotton yarn, salted eggs and oil, while imports included betelnut, ivory, gold, silver and opium, 'to which the inhabitants are unfortunately much addicted'.

Raffles had championed the notion of the Balinese as noble savages, but as soon as he left and the Dutch returned, they were regarded as just savages again, and uncontrollable ones at that. Raffles was furious about being deposed, and the Dutch believed he was about to make his own attempt to colonise Bali for the British. In fact, his eyes had already fallen upon the Malay Peninsula and the island of Singapore, but the Netherlands government acted quickly in sending a delegation to establish formal contact with the Balinese rajas and get them to sign a 'contract' authorising Dutch control. The Dutch mission was headed up by H.A. Van Den Broek, a taxation official who was accompanied by twenty armed guards as he trooped from regency to regency. He expected some support from the raja of Buleleng, who had asked Batavia for arms and rice to relieve famine on the northern coast, occasioned, he claimed, by British attempts to stamp out his livelihood from the slave trade. When Batavia came to his aid with a shipload of guns and rice, the raja sent three slave girls in payment.

But by the time Van Den Broek reached Bali, Buleleng and Karangasem were at war and the other rajas had aligned themselves with one side or the other. With no hope of getting consensus on his contract concept now, the civil servant became increasingly belligerent at court and the Balinese refused to have anything to do with him. Meanwhile, the raja of Buleleng stepped up his involvement with the slave trade, at one point allowing up to ninety pirate slave boats to use his small harbour in return for a substantial tax on their opium cargo.

While the Dutch kept their distance, Bali flourished in the 1820s and 1830s, with trade increasing dramatically, particularly with the Raffles-created British colony of Singapore. Once more afraid of a British takeover, the Dutch renewed their attempts to get the rajas to sign up to sovereignty, or at least to trade regulations that would protect Dutch monopolies. This time they used the old Gelgel concept of World Ruler to get the other rajas to fall in line with the Dewa Agung of Klungkung. But the rajas claimed

Chapter 2 Blood on the Bamboo

they had never actually signed such an agreement and continued to ignore its existence. For the Dutch, this was further proof of the treachery of the dope-addled Balinese despots, and they considered that a binding agreement with the rajas was in place, and could be used to control Bali in the future.

That solved, they turned their attention to the vexing problem of a Danish trader who had thumbed his nose at all bureaucratic attempts at control of Bali's commerce and had set up a thriving business on the south coast at Kuta.

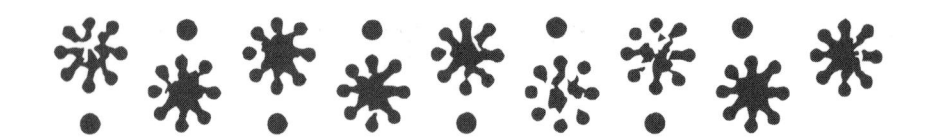

Chapter 3 The *Bule* Raja of Kuta

Ever since the Crusades of the early Middle Ages, European men have day-dreamed of ruling over docile and graceful natives, with free access to their wealth and their women. It is a dream that sustained the momentum of European imperialism in all its varied forms, from the systematic enterprise of governments to the romantic adventurism of bold and sometimes eccentric individuals.

Bob Reece, 2004

In frantic, modern Kuta, just beyond the underpass on the road to the airport, a few paces down Jalan Tuan Lange, there is a tiny Chinese graveyard. To one side of the overgrown, neglected monuments, through a small gate guarded by a statue of a Dalmatian hound, is a well-kept and rather large black-and-white obelisk built over a tomb.

A plaque bears Mads Lange's name in Roman and Balinese letters, and below is the inscription: 'Sacred to the Memory of Mads Johansen Lange, Knight of the Nederland, Leeuw and Danish Gold Medal, born on the Island of Langeland, Denmark, Sept. 18, 1807. Departed this life at Bali, May 13, 1856, after a residence of 18 years on this island.'

On the day I visited, dried flowers and leaves were scattered on the ground, the remains of the simple Hindu offering of fresh flowers and leaves arranged on a bed of young coconut leaves. These are left everywhere, every day, all over Bali, but only in places of significance to someone. A young Balinese woman came hurrying out of a small house adjacent to the graveyard, clutching a visitor's book and a money jar for a donation towards the upkeep of the monument. This was Ni Made Widi, a descendant of the deceased.

I made a donation and asked to see the visitor's book. Before I signed it I looked back over the pages that had been filled since the monument had

Chapter 3 The *Bule* Raja of Kuta

been built above Lange's gravestone to commemorate the 200th anniversary of his birth. Mostly, they were Danish names and several were family members on a peculiar pilgrimage. Occasionally, they were just bewildered tourists who had no idea why their guide had brought them here, and hoped that they would soon be transported across the street to the more congenial air-conditioned designer stores of the Bali Galleria.

I asked Made if she knew the story of the man for whom the memorial had been created. She smiled sweetly and said: 'Yes, very good man, live in Kuta long time ago.'

Well, yes he did, and certainly in some ways he was, but there is so much more to know about the *bule* raja of Kuta, an adventurer who made much of his money trading slaves and opium, and yet sacrificed his own financial empire to broker an uneasy peace between the Balinese and the Dutch invaders.

Lange was born in the port of Rudkobing on the island of Langeland, Denmark, at the end of a summer during which the Danish ports had been trying to recover from the British naval blockade of Copenhagen, when the Danish fleet had been blown apart or towed back to England, rather than see it fall into the hands of Napolean's French Empire. Rudkobing was a seafarer's town and Lange's early years were spent in an atmosphere of depression and poverty. His father, Lorents Lange Pedersen, was a trader and distiller, but his business, like everyone else's, fell into a slump that lasted many years.

When Denmark began to emerge from its economic doldrums, a new class of merchant seaman was also emerging, the freewheeling privateer who was prepared to go to the ends of the earth to seek his fortune. At seventeen Mads Lange left his parents, eight younger brothers and one baby sister, and went to sea on the *Norden*, a schooner bound for the Spice Islands. On the voyage he became friends with the captain, a young man named John Burd, born in Denmark of Scottish parents, and on his first command. Burd took the teenager under his wing, and in seafaring knowledge and enthusiasm they soon complemented each other.

In the Far East their first base was the Indian port town of Tranquebar, on the south-west coast, which had been leased to the Danish East India Company for two centuries. Here they could buy the commodities needed to trade further east—cotton, guns, powder and opium—and they were soon doing good business. In 1831, however, the *Norden* was wrecked on a reef during a storm off the South Indian coast, and Lange and Burd were lucky to reach shore alive. The two men resolved to start their own business, Burd was able to purchase cheaply two Danish ships, and they took a year off to sail home and see family before starting the long journey of building an empire. At home Lange fell in love with his sixteen-year-old cousin, Ida Bay, but he held to his plan and sailed for the East on board Burd's third and latest ship acquisition, with three of Lange's younger brothers signed on as crew.

Although Lange's youngest brother was tragically lost at just fifteen years of age in a shipwreck soon after their arrival in the Spice Islands, the rest prospered, sailing contract voyages for the big Singapore trading houses and, as Burd's fleet grew, setting up their own trading posts. After months of searching for a post he could call his own, Lange finally decided on the island of Lombok, Bali's next-door neighbour but with a much larger rice crop. Establishing trading bases on Bali or Lombok had proven immensely difficult for the Dutch, and even when they had been allowed to build small facilities on the coast, they were forbidden by the rajas to travel inland to deal direct with the farmers. But Lange, although short in stature, was a formidable man with a pleasant manner and a way of looking directly at the subject of his attention with his clear-blue Scandinavian eyes that inspired trust. He was a born salesman and the raja of Karangasem-Lombok soon warmed to him and his proposals, for not only was Lange a charmer, but he had somehow learned to charm in the three languages needed to address different castes.

At that time Lombok was ruled jointly (and uneasily) by the powerful and warlike Hindu raja of Karangasem and the Muslim raja of Mataram. Their seats of power, Chakra Negara and Mataram, were only a few kilometres apart and both shared the seaport of Ampenan, which had emerged as an important regional trade centre, servicing the heavy traffic of the shipping route between China and Singapore and Australia. After beguiling the raja of Karangasem-Lombok and showering him with gifts, Lange was given the position of *shabander*, or harbourmaster, and allowed to build a vast shipyard and warehouse at Tanjung-Karem, just along from the port. From here he could load huge quantities of cheap rice he had bought direct from the farms and, using Burd's fleet, ship it to the markets of Singapore and Canton. For the return journey, in Singapore he took on guns for the raja and in China *kepeng* coins, which had become the currency of Bali and Lombok. (Lange bought them at 1400 to the dollar and sold at 700.)

Chapter 3 The *Bule* Raja of Kuta

Lange and his brothers were well on the way to making their fortunes when another *bule* trader arrived, courted the raja of Mataram-Lombok, and set up shop along the bay in opposition to them. George Peacock King was a Bengal-born Englishman who had skipped out on a trail of debt in Surabaya and was looking to start afresh. Initially, there was enough money to be made to keep both men happy, although Lange's attempts to turn the rajas against King were always in the back of his mind. Lange's Danish biographer, Aage Krarup Nielsen, wrote: 'They advertised their cheap Lombok rice in newspapers in Singapore, China and Australia, and their presence at Ampenan soon attracted many European ships … Different reports mention a yearly export of 10,000 to 14,000 tons of rice.' Ampenan also attracted British convict transportation ships returning from Australia that would take on rice for the European markets.

Urged on by their *bule* trading partners, the rajas of Mataram and Karangasem engaged in an increasingly nasty verbal squabble, mostly about alleged incest, but touching on all manner of wrongdoing. It finally got physical, however, over the mundane matter of water rights, and in 1838 escalated into a full-blown land and sea war. King and Lange became admirals of the fleet for their respective rajas and, instead of shipping rice, started firing cannons at each other. The Lombok Wars raged on and off for two years, but what finally turned the tide against Lange was the intervention of the Dutch. They had watched helplessly as King and Lange, with the patronage of their rajas, had made a fortune in trade, and now they saw an opportunity to gain some control over the victor. By 1839 King's ships were flying the Dutch flag, Lange's the Danish.

The Mataram forces sacked the fortress at Chakra Negara and the raja was initially lucky to escape with his life, only to be caught and executed six months later. Depending on which of the written accounts you believe, Lange was either given one hour to leave Lombok on his ship, *Venus*, or he fought valiantly all the way to the shore, where he jumped on his horse and galloped, then swam, to the *Venus* at anchor in the bay. Either way, he left Lombok with nothing but his clothing, his horse and his ship.

There was no question about where Lange would go next. In his travels around the islands, he had visited South Bali and had an audience with the raja of Kesiman in Badung (now Denpasar), and the raja, in true raja style, had offered him the opportunity to operate a trading post on the coast at Kuta, in return for opium, guns and money. Now, penniless and deeply in debt to Chinese merchants in Singapore and Canton, Lange simply started again.

Lange built a fine residence for himself and his brothers, added a factory and expanded the existing warehouses, securing all of it behind high, thick walls. Adjoining the narrow Dawan River that at high tide was navigable to Kuta Bay, the compound was also directly opposite the Dutch government trading post, operated intermittently and without much success since 1826, other than in rounding up slaves to fight wars in Java. Now the Dutch just looked on in petulant amazement as Lange used his wealth of contacts to secure new trading deals.

Once his business was up and running, Lange launched a charm offensive on Bali's rajas, visiting each kingdom on his huge white steed, lavishing gifts on them and their favourite wives, and sitting in court respectfully below them while he sought their blessing for his commerce. Everything came at a price, of course, and Lange soon became a major supplier of both arms and opium to the courts of South Bali.

Although it was a physically beautiful place, located on an isthmus with a long white-sand beach and protected waters inside a fringing reef to one side and a mangrove-edged deep natural harbour to the other, Kuta had long been considered a place of evil spirits, its mangrove marshlands carrying disease and fever. Over recent centuries it had become the dumping ground for undesirables, which was why the Dutch had set up a slaving station there. The rajas of South Bali had a fairly simple approach to justice. Heinous crime was punished by death, usually a *kris* sword through the heart, after the executioner had first secured the victim's verbal consent to kill him; lesser but still serious offences often attracted banishment to the dry Bukit Peninsula, where wild beasts roamed and evil spirits abounded (no one ever came back); and serial small-time pests, like bankrupts, pickpockets, con men, fraudsters, prostitutes and pimps, might be banished to Kuta, where they could carry on without offending people of high caste, and with any luck would be sold as slaves and never be seen again.

The most vivid description of Kuta around the time that Lange set up shop is from Frenchman Pierre Dubois, who ran the Dutch trading post between 1827 and 1831:

> The population consists of approximately 30 Chinese, mainly refugees from upper provinces who do their trading here, and approximately

Chapter 3 The *Bule* Raja of Kuta

30 Muslim Balinese who do not have the best reputation, and approximately 400 Balinese families of which 100 are fishermen. The remaining 300 families are mainly refugees from the other kingdoms who, after committing a crime, have come to seek refuge under the Badung Government ... No smart government would ever have such a group in the middle of a trading area. On the other hand, probably there is no better place to put them in the kingdom, since it would have been even worse to place them in the *kampoeng* or villages among the farmers. And they would have probably done fine, if among them they didn't have the approximately 40 poor, lazy and not very trustworthy Gustis, who were the relatives of the king ... Goesti Ngoerah Ketoet, who had already been expelled three or four times for murder and robbery, but as a nobleman could not be sentenced to death and therefore was forgiven and placed in Koeta.

Dubois reiterated the widely held view that Kuta was a detrimental place to live: 'The trading station was very unhealthy, being placed on a very narrow piece of land, one mile wide and along a town river in which the sea water would rise so that both the drinking water and the air would become very unhealthy.'

Aage Krarup Nielsen, writing nearly a century later, claimed that at this time Kuta was a shockingly violent place, with 'terrible fights among the collected slaves since an angry Balinese does not for long think of his own life but wants to see blood'.

And then, of course, there were the opium wars. Every trader in town, Lange included, was having a crack at profiteering from this lucrative import, but once the Dutch had bowed to world opinion and abandoned slavery (officially, at least), they sought to wrest control of the opium trade from Bugis and Chinese privateers. When Lange arrived in Kuta in 1839, the Dutch were doing virtually no exporting, but their little Kuta post was importing 300 cases of raw opium annually, originating from Turkey, Persia and British Bengal, and purchased by Dutch agents at the Calcutta markets or on the docks of British Singapore. Legal opium was strictly controlled, the number of dens operating in Bali regulated according to population size.

But in their efforts to achieve a monopoly and control supply, the Dutch merely created greater demand for an alternative source. Illegal opium was cheaper and just as available, and while most of the opium brought into

Bali: Heaven and Hell

Bali was transhipped to the much bigger market of Java, by the 1840s more than half the domestic consumption was contraband. It arrived in a variety of ways, ranging from adventurers smuggling in a suitcase at a time, to big Chinese merchants purchasing through shady Armenian traders, like the firm of Polack in Surabaya, and paying for their wares through bills of exchange drawn on the leading colonial banks. Friction between the different arms of illegal supply led to frequent violent clashes between the Dutch and the middlemen of the Chinese and Bugis pirates, at both Buleleng and Kuta.

In the middle of all this mayhem, Mads Lange created a paradise of sorts. His vast compound included well-appointed guest residences, an open-dining pavilion where his kitchen staff and servants could present sumptuous feasts with wine from his well-stocked cellar, a billiard table and a music room. His personal quarters included plenty of space for his wives, concubines, children, servants, slaves and two large Danish Dalmatians. A pragmatic man, Lange had taken two wives. The first, the daughter of the biggest Chinese trader in Kuta, shored up his relationship with those sometimes bitter rivals, while his high-caste Balinese second wife gave him credibility and family ties to the ruling class.

Traders, merchants, smugglers, sea captains, botanists and linguists all came knocking at Lange's elaborate door and he entertained them generously and lavishly for as long as they wanted or needed to stay. A young Danish adventurer named Ludvig Verner Helms knocked on the door in April 1847 after a long and difficult journey:

> It was past midnight when an opening in a palm forest appeared and the boat was tied up on shore and I jumped onto land. In front of me was a huge wall with a massive gate, on top of which a flag was blowing in the wind ... We hammered on the gate for a long time without any reactions. Finally we heard voices ... a side door was opened slowly and a strange-looking person held a light in front of me and inspected us curiously ... Finally we were allowed into a big yard full of trees, surrounded by low buildings of different character ... When the sailors had been sent away, my guide took me across the yard to an open hall that was the eating area. It was lit by a small lamp and had a billiard table at one end ... the owner of the establishment stepped into the room, gave me

Chapter 3 The *Bule* Raja of Kuta

his hands in a very forward way, and asked me in English about
my business ... he acted like a man who was used to ruling.

Thus began a two-year stint in Lange's employ. Young Helms was amazed at how much responsibility he was given, running the day-to-day business of the post and supervising the loading and unloading of cargo. He was often frantically busy, but he was also rewarded with countless leisurely nights at Lange's table, being kept amused by the guests from around the world, by the Lange brothers' late-night renditions of bawdy Danish songs around the piano, and by the company of exotic slave girls in his quarters.

Throughout the 1840s Bali became the granary of fast-growing Singapore, and while he would trade anything that turned a profit, Lange's second fortune was principally built upon the abundance of high-grade, low-cost rice. His fleet grew to more than ten schooners and brigs capable of handling multiple 1000-tonne rice cargoes. While there is no record of how much business he did with Singapore and China, it is likely that it was much greater than the million guilders a year he did with Java.

Much of Lange's commercial success was related to his deft playing of the political card with the Balinese kingdoms, and his ability to negotiate in a civil manner with the Dutch at the same time. Soon, he had become invaluable to both sides, a fact that was demonstrated when the Dutch frigate *Overyssel*, on its maiden voyage from Plymouth to Surabaya with a cargo of machinery to establish a sugar mill, struck the reef at Benoa, just beyond Kuta, the captain mistakenly believing they were on the coast of Java. Since they had been a presence in Bali, the Dutch had been in conflict with the rajas over the ancient concept of *tawan karang* or reef rights, which the Balinese claimed gave them rights of possession over any ship that came to grief on their shores, the bounty of Baruna, the sea god.

Lange was well aware that reef rights were going to be an issue, but when he received word of the *Overyssel*'s plight he was commendably only interested in ensuring the safety of the more than fifty passengers and crew. Lange and his men got onto the reef in small boats and ferried the people ashore without loss of life, but they were met on the beach just on dark by Gusti Ngurah Ketut, Kuta's highest-born thug, and twenty or thirty of his armed henchmen. Only Lange's presence prevented violence, and the band of survivors was taken to spend the night at Lange's compound and the residences of the Dutch trading post.

The following day, however, the powder keg almost went up again. When Lange led his men back to salvage luggage and personal effects, the Gusti gang bailed them up, demanding to know what valuables were on board. A scuffle broke out and one of Lange's Chinese servants cuffed a Balinese man across the head, the ultimate insult to a Hindu. Gusti and his men demanded the Chinese be handed over to face the death penalty, and when Lange refused, they threatened to torch his compound and kill the survivors of the wreck. Showing his usual grace under pressure, Lange appeased the mob with 200 guilders and four crates of opium. Interestingly, he seems to have rather enjoyed a somewhat friendly adversarial relationship with Gusti.

As it turned out, there was not much on the *Overyssel* that the Balinese wanted, and Lange ultimately purchased it for spare parts, but the dispute over its ownership and the broader issue of the legitimacy of *tawan karang* festered for months and then years as the Dutch governor-general, Huskus Koopman, drew up new sovereignty contracts and the rajas ignored them. After several more reef incidents along the north coast, matters came to a head in 1844 when the Dutch sent a tough new commissioner, Ravier de Lignij, to enforce the contracts. In Buleleng, the newly appointed chief minister, a young prince named Gusti Ketut Jelantik, answered on behalf of the kingdom in words that inspired new opposition to the Dutch: 'Not by a mere scrap of paper shall any man become the master of another's lands. Rather let the *kris* decide.'

Everyone knew war was inevitable, but some rajas welcomed it more than others, who blamed Buleleng for the dire situation in which they found themselves. When the Dewa Agung of Klungkung, still the supreme leader in the eyes of many, gave his tacit endorsement to war, all the rajas bar Badung and Tabanan in the south, who wanted nothing to stand in the way of their lucrative trading, went along with it. When the raja and Jelantik refused to pay reparations for two looted ships, the Dutch navy invaded in June 1846 with a force of 1700 men. They bombed the royal palace at Singaraja into the ground, but met fierce resistance in the foothills and were in danger of being humiliated until Lange and his archenemy, George King, jointly brokered a face-saving treaty. The Balinese promised to pay a settlement (300,000 guilders over ten years) and accept a garrison, and the Dutch left.

Just how Lange came to partner up with King to achieve this objective was not so much a mark of the character and integrity of the traders as it was

Chapter 3 The *Bule* Raja of Kuta

of their all-consuming need to get back to the business of making money. The two men sat at anchor in their respective ships while they advised their respective rajas, but it was Lange who rode on horseback into the foothills to finalise the treaty with the raja's court.

It was not to last. The Balinese did not pay the first instalment of their settlement, and the Dutch came back in 1848 with a land force of 2400 men backed up by a naval fleet and 740 sailors. But Jelantik had organised an army of 16,000 men with about 1500 firearms. He was a fearless leader and a clever tactician, and although he lost more than 2000 of his men when the Dutch attacked, the Balinese killed at least 200 and sent them into another humiliating retreat. This time there was no face-saving treaty: the Dutch simply fled.

The Dutch returned in April 1849, this time unleashing the full force of 5000 men backed by a fleet of one hundred vessels. Adopting a more cautious approach, they began well by capturing the hill station of Jagaraga. The Balinese regrouped and appeared to be gaining ground, but then dissent between the kingdoms reared its ugly head again when the Balinese king of Lombok helped the Dutch attack South Bali. In the ensuing battles Jelantik and his raja were killed, and the king of Karangasem committed suicide. The Dutch then marched west to invade the prize regency of Klungkung, but the tide turned again when they were met by a force of 33,000 Balinese and their revered commander, Major General Michiels, was killed in the first exchanges.

The Dewa Agung vowed to fight on to the death until the bizarre arrival of Mads Lange on horseback, accompanied by the rajas of Badung and Tabanan and some 16,000 of their men. They convinced the Dewa Agung to seek an honourable peace and Lange and a company of men then rode to Padangbai to deliver the message to the advancing Dutch. It was an audacious, and some would say foolhardy, strategy, but it worked. Both sides agreed to travel to Lange's compound in Kuta to thrash out the terms of the peace, before celebrating with feasts and ceremonies that lasted several days.

As peace broke out Lange was acknowledged as a hero by both sides of the conflicts, but the years of war, commercial uncertainty, a deadly smallpox epidemic in Kuta, and Dutch blockades and trade embargoes had all taken their toll on his trading post, while rat plagues and water shortages had reduced the hinterland rice crops to a fraction of what they were. Moreover, the shipping routes of the Indies were changing. The new steamships could not use Kuta's surf-washed bay or Benoa's shallow harbour, while Buleleng, now under the total control of the Dutch administration, had re-emerged as the opium trading capital, and Ampenan on Lombok was better positioned for trans-shipping and export on the main north-south route.

Lange was the official Dutch agent at last—he flew the Dutch flag from the *Venus* and he had been made a Knight of the Dutch Lion in 1848—he had all the trappings of success and he was going broke fast. However, he was not the kind to mope. He spent much of his time sailing the Bali coast on his *Venus*, while one of his brothers ran the store, and began dreaming about going home to Denmark and reuniting with his first love, Ida Bay. Meanwhile, he continued to enjoy the company of his two wives, Balinese Nyai Kenyer, with whom he had two daughters, and Chinese Ong Sang Nio, with whom he had a son.

As the political situation worsened in South Bali due to internal conflicts in the royal families, Lange made ready to leave his Balinese family and sail back to see his homeland a final time. As the date of departure drew near, however, he decided to accept an invitation from the raja of Badung to attend a banquet at the Den Pasar Palace.

There is evidence (in a letter he wrote to the raja of Tabanan) that Lange had been unwell for some days before the banquet, but when he returned to the Kuta compound after it he became violently ill, coughing up blood. His doctor was summoned and concluded that he had been poisoned. There was little they could do but wait and hope. Lange drifted in and out of consciousness before dying on 13 May 1856, at the age of forty-eight.

Lange's brother, and later his son, tried to keep the trading post alive, but neither had the power and charisma of the *bule* raja. Kuta's few sandy streets were still full of slavers and opium dens, but times were changing in Bali, and Mads Lange's time had passed.

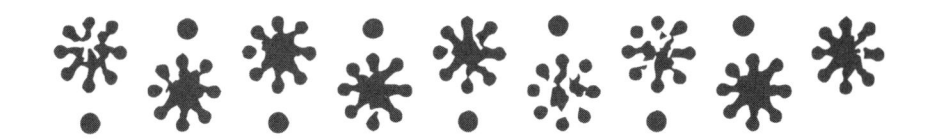

Chapter 4 *Puputan*

Happy the warrior to whom the just fight comes unsought. It opens for him the door of heaven.

Vicki Baum, 1937, paraphrasing the Bhagavad Gita

The peace between Bali and the Dutch did not last long. Batavia sent forces in to put down uprisings in 1858 and again in 1868, and in 1882, ushering in a new phase of Dutch imperialism, Bali and Lombok were combined into a single residency once more in the hope that the placid Lombokese would be a good influence on their neighbours. It didn't work. The Balinese rajas responded by waging war.

By the 1890s, however, the kingdoms were mainly warring with each other. Badung conquered Mengwi, and Klungkung battled Karangasem across the strait and into Lombok. It was all-out civil war until the Dutch imposed a naval blockade on Lombok and forced a ceasefire.

Although it seemed that war had become a constant state in most of the kingdoms of Bali, in fact the Dutch colonialists were slowly chipping away at the independent spirit of the Hindu islanders. From 1855, by which time Batavia felt it had some control over Buleleng and the north, a Dutch 'resident *controleur*' set up office in the raja's palace in Singaraja, his mission being to get Bali to start acting like a colony.

The main agreement to come out of the 1849 'peace' had been signed with the Dewa Agung, the ruler of Klungkung, whom the Dutch recognised by treaty as the emperor of all of Bali. In return for pledges not to enter into agreements with other 'white men', to refrain from intruding on Dutch shipping, to provide assistance to shipwrecks and not loot their cargos, and to allow Dutch representatives to remain permanently on the island, the Dutch promised they would not 'interfere with the governance of the Emperor'. The agreement continued: 'The Government of the Dutch Indies states that so long as the Emperor in the lands of Klungkung complies with the above agreements, the Government shall not in any way attempt to establish itself in this land.' But in reality these assurances meant very little, and having instituted themselves in the north, the Dutch began looking for ways to extend their power over the south.

The first resident *controleur*, Bloemen Waanders, banned the practice of *suttee* (widow burning) in 1859 and took steps to abolish slavery, although his immediate move was to tax it. By far the greatest mission of the Dutch residents, however, was to regain control of the lucrative opium market and derive revenues from it while simultaneously controlling its supply within Bali, in the hope that they could stem the rising tide of addiction. If this seems a little like having your cake and eating it too, so did much of the Dutch approach to managing Bali in the nineteenth century. Once confined to the 'drug-induced haze of the courtly world', opium had become ubiquitous, and as the caste system began to break down with the emergence of a merchant middle class, people from all levels of Balinese society were becoming hooked.

Opium imports were taxed considerably by the rajas and then generally placed in the hands of the Chinese *opiumpachters* (opium farmers), who paid a handsome licence fee for a dealership monopoly. It was a relatively civilised cartel when opium was a drug of court, but once demand spread across the broader community, things got out of hand. In the kingdom of Bangli, for example, two chests of opium a year met demand in 1860, but by 1870, fifteen chests were not enough.

Some in the colonial government of the Dutch East Indies favoured total prohibition, but saner heads realised that the opium culture had become ingrained and an attempt to enforce prohibition would probably lead to an end of the fragile peace. Instead, they introduced an *opiumregie*, which was more or less a refinement of the government monopoly they had made several attempts at initiating previously, but this time based on the successful model that the French had instigated in Indochina.

It's difficult to comprehend now, but at the end of the nineteenth century it seemed the entire Far East was stoned on cheap opium. A partial explanation for this may be found in a brief look at the wretched times in which the Balinese lived. Between 1850 and 1884 smallpox epidemics killed more than 30,000, often almost wiping out entire villages. In Sempidi in 1872,

Chapter 4 Puputan

for example, smallpox took out 700 of the 1000 residents in just a few months. Cholera killed thousands more and rural life was a cycle of crop failure and mice plagues. 'South Balinese society was constantly threatened by visible and invisible dangers which disrupted the continuity of life,' wrote Asian studies scholar Henk Schulte Nordholt. 'The building of temples and many of the large public rituals were intended to secure some protection against the ever returning ravages of epidemics and crop failures.' But while their Hindu belief system sustained many starving peasants, across Balinese society vast numbers of people were discovering that opium offered more immediate solace, however temporary it might have been.

The opium black market didn't go away, but from its introduction in Madura in 1894, and then throughout the Indies the following year, the *opiumregie* began to have an effect, first on revenues and then on market control, and by the 1930s opium consumption was out of sight and out of mind again. The *opiumregie* remained in place, however, until the Japanese invasion in 1942, and for perhaps twenty years of this period, opium not only fuelled the economy of the Dutch East Indies but also supported the Netherlands itself. In the latter part of the nineteenth century, in Dutch-controlled North Bali, the income from taxes on opium amounted to two-thirds of total annual revenues, with rice accounting for most of the remainder. But from 1894, the plan was to increase government revenues throughout Bali.

Whereas previously they had just taxed the *opiumpachters*, under the *opiumregie* the government assumed direct control over all aspects of the trade. Packaged opium was manufactured in government-controlled factories that looked rather like modern distilleries, and was supplied from a central depot in Singaraja to 124 salesmen, under the supervision of five assistant collectors. Some 127 outlets were established to sell opium in Balinese towns and villages. Wholesale and retail merchants, smoking shops and dens all had to apply for a licence, and chartered opium pharmacies were established to sell to registered addicts. Run like a franchise, each opium den had to display a numbered wooden signpost in Dutch, Balinese and Chinese. Usually open between 11 pm and 6 am, the dens accepted only cash transactions with no credit extended.

The profits for the government were enormous. In Madura in 1894 the pilot scheme had yielded revenues of 17.5 million guilders. By 1914 the opium monopoly across the Indies had generated total revenues of 500 million guilders (which equates to billions of dollars in today's terms). The Dutch were prepared to use force if necessary to keep the money flowing, but in the new century they took great pains to keep details of this unsavoury trade hidden from the rest of the world. 'It will come as no surprise that the opium monopoly was not a favourite topic of colonial scholarship, particularly by government officials,' wrote J. Stephen Lansing.

In 1914 Dutch administrator and socialist politician Henri Hubert van Kol wrote of the government's attitude:

> Anywhere the monetary interests of the government are involved ... the damages of opium sales are often denied and attempts are made to excuse it because of the small amounts used ... The native becomes poorer, and brings his jewelry, clothes and tools to be pawned. He pawns his land and would rather commit a crime than work.

Arguing that the Netherlands should extricate itself from this sordid mess on both moral and economic grounds, he concluded:

> The loss of opium monies will be recompensed by the increasing prosperity of the population whose productive force will no longer be paralyzed, and the enormous amounts presently spent on this juice will be used for the purchase of necessities which will increase tax income. Moreover, this will be income to which no tears are attached.

By the early years of the new century, the eight kingdoms of Bali had entered a period of relative calm, during which the opium haze that hung over the whole island must have helped numb the pain of increasing dominance of Balinese life by the Dutch colonial government. The Dutch *controleur*, H.J. Schwartz, operating out of Gianyar, began to draw South Bali into his administrative web, collecting taxes and using them to improve roads and irrigation systems. But the Dewa Agung in Klungkung and the rajas of Bangli, Tabanan and Badung remained firm in their resolve to keep the Dutch out of their affairs, launching nuisance campaigns, like disguising sharpened bamboo in the rice fields as hazards to surveyors drawing property lines, and frequently harbouring fugitives from colonial law.

By far the biggest thorn in the side of the Dutch, however, was the insistence of the rajas on claiming salvage rights over shipwrecks along their coasts. After a series of such incidents along the Buleleng coast, matters came

Chapter 4 *Puputan*

to a head after the looting of the *Sri Kumala*, a Chinese steamer from Borneo that came to grief on reefs off Sanur in May 1904. The villagers stripped the hull of everything of value within a few days. The Chinese owners protested to the colonial government and presented the *controleur* with a vastly inflated bill for the damages. Even two years later, when this had been watered down to a more realistic assessment of 2500 guilders, the raja of Badung refused to acknowledge that there had been any responsibility on his part or wrongdoing by his people. The Dewa Agung and the raja of Tabanan both backed him in opposing the fine.

The Dutch were furious, but the more pragmatic of them saw this as an opportunity to permanently squash the remaining cells of rebellion. In June 1906 the Dutch blockaded the coasts of Badung and Tabanan while they prepared a punitive military expedition. What happened next remains one of the most tragic and yet strangely inspiring episodes in modern Balinese history, touching on both the strength of their Hindu beliefs and their proud, brave fatalism.

In early September three battalions of infantry, a detachment of cavalry and two batteries of artillery arrived off the Badung coast under heavy naval support. The Sixth Military Expedition, under the command of General Rost van Tonningen, landed at Sanur on 14 September, and, meeting no serious resistance, marched towards Kesiman and Denpasar. In Kesiman they discovered that the elderly raja had been murdered by his own high priest for refusing to rally some resistance. The Dutch pressed on, believing that taking Denpasar would be like taking Kesiman—a mere formality.

There are many accounts of the events of 20 September 1906, but virtually none of the days and hours of preparation for death that preceded the arrival of the expedition in Denpasar.

At dawn the Dutch marched on Denpasar and found the city square apparently deserted, with smoke and flames rising above the walls of the raja's palace. Then the soldiers heard the beating of drums from behind the walls, and slowly, deliberately, a silent procession emerged from behind the gates, led by the raja himself, carried by four bearers and looking magnificently defiant in white cremation garments and glittering jewels, a heavy *kris* sword in his hand. Behind him came the officials of court, the priests and his guards, followed by the raja's wives and children and his retainers, all of them resplendent in white, with flowers in their hair, all of them armed with swords.

Bali: Heaven and Hell

As the procession came within firing range, the stunned Dutch aimed their guns. At this point the raja gave a signal and a priest plunged a *kris* into the raja's heart before proceeding to kill himself. As they continued to advance towards the troops, men, women and children followed suit, plunging knives into each other and slitting each other's throats. Horrified, the Dutch began to fire indiscriminately at the mounting piles of dead and dying. But still the white-clad Balinese poured forth from the palace and proceeded to 'open the door of heaven', some of them managing to take a soldier or two with them.

When the carnage was finally over, more than 1000 Balinese and a dozen or so Dutch lay dead. The soldiers then looted the corpses for their jewellery and the ruins of the palace for coins and artefacts before moving on to their next conquest. Badung had fallen and Tabanan followed within a few days, although the raja and members of his court preferred suicide in prison to ritualistic slaughter in the streets. Nevertheless, word of the *puputan* (literally, the ending) of the court of Badung in the face of the Dutch invasion spread across the island and inspired other kingdoms to seek death with honour, rather than life under foreign rule.

In 1908 Bangli and Klungkung were the final kingdoms to fall to the Dutch, the latter in another bloody *puputan* in which the Dewa Agung and 300 of his family, staff and followers butchered themselves in the face of the soldiers. The Dewa himself was felled by Dutch gunfire, which inspired his six wives to slice each other to death in a frenzy of grief above his crumpled body. Klungkung, the largest, oldest and most sacred of all Balinese palaces, was blown to rubble by Dutch artillery, and the last king and his entire court chose death over defeat.

Having received damaging international press coverage over its role in the Denpasar *puputan* two years earlier, the colonial government sought to blame resistance to the opium monopoly for the slaughter and the subsequent fall of Klungkung. Batavia's *Bataviaasch Nieuwsblad* reported:

> At the establishing of the opium monopoly, troops were sent without warning to look for clandestine opium. It was the advent of these troops which made the population go for its arms ... The role of the opium monopoly in this rebellion becomes even clearer when one learns that after the departure of officer van Schauroth from Klungkung to the coast, all of the salesmen of the opium selling points were murdered.

Chapter 4 *Puputan*

The defeat of the Balinese kingdoms gave the Dutch complete control of the island. 'The era of clever plots and invasions was over,' wrote J. Stephen Lansing. When the first reports of the fall of Klungkung began to come in, a leading newspaper in Batavia editorialised, 'It seems clear to us that the government will switch over to direct government of the whole of Bali.'

After 600 years, the descendants of the Majapahit emperors had been decimated, and for the first time since the traders had set up camp on the northern coastline, the island of the gods was now unquestionably the island of the Dutch. But the violent end of the rule of the rajas had not gone unnoticed, and in the wider world it was felt that Batavia and the central Dutch government in The Hague had a lot to answer for. No one knew the full story, but in the great capitals of the world there was a strong suspicion that the conquest of the Indies had been less than humane. Within the Netherlands itself, there was a widely held view that the time had come for some restitution, if the Dutch were to retain the position they believed they still held as the world's leading colonists.

The Dutch humanitarian and clergyman Wolter Robert van Hoëvell, president of the Royal Batavian Society for the Arts and Sciences and publisher of the *Journal of the Netherlands Indies*, was probably the first to spread some enlightenment about the native culture of the Indies, and in particular of Bali, in articles written in the late 1840s. Van Hoëvell used as his base the Kuta compound of his friend, Mads Lange, while he travelled around Bali gathering information, and while it may seem odd for a humanitarian to seek support from a sometime slave trader, van Hoëvell's long stays with Lange gave him the intellectual materials to push into acceptance what would eventually become known as the Ethical Policy, acknowledging Dutch responsibility for the exploitation of the Indies natives and seeking to make recompense for it.

If van Hoëvell's friendship with Lange seems strange, the Dutch Reformed Church pastor's association with a German Sanskrit scholar named Friederich is far stranger. Despite being a chronic drunk who habitually beat his servants with a horsewhip, Friederich wrote one of the first accounts of the relationship between Hindu religion, literature and society in Bali, laying the groundwork for the concept of the island as the museum of the classical culture of the Indies. Friederich was the Royal Batavian Society's principal agent on the island, but he was not a great ambassador. Mads Lange, who also had his moments, wrote in a letter to the resident: 'Mr Frederick has turned raven mad [sic] ... he have [sic] flogged an Ida at Suny ... and the other day at Deva Mate Reis feast he floked hes [sic] Brother—Deva Mate Kareng ... He quarrels with every one.'

Long after van Hoëvell had returned to the Netherlands to continue his fight for native rights in the parliament, scholars Herman van der Tuuk, Julius Jacobs and F.A. Liefrinck continued his work. Malaccan-born van der Tuuk continued the tradition of eccentricity by completely adopting the Balinese lifestyle and carrying out his business barefoot and in pyjama trousers, but he advanced the notion of Bali as a place of culture and learning, and devoted decades of his life to compiling a dictionary of the Balinese language.

Jacobs, a doctor who came to Bali to work on a smallpox vaccination program, also adopted the lifestyle while becoming obsessed with documenting Balinese sexual practices. His published output pioneered what would become a frequent theme in later works on Bali—the idea of Bali as a sexual paradise where beautiful bare-breasted women lived in harems and were liberal with their sexual favours. Jacobs spared his readers no detail, ranging from 'the strongly developed clitoris, with which experts say many Balinese beauties are blessed', to *'masturbatie'*, which he claimed was often performed using the bounty of the kitchen. 'Yams and bananas are much used by the Balinese girls as delicacies, but not only for eating.'

In marked contrast to Jacobs and van der Tuuk, Frederick Albert Liefrinck was a dour civil servant who became Resident of Bali and Lombok in 1896, but his work was no less important, particularly his development of the concept of the 'village republic', through which he explained the structure of Balinese society.

The Ethical Policy got a further boost in 1902 with the visit of the influential Dutch socialist politician Henri Hubert van Kol. Although he is sometimes described as Bali's first tourist, and he was in the sense that he travelled to his own timetable and at his own expense, van Kol's was a fact-finding mission. He wanted to gather more information on what was happening in the Indies than any of his colleagues had and thereby influence colonial policy, particularly in regard to Bali. A byproduct of his extensive travels was a huge 826-page travel book, *Uit Onze Kolonien (Out of Our Colonies)*, published in 1903.

Van Kol had been in Bali before, working as a civil engineer in the 1880s, so he had some idea of what to expect, but that didn't stop him falling

Chapter 4 *Puputan*

head over heels in love with the place. Although he travelled without an entourage, van Kol did so in style. He was met at the docks by the Dutch *controleur*, who provided him with a handsome steed like his own, and the two men galloped off to a royal reception in the palace at Karangasem, after which van Kol was shown to a sumptuous guest room, his home for as long as he needed it.

The politician found that not everywhere he journeyed lived up to the standards of the royal palace, noting that some of the lodgings he was offered in his ride through every regency except Jembrana were 'stifling, filthy, vermin-ridden and stained with betel nut spittle'. He advised carrying disinfectant soap at all times.

Apart from being snubbed by the Dewa Agung in Klungkung (which he took as a personal insult), van Kol found the colony to be in generally good shape.

> We remain true here to the well-proven tactics of our colonial
> policy and to this we owe our greatness ... We remove abuses, and
> those which remain will yet disappear ... In Bali there is great
> and noble work to be done, and hail to the Dutch if we proceed
> with this beautiful task in a spirit of dedication and selflessness.

This glowing report card, contained within the mammoth tome that was published only in Dutch and which very few people read, was possibly somewhat influenced by van Kol's friendships with the *controleur* and most of the rajas, rather than by his socialist sensibilities. When he returned in 1910 to a Bali still in shock after years of carnage and conquest, his view was less sunny:

> It is our sacred duty so to conduct ourselves that the results of
> our rule will be beneficial to the people, as will happen only
> if we are guided by humanitarian rather than selfish motives.
> Then, sooner perhaps than many persons think, the time
> will come when our own task will be completed, our own
> pledges will be fulfilled, and the Balinese will regain their
> freedom. May the Dutch in Bali work toward this end.

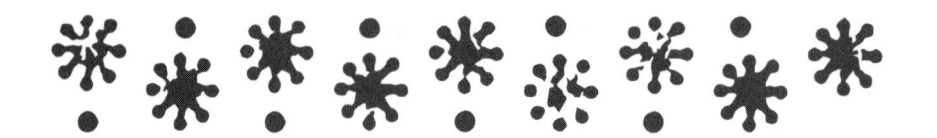

Chapter 5 'Bali Is Ruined'

Although I was in Bali only a few hours, it seemed I had always lived there ... How easy man falls into his natural state. What does a career, a civilisation matter in this natural way of living? From these facile people one gleans the true meaning of life—to work and play—play being as important as work to man's existence. That's why they're happy. The whole time I was on the island I rarely saw a sad face.

Charlie Chaplin, 1933

The blood of the Klungkung martyrs had barely dried on the square outside the palace when a new form of colonialism raised its head, with the opening of an 'Official Tourist Bureau' in Batavia, its aim being to promote visitors throughout the Dutch East Indies. In 1908 tourism was in its infancy around the world, but already the South Pacific and the Far East had been identified as the most romantic and exotic destinations on earth, and while the American Matson liners had begun to create their version of cruise-ship nirvana on the Waikiki shore of Honolulu, the Dutch Royal Packet Navigation Company (KPM) saw an opportunity of its own in the newly united, peaceful, colonised Bali.

KPM had been running steamships down the archipelago to Buleleng for more than a decade, but their cargo had been pigs, not people, bound for export to Singapore and beyond. Pigs, however, had no use for cabins, so KPM made its first moves into the new business of tourism, offering passages on a route that soon became known as the *Babi Expres* (Pig Express). Unconcerned about cruel nicknames, KPM went on a marketing offensive after the Dutch military occupation force was withdrawn from the island in 1912, with brochures proclaiming Bali as 'the gem of the Lesser Sunda Isles' and advertisements that showed palm trees, rice-field terraces and, most

Chapter 5 'Bali Is Ruined'

importantly, beautiful native women alongside the words: 'You leave this island with a sigh of regret and as long as you live, you can never forget this Garden of Eden.'

This was not the first time KPM had engaged in marketing exercises. As early as 1897 the company had sponsored the publication of a slim *Guide to the Dutch East Indies*, with advertisements for its routes front and back. Compiled by a natural history academic and a retired colonel, the booklet offered basic advice on cruising the islands of the archipelago, such as what to wear, language, tipping, where to get your washing done and ways to combat on-board boredom.

According to turn-of-the-century travel writer E.R. (Eliza) Scidmore, the Dutch colonial authorities in Java did not encourage tourists nor make them feel welcome, for fear that they would 'tell disagreeable truths about Dutch methods and rule'. Given the fact that the Dutch were the biggest opium dealers in South-East Asia at the time, there may have been some truth in this. Interestingly, when Scidmore returned to the Indies in 1912, she reported:

> The Netherlands officials have greatly relented in their attitude to travellers, and really welcome them. There are guidebooks, even an official tourist bureau, and one may be personally conducted or go with his own coupons everywhere. The hotels have been enlarged and modernised, and the automobiles have made a driving tour over the beautiful country even more enjoyable.

KPM was helped in its marketing efforts, particularly with respect to Bali, by the increasingly high profile of the island being created by the work of two photographers. Gregor Krause went to the Dutch East Indies after finishing a medical degree in Germany and receiving Dutch medical papers in Leiden. He arrived in Bangli, Bali, in August 1912 to take up a position as a medical officer in the Dutch colonial army. Like many army doctors of the time, Krause was also an amateur photographer who intended to use his skills to document his work. But he'd only been in Bali five minutes when he realised that there was a whole new world of photographic possibilities around him.

Between 1912 and 1914 Krause took more than 4000 photographs depicting all aspects of village life in Bangli, but his most striking images showed beautiful, near-naked Balinese women going about their lives, fetching water or bathing in mountain springs, making the daily offerings or sitting in the markets with their wares. Krause may not have set out to create the image of a bare-breasted Bali, but he was certainly appreciative of the female form he photographed:

> Balinese women are beautiful, as beautiful as one can imagine, with a physiologically simple and dignified beauty, full of Eastern nobility and natural chastity. Their shoulders are almost of the same breadth as their hips. Carrying every burden on their heads with raised arms develops their shoulders and their muscular system, and the always powerful great chest muscle provides the most favourable foundation for beautifully formed breasts. The hips are strikingly slim, as are the legs, yet they are of almost masculine strength, a consequence of walking daily through steep valleys.

Back in Europe Krause became acquainted with W.O.J. Nieuwenkamp, the first foreign artist to base himself in Bali in 1904. Nieuwenkamp was a collector as well as a painter, and when he saw the quality of Krause's photography he suggested they stage a joint exhibition of photographs, paintings and Balinese pieces from his collection. The 'Exhibition of Balinese Art' at the Arti et Amicitiae Society gallery in Amsterdam in 1917 was the first significant exposure of Bali to the European art community, and it later toured museums in Munich and Paris. As a result, Krause was contracted to produce a book of his photographs.

Insel Bali was published as a two-volume set in 1920 and sold out of its first print run within six months. It then enjoyed new sales success in 1922 when it was condensed into one volume, and is still in print today. Of 176 photos of women in the 1922 edition, only twenty-six were nudes, but the combination of exotica and erotica was enough to make it a roaring twenties publishing sensation.

Margarethe Mathilde Weissenborn, known as 'Thilly', was born in 1889 in Kediri, East Java, where her parents had a coffee plantation. When she was three her mother took all the children back to The Hague for an education, but in 1913 Thilly returned to the Indies and found a job in a photographic studio in Surabaya. In 1917 she moved to Garut and opened her first 'Foto Lux' studio. Although her work lacked the sparkle of Krause's, she was a talented photographer and soon found herself with commissions to

Chapter 5 'Bali Is Ruined'

travel through the archipelago shooting for major Dutch companies, including KPM. In 1924, to celebrate the start of a weekly steamship service from Batavia to Surabaya, Makassar and Buleleng, KPM funded a special issue of *Inter-Ocean* magazine, formerly *Sluyter's Monthly*, on Bali. Weissenborn did all the principal photography and KPM subsequently published Bali pamphlets illustrated with her dancing-girl photos. Thilly became the 'it girl' of Bali photography.

Down the centuries Western entrepreneurs have always flocked to a new industry like bees to a honey pot but, interestingly, it was a Balinese woman who was first to seize on the opportunities offered by the KPM tourists. Mah Patimah's story was that she had been one of the wives of the late Dewa Agung who had gone into hiding to escape the funeral pyre when the wives committed *suttee*. Once the rajas had fallen she emerged from the shadows to help the *controleur* and his staff run tourism services.

Although part of this unofficial responsibility involved the oldest branch of the hospitality industry—Patimah, laden with bunches of flowers and a bottle of booze, would get a boy to row her out to the ships as they arrived—she soon developed other, even more lucrative lines of business. She subcontracted silver workers from the villages around Buleleng to copy *bule* jewellery designs and opened a showroom at the port to display their wares. Soon she had reinvested her profits in a fleet of Buick taxis that took the tourists on day trips to see the sights, with plenty of shopping opportunities at Patimah-controlled craft shops along the way.

In those first years tourists arrived in Bali aboard a weekly cruiser that berthed in Padangbai on the east coast for one or two days, but from 1924 the weekly KPM steamship in and out of the port of Buleleng offered tourists a better deal. Passengers disembarked on Friday morning and departed on the same boat when it returned from Makassar on Sunday evening, allowing just enough time to see the island by Patimah's luxury taxi service. When the KPM agent in Buleleng was appointed the Tourist Bureau's representative in Bali, he soon got permission for visitors to use the official *pasanggrahan* (rest-houses) originally designed to accommodate Dutch officials on their rounds of the island, thus enabling tourists to stop overnight along the route.

When in 1928 KPM replaced the Denpasar *pasanggrahan* with the Bali Hotel, the island's first hotel worthy of the name, Mah Patimah's monopoly on 'tourist services' ended, but she continued to pump up her own legend and live like the Balinese princess she claimed to be. 'One of the first persons the traveller is likely to hear about on landing at Boeleleng [Buleleng], on the island of Bali, is the rather mysterious person who signs herself "Mah Patimah, Princess of Bali",' an Australian newspaper noted in 1930 in a feature article headed, 'Mah Patimah, Princess of Bali—Picturesque Personage a Motor User'. The article concluded:

> It is probable that she is no longer of Hindu faith and although she makes no open profession of any particular religion, it is said that her children are being brought up under Christian influence. There are some who claim that Patimah was not of royal blood, but merely a slave in the household of the Rajah who died, but most of the people who know her today prefer to believe that she has the right to sign herself as she does.

Arriving at Buleleng in early 1930, the Mexican artist and writer Miguel Covarrubias and his American wife, Rose, were met by:

> a gay and dignified middle-aged Balinese 'princess' from whom one rents a car to go to the south of the island. Patimah is a famous woman: tales go about that she was saved by the Dutch from being burned alive at the cremation of her husband, the king of Bali. The truth is that she was visiting in Buleleng at the time the Radja of Klungkung was killed with his whole court when he opposed the Dutch army. Patimah escaped death by submitting quietly and remaining in Buleleng. There she married a henpecked Mohammedan, changed her religion and became the prosperous owner of a silver and brocade shop and a fleet of fine motor cars for hire. The traveller succumbs easily to her charm, her lively sense of humour, and her hospitality when she serves coffee on her veranda ... But some Babbitt has taught unsuspecting Patimah that a typical American greeting is: 'Shake the bottle!' followed by a significant gesture of the hand. This is the only English she knows.

Patimah's first rival in the taxi business was an Armenian businessman named M.J. Minas, who had established Bali's first movie theatre in Buleleng in 1919 and the following year started picking up tourists from the docks to take them there. Soon he had employees running his taxi business, the cinema

Chapter 5 'Bali Is Ruined'

and his portable projector travelling picture show that toured the villages, while he controlled the cash flow and looked for new investments.

In 1924 Minas was joined in his rapidly expanding tourism business by a well-connected new arrival named Andre Roosevelt, the French-born first cousin, once-removed, of American President Theodore Roosevelt. Born in Paris in 1879, Roosevelt's career had been chequered despite his connections, but in 1917 he regained some credibility when he served as a production manager on director Wesley Ruggles's wartime propaganda picture, *For France*. Now Roosevelt planned to develop film projects in the Far East, but after seeing where Minas was making his money, he detoured into tourism, using what influence he had left in high places to bring the patronage of American Express and Thomas Cook and Sons to the partnership he formed with Minas.

Roosevelt was long on ideas but short on cash. Minas was wealthy by local standards but not fond of spending his own money. They were both wildly eccentric but convincing salesmen, and somehow the partnership worked and they became the only serious opposition to the government-owned KPM, if you leave to one side Mah Patimah's increasingly desperate and now independent perfume-soaked pitch for the tourist dollar.

One of Roosevelt's more ambitious plans involved turning much of Bali into a kind of national park, within which the natural environment and native culture and lifestyle might be preserved for future generations of tourists—more or less a literal version of the concept of Bali as cultural museum touted in the late nineteenth century. He felt that the best way to give these ideas wide currency was to write a book, but although he was a competent photographer and cinematographer, he was the first to admit he lacked the skills of the writer. Fortuitously, he met a young American journalist named Hickman Powell, who was spending a few days holidaying on Bali at the end of a tour of the East. Roosevelt later wrote:

> After an hour or two spent with Powell I realised that this keen young American newspaper man had assimilated in a few hours infinitely more than the average person would have in the same number of months. He had that peculiar knack which is characteristic of the good newspaper reporter of digging deep below the surface and delving into the psychology of things unseen; he was also avid for facts, exact facts, and added to this, he had the soul of an artist.

Bali: Heaven and Hell

> When I discovered that he could write, I felt that he was just the man I had been looking for. He was ambitious. When I suggested he remain in Bali to write the first book in English about the island and its people, he could not resist the temptation.

Although he has sometimes been described as an 'American dilettante' with 'more money than sense', Powell was in fact a diligent worker from Duluth, Minnesota, who had graduated from the University of Wisconsin in 1923 and worked his way up through regional newspapers to a crack job at the *New York Morning World*. He took a year's leave without pay to travel the world, then extended it so that he could write his Bali book. When he returned to New York he covered politics and crime for the *New York Herald Tribune*, reporting on the Lucky Luciano racketeering trials (which resulted in his bestselling second book, *Ninety Times Guilty*) and eventually worked as speechwriter and adviser for presidential aspirant Thomas E. Dewey.

In 1928 Powell was set up with a family in the village of Bengkel, which he used as his base to paint a fascinating if sometimes breathless—'South Bali lay before us, a teeming, pregnant woman, and in her eyes burned afterglow of fallen empires'—account of village life in Bali, interspersed with a potted history, his own occasionally bawdy observations ('Roads streaming with girls. Heads proudly bearing burdens. Ankles, elbows, balanced curve of breast and armpit') and the inevitable paid political announcements of his mentor.

Powell's guide to village life was a man named Kumis, and the young journalist fell head over heels in love with his beautiful niece, Renang. Powell, like so many *bule*s before and after, had become besotted with the idea of the Balinese woman, and happy to share his views whenever possible:

> One day, on a ship westward bound, I was telling these things [about Balinese beauties] to a young woman who had been visiting in Malaya. Her hair had been waved by an expert coiffeur; her nails were fastidiously polished; Paris had cultivated the charm and precision of her dress. Every device that little Renang knew not, she had used to enhance her natural beauty; though being British, she walked like an Englishwoman. 'But why,' she exclaimed with a lady-like shudder, 'didn't you live in a bungalow, with servants? I never heard of anybody wanting to live with natives.' So, after

Chapter 5 'Bali Is Ruined'

paying what tribute was due to her own lily whiteness, I told her things about the people of Bengkel: that they had developed a civilisation which was not one of germicides and bathroom fixtures; that they were far advanced in some respects in which we were generally barbarians; that they were beautiful. She interrupted me. 'But if you married one of them, you'd soon get tired of her!'

The Last Paradise is a well-crafted book. The simple poetry of his short opening paragraph is etched in my memory: 'Out in the Dutch East Indies, a week east of Singapore, a night east of Java, and just south of the equator, lies the little island of Bali.' When it was published in the United States in 1930, it attracted rave reviews. 'Once or twice in a lifetime one reads a book that perfectly expresses one's own reaction to a circumstance or place … In his epic of the Balinese Mr Powell has done this,' said *The Saturday Review of Literature*. But the book had no impact on colonial policy, and the tiny group of Western expatriates on Bali continued to meet over drinks to despair about the future. Even while Powell was writing his book, however, Roosevelt was befriending another creative talent who was to play a far greater role in shaping Bali's immediate future.

Attempting to explain his campaign to save the Balinese from progress, Roosevelt writes in his introduction to Powell's book: 'Having leisure, my friend Spies and I started a scheme which would tend to slow down the invading forces from the West and keep the Balinese in their happy, contented ways for a few decades longer.'

Roosevelt's 'friend Spies' was the artist and musician Walter Spies, who had arrived in Bali from Yogyakarta in 1927. Spies's biographer, John Stowell, writes:

> Born to wealthy German parents in Czarist Moscow in 1895, Spies had not quite finished his schooling in Dresden when World War I and the Russian Revolution stripped the family of its fortune and sent Walter into internment in the southern Urals. Turbulent years in post-war Germany, spent in close contact with leading figures in the arts, especially with Friedrich Murnau and the new art of the cinema, ended abruptly in the decision to seek a better life elsewhere. After working his passage to Batavia … Spies spent four years in Java, working for much of that time as director of the Western Orchestra

of the Sultan of Yogyakarta while he steeped himself in the music and associated arts of the courts of the principalities of Central Java.

In a letter written years later, Spies told of his early years in Java:

> Since I arrived completely without any money, I first played the piano in a cinema in Bandung for 80 guilders a month ... [In Yogyakarta] I played the piano in the palm-court orchestra of the Soos [the European Club] for rather more money [800 guilders a month] ... To the shock, horror and shaking of heads of many of my friends, I turned down amazing offers of almost 1000 guilders a month ... to carry on playing ... in hotels and nightclubs ... and took the position [Master of Music] at the Sultan's court for 100 guilders a month. I worked in the Kraton for 4½ years ... In 1927 I took leave from the Kraton and moved to Bali, never to leave it again.

In Bali Spies focused on his art, developing a bold hybrid style that combined elements of European painting set in a Balinese landscape, but he was also a skilful photographer, filmmaker and musician. Despite a lack of formal studies, he was competent in seven or eight languages and fluent in several. His comprehensive knowledge of Indonesian life and culture embraced many fields. As one friend said, little escaped his 'relaxed yet sharply perceiving attention'.

Spies built a charming Balinese-style compound by the river at Campuhan, near Ubud, which soon became known as 'Puri (palace) Campuhan', a salon where the small group of *bule* expats (the uber-eccentric Roosevelt among them) came to mingle with Balinese aristocrats and artists, and a never-ending procession of handsome young boys. Blond-haired and blue-eyed, the devilishly handsome Spies set female hearts fluttering wherever he went, but he had made his sexual preference very clear since his arrival in the Indies.

While they did not have a lot in common, both Spies and Roosevelt had dabbled in film enough to see Bali's environment and culture as subjects of global appeal. Since about 1920, still photographs of Bali had been seen widely, particularly the high-quality images of Gregor Krause and Thilly Weissenborn, but the first flickering moving pictures were seen only in 1926, after Roosevelt's arrival and just before Spies's, when two short German

Chapter 5 'Bali Is Ruined'

actualities, *Cremation* and *Sang Hyang and Kecak Dance*, made by W. Mullens (of whom nothing is known), were shown in Europe. The following year a drama set in Bali, *Calon Arang*, gave human form to the traditional demon, Rangda, with the wicked witch wreaking havoc around 'the inevitable bevy of dusky beauties', but the film was rarely seen and soon disappeared.

Roosevelt and Spies began working on a film originally called *The Kris*, which was primarily a simple story of the love between a native prince and a servant girl, wrapped around documentary footage of village life and scenic wonders. According to Spies, he found and developed the story, planned the film, chose the cast from thousands of eager villagers and did most of the direction, while Roosevelt operated the camera. They worked through the dry season of 1928 and by November had almost shot the entire film. Then Roosevelt made the mistake of sending the cans to Surabaya to be processed and most of it was ruined. With the two men at loggerheads, Roosevelt went back to the US to get more funding and new equipment, returning to Bali in May 1929 to reshoot, but this time Spies played no part.

Roosevelt finished his film in collaboration with the Belgian documentary filmmaker Armand Denis, renamed it *Goona-Goona, An Authentic Melodrama*, and released it in the US in 1930, where it became a smash hit, running for nine weeks at the Cameo Theater, and inspired a *goona-goona* Bali craze. *Goona-goona* (or correctly *guna-guna*), the Balinese term for 'magic', became New York patois for sexual allure. Roosevelt and Denis sold global distribution rights for $35,000 and the film ran for sixteen weeks at the Marigny Theatre on the Champs-Elysses, Paris.

In 1932 in Los Angeles, California, a short, stocky, redheaded young woman paused to look at a cinema billboard as she walked down Hollywood Boulevard. Muriel Stuart Pearsen, as she was known then, would later write:

> I stopped before a small theatre showing a foreign film and on the spur of the moment decided to go in. The film was entitled *Bali, The Last Paradise*. I became entranced. The picture was aglow with an agrarian pattern of peace, contentment, beauty and love. Yes, I had found my life. I recognised the place where I wished to be. My decision was sudden but it was irrevocable.

Pearsen, or K'tut Tantri, as she became infamously known in Bali, along with 'Surabaya Sue' and other aliases, was certainly inspired to go to Bali, but she confused the movie she saw with the title of the book by Hickman Powell. The only film about Bali released at that time in the US was *Goona-Goona*, but the fascination was set and more films were in production.

While Roosevelt and Denis were finishing *Goona-Goona*, Walter Spies had begun working with the German team of Baron Victor von Plessen and Dr Friedrich Dalsheim, both alleged experts in 'primitive culture', on a film to be called *Island of the Demons* (although also sometimes called *Black Magic*). Another story about love between two peasants being thwarted by a witch, it gave Spies a blank canvas on which to present his own interpretation of Bali life. During 1931, Spies's house in Campuhan was packed to its thatched roof with film people. They enjoyed the lavish hospitality that Spies always managed to provide, while he worked at remodelling the *kecak*, or monkey dance. He increased the number of participants to more than one hundred young men sitting in a circle, and also introduced the figure of the dancer-narrator who recites, in the light of a central standing lamp, tales from the Ramayana.

Although *Island of the Demons* was well received when it was released in 1933, by then a Hollywood blockbuster that would provide the last word on the *goona-goona* genre was in production in Tampaksiring. Frenchman Marquis Henry de la Falaise de la Coudray (known professionally as Henry de la Falaise), was a Hollywood socialite who had been married to screen siren Gloria Swanson, and was now onto his second (albeit lesser known) celebrity wife, the actress Constance Bennett. But Bennett had money and her Bennett Pictures Corporation funded *Legong: Dance of the Virgins*, one of the last silent films to be released commercially. It featured so many topless Balinese women that three different versions had to be made for the censors in the US, Britain and France, and in the US almost half of it was cut, so that it ran for just over an hour.

Falaise bought some local credibility for his production by hiring Spies, Roosevelt and Denis to scout locations and choreograph scenes, but there was no getting around the fact that *Legong* was a sexploitation film, or '*goona-goona* epic' as some of the New York film critics were labelling the genre. But *Legong*, shot by three-time Academy Award winner William Howard Greene in two-colour Technicolor (almost the last time it was used), had enviable production values and was given a major release in 1935.

The film opened in New York on 1 October at US$5 a ticket (more like $100 today). *The New York Times* reviewer found it 'a pleasant venture

Chapter 5 'Bali Is Ruined'

in the filmic literature of escape ... a pretty tale, and the photoplay recites it simply and with faith'. *Variety*, on the other hand, considered that it offered 'nothing especially refreshing ... follows usual procedure for this type of native stuff'. But ten weeks later *Film Daily* reported that *Legong* was still playing in New York. Part of its appeal may have been Bennett Pictures' in-your-face marketing. Posters and full-page advertisements screamed: 'NUDITY WITHOUT CRUDITY: A FILM FOR ALL AUDIENCES! Bali ... a garden of Eden with dozens of "Eves"!'

While the *goona-goona* phenomenon was gathering momentum, the most famous movie star in the world had run out of puff. Seeking relief from a faltering career (his latest release, *City Lights*, had been panned by the critics), a messy divorce from second wife Lita Grey and his hair having turned white from the stress of it all, forty-two-year-old Charlie Chaplin decided to go travelling. A decade earlier he had escaped a turbulent time in his personal and professional life by taking off across Europe and writing about his travels in *My Trip Abroad*, a slim volume of essays that pioneered the twentieth-century celebrity-tourist book genre. In 1931 he put some distance between himself and his midlife crisis by embarking on a long world tour with a couple of friends and his brother, Syd.

Chaplin's entourage in Europe was burdened somewhat by the depressing presence of his New York friend, Ralph Barton, whose fifth marriage had just ended. On the Riviera, Barton left the tour by mutual consent and suicided two weeks after his return to New York. But things brightened up when Charlie found a new girlfriend in dancer May Reeve, with whom he frittered away the late summer of 1931 at Juan-les-Pins. By the time they headed for the Far East however, Reeve had disappeared and it was just Charlie and Syd steaming across the Mediterranean. 'We were nearing Port Said when my brother brought me a book on travel,' Chaplin later wrote. '"Here is an interesting article on Bali," he said and added: "There are two young American boys on the boat who are going there." During the day, I browsed the book and after reading a chapter I was sold.'

While Chaplin doesn't name the book, a letter from his brother to his friend, R.J. Minney, written at the time, lists the books they had with them, and Hickman Powell's *The Last Paradise* was one of them. The English edition, which is the one Syd most likely would have had, features bawdy illustrations by Alexander King and *National Geographic*–style photos by Andre Roosevelt of half-naked young women. At the time this was the acceptable face of soft porn, and certainly the incentive for many *bule* men to make the extra effort to visit Bali.

Charlie and Syd Chaplin arrived in Java in March 1932, and in Bali at the beginning of April. Although it was a private vacation, the Chaplin brothers had it filmed for posterity by Dutch filmmaker Henk Alsem. The extant footage, which can be found on YouTube, enables us to share the high-end tourist experience available in 1932, and offers a fascinating insight into the extent to which Western culture had permeated Bali at that point. Charlie Chaplin is seen alighting from a native *jukung* (outrigger canoe) on the beach at Buleleng, admiring the jungle forests and feeding the monkeys, before pulling into the driveway of the Bali Hotel in what is quite possibly one of Mah Patimah's Buick convertibles.

In later scenes Chaplin is shown sitting next to a pretty, topless teenager during a village ceremony, then amusing villagers by attempting to mimic the intricate moves of the *legong*. The audience is laughing, and later they are seen mobbing Chaplin, but whether they had any concept of how big a star he was is open for conjecture. Perhaps they recognised him as the star of the films they saw in Minas's cinema, or perhaps they just saw him as a funny man who had come to visit.

Channelling his 1921 travels, Chaplin had accepted a commission from *Woman's Home Companion* magazine to document his world tour in a series of illustrated articles to be titled, 'A Comedian Sees the World'. The series had started well, but by Bali Chaplin was in the home straight and his heart was no longer in the project, despite the fact that he had a ghost writer, an editor, an illustrator for every leg, and he had loved Bali from the moment he stepped ashore.

He wrote:

> As we travelled, the country became progressively [more] beautiful. Green rice shoots were growing in silver-mirrored fields, and wide green steps terraced down the mountainside. We passed through villages with beautifully built walls and imposing entrances along the roadsides. They were like the enclosures of some fine old estate. They looked like the remnant of some western influence. But no. They were the walls that surrounded the native compounds and built to keep out evil spirits. They were paradoxical—these magnificent walls and the primitive buildings they surrounded.

Chapter 5 'Bali Is Ruined'

In Bali, Chaplin connected with the young New York illustrator and cartoonist Al Hirschfeld, who had met the Mexican artist and writer Miguel Covarrubias in Tahiti and been convinced he must visit Bali. Chaplin not only commissioned the young man to illustrate the fifth and final instalment of his magazine series, he bought four of Hirschfeld's latest works, enabling him to return to New York and begin a career as one of America's foremost black-and-white artists.

Inevitably, Chaplin also met Walter Spies and spent some time at the Campuhan salon and on the road with him, as Spies's biographer, John Stowell recounts:

> When Chaplin came to Bali ... he was treated as a celebrity and paraded at formal dinners and receptions given for the European community but including some Balinese princes. Spies was invited to attend as interpreter and Bali expert, and he responded to Chaplin's plea for liberation from the social round by carrying him off to see the special places and ceremonies of Bali as a private person and not as the great entertainer. They shared their sorrows, and Chaplin delighted his host and the Balinese guests with his gifts of mimicry ... Invitations were extended for Spies to bring his piano reductions of *gamelan* music to America, where Chaplin would organise a concert tour.

But none of these meetings and adventures in Bali inspired Chaplin's literary mojo. When his editors at *Woman's Home Companion* complained (through his agent) that the later instalments were almost unusable, it was feared that the series would just fade away. But Chaplin was not usually a quitter, and academic researcher Lisa Stein found at the Association Chaplin in Paris a single page of handwritten (and somewhat illiterate) notes that reveal that the comic master was working, however incompetently, towards finishing his Bali coverage.

The final article of the series appeared, as scheduled, in January 1934, perhaps more a testament to the brilliance of the ghost writer than to Chaplin's diligence, but his glowing endorsement of the island was yet another factor in the emergence of Bali's golden age of tourism in the 1930s.

Ironically, when Chaplin returned to Java and Bali in 1936, this time accompanied by his new leading lady and fiancée, Paulette Goddard, and her mother, Alta, he stayed but a short time, barely popped into the Spies salon at

Campuhan, and was quoted widely but without verification as having said: 'Bali is ruined. I shan't be back.'

Perhaps, like 'Play it again, Sam' in *Casablanca*, it was a line that was never actually spoken, but Charlie Chaplin's rebuff of Bali—real or imagined—was the first time the world at large heard what would become a familiar chorus.

Chapter 6 The Golden Age

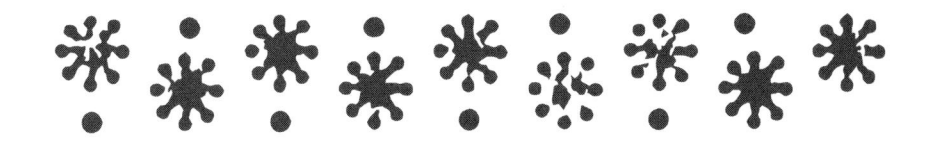

With my own eyes I saw how one of the best-known Europeans in Bali—in this case not a Dutchman—arrived in Denpasar in an open car surrounded by six of his best-lobed boys! A degrading mockery of decent behaviour, wilfully bringing about the degeneration of the much-vaunted good qualities of this people, whom Protestant and Catholic missions might otherwise corrupt.

Journalist Mary Pos, 1936

As tourist numbers grew in Bali (from one hundred a month in 1920 to 250 a month by the 1930s), so, too, did the numbers of part-time or full-time foreign residents, or expats. Spending longer periods in Bali became easier for *bule*s with the easing of the *toelatings-kaart* (literally, admission ticket) system that had applied to all visitors to the Indies.

In a 1908 series of articles about the Indies for Singapore's *Straits Times*, Thomas H. Reid noted:

> One of the first things one ought to do after arrival is to obtain the *toelatings-kaart* at the Town Hall. Armed with this document, which, most probably, he will never be called upon to show, the tourist may travel in the interior. Without it, he may have trouble.

When she returned in 1912, having experienced downright hostility in 1897, travel writer Eliza Scidmore also noted a general easing of bureaucratic restrictions on tourists, although 'it was … difficult for private individuals to settle … for long periods because of this system of permits. Each newcomer had to find two people to stand as financial guarantors, which meant that periods of stay were usually quite short.'

Bali: Heaven and Hell

But a few hardy souls, intent on beginning a new life in the tropics, managed to find their way around the red tape, and among them was a small colony of artists. Although Walter Spies, who was to become the best-known of them, is often given credit for establishing an artists' community when he arrived in 1927, its pioneer was in fact W.O.J. Nieuwenkamp, who first came to Bali in 1904, and lived there on and off until 1937. History has probably overlooked Nieuwenkamp as an artist because he was not a particularly good one, but he nevertheless made a significant contribution to Western understanding of Bali even before his European exhibitions with Gregor Krause.

Born in Amsterdam in 1874, Wijnand Nieuwenkamp attracted some early attention as a promising graphic artist, but his nickname from youth was *De Zwerver* (The Wanderer) and when he married Anna Wilbrink in 1900, he put his career on hold, built a houseboat, named it *De Zwerver* and took off river cruising through Holland, Belgium and Germany, selling his ink drawings from on-board exhibitions in the bigger ports. Next he turned his attention to the Middle East, and then the Far East, visiting Batavia and Bali in 1904 and then spending most of 1906 and 1907 in Bali and Lombok. During his first visit, he wrote: 'There are so many beautiful things to see and to portray, which have not yet been noticed as beautiful, let alone discussed. Therefore I have decided to make a book with plates about Bali, the loveliest land I know.' He travelled by bike, on foot and on horseback, stayed with Dutch civil servants, in *pasanggrahan*s and in palaces, but also from time to time in a makeshift tent covering his camp bed.

His second trip to Bali coincided with the Dutch military expedition to Badung and Tabanan in July 1906, and he gained permission to travel from Java on board one of the ships. But for security reasons he was not allowed ashore during the landings on the southern coast, so he steamed back to Surabaya and took a commercial ship straight to Buleleng, then travelled overland, meeting the Dutch military outside Denpasar in September, just after the bloodshed and the sacking of the city.

Having witnessed the turmoil of the *puputan* and its aftermath, he painted *Ruins of Den Pasar*, which was one of many illustrations in his published albums, *Bali en Lombok*, still regarded today as an important ethnographic study of a period in which documentation was rare. This stay in Bali completely changed Nieuwenkamp's view of colonialism and he became strongly critical of the Dutch government in the pages of the newspaper *Algemeen Handelsblad*.

Chapter 6 The Golden Age

The Dutch painter Willem Dooijewaard was the next to become a resident of Bali, arriving in 1913 and spending almost twelve years on the island. Dooijewaard introduced the Austrian artist Rolland Strasser to the pleasures of his new home, and the two painters often shared a model, working side by side in the open air. Then came C.L. Dake, a successful impressionist who arrived in 1915 and became part of the *Mooi Indië* (Beautiful Indies) school of landscape painting, much-maligned at the time but which later would achieve a kind of kitsch chic.

In the 1920s another Dutch painter, Rudolf Bonnet, was travelling in Italy when he happened upon Nieuwenkamp, now dividing his time between Bali and a villa near Florence. The two artists became friends and Nieuwenkamp convinced Bonnet that Bali was heaven for young men of artistic inclinations. Bonnet continued on his travels through North Africa, but he kept the older man's recommendations in mind, and in 1929 he sailed for the Indies.

On arrival in Bali he met Dutch musicologist Jaap Kunst, who persuaded him to travel to the island of Nias off the west coast of Sumatra, where Kunst was studying *gamelan* music. Bonnet spent April and May of 1930 exploring Nias with Kunst, and became so enamoured of the remote island he then went back and spent more than six months making sketches and photographs that he would later use in his art. He had been considering living on Nias but, eventually, the tragic impact the Christian missionaries were beginning to have on the villagers filled him with despair and he fled, stopping off in Java, where Kunst gave him a letter of introduction to Bali's leading European artist, Walter Spies. Bonnet disembarked at Buleleng and made directly for Ubud.

While Bonnet had been adventuring in Nias, an artist of rather different background had arrived in Bali and immediately fallen in with the Spies salon at Campuhan. Miguel Covarrubias was just twenty-six when he disembarked with his new wife, Rosemonde Cowan, a beautiful Mexican-American dancer (stage name Rose Rolanda) nine years his senior. Covarrubias was Mexican, but he had been Americanised by working since his teens in New York where his illustrations had first appeared in *Vanity Fair* and *The New Yorker* in 1924. That same year he had his first exhibition at Whitney Studio Club, and the following year a one-man show at the Dudensing Gallery. Falling in love with Rose turned out to be a good career move and the couple was soon the toast of New York, hanging out with luminaries of the art and literary scene such as fellow Mexicans Diego Rivera and Frida Kahlo.

In New York Covarrubias had met Andre Roosevelt, who had waxed lyrical about his adopted home and given him a letter of introduction to Walter Spies, and on arrival at the port of Buleleng, the KPM tourist officer, Bob Morzer Bruyns, organised the Covarrubiases' transport to Denpasar with Mah Patimah, and promised to personally take them to meet Spies in a few days when they had settled in at the Bali Hotel.

Although Covarrubias and his wife had been impressed by the majestic dawn they had seen as their ship arrived in Buleleng, the town itself left them cold:

> As we were rowed ashore, Buleleng came out of the mist: the eternal tin roofs and dilapidated Chinese houses, the concrete steamship office and the scraggy coolies of every small port of the Indies ... the car darts through narrow streets lined with dingy little shops of cheap crockery and cotton goods run by emaciated Chinese in undershirts or by Arabs with forbidding black beards. Javanese in black velvet skull-caps mingle with Dutch officials in pith helmets and high starched collars, but the beautiful Balinese of steamship pamphlets are not to be seen anywhere.

The Covarrubiases saw snatches of beauty as they were driven south over the mountains, but Denpasar proved to be another disappointment: 'Denpasar is a glorified Buleleng ... The business street leading to the market consists, as in Buleleng, of the same squalid shops, provision stores, gasoline pumps, a small Chinese hotel, and curio stalls with mass production "Balinese art".' The KPM-owned Bali Hotel, their home for the first days of their stay, fared little better: '[We were] shown to a clean and sanitary room with a hospital bed through the middle of which, lengthwise, stretches a hard, round bolster, the so-called "Dutch wife".'

The Covarrubiases found the 'real Bali' soon enough, and were to spend the rest of 1930 touring around it, mostly in the company of Walter Spies, but it is interesting to compare Covarrubias's first impressions of Denpasar with those of Colin McPhee, the Canadian-born musicologist who crossed paths with the Covarrubiases in Paris as they were on their way home from Bali:

Chapter 6 The Golden Age

> Den Pasar was a rambling town of white Government buildings, a dozen European houses, and a street or so of shops, surrounded by an outer layer of huts crowded beneath a tangle of trees and palms. There was peace and order in the large square around which the European houses were set. The shops were a repeat of Buleleng—a line of Chinese grocers and goldsmiths, Chinese druggists, photographers and bicycle agents. There was also a single Japanese photographer who did little business, but whose shop was strategically placed at the main crossroad where you could see the European offices and houses as well as the Chinese shops. On a side-street Arabs sold textiles and cheap suitcases. In the Javanese ice cream parlour you could buy hilariously coloured ices when the electric equipment was in order. There was no church, but the Arab quarters contained a mosque; a small cinema ran Wild West pictures twice a week. At one end of the main street lay the market, where people picked their way through a confusion of pigs and pottery, batiks, fruit, brassware and mats.

McPhee's acute powers of observation are all the more impressive when it is realised that he was writing many years after his time in Bali, but since music was his life, he is at his best when describing the sounds of Denpasar:

> During the day there was the incessant clang of bells from the pony carts that filled the streets, and the asthmatic honk of buses and cars forever driving in and out of town. The crowing of a thousand cocks, the barking of a thousand dogs formed a rich, sonorous background against which the melancholy call of a passing food vendor stood out like an oboe in a symphony. But at night, when the shops had closed and half the town was already asleep, the sounds died so completely that you could hear every leaf that stirred, every palm frond that dryly rustled. From all directions there now floated soft, mysterious music, humming, vibrating above the gentle, hollow sound of drums. The sounds came from differed distances and gave infinite perspective to the night.

McPhee was also somewhat kinder than Miguel Covarrubias to the Bali Hotel: 'The hotel with its cool lobbies and tiled floors was an oasis after a few hours in the glare and heat that I loved, but which drained me of the last drop of energy ... After a walk through the town I would collapse on the bed, which, like all beds in the Indies, had no springs.'

Although McPhee had yet to meet Walter Spies as he spent his first nights at the Bali Hotel, Spies was the indirect reason he had come to the island. In August 1928 representatives from the German record companies Odeon and Beka arrived in Bali to record the indigenous *gamelan* music. At this point Spies had only been in Bali a year, but already he was regarded as the most knowledgeable *bule* on matters of local culture, and he had previously worked on a recording project for Odeon while music director of the Kraton in Yogyakarta. He became point man for the Bali recording project, which resulted in ninety-eight recordings on 78 rpm discs, representing the widest possible range of styles. While all the music was released commercially for the Asian market, only five sides were published internationally as *Musik des Orients*.

At a party in the New York apartment of photographer, music critic and novelist Carl Van Vechten in late 1929 or early 1930, with his anthropologist girlfriend, Jane Belo, McPhee heard *gamelan* for the first time on the host's gramophone. It was a sampling of the raw, unreleased Odeon sessions, brought back from the East Indies by the artist Gela Archipenko and anthropologist Claire Holt. As complex and energised as jazz, the music of the Indies had McPhee mesmerised from the start.

The social circle that McPhee and Belo moved in revolved around the larger-than-life figure of Van Vechten, who seemed to know everyone of consequence in New York. Parties at his sumptuous West Side apartment would include celebrities such as Paul Robeson, Helena Rubinstein, Somerset Maugham and Bessie Smith, and it was at these soirees that McPhee and Belo met Miguel Covarrubias and Rose Rolanda.

The two couples married within weeks of each other in the spring of 1930, but the McPhee–Belo union was rather different from the hot-blooded relationship of the Covarrubiases. Belo knew from the outset that McPhee was homosexual, yet they had an affair while she was still married to her first husband, the artist George Biddle. 'My present stage of being in love with a feminine man has aspects of masculine protest and narcissm [*sic*] on my part,' she wrote to a friend. 'Heaven knows what stages of change I still have to go through, and how long it will take before I can become the mature female.'

Chapter 6 The Golden Age

Born in Texas to wealthy parents, Belo was typical of the college-educated society belles of New York in the roaring twenties, always seeking the exotic, the next big thing, whether it was a new black honky-tonk in Harlem or a new island paradise. But she differed from many of her friends in that she shared with McPhee a passion for understanding new cultures, as well as being excited by them. And it was this shared ardour for the exotic that kept them together as man and wife long after friends thought the marriage had run its course.

In June 1931, McPhee and Belo sailed for Europe for the summer, after which they planned to continue on to the Far East and Bali. Belo's trust fund paid the fares, as well as the swank hotel in Paris, where the International Colonial Exposition had just opened and was the talk of the town. 'By great good luck we ran into Rose and Miguel Covarrubias on the Rue de la Paix,' Belo later wrote. 'They had just returned from their first six months stay in Bali and were bursting with enthusiasm.'

The four friends took a taxi to the exposition site at the Bois de Vincennes, where they attended the first performance in the Dutch East Indies Pavilion of the Balinese dancers and musicians from the villages of Ubud, Mas and Peliatan, a troupe put together by Walter Spies. This was the first Balinese music and dance that had been performed in Europe, and for McPhee it was his first experience of the live sound of the *gamelan* orchestra. As McPhee sat spellbound, Covarrubias explained that Spies had been heartbroken on the eve of their departure when KPM and government funding for him to travel to Paris with the troupe had fallen through. 'It's this wretched financial crisis,' he said, pouring champagne for his friends. 'It's starting to affect everyone.'

After the performance the Covarrubiases introduced McPhee and Belo to two of the leading musicians, I Made Lebah and Anak Agung Gede Mandera, both from Peliatan and musical collaborators of Spies. Full of technical questions, McPhee had to be prised away from the exhausted Balinese.

The Balinese troupe proved to be the sensation of the exposition, performing nightly to fair crowds until a fire at the end of June burned the Indies Pavilion to the ground. The musicians and dancers, who slept behind the stage, found themselves headline news across Paris the next morning, and thereafter they played to packed houses every night in a makeshift marquee. Over the six months of the exposition more than eight million people from all over Europe visited, and the most enduring image of the entire event was that of Bali, an island paradise where high culture and beautiful semi-naked women went hand in hand.

In Bali in the late northern summer of 1931, McPhee and Belo escaped the Bali Hotel's austere atmosphere and rented a house in the village of Kedaton, on the outskirts of Denpasar, where they stayed for six months while slowly infiltrating Walter Spies's exotic salon. Then they returned to Paris for a reality check—perhaps to pinch themselves and test whether they had been dreaming—before sailing back to Bali to make it their home. Spies helped them find a beautiful plot of land on the Sayan Ridge outside Ubud, overlooking the Ayung River, designed a traditional compound for them, then rented them his own house at Puri Campuhan while theirs was built.

By this time Bali's expat community had changed considerably from the 1920s, when it consisted almost entirely of shady entrepreneurs and stolid middle-class Dutch working for the government or the trading companies. In both cases the expats were there for the money and would have preferred to be somewhere else, and tended to live outside and separate from the native community. In contrast, the new expats were passionate about their adopted home, learned to speak Malay (and some even Balinese) and interacted with the villagers as much as they did with the Dutch colonialists. The majority based themselves in and around Ubud, where Spies had become the leader of the pack, or at Sanur, on the beach not far from Denpasar.

The reef-fringed, white-sand beach of Sanur had seen a lot of trouble and strife in the early years of the century, but by the 1930s it had become an idyllic playground for expats, a short drive on reasonable road to the essential services of Denpasar, including cocktail hour at the Bali Hotel. American photographer Jack Mershon and his wife, Katharane, a dancer and choreographer, had built a roomy beachfront home, 'thatched in the native style, with a carved and gilded doorway and modern bamboo furniture on the porch', where their house guests often included the rich and famous. But they were also typical of the new expats in that they didn't spend all of their time sipping gin and tonics under the palms. Jack involved himself in photographic projects while Katharane studied Balinese mystical lore under Ida Pedanda Made Sideman, a high priest. Sanur was, in fact, regarded by the Balinese as an important centre of sorcery, and this was another attraction for the more exotically inclined *bule*s.

Along the beach from the Mershons, the German Neuhaus brothers, Rolf and Hans, had built an art gallery and aquarium. The aquarium

Chapter 6 The Golden Age

attracted the cruise boat tourists and the gallery became a clearing house for local arts and crafts, which the canny brothers offered at prices cheaper than the Chinese art shops in Denpasar. Sanur also had its own resident artist (the first of many) in Belgian aristocrat Adrien-Jean Le Mayeur de Merpres. Le Mayeur was connected to the Belgian royal family, but in Bali he was chiefly famous (and somewhat notorious) for his marriage to the young Balinese dancer who modelled for his paintings, the exquisitely beautiful Ni Polok. Visitors to the Le Mayeur beachside compound were amused to be greeted by the painter, then in his fifties, naked except for a sarong knotted under his considerable belly. But they were rendered speechless by the arrival of Ni Polok, bearing the drinks tray on her head, her stunning breasts and tight brown stomach bare above her sarong. One 1930s visitor wrote:

> A tall young woman came sedately towards us, her smooth,
> brown body, clothed only in a sarong, was broad-shouldered and
> narrow-hipped. Her breasts floated in vigorous curves. Her face
> had the dignity of a Greek marble, with large eyes and sensual
> but clean-cut lips. Her black hair was brushed back and her
> pierced earlobes were distended with gold plugs. She would have
> been a sensation in any drawing room, in any kind of clothes.

In Ubud Rudolf Bonnet, now ensconced at the Water Palace within the Sukawati Puri, had joined forces with Walter Spies and the new district officer, C.J. 'Han' Grader, to develop two separate but linked initiatives designed to preserve and foster Balinese art and culture. The first of these was to be the creation of the Bali Museum in Ubud, for which a committee was set up in June 1932. Spies was appointed curator, and:

> ... took most pleasure in collecting trips to remote villages
> where he knew special artefacts were to be found. Grader
> recalled how they would take the Overland Whippet as far as
> it would go along the mountain tracks and return to town with
> it slung about with the most varied treasures, such as richly
> carved doors and barge-boards ... the collection rapidly grew
> in size and value, numbering more than 2000 items by 1937.

The second initiative was the establishment of Pita Maha, an artists' association whose charter was to encourage traditional Balinese art and present it to the world, while discouraging commercialism in its themes. Bonnet was on the committee of the museum, but he made Pita Maha his baby, and actually lectured Balinese artists on the content of their work. While they appreciated the help in selling their art, the Balinese were somewhat confused as to why Bonnet and other *bule* artists wanted to stop them from doing what they had always done—depicting daily life as they saw it, even if that meant painting tourists with cameras visiting a temple or a market.

Spies was busy with numerous other projects, too—he collaborated with Dr Roloef Goris, an expert in the languages of the Indies and of ancient Bali, to produce a tourist guidebook on religious ceremonies, published by KPM for the benefit of its customers in 1931, and by 1934 he had begun work on a major study of Balinese theatre with the celebrated English expert on dance, Beryl de Zoete.

Born in London of Dutch descent, de Zoete, like McPhee, first saw Balinese dance at the Colonial Exposition in Paris in 1931. She was overwhelmed by it and wrote to an old friend she had studied with who was now living in Bali, requesting his assistance in learning more about it. Walter Spies responded that he was happy to help. After a short visit in 1934, de Zoete returned to Bali in 1935 to begin work on what would become *Dance and Drama in Bali*, the definitive work on the subject for generations.

Meanwhile, the Covarrubiases had returned and were working hard, with Spies's frequent assistance in making contacts and getting access, on the first detailed study of Balinese life and culture in words and photographs, *Island of Bali*. German-born novelist and screenwriter Vicki Baum had also arrived and was being guided by Spies through the history of the 1906 Denpasar *puputan*, which would become the centrepiece of her novel, *Love and Death in Bali*.

Colin McPhee was travelling around the back roads of Bali, again often with Spies, recording music on film (there being no tape recorders) and learning of its origins for his own masterwork, *Music of Bali*, which would be published posthumously in 1966, long after he had given up his decades-long battle with the bottle. Belo was studying the phenomenon of trance, encouraged by the recent arrival of her New York friends, the recently married anthropologists Margaret Mead and Gregory Bateson, who would set up house in the remote hill village of Bayung Gede and do their own somewhat controversial analysis of Balinese behaviour, *Balinese Character: A Photographic Analysis*.

Chapter 6 The Golden Age

As well as having established herself as the world's leading female anthropologist at a very young age, Mead was also a pioneer of lifestyle freedoms of the kind that would become known decades later as 'free love'. She had met Bateson while doing field work in New Guinea with her second husband, New Zealander Reo Fortune. The two began an affair in full view of Fortune and in a field camp environment where there was little chance of him getting away from it. Mead later described the period as 'the closest I've ever been to Madness'.

Mead and Bateson went straight to Campuhan, where their libertarian views were barely noticed in the hotbed of twisted relationships and fiery sexuality that the Puri had become, but soon they made their way to Bayung Gede to begin the hard work and deprivation, as she described in a newsletter:

> Last week we went 'down below', our first excursion out of the mountains since we came up here for four months. We have walked to feasts in nearby villages but we had not been in a motor car or a town in that time. We had a beautiful time.

If the gathering together of this incredible creative stew in Ubud in the mid-1930s sounds like all work and no play, rest assured that in the court of Walter Spies at Puri Campuhan, extravagant leisure was always foremost on the agenda. As biographer John Stowell noted:

> [Work was] put aside when exciting new visitors arrived, announced by a letter of introduction from Miguel Covarrubias. They were Barbara Hutton, the Woolworth heiress and her best friend Jean, newly married to Morley Kennerley, a junior member of the publishing firm Faber and Faber. They stayed at the Bali Hotel but spent a month on the island being shown all the sights by Walter ... Barbara paid a handsome price for Village Vista (1933). With the money Walter not only cleared his debts but also ordered a swimming pool to be built, carved from the rock of a terrace below the house. Most of the work was carried out while he was Barbara's guest in April when they flew in a private airplane through Java and then to Bangkok where the King of Siam gave a reception in Barbara's honour.

Bali: Heaven and Hell

Stowell records that only a few months later:

> There was a spate of short-time visitors of stage and screen. Cole Porter and his wife Linda, Monty Woolley and Moss Hart came shortly after Vicki Baum left ... then followed a ten-day visit by Noel Coward who played and sang all the latest songs from the shows and was said to be a most amusing guest ... On his departure he left a gracious poem of thanks in the guest book:
>
> To Walter Spies
>
> Bali 1935
>
> Oh Walter dear, Oh Walter dear/ Please don't neglect your painting ... Neglect your overwhelming wish/ To gaze for hours at coloured fish. You may delight in flowers and trees/ And talking to the Balinese But they, alas, tho' gay and sweet/ Are, notwithstanding, most effete And not conducive to the state/ You need in order to create.
>
> So Walter dear neglect to drink/ Neglect to eat or wash or think/ And when at last you madly rush/ To squeeze your pain and grab your brush/ Do not neglect in memory/ To give a kindly thought to me!

Whether Spies was in residence or not, life was never dull at Puri Campuhan. The 'happy few' kept pouring through the door, usually waving a letter of introduction from someone in Spies's ever-expanding network of friends.

If there was always a party brewing at Puri Campuhan, there was almost always someone stealing away to a vacant bed for a steamy tryst. All of *bule* Bali was a bit like that in the 1930s, but nowhere more so than Ubud and Sanur. Not only were the expats involved in complex liaisons between themselves, but there was an increasing number of interracial relationships, frowned upon by the Dutch colonialists, who had done their best to get pretty Balinese girls to cover their breasts, at least while in the towns, so as not to arouse *bule* passions. English travel journalist Theodora 'Roby' Benson wrote:

> I have been told that no country girl of decent Balinese family will have a liaison with a European. But I have also been told that it is not the difficulty but the danger that should hold the European in check; inasmuch as though the race shows

Chapter 6 The Golden Age

> no signs of disease, seeming in course of time to have become almost immune, white people very often find them infectious. I cannot judge of the reliability of my sources of information.

Benson also quoted an amusing entry she had seen in the guestbook of the Bali Hotel: 'I hate Bali! signed N. Ipple, Pres: Amalgamated Brassiere Co., Buston [*sic*], Mass.', which would indicate that the Dutch cover-up campaign was not working terribly well.

Another travel writer of the day, Mrs Larz Anderson, also saw Balinese girls as a danger to husbands:

> These coffee-coloured girls of Bali walk with a lively free grace and seem very strong. They have a Chinese slant to their eyes and long thick hair, which they do up very untidily without hairpins and sometimes with the help of a scarf. Such morals as the people have are, at their worst, we must remember, according to a code of their own.

Soon after his arrival, Colin McPhee had been told by the Dutch administrator: 'In the old days Hollanders married natives; to-day it is different. Take them to bed if you like, but see they come in the back door.'

Such attitudes were hardly rare in the colonial Far East, but they seemed to have been exacerbated in Bali by the Dutch policy of presenting the island to the world as a bare-breasted paradise. Curiously, it took people who lived at the cutting edge of sexual behaviour to put some perspective into the argument. Geoffrey Gorer, a writer and budding anthropologist who had been noticed by Margaret Mead, wrote:

> The physical beauty of the Balinese has to my mind been greatly exaggerated by people who have written about them. They are well-made and healthy looking; actual ugliness among them is uncommon, but so is outstanding beauty. I know of at least half a dozen races in different parts of the world where in an ordinary crowd you will find more satisfying physical types. The reputation of the Balinese is, I believe, founded on two facts; firstly, they photograph extremely well, their brown and even skin, with the contrasting hair and

well-marked features being pre-eminently photogenic; and, secondly both sexes habitually go naked except for a sarong.

Gorer didn't find them particularly sexy either:

> ... the Balinese attitude towards sex is unparalleled anywhere; they have neither modesty nor immodesty; they are in no way romantic about sex; they treat it as any other part of the ordinary business of life; it has no more intrinsic emotional importance than eating ... There is, however ... one generalisation that can be made about Bali; the Balinese are a very happy people ... In Bali I saw the only happy large community I have seen in my life.

Gorer was a Cambridge graduate who published his first book, *The Revolutionary Ideas of the Marquis de Sade*, in 1934. The following year in Paris his friend, the Russian artist Pavel Fedorovich Tchelitchew, introduced him to Francois 'Feral' Benga, a Senegalese dancer from the Wolof tribe who was fast becoming the gay sensation of the Folies Bergere, the male counterpart of Josephine Baker, with whom he often appeared. Gorer joined the large team of artists and intellectuals who were infatuated with Benga's muscular black body and sexual allure, including the sculptor Richmond Barthé (who immortalised the black man in his greatest work, the bronze nude *Feral Benga*), Tchelitchew, the New York society host and photographer Carl Van Vechten, and filmmaker Jean Cocteau. '[His] position in Paris was rather like that of the fashionable divorcee in the nineteenth century: a person whom it was chic to be seen with in the right places, but whom one did not always recognise in public, should it be compromising to one's companions,' Gorer wrote. But rather than continue to play pass the parcel around the studios and bedrooms of Paris, Gorer whisked Benga off to Africa, where the dancer introduced him to traditional dance. The result was Gorer's 1935 book, *Africa Dances*, which gave him entrée into Mead's world.

In 1936, Gorer spent several months travelling through Sumatra, Java, Thailand and Cambodia, before coming to rest in Ubud where Mead, Bateson and Spies inspired him to begin *Bali and Angkor*, a work that cemented his reputation as an anthropologist but raised some interesting questions about how he related to the people of the Indies. He wrote:

Chapter 6 The Golden Age

> I think it may be said as a generalisation that Orientals despise Europeans, even when they are afraid of them, thinking them ugly, and clumsy and gross and stupid: for Hindus and Mohammedans they are also infidels and unclean. This attitude is on the whole unjustified; although Orientals have not yet made as much of a mess of their lives as we have, although they are not yet faced with apparently ineluctable death from starvation or poison gas, their escape is I think chiefly due to inertia.

Perhaps the Orientals of Ubud only despised *bule* men who wanted to have sex with them. Certainly the Spies circle, led by Spies himself, was getting a reputation for aggressive and predatory sexual behaviour. Spies didn't introduce homosexuality—indeed there was a long tradition of same-gender sex and cross-dressing (*bebancihan*), and the erotic dance *Gandrung*, in which young men played the roles of young women, had been the trigger for homosexual orgies in the courts of Bali for centuries—but the court of Puri Campuhan rubbed its licentiousness in people's faces, sometimes quite literally.

The visiting Dutch journalist Mary Pos was not the only one to be appalled by Spies's 'degrading mockery of decent behaviour'. Teenage boys in Ubud were warned by their parents to stay away from Puri Campuhan, and the Dutch authorities started sending undercover police into the town to gather evidence against Spies. 'Homosexuality and pederasty ... had been targeted by the guardians of morals as the chief source of moral turpitude in Bali,' wrote John Stowell. 'Police spies were sent out to gather incriminating material against possible offenders and Spies was careless about protecting his reputation.'

The morals campaign soon became a witch-hunt and, inevitably, Spies was arrested on charges of having had homosexual relations with minors and tried. Despite Mead, Bateson and Jane Belo writing compelling essays in defence of his good character and his cultural contributions to Bali, Spies was found guilty and sent to prison in Java from 31 December 1938 to 1 September 1939.

When he returned to Bali in early 1940, Germany, the country of his birth, was at war with the rest of Europe, and his future in the East was uncertain. The Puri Campuhan salon had evaporated in his absence, its members departing for New York or London. The Golden Age was over, but its legacy would remain.

Bali: Heaven and Hell

Michel Picard wrote:

Special mention should be made of the small community of foreign residents—artists and anthropologists for the most part—which constituted a kind of avant-garde as well as a cultural asset for the elitist tourism which developed between the wars. The accounts, photographs, and films which recorded their stay on the island, contributed to forging a brilliant image of Balinese society, an image which would be relayed through the promotional services of the nascent tourist industry.

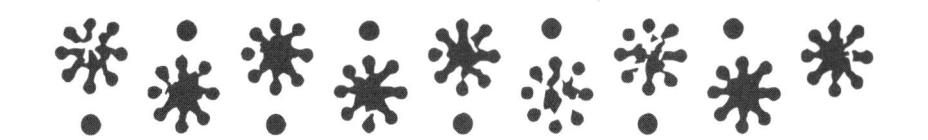

Chapter 7 Our Hotels in Kuta

'I will tell you what we will do,' Wyjan replied calmly. 'We will start to build another hotel—the kind of hotel of which you have dreamed. It will be right here on this beach, and built like a rajah's palace ... And when it is finished the foreign guests will surely come to you and you will make a fortune. We will call it Suara Negara—The Sound of the Sea.'

K'tut Tantri, 1960

As the Western world began to move out of the Great Depression, tourism in Bali continued to grow, particularly after a ferry service between Banyuwangi in Java and Gilimanuk was introduced, enabling people to travel from the big Javanese cities by motor vehicle. But the journey was no picnic. The two Germans who ran the ferry service would often disappear on a bender for a couple of days, leaving motorists to turn around and go home, or explore the limited attractions of Banyuwangi while they waited. The road from Gilimanuk was rough, with dangerous hill climbs, and by night tigers roamed along it.

The mysterious K'tut Tantri (Mrs Muriel Pearsen) claimed to have driven the road in late 1932, having crossed the Java Strait sitting in her car, which was strapped to a native *prahu* (canoe).

> The road from Gilimanuk plunged into a deep, dark forest; the jungle symphony was music to my ears, and I drove many miles and crossed many narrow flimsy bridges before I saw the golden-skinned, graceful little men and women who are the people of Bali ... Much of the way the road followed winding streams. Frequently I saw natives bathing, washing their buffaloes, and even attending to other bodily functions, all in the same stream.

Bali: Heaven and Hell

Around this time direct air travel to Bali also became possible, although this, too, was somewhat dangerous. The first survey flight in 1932 crashed into Gunung Batukaru, but in 1933 a weekly commercial flight from Surabaya began, landing at a rough airstrip on the dusty Bukit Peninsula that could only be used when there was virtually no wind. It was only in 1938, when a better-maintained strip opened at Tuban, close to Denpasar and Kuta, that Bali became an international stop-off, with the weekly KNILM (an affiliate of KLM) flights to Makassar and Australia servicing the increasing number of Bali tourists. But the Tuban airport was just a one-shed affair, with a siren to warn villagers of incoming flights so that they could move cattle and children off the paddock.

The new airport drew attention to the nearest village, the former slave-trading post of Kuta, long considered to be a haven for low-lifes and a danger to health, with its swamplands a breeding ground for malarial mosquitoes and vermin. But this was not the Kuta that K'tut Tantri saw for the first time in 1936:

> I finally came to the village of Kuta on the west coast facing the Indian Ocean. The beach was magnificent and without a house or a hut ... What a site for a house! I revisited the beach frequently and it was here that the idea entered my head of building an exclusive hotel ... If only I had the land ... under the Dutch no white person could own land, I was told. I talked with the villagers who owned the beach. They could lease me the land, I learned, for the amount they would have to pay the government in taxes. This was such a ridiculously low sum that I leased from two families practically the whole of Kuta Beach.

And so begins the story of Kuta as a tourist resort, or so Tantri would have us believe. In fact, there are many versions of this complex story, and to even begin to understand them, it is necessary to provide some background on this bizarre woman.

Having been inspired by seeing *Goona-Goona* at a Hollywood cinema in 1932, Mrs Muriel Pearsen (nee Walker, born in Scotland in 1898, married to an American, Karl Kenning Pearsen, at some point between 1930 and 1932) left her husband and sailed to Bali, where she was taken in by the royal court of Bangli and given a Balinese name by the raja. She became

Chapter 7 Our Hotels in Kuta

'soul-mates' with the raja's son, Prince Ngurah, and may have had a sexual relationship with him. Certainly, this was the rumour at court, and possibly the reason she had to leave the Bangli *puri* (palace) in 1935. While most of the details of her life in the *puri* cannot be verified, Tantri's claim that she had to dye her auburn hair black so that she wasn't mistaken for the mythical character of Rangda, the evil witch, was found to be true by her biographer, Timothy Lindsey, whose forensic exposé of her farrago of falsehoods was made somewhat difficult by the subject's late-life friendship with the author.

A short, frumpy woman who affected native-style dress by wearing sarongs fashioned into a 'Mother Hubbard' look, Tantri was ridiculed and despised by many in the expat community. In a 1935 letter to Jane Belo, complaining that all his friends were leaving the island, Walter Spies wrote: 'Only Bonnetchen [Rudolf Bonnet] and the Egyptian Manx (who is AWFULLLL!!) and I shall remain.' 'Manx', or 'Manxie', another of Tantri's names, derived from the fact that her parents were Manx, and Tantri had grown up on the Isle of Man. The Egyptian reference was to her dyed black bangs. Filmmaker Hans Van Praag described her as the most disliked expat of the period: 'She was a horrible woman. Short, ugly, manipulative and very cunning.'

Kicked out of the *puri*, Tantri moved rent-free into a house nearby, owned by one of the royals, and, by her own account, turned it into an 'Arabian Nights' boutique hotel. Again, there is no evidence that any guests ever paid to stay there.

Apparently, the hotel in Bangli did not cover her living costs because by 1936 she was working part-time as a tourist guide at the Bali Hotel, which was where, on a hot August afternoon, she met Americans Robert Koke and his partner, Louise Garrett. Koke recalled: 'On the second or third day [after arriving in Bali] we were having drinks on the veranda and who should show up but a dumpy woman in a sarong, horn-rimmed glasses, black hair, and she spoke English. She rented us a car and ... showed us Kuta Beach.'

Koke was a tall, slim, very fit man who had been a tennis professional. Born in Los Angeles in 1910, he studied at the University of California, Los Angeles, before getting a job in the production department at MGM, where one of his first assignments was to travel to Hawaii as assistant to director King Vidor on the 1932 film *Bird of Paradise*, starring Dolores Del Rio. Although he had grown up not far from the beach, this was Koke's first real experience of surf culture, and he loved it. Soon he was riding big redwood surfboards alongside the beach boys at Waikiki.

Bali: Heaven and Hell

Louise Garrett was a young painter married to the Hollywood screenwriter and director Oliver H.P. Garrett (*A Farewell to Arms* and many other early talkies) when she met and quickly had an affair with the handsome young tennis pro. Oliver Garrett was away in Hungary at the time, having, as it turned out, an affair with a model he subsequently brought back to California with him. This was too much for Louise, who filed for divorce and ran away to the Far East with her boyfriend. The couple left Los Angeles in October 1934, bound for Yokohama, then travelled through Japan, Shanghai and Hong Kong before arriving in Bali in August 1936. Just like Tantri, Hollywood and a broken marriage had led Louise Garrett to Bali, but the two women had nothing else in common. In the Indies the Kokes passed themselves off as a married couple, but in fact they did not marry until their return to the United States in 1942.

That K'tut Tantri and the Kokes became partners in a hotel venture in 1936 is not in dispute, but practically everything else is, a situation helped not at all by the fact that both parties published books years later purporting to document the period. Timothy Lindsey has devoted an entire book to working out how much truth is in Tantri's accounts of anything important in her life, without a great deal of success. In the early editions of *Revolt in Paradise*, published in 1960, Tantri makes her business partner 'a Frenchman' and trivialises his role in the endeavour. In later editions the Frenchman becomes 'an American couple'. Louise Koke's book, *Our Hotel in Bali*, written in 1942 when the Kokes and Tantri were still possibly involved in litigation, does not even mention their one-time partner, and it is Jack Mershon, not Tantri, who introduces them to Kuta. But in correspondence with Lindsey in 1993, Bob Koke concedes that it was Tantri who first showed them the beach, and took them back there when he told her of his idea for a hotel on the beachfront: '[We] went back next day and found a man called Gudir who owned the beachfront coconut grove, and he would rent it for 90 guilders [about $50] a year on a ten-year lease ... We drew up a contract with Manx [Tantri], outlining her duties and mine.'

The Kokes claimed that the lease contract was signed by them in front of the Dutch Resident in Denpasar, with Tantri witnessing it. Tantri claimed that she had signed the contract and paid the lease months before, and the Kokes merely agreed to fund the building of a hotel. The actual lease was 'lost' before the lawyers got involved, so it was always the word of one side against the other, but all of this was to come later. As the wet season of 1936

Chapter 7 Our Hotels in Kuta

descended on them, the Kokes and Tantri were at least momentarily united in their resolve to create Bali's first beach bungalow hotel.

But first they had to find a builder. When attempts to locate one in Kuta failed, they were advised to seek the guidance of Walter Spies. Spies hosted them to poolside drinks at Puri Campuhan with his house guests, Vicki Baum and her brother, pouring them whisky and gin as he lay in the cool water, watching lustfully as a young Balinese man glided up and down the pool. While Louise Koke hints at the decadence of the scene ('I sat up to my waist in the cool mountain water, holding a glass of Holland gin and imagining what exotic parties could take place in that hidden ravine'), she is also extremely impressed with the 'tall and elegant' Spies, who, more to the point, gives them the name of a builder to contact in Denpasar.

Krinting, the builder, proved to be everything they were looking for, taking charge of their 'indolent coolies' immediately and preparing the large plot of land in front of the coconut groves for construction. The Kokes sat up late at nights planning a compound of four thatched-roof guest bungalows fanning out from a central lounge and dining area, with all rooms facing the sea, and Krinting produced a quotation for building the entire thing, except for 'carvings and gold doors', for US$1375. This was more than the Kokes had, but Krinting agreed to accept half up front and then be paid off at intervals as the hotel took in paying guests. Bob Koke's plan was to double the number of bungalows if business was good.

The leasehold was in two parts, the larger of which covered the beach-front to the immediate north of what would later become known as Jalan Pantai Kuta (Kuta Beach Road), and the other a smaller block on the south side of the sandy dirt track. Included in Krinting's remit was the construction of a manager's bungalow for the Kokes on the north block, and a two-room bungalow for Tantri on the south block.

Before construction had finished, the Kokes visited the Mershons at Sanur and were shocked to hear the low opinion the couple held of their business partner. Bob Koke recalled: 'Were they against Manx! She was a liar and a cheat and couldn't be trusted … we decided to go on with it anyway and didn't see much of the Mershons for a long time, until Manx had done everything they said she would.'

The Kokes planned to open the hotel from March 1937, but during the construction period Louise Koke had started a marketing campaign by writing to all the friends she had made in the East since their arrival in 1934, asking them to spread the word about this new concept in hotels. It paid dividends almost immediately, with a booking for late January. The Kokes were now on a tough deadline for completion, but things got worse before Christmas when a young American tourist turned up unannounced. He had heard about the new place, the Kuta Beach Hotel, in Denpasar and wanted to stay a few nights. Although the Kokes could only offer him a mosquito net over a daybed on the veranda, Bill Dunbar was happy enough with it, and over subsequent regular visits he became a roving ambassador for the hotel.

K'tut Tantri seems to have gone underground during this busy period, and Bob Koke's later explanation for that is that she was only a minor partner anyway. Certainly, she was not involved in attempting to resolve the worsening relations between the Kokes and the Dutch authorities over a range of issues, from late payment of a building permit to the more general KPM-led criticism of their 'dirty native huts'. (To further confuse the issue, Tantri would later claim that the Kokes were too 'pro-Dutch' for her liking.)

The KPM campaign against the Kuta Beach Hotel backfired. It seemed that a lot of Western tourists found the Bali Hotel and the cheaper Denpasar options too restricting. The Dutch colonialists were horrified to discover that a significant number of people actually wanted to live rough on the beach, and once the Kokes had properly opened their hotel, they were busy most of the time. There were some appalling teething problems, stemming from their inability to find good staff and their own complete ignorance of the fundamentals of hotel management, but as adventure travellers themselves, the Kokes understood that in remote Bali their clientele needed to be guided through a cultural experience, possibly even more than their need for a decent meal and a bed with springs, although their goal was to provide all of this as well. Some things just took longer to achieve than a friendly greeting and good travel advice.

Bob Koke's photos of the relaxed dinner parties and drinks sessions on the lawn of the Kuta Beach Hotel paint a now familiar scene, although the custom-made bamboo furniture owes more to the Hawaiian lanai style than to traditional Balinese. But that was really where the Kokes pioneered the concept of the Bali resort, offering a combination of the exotic and the familiar. Part of the Kokes' package was the surfing experience. As a tyro surfer himself, Bob Koke recognised immediately the wave-riding potential of Kuta Beach, and sent back to Hawaii for a redwood plank. But even before it had arrived he worked with his yard staff to carve out a couple of shorter wooden

Top: Kuta's pain was still evident in the rubble as the first anniversary of the 2002 Bali bombings was held at Ground Zero. Bottom left: A bloodied victim of the 2005 Jimbaran bombing is helped to a stretcher. Bottom right: A young volunteer at the bombsite sums up the Balinese sentiment in a T-shirt. All photos Jason Childs.

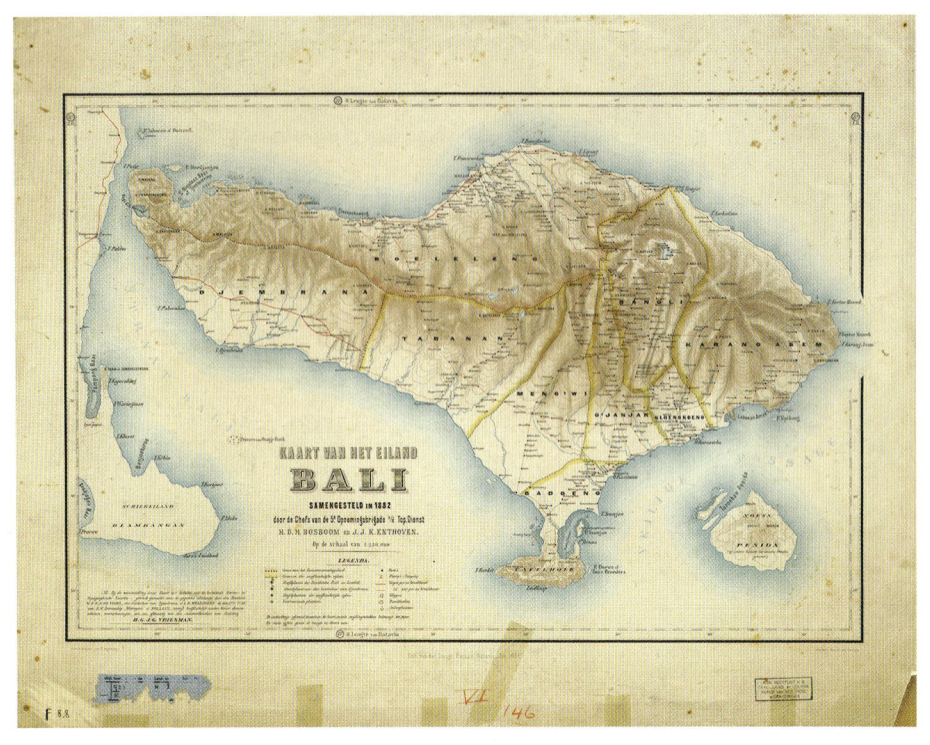

1882 Bali map showing regency borders. HDH Bosboom, Batavia (KITLV).

Dutch cavalry on the move, Badung, 16 September 1906. Photo HW van Weede (KITLV).

Pottery market, Gianyar, 1912. Photo Gregor Krause (KITLV).

Left: Young dancers, Bangli, 1915. Photo Gregor Krause (KITLV).
Right: Bather, 1914. Photo Gregor Krause (KITLV).

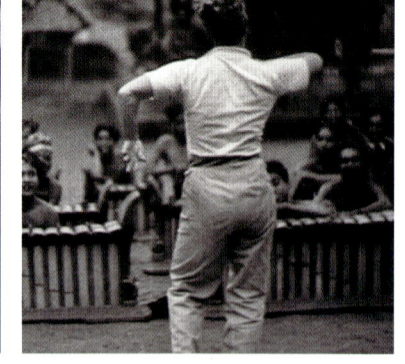

Top: Walter Spies at home in Campuhan, 1935. Photo courtesy Afterhours Books.

Above: Charlie and Syd Chaplin living it up in Bali. Still frames from *Trip to Java and Bali 1932* (Association Chaplin).

Right: Hotelier Robert Koke on his Kuta beachfront property, 1937. Photo Louise Koke.

Left: Miguel and Rose Covarrubias, 1930. Photo Nickolas Muray.

Above: Poster for Andre Roosevelt's *Goona Goona*, released in 1932.

Safe harbour at Benoa, 1926. Postcard by Cornelius (KITLV).

Top left: Villagers flee from the eruptions at Gunung Agung, March 25 1963. Photo Associated Press.

Top right: Eyewitness to history, Lelia Lewis. Photo Phil Jarratt.

Above: Suspected communists being slaughtered in an open grave. Photo courtesy KITLV.

Right: PKI interrogation. Photo courtesy KITLV.

Donald Friend at home in Sanur, 1975. Photo Ross Dearing (National Library of Australia, an24079807).

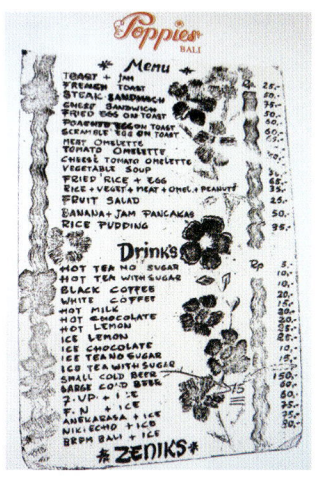

Poppies staff, 1973, and a very early menu. Photos courtesy Poppies.

Top: Tony 'Doris' Eltherington under the Padang Padang lip, 1975.

Above: The crew at Kodja Inn, Kuta, 1973. David 'Mexican' Sumpter, surf adventurer Peter Troy and photographer Jack McCoy seated centre.

Right: A Kuta cowboy entertains at Kodja Inn, 1973. Wayne Lynch in background looking amused. All photos Dick Hoole.

Chapter 7 Our Hotels in Kuta

boards in the Hawaiian alaia style, sensibly thinking that they could be used by guests with no experience to ride either standing or prone. When his own redwood board arrived, Koke showed his young Balinese employees how it could be ridden on the Kuta Beach breaks. Koke, no master himself, couldn't get his boys up and riding on the big board, but they soon became proficient enough on the shorter boards to guide guests through the thrill of a glide along a surging wave.

The Kokes had all kinds of takers for their surfing lessons, including at least one elderly aristocratic dowager, as Louise Koke later wrote:

> Down from the hotel came Lady Hartelby, in a severe black bathing suit, her stern English features lit with determination. My heart sank. Only a few days before she would have drowned in a deep and turbulent spot had not Bob been there to grab her. She could not swim, she was nearing 70, and now she wanted to go surfing. I tried to dissuade her but the undaunted spirit of the British Empire won … Over and over I pushed Lady Hartelby off, until she was carried all the way to shore, more than enough for the first day. But not enough for Lady Hartelby. Though she was worn out, she struggled back for more …

According to Louise Koke, Lady Hartelby lived to fight another day, but according to *Burke's Peerage*, the authoritative guide to the British peerage since 1826, no such noblewoman ever existed. At some points in her narrative, Koke acknowledges that she has changed names (presumably to protect the innocent), but her book cannot be considered a reliable source of information about early visitors to Bali. In fact, both Louise Koke and K'tut Tantri produced totally unreliable memoirs, and Bob Koke's late-life memories are also highly suspect. Readers must draw their own conclusions.

By the end of 1937 the Kokes and Tantri were at war over a number of issues. Tantri claimed that the Kokes were racist, like many of their Dutch friends on the island, and had instituted a 'colour bar' at the hotel. Interviewed by Timothy Lindsey years later, Bob Koke dismissed this as 'wholesale bullshit', while conceding that he and Louise had become great friends with the assistant resident, Joop Van Beuge, and his wife. Koke claimed there were no restrictions on guests at the Kuta Beach Hotel but that their clientele was almost exclusively white because these were the people who booked the rooms.

Bali: Heaven and Hell

According to Tantri's account, a 'rich American, Mr Tenney', helped broker a settlement by buying her partners out of the property on the southern side of the beach road, gifting her his car and then conveniently disappearing. Tantri, with the help of loyal and asset-rich Balinese staff, then set up her own hotel adjacent to the Kokes', calling it Suara Segara (The Sound of the Sea), and went head to head with her former partners for the tourist dollar.

Although Tantri paints the hotel she expanded from a simple bungalow as a luxurious and opulent resort, Bob Koke claimed that it was little improved from the original building, and that it was known, less glamorously, as Manx's Rooms and Bungalow, the name that appeared on her letterhead. Koke also claimed that Tantri's 'rich American' was Virgil Tenney, a knockabout drunk from Hawaiian missionary stock who had to leave Bali in a hurry and left a beaten-up Buick with Tantri. He was rumoured to have fallen overboard and drowned while steaming home. Strangely, this story also appears in Louise Koke's book, but the character is a troublesome guest of theirs named Morgan.

Had Bob Koke become confused in old age, or was it simply that neither party could lie straight in bed? Either way, they ended up in court in 1938 over Tantri's claims that she was entitled to a much greater share of the partnership assets than just her bungalow/hotel. Tantri's case was funded not by Balinese royalty but by the wealthy Dutch planter Daan Hubrecht, who travelled to Surabaya with her for the interlocutory hearing, which appears to have been won by the Kokes after damning testimony against Tantri from the hotel chef, Nyoman Tampa. This was not the end of it, of course, but the Kokes and Tantri do seem to have settled into an uneasy truce while they each tried to destroy the other's business, often both representing themselves as the 'Kuta Beach Hotel'.

We are given an idea of what Tantri's hospitality might have been like when Walter Spies's film associate, Baron von Plessen, his wife and posse of taxidermists were asked to vacate Puri Campuhan and 'staff and stuffing' were removed to Tantri's at Kuta. The Germans, like Spies, found her so intolerable they hastily moved on to Sanur to stay with the Mershons, who despised her as well.

It seems clear that Tantri was deluded when she claimed years later that Suara Segara had been 'very luxurious, had a twenty-four-hour meal-and-drink service, [and] was designed and furnished in the native style'. And that it had carved doors decorated with gold leaf and a *bali gede*

Chapter 7 Our Hotels in Kuta

(one-room pavilion), complete with parchment ceiling panels and a four-poster bed, donated by the rajas. 'Her description is beyond belief. It was just cluttered with bananas and papayas,' said Bob Koke, who only spoke to Tantri after the split when he knocked on her door to advise her to get out ahead of the Japanese invasion in 1942.

But Koke can't be trusted on this either. Tantri may have gilded the lily, but her hotel appealed to some. Guelda Pyke of Melbourne stayed there for two months in 1939 and was there when war was declared. She recalled: 'I stayed with a woman who introduced me to writers, filmmakers and artists ... she arranged for me to learn carving ... my experience in Bali generated a desire to know more about art.' Pyke later became a successful painter and a member of the George Bell school. She remembered fondly Tantri's hotel as basic bungalows set in a palm and banana forest. There were no golden doors that she recalled.

Tantri claimed that KPM and the Dutch officials had branded her hotel as the 'scene of shameful orgies, unmentionable debaucheries', which can't have been bad for business at all, since Duff Cooper, also known as Lord Norwich, the British Minister for the Far East at the outbreak of war, bypassed the colonial government and booked a stay at chez Tantri by personal telegram while en route to a safer haven in Australia with his glamorous wife, the actress Diana Manners. Manners recalled the stay years later, describing her hostess as 'no disappointment, old girl Manx, fifty, 4 ft high, a mop of black hair and a Mother Hubbard garment'.

In May 1940, Hitler invaded the Netherlands and the Dutch Resident and his men began rounding up German nationals, including Walter Spies, for internment in Sumatra. For the second time in a year, Spies found himself leaving his Bali life behind for a primitive cell. Over the next eighteen months Bali was transformed from tourist paradise to military outpost. All able-bodied Dutchmen in the Indies were conscripted and native volunteers were dressed in heavy Western uniforms and formed into their own platoons. While the volunteer home guard practised the use of the machine gun in the coconut groves behind the beach, Dutch bombers took over Tuban airport and had target practice just a few hundred metres along the beach from the bungalow hotels of Tantri and the Kokes. Denpasar, Kuta and Sanur were deserted by civilians who fled to family or friends in the hills. For those with neither, the enterprising Chinese rented or built cheap homes in the hills and made them available to the terrified Balinese at huge profit.

Tourists stopped coming, and the Kokes realised that it was only a matter of time now before they would have to abandon their dream. Bob Koke had been building a nine-hole golf course on land next to the airport, but the Dutch officers made him bulldoze it as they barricaded around the strip with barbed wire. It didn't matter: no one was coming to play golf now. After a Japanese trade mission to Batavia had failed to get concessions, the threats from the north became more pronounced, and it was clear to anyone on Bali that if the Japanese were to take the Malay Peninsula, the island would be a stepping stone into Java.

On 7 December 1941, Japanese bombers attacked Hawaii's Pearl Harbor and the war in the Pacific had begun. Bali virtually shut down overnight. The few guests at the Kuta Beach Hotel—families of Dutch servicemen—immediately headed back to Java for new orders. Denpasar went into a sunset blackout and across the island the outside use of kerosene lamps was forbidden. The streets became deserted after dark. When the Balinese met in clusters during the day, there were two schools of thought as to what might happen. An overriding fear was that Japanese bombers would destroy their homes and villages and many would die, but there was also a widespread belief that Japanese occupation would not be so bad, that their oriental brethren could not be worse than the Dutch. Japanese propaganda reinforced this notion with slogans such as 'Asia for the Asians' and the 'Greater Asian Co-Prosperity Sphere'.

For the Kokes, however, staying in occupied Bali was not an option. Bob Koke maintained the Japanese would never get that far south, but he knew Louise could not stay in fear, and he wanted to get to Surabaya to join the American army while that was still possible. They provisioned the hotel, leaving the most senior staff in charge, Bob paid his visit to Tantri, who scoffed at his cowardice in leaving, and on New Year's Eve, 1941, the Kokes drove their Chevrolet to the Java ferry, their eyes moist with tears the whole way.

As the Kokes arrived in Surabaya and Bob made plans for Louise to ship out, Walter Spies was one of several hundred German nationals being loaded onto a transport ship for the voyage from Sumatra to a much bigger POW facility in Ceylon. The *Van Imhoff* set sail on 18 January 1942, but a day later off Nias it was hit by a Japanese torpedo boat. The Dutch crew abandoned the sinking ship, leaving the 411 German prisoners locked away on board. Walter Spies was among the 340 who drowned.

Chapter 7 Our Hotels in Kuta

The Puri Campuhan salon had long since fallen apart, and it would be years before most of Spies's friends would learn of his fate.

Tantri continued to run her bungalow hotel, mainly for the benefit of Dutch fly-boys who would come from Java on three-day training flights. According to her own account, the aviators loved staying there, but the Dutch Air Force soon had it declared off bounds because of the possibility that she was a spy. The order was later revoked, but by then Singapore had fallen. Tantri made ready to flee to Java, but the Japanese were already landing at Sanur before she finally made the journey by car to Gilimanuk in the dark night and had some Madurese fishermen take her across the strait.

On 1 March 1942, the Japanese forces invaded Java and K'tut Tantri began a controversial and contradictory period as prisoner or collaborator of the Japanese. Maybe a bit of both.

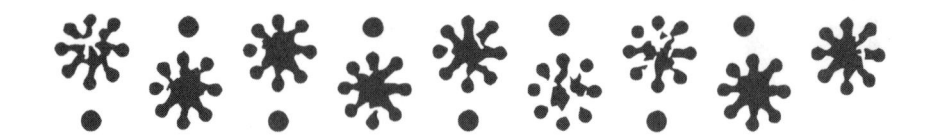

Chapter 8 *Merdeka!*

It is impossible at present to give further particulars of the magnificent successes of the Allied sea and air forces. The invasion of Bali means a Pyrrhic victory. The enemy has paid a high price.

The West Australian, 24 February 1942

The attack on Pearl Harbor was the starter's gun for a major Japanese military thrust into South-East Asia, with the oil fields and refineries of the Netherlands East Indies their pot of gold at the end of the peninsula. Since 1937 Japan's war on China had demanded massive quantities of oil and other natural resources, and the Nippon military machine had long seen a Pacific war as an opportunity to consolidate the Empire's resources base. While more than half of the necessary oil had previously come from the United States, a critical 25 per cent was from the East Indies.

German occupation of the Netherlands in May 1940 led to Japan's demand that the Indies government supply it with fixed quantities of vital natural resources, especially oil. Further demands were made for economic and financial integration of the Indies with Japan. The Indies government played for time but, in 1941, it followed the United States in freezing Japanese assets and imposing an embargo on oil and other exports. Tokyo immediately announced its 'advance south' policy.

As they prepared for the onslaught, the Allies formed a joint command of American, British, Dutch and Australian forces, known as 'ABDA'. According to military historians, ABDA was a shambles and so was the defence strategy it constructed.

Through December 1941 and January 1942, the Japanese seemed to have free rein over the Western Pacific, attacking the American bases

Chapter 8 *Merdeka!*

in the Philippines before advancing on the 'impregnable' British-held Singapore, while bomber attacks on Darwin more destructive than Pearl Harbor wiped out ABDA's main supply base. By February, the Dutch forces were concentrated on the defence of resource-rich Java, which ultimately depended on the arrival of air reinforcements from Australia. The air route from Australia to Java consisted of a string of primitive airstrips stretching from Darwin to Surabaya, via the islands of the eastern archipelago and neighbouring Bali. The Japanese strategy was to claim the islands along the route and isolate Java.

Initially, however, they were not concerned about Bali since they already controlled the airport at Kendari in the Celebes, one of the best-equipped fields in South-East Asia whose paved runways had only been completed in 1940. From Kendari their bombers could target Surabaya, but they soon discovered that wet-season conditions restricted their flying time to a minimum, so they took a fresh look at the Tuban airfield near Denpasar, much closer to all their Javanese targets. From Bali, they could also block ABDA's naval movements. Suddenly, Bali was back on the Japanese radar.

The long-accepted notion that the Japanese simply landed at Sanur and took control with little or no resistance from either the Dutch or Balinese is at variance with the account of military historians. In fact, the Japanese considered their invasion vulnerable to air and sea attack, so their strategy was to land ground troops and clear out their ships before ABDA could retaliate. The invasion force left Makassar in the Celebes on the night of 17 February 1942. The convoy was made up of two troop transports escorted by four destroyers, with another three destroyers providing a distant covering force. The landing force consisted of one battalion (minus one company), one mountain-gun platoon, radio and field units, an engineer platoon and part of an infantry division, all of which had been withdrawn from the Philippines at short notice when the Japanese couldn't put together enough troops from Borneo.

ABDA's air reconnaissance soon discovered the convoy, but could do little to respond, since most of their ships were deployed off western Java, where they had recently failed to repel the invasion of Sumatra. They also assumed that the destination was Timor. By the time they realised the convoy was heading for Bali, the best that Dutch Rear Admiral Karel W. Doorman could do was to redeploy his scattered ships and steam for the Badung Strait and the Lombok Strait to meet the Japanese.

Bali: Heaven and Hell

The attempted defence of Bali came in three waves, each attacking independently without support. It was not a great plan but it was the best Doorman could come up with. The first wave was to approach through the south entrance of the Badung Strait, a 15-mile-wide channel separating Bali from Nusa Besar Island (Nusa Penida), shortly after midnight on 19 February. By that time, however, Japan's Admiral Kubo had already landed his full complement of troops at Sanur, having managed to avoid British and American submarines patrolling the strait. After getting lost and running aground in a tragicomedy of errors, the British sub *Truant* and the American *Seawolf* finally engaged the Japanese destroyers off Sanur. Both survived a hammering from the enemy but failed to score one torpedo hit on the Japanese.

American planes from Java arrived over the strait at dawn and by evening they had made eighteen attacks on Japanese positions, but their claims of four direct hits and twelve near-misses, with many ships sunk and damaged, proved to be somewhat exaggerated. Only the transport ship *Sagami Maru* received heavy damage from a bomb hit on her engine room.

Meanwhile, the garrison of 600 Balinese militia deserted almost immediately after the Japanese landing, failing to blow up the Tuban airfield as they fled. So Bali had been lost even before Doorman's second and third waves arrived. All the ABDA fleet could do was engage the retreating Japanese ships as they headed back to Makassar, but in both the Battle of Badung Strait and the Battle of Lombok Strait, the Japanese emerged victorious, with heavy loss of life when the *Piet Hein* was hit by nine Japanese torpedoes and sunk instantly.

According to military historian Tom Womack:

> The Battle of Badung Strait was a disaster for the ABDA command. Despite heavy air attacks and the efforts of two submarines, three light cruisers, seven destroyers and seven MTBs (torpedo boats), the Japanese suffered severe damage only to an empty transport and one destroyer (although 96 lives were lost when the *Michishio* was attacked), with light damage to a second destroyer. Even more depressing, the mass of Allied firepower never faced more than two destroyers at one time.

The loss of Bali was a death blow for the defence of Java. Japanese control of the Tuban airfield ensured that ABDA would receive no more air

Chapter 8 Merdeka!

reinforcements. Japanese planes now dominated Java, and, combined with airpower on southern Sumatra, they now ruled all Javanese airspace.

Womack wrote:

> The boldness of their plan paid great dividends for the Japanese. They quickly intensified air sweeps over Java and soon eliminated most of the remaining ABDA air power. As Japanese invasion convoys neared Java, they faced virtually no opposition in the air … Admiral Doorman's battle plan at Badung Strait had been weak and perhaps even fatally flawed.

In the eyes of the propaganda-driven Western media, the Japanese invasion of Bali was just collateral damage with no serious impact likely on the stability of the region. Perth's *West Australian* reported, under the headings, 'Bali Invasion' and 'Japanese Take Airport': 'It was announced in a communique issued in Batavia today that Japanese troops who succeeded in making a landing on Bali had overrun part of the island and were in control of the airport at Den Pasar, the capital.' The communique added, 'On the other hand, the strong Allied naval and air offensive against the Japanese expeditionary force has been so successful that not one single enemy warship or transport remains near Bali to give the Japanese support or supplies.'

The report continued:

> Details of the Japanese losses in the landing operations are not yet complete, but the losses are understood to be heavy. The Netherlands East Indies Information Bureau in London, giving further news of the air and sea battle around Bali, said today that it could be assumed that the Japanese fleet sent for the conquest of the island had been for the greater part destroyed or badly damaged. A single ship which succeeded in escaping destruction had fled.

But not everyone was as optimistic as the NEI Information Bureau. The 'special representative' of the Australian Associated Press in Batavia reported:

> At any moment the greatest blitz yet launched by the Japanese will be directed against Java. The mere fact that the invasion has been delayed for some days is an indication that the

Bali: Heaven and Hell

> Japanese are not under-estimating the strength of the defences, but are bringing up reinforcements and preparing bases before striking. To get fabulously wealthy Java, with every raw material that Japan needs and 47,000,000 natives for cheap labour, was Japan's primary object when she started this war … When she strikes, it will be with her full strength, aerially, navally and with heavy troop landings, probably at several points.

The AAP reporter continued, painting a fascinating picture of Batavia fiddling while Bali burned:

> The Dutch here see themselves in the same position as England after Europe was conquered. They say: 'Hitler got everything but what he wanted—England. The Japanese have got everything but what they want—Java. If we can hold Java, we shall turn the tide of the war.'
>
> In Batavia today, I sat on the terrace of a luxury hotel and listened to an eleven-piece orchestra which, with unconscious cynicism, was playing selections from 'The Mikado'. The all clear had just sounded outside and natives milled through the streets, with here and there a dash of khaki, a digger's slouch hat or the green of a Dutchman's uniform. Inside, officers drank and swapped stories, while Dutch and English girls, greatly outnumbered and revelling in it, held court.
>
> Last night the dance floor was so crowded that it was uncomfortable. The bar was jammed and so was the dining-room, which is understandable, as the guests are sleeping five to a room. There is no sign of depression, fear or foreboding. I had seen the same thing in Bandung and Surabaya. War, even on an island smaller than New Zealand, cannot kill gaiety.

In Tokyo, the *Asahi Shimbun* newspaper reported that the fall of Java was certain: 'Batavia will be a second Singapore. The loss of the N.E.I. will be the funeral bell for Australia.' They were half right. The invasion of Java began four days later and the Allies surrendered on 12 March. The battle for the Netherlands East Indies was over.

The Japanese occupation of Bali brought to an end the brief but hugely influential period of Dutch colonial rule. In its place, and in contrast

Chapter 8 *Merdeka!*

to what happened in other parts of the Indies, the Japanese created a strictly authoritarian but mostly peaceful regime that many Balinese at first regarded as an improvement upon the Dutch model.

'The Indonesian residents of Bali Island are enjoying a peaceful life under the control of the Japanese forces,' claimed a Japanese propaganda radio broadcast of 17 March 1942. 'Buses are running as before and highways destroyed by the Dutch have been repaired by the Indonesian Voluntary Labor Corps.' Bali had neither buses nor highways in 1942, and it is doubtful that many Balinese were 'enjoying' the occupation, but there was nevertheless a degree of truth in the mood of the report.

The occupation force offered opportunities for young Balinese men to learn new skills, and while they were wisely kept out of the firing line in domestic operations, most people felt positive about this. The concept of collaboration was not one that occurred to them in this context. They had simply substituted one colonial power for another, and this one shared the same gene pool. The one bone of contention, however, was the increasingly harsh taxing of their crops to feed Japanese troops.

The Japanese divided the East Indies into three jurisdictions: Java and Madura were placed under the control of the 16th Army; Sumatra, for a time, joined with Malaya under the 25th Army; and the eastern archipelago was placed under naval command. Java's economic value lay in its huge labour force and relatively developed infrastructure. In Sumatra and the east, the overriding concern of the occupiers was the maintenance of law and order and the extraction of needed resources. In Bali this meant such severe taxing of the rice crop that many went hungry.

The occupation was not always benign throughout the Indies. Japanese troops often acted brutally against locals, with the Japanese military police especially being feared. Food and other vital supplies were confiscated, causing widespread misery and starvation, but the worst abuse was the forced mobilisation of some 4 million manual labourers, or *romusha*, most of whom were put to work on construction projects in Java. About 270,000 *romusha* were sent to the outer islands and Japanese-held territories in South-East Asia, but only 52,000 were repatriated to Java.

The eastern administration area consisted of about 2.4 million people, made up of 1,250,000 in Bali, 820,000 in Lombok, and 320,000 in Sumbawa. The Japanese Navy's civil administrative unit calculated 'work force' to be men from the age of ten to fifty. Each unit was given a score out of 100.

From ten to fifteen and from forty-one to fifty were considered 'half units'. Estimated this way, Bali had 90 million, Lombok 57 million, and Sumbawa 23 million units of labour per year. The demand for labour in Bali in 1944, not including the demands by the military, was calculated to be 116 million (68 million for agriculture and 48 million for everything else), so there was not enough manpower left to get even the basics done. The Japanese may not have been violent but they were cruel, and the native population soon became malnourished and sickly.

Adding to their woes was the fact that virtually all cotton production had been seconded to the military, and all imports of clothing had stopped. Before the war, Bali, like most of South-East Asia, was self-sufficient in food but far from it in clothing, importing mainly from Japan and China. Now the people wore rags, and as the occupation wore on, many were reduced to wearing clothes made from jute gunnysacks. A factory in Solo, Java, stopped making new gunnysacks and devoted their entire operation to converting their existing stock to crude items of clothing. Meanwhile, hospitals ran out of bandages and had to use banana leaves, and women began to make their own sanitary napkins out of kapotex, a crude fibre made from kapok.

Perhaps the worst thing about all of this was that the Japanese knew exactly what would happen, and considered it nothing more than an unfortunate but inevitable consequence of war. Finance Minister Kaga Okinori explained to the Imperial Conference on 5 November 1941:

> The southern regions to be occupied have been importing considerably large amounts of various commodities. When we occupy the areas, importation of those items will stop. If the local economies were to be maintained effectively, we should be supplying those commodities. However, we do not have the necessary capabilities. For a considerably long period we cannot afford to pay attention to the economic wellbeing of the local people. We cannot but adopt so-called exploitative policies ... We must push on forward ignoring for the time being the economic confusions in the occupied land caused by the fall in the value of the currencies and so on. Local inhabitants are, however, culturally primitive and their lands are rich in natural resources. Maintaining their lifestyles would, therefore, be relatively easy in comparison with some other areas.

Chapter 8 *Merdeka!*

The Japanese occupation was a watershed in Indonesian history. Despite the fact that the Dutch re-established their rule after the Japanese surrender, there had been a significant shift in thinking in the Indies, and acceptance of colonial rule was never going to happen again. Java was far more developed politically and militarily than the other islands, and the Japanese occupation had actually furthered the cause of Indonesian nationalism. In administration, business and cultural life, the Dutch language had been discarded in favour of Malay and Japanese. Committees had been formed to standardise Bahasa Indonesia and make it a truly national language. Although the occupiers had constantly preached the gospel of Japanese leadership of Asia, they had not tried, as they had elsewhere, to promote Japanese culture above the local. Instead, their approach had been that Indonesians, as fellow Asians, were essentially like themselves but had been corrupted by three centuries of Western colonialism. What was needed was a healthy dose of *samurai* values.

Perhaps the most significant legacy of the occupation, however, was the opportunity it gave Indonesians to participate in politics, administration and the military. With all the Dutch officials interned, Japanese officers had taken over the highest positions in commerce and government, but they filled the middle and lower ranks with Indonesians. Over almost four years of occupation, this saw the beginnings of a home-grown bureaucracy, although after the Japanese surrender, some of the higher-profile bureaucrats were put to death as collaborators. One notable collaborator who escaped this fate was the best-known nationalist in the Indies, Kusno Sosrodihardjo, known as Sukarno.

Born in Surabaya in 1901 to a Javanese schoolteacher and his Balinese wife, Sukarno was renamed, according to custom, after surviving a serious childhood illness. Henceforth he was Karno (a Javanese word meaning 'good karma') with the honorific Su, or Bung. Still in his teens and a college student, he married the daughter of his boarding-house landlord, but when he moved to Bandung to study engineering and architecture he immediately took up with Inggit Garnasih, the wife of the boarding-house owner who was thirteen years his senior. Although Inggit was to be the last of his boarding-house romances, she was certainly not the last of his wives; a pattern of infidelity, polygamy and playboy lifestyle had been set for Bung Karno.

Like many young Javanese intellectuals, Sukarno despised the constrictions of both traditional feudalism and Dutch colonialism. Sukarno and his close friends were nationalists and socialists (although with Hitler on the rise in Europe, those words could not be paired), and in 1927 they formed the Partai Nasional Indonesia (PNI), with Sukarno elected leader. Since the communist party (PKI) had been crushed after a failed rebellion the previous year, the young Left came flocking to the PNI and it became a powerful political force.

Inevitably, the Dutch colonialists soon had heard enough insurrection. Sukarno and other key PNI leaders were arrested on 29 December 1929. Sukarno used his 1930 trial as a political platform and his speeches from the dock made him an international figure, but he was sentenced to four years in prison which he began serving in Bandung. International pressure on the Dutch, however, forced them to release him after two years. Sukarno was now an Indonesian hero, but in his absence in jail his party had splintered. When PNI was disbanded by the Dutch, out of its ashes came Partai Indonesia (Partindo) that promoted action by the masses.

In 1933 Sukarno published a manifesto entitled, *Mentjapai Indonesia Merdeka* (*To Attain Independent Indonesia*) and was promptly arrested again by the Dutch, who used their 'emergency powers' to send him and his wife into exile on the island of Flores without trial. When malaria broke out on Flores in 1938, Sukarno and Inggit were moved to Bengkulu on the west coast of Sumatra, where he began an affair with Fatmawati, the precociously beautiful fifteen-year-old daughter of a local Muslim leader, a situation he justified by explaining that Inggit had yet to bear him any children, and was not getting any younger.

Sukarno was still in Sumatran exile when the Japanese invaded in 1942, but he and Mohammad Hatta, leader of the rival Pendidikan Nasional Indonesia (PNI), were able to communicate and agree that both would cooperate with the Japanese.

The Japanese occupiers soon saw the value in Sukarno, who wrote: 'The Lord be praised, God showed me the way ... Yes, independent Indonesia can only be achieved with Dai Nippon ... For the first time in all my life, I saw myself in the mirror of Asia.'

In July 1942, Sukarno was sent back to Batavia (now being called Jakarta), where he was reunited with other nationalist leaders who had been released by the Japanese, including Mohammad Hatta. Sukarno was willing to support the Japanese, in exchange for a platform to spread nationalist ideas, while the Japanese needed Indonesia's manpower for their *romusha* labour program. To his eternal shame and regret, Sukarno, as head of the

Chapter 8 *Merdeka!*

labour movement, became the instrument and advocate of that cruel regime that resulted in the famine in Java that killed close to a million people.

While many in Java were slowly starving, Sukarno lived well in a comfortable house provided by the Japanese. When Inggit refused his request for a polygamous marriage (as a Muslim he was entitled to four wives), he divorced the older woman in 1943 and married Fatmawati, who soon bore him children, including a daughter, Megawati.

In September 1944, Sukarno and Hatta got their payoff for collaboration when the Japanese promised to grant independence to Indonesia, but no date was set for it, and the war had started to go very badly for them.

After the atomic bombs were dropped on Hiroshima and Nagasaki, Sukarno was urged by the more radical nationalists to proclaim the independent republic of Indonesia without delay, but he wavered, fearing both a final bloodbath from the defeated Japanese forces, and the future enmity of the Allies. Finally, on the morning of 17 August, Sukarno proclaimed independence in front of a crowd of 500 jubilant supporters. But the battle for independence was just beginning.

On 19 September, Sukarno addressed a crowd of one million people at what is now Merdeka Square in Jakarta, to celebrate a month of independence, and show the world the strong level of popular support for the new republic, at least on Java and Sumatra, where the Sukarno government had quickly established control while the remaining Japanese waited in their barracks for the arrival of the Allied forces.

It was a very different story on Bali. Despite the fact that he had Balinese blood, Sukarno was not the popular hero in Hindu Bali that he was in Muslim Java and Sumatra, and by the end of 1945 many people were too preoccupied with the growing famine to fight on behalf of someone else's new republic. Besides, there was no one for them to fight for almost six months until the Dutch eventually returned. During this curious void, when Bali was more or less independent by default, any outbreaks of violence were most likely to be payback attacks on real or imagined collaborators.

The return of the Dutch had been stalled by the insistence of the British South-East Asian Command that they meet certain guidelines regarding their control of the people, rather than picking up where they'd left off in 1942. But when the soldiers and administrators of the Netherlands Indies Civil Administration, under the command of Hubertus van Mook (who had led the Netherlands Indies Government-in-exile in Brisbane), arrived in Jakarta, a shooting war with the Indonesian Republicans soon developed. The situation became so dangerous that Sukarno and most of his government fled to Yogyakarta, where they could operate under the protection of the Sultan's guard. Meanwhile, the British were engaged in an air and naval bombardment against the Republicans of Surabaya.

The Balinese were not oblivious to all of this, but still the island was divided between those who wanted to be part of Sukarno's independent Indonesia, and those who believed that it would never happen and a better deal from the Dutch was the best they could hope for. It would take the emergence of their own revolutionary hero, and his tragic death, to sway public opinion in favour of the Republic.

During the second half of 1945, twenty-nine-year-old Colonel I Gusti Ngurah Rai had transformed the Prajura Corps (or Bali Defence Force) from a lacklustre 'dad's army' into an efficient Balinese army, boosted by young volunteers from the Republican support bases in Badung, Buleleng and Tabanan. When the Dutch returned and started arresting Republican sympathisers, Ngurah Rai took his men into the hills, where their mission was to disrupt the Dutch takeover with small strikes against working parties. Like Robin Hood and his merry men, Ngurah Rai's bandit soldiers gained more support with every strike, but in late 1946 they met serious Dutch opposition in a series of skirmishes near Tabanan. As more Dutch troops joined the battle, Ngurah Rai made the strategic decision to run for the hill country. At Marga, west of Ubud, however, they were cut off by another Dutch platoon. Ngurah Rai elected to fight to the death, and with the assistance of an aerial bombardment from a lone B-25 bomber, the Dutch systematically slaughtered the young colonel and all of his men.

The battle of Marga was a shattering defeat for the Balinese resistance movement, but a major psychological turning point for the independence struggle in Bali. This wasn't about intellectuals and the high-caste cadre anymore. It was personal now, resistance had a human face, and it had become the fight of the common man. Nevertheless, with no army, all organised resistance to the Dutch stopped, to be replaced by random protests and acts of civil disobedience.

Bali became part of the Dutch-controlled Republic of East Indonesia, set up in opposition to Sukarno's independent Republic, then in 1948 it was given autonomy within that alleged republic. But much of life in Bali was still controlled by the Dutch, and their policy was to divide and conquer,

Chapter 8 *Merdeka!*

setting Balinese villages and towns against each other by making claims and counter claims of collaboration against both sides. By late 1949 more than 2000 Balinese had been killed by their own people over the issue of independence and how to achieve it. Not for the first or the last time, the *kris* sword had become the final arbiter.

Meanwhile, Sukarno tried to negotiate a settlement with the Dutch, but two agreements were made and broken before the major powers began to tire of the never-ending conflict and threatened the Dutch with political and economic embargoes unless they granted the Indies their independence. The Dutch made one more crude attempt at a military solution, bombarding Yogyakarta, arresting Sukarno, Hatta and other ministers and jailing them in Sumatra, before finally bowing to pressure from an outraged United States and United Nations, and releasing the Republican leaders. Sukarno had made no real attempt to avoid incarceration, for he knew that the game was up for the Dutch. The more they attacked his liberty, the sooner they would be gone.

Finally, on 27 December 1949, at the Dutch–Indonesian Round Table Conference held in The Hague, Queen Juliana of the Netherlands transferred complete sovereignty to Indonesia. On that same day, Sukarno flew from Yogyakarta to Jakarta, making a triumphant speech on the steps of the governor-general's palace, renamed the Merdeka Palace. Indonesia was independent and President Sukarno was 'father of the nation'. It was a gloriously triumphant moment, but now his problems really began.

✳ ✳ ✳ ✳ ✳

In March 1946, just as the Dutch landings began on Bali, a tall, tanned American stood on the beach at Kuta, shaking his head at the panorama of rubble that extended from his feet to Jalan Pantai way to the south. Bob Koke took off his army cap, wiped his brow and kicked at the dirt, revealing the remains of the concrete wall of the laundry block that had once been part of the Kuta Beach Hotel.

The beach was still there, still beautiful, still untouched, and the line of the bay was the same, and now, an hour or so before sunset, he could see the fishermen in their *prahu*s heading out beyond the reef. But the Kuta Beach Hotel was just a memory, a crazy, funny, wonderful piece of the past that he and Louise, now back in the US, would never forget.

Bali: Heaven and Hell

Bob Koke was thirty-five, and he had served with distinction in the Office of Strategic Services in Batavia and later Shanghai, been a senior officer in the Singapore occupation force and was now with the South-East Asia Command. There was no place for him in Bali; that time had passed. He took one last look at his field of dreams, climbed into the jeep and nodded to his driver to take him back to the recently reopened Bali Hotel. He felt a cocktail coming on.

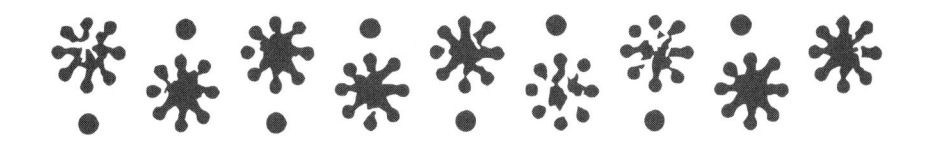

Chapter 9 Our Mission in Bali

In the name of the Lord Jesus, I deliberately set my feet on the soil of Bali and claim it for Him. The light of the gospel, preached by Spirit-filled missionaries, will drive out the millions of demons of darkness, and these people, enchained by the devil so long, will be set free.

R.A. Jaffray, 1928

In the dark, wood-lined sitting room of a large, Dutch-style home in Sanur, an elderly woman rises from her comfortable bamboo chair and glides to the door to greet her guests. She moves slowly but assuredly, a purple sarong draped around her long, fine neck, a mauve print dress just touching the floor. Her smile is warm, revealing even white teeth, her grey-white hair groomed just so. Her hands, pushed forward in greeting, are slender and dainty. Everything about her is elegant.

Although we are well and truly into the dry season, the rain has been pouring down all afternoon. The sky outside is leaden and it is almost dark inside the house. 'A little rain is good for the garden,' says Mrs Lelia Lewis, motioning for us to sit, 'but it is a bit steamy. Would you like a cold drink?' She repeats the conversation in perfect Balinese for the one Balinese guest. Then she sits back down in her bamboo chair, straightens her sarong and asks, 'Where would you like me to begin?'

Lelia Lewis, then in her mid-twenties, arrived in Bali in December 1953, with her husband, Rodger, and first child, Helen, who was eighteen months old. She was pregnant with second daughter Frances. The Lewises hadn't come for a vacation. They had come to stay for as long as it took. They were evangelical Christian missionaries, sent out from the US by the Christian Missionary Alliance as part of a new wave of soul saving made possible by

President Sukarno's declaration of freedom of religion in the new republic and his revoking of the long-standing ban on evangelical missionaries.

For more than a century the majority of Balinese had struggled to understand the motivation of these missionaries, who seemed to want to tear down Balinese belief systems and substitute their own rather flawed set. It didn't make any sense. The story of the first Christian convert had become legendary, and many Balinese could quote it in defence of their intense dislike of the missionaries. It went like this.

In 1830 the Dutch tolerated the mission of a Reverend Ennis, an Englishman who set up a church in Buleleng, but in the course of them negotiating treaties with the Balinese, the Dutch began to favour a laissez faire approach to native culture and religion. Ennis went home without a single convert, and there was no further attempt to save the heathens until 1866, when the Utrecht Missionary Union sent out the Reverend R. van Eck, who immersed himself in the Hindu culture and only found time to convert one native—his servant, Gusti Wayan Nurat Karangasem, whom he renamed Nicodemus. Although he was ostracised by his village and family for adopting the *bule* faith, Nicodemus seemed quite content with his lot in life until the Utrecht Union read one glowing report too many about Hindu culture and called van Eck home, replacing him with the Reverend J. de Vroom, an energetic fundamentalist who believed that any means were justified in getting heathen bums on church pews.

Nicodemus was sent amongst his own people to bring them to de Vroom's church or suffer the wrath of God in the form of the Reverend's whip. Regarded as 'morally dead' by his own people and unable to deliver a single soul to the Lord, Nicodemus broke down in mind and spirit. In June 1881, de Vroom was found brutally murdered in his home, and two servants were soon arrested. When they testified that they were acting on instructions from Nicodemus, he was hunted down in Mengwi. Seemingly resigned to his fate, he stared straight ahead as he was paraded around the kingdoms in a bamboo cage before being beheaded.

This shocking case aroused strong emotions amongst both the Balinese and the Dutch administrators, with the Balinese resolved that they would no longer tolerate missionaries, and the Dutch convinced that their first policy of religious tolerance had been the right one. Utrecht was told to send no replacement, and a new law was put in place forbidding missionaries to settle in Bali. This law remained in force until 1951, although it was amended

Chapter 9 Our Mission in Bali

in the 1920s to allow a small number of American missionaries permanent residence with the proviso that they minister only to existing Christians and not seek to convert anyone.

This directive was an impossibility for a missionary of such powerful faith as Dr Robert A. Jaffray. Jaffray didn't found the Christian Missionary Alliance, but as soon as he heard the man who did, the Reverend A.B. Simpson, preach in New York, he immediately enrolled in the New York Missionary Training School and in 1897, at the age of twenty-four, he went into China to save souls. Simpson had started out in 1884 by sending his first overseas missions to the Congo, but by the turn of the century the CMA had outposts all over the world and Christian zealots ready to serve in them.

Although he had been born into wealth and privilege (his father was a Canadian senator who owned and published the influential *Toronto Globe* newspaper), Jaffray built a new life from nothing in China, marrying fellow missionary Minnie Donor in 1900 and founding the South China Press, which published *The Bible* magazine in Mandarin, reaching Chinese communities all over the world. But when his father died in the late 1920s and left him an inheritance, he turned his missionary eye to the greatest challenge in the Far East—the Muslim hordes of the Dutch East Indies and the unreachable Hindus on Bali.

The Jaffrays made several largely unsuccessful attempts to spread the gospel through Bali, but they were living in Makassar in Sulawesi at the outbreak of World War II where they were interned, and Dr Jaffray died in a work camp a month before the Japanese surrender in 1945. As well as being a powerful evangelist, Jaffray had been a thinker who helped shape the CMA philosophy of muscular fundamentalism, stressing that Christ's return was imminent, that adultery was the work of the devil, divorce unthinkable and homosexuality the 'basest form of sinful conduct', although it is doubtful that his philosophies had anything to do with CMA's much later opposition to abortion, stem-cell research, euthanasia, marijuana and ordained female clergy.

Eight years after his death, little remained of the Jaffray legacy in Bali when Rodger and Lelia Lewis began their mission in Klungkung. There were a few Christian churches in Denpasar and a couple more scattered across the island, mostly to serve the *pendatung* (inter-island migrants who had come to Bali for work) and the Chinese merchant Christian community. But in Klungkung there was just one other missionary couple and a Catholic priest. 'That was it,' says Lelia, 'the entire expat population of Klungkung.'

The former accommodation of the Dutch *controleur* within the palace of the Dewa Agung had been made available for rent to the missionaries, courtesy of the Dewa, the raja of Klungkung and still the acknowledged ceremonial head of state of Bali. 'It wasn't very palatial,' Lelia recalls with a chuckle. 'But the Dewa was a jolly old guy, a very interesting landlord, who had thirty-nine wives kept in three separate houses within the palace.'

Life in Klungkung was tough by anyone's standards, but Rodger and Lelia fell in love with the lush landscape of their new home. Lelia remembers:

> It was a peaceful, beautiful island. You didn't have the malls or the hotels back then. The flutes that you'd hear at night, those liquid notes ... and there was a type of jasmine flower that doesn't grow anymore. And, oh, the fireflies ... we'd just go out walking in the dark night, knowing each of the few vehicles that might come by, and you'd just see fireflies and the stars. It was very, very beautiful.

Both Lelia and Rodger were born to be missionaries, of missionary stock, but she had the better grasp of the highs and lows of life on a remote station, having been born on the mountainous borders of China and Tibet, where her father died and was buried. After that tragedy, she and her mother returned to America where, in time, she met and married Rodger Lewis, and the young couple set out again to the far parts to do the good works of God and the CMA. But this was not a feel-good adventure for the righteous young, a brief experience to look back on later in life. The CMA did not send out their missionaries for three or five years' experience in the front line. They demanded a commitment for life. When Lelia Lewis arrived in Klungkung in 1953 with a child in her arms and one in her belly, she had no expectations of ever returning to the place she called home but had never really known. She was resigned to that reality, if not entirely comfortable with it. It helped that Bali was soon in her blood.

> You had a people who were very friendly, an agrarian society, lots of rice fields, fairly decent roads that the new government had put in. But mostly there just wasn't the rush that you find now. You could trust the Balinese. We could leave the windows open, you didn't

Chapter 9 Our Mission in Bali

> have to lock doors, nobody stole. This was part of what they learned in the *banjar* [village council]. Back then there was still quite a distinction between the castes, and that has broken down now, which is good. When we first came, there was an article in *Reader's Digest* in which the writer said, 'I never saw a fat woman in Bali.' And that was true! We lived in the mountains and we'd see women walking up and down ravines with their wares on their heads, so erect and graceful. And the women would work so hard on the roads or in the fields while the men took care of their fighting roosters. Now I look at the women in my *banjar* and they are all quite, ah, healthy.

Lelia paints an idyllic picture of those early years in Klungkung, but in fact, it was hard living, without running water or refrigeration. 'Oh, we had running water,' she corrects. 'When we needed water the boy who worked for us would run and get some.' Lelia smiles so sweetly as she delivers her punchline that it is impossible to take offence at the paternalistic inference.

> Then we'd have to treat it to make it drinkable. We had all these lanterns and every night we'd have to light them all. It was hard work but it was enjoyable, and I miss it so.
>
> Back then shopping was easy because every day the fish lady would come with fresh fish caught in unpolluted waters, the butcher would come to the door with beautiful cuts of beef. Fruit was cheap and every day we had papaya. The Balinese didn't eat it, and they were always surprised to see us devour it for breakfast. They would only use it as a vegetable before it was ripe. We ate very well on what was fresh and available. Maybe once every two weeks we'd come into Denpasar to buy staples. The thing I longed for the most was cheese, but all you could buy was this horrible tinned cheese, so we would buy that to have with our home-baked bread.

Lelia Lewis's memories of Bali in the early 1950s are invaluable because there are very few accounts of ordinary life during the first years of independence under Sukarno, a time when, despite Lelia's rosy picture, economic circumstances were becoming very difficult for many Balinese. It was a time of significant social change, particularly in the cities, yet historians have had to rely on short fiction published in magazines for glimpses of city life.

Bali: Heaven and Hell

Damai magazine in Denpasar and *Bhakti* in Singaraja both published stories by local writers with themes such as foreign films (shown at the Hollywood Cinema) making some people fantasise about wealth and luxury, or the rise of street-side cafes known as 'depots', and the social scene at the night markets. Other writers focused on the adaptation of young people to Western clothing and cosmetics, or the rapidly changing nature of traffic in the crowded city streets. (A survey taken in January 1953 showed that there were 1497 motor vehicles on Bali and 1827 human- or animal-powered vehicles, but cars were rapidly catching up.)

A growing obsession amongst city people with the wealth and luxury they saw depicted in films resulted in many aspiring to a *rumah kantor* (literally a company house but meaning a Western-style, free-standing home with mod cons). Such a home would boast a cabinet radio, a glass-fronted bookcase filled with books, a sewing machine and a modern kitchen. Electricity and running water were also important, but it was the look of the place that was all-important. While these dreams were innocent enough, the pursuit of wealth against all odds had a significant downside, with the rise of corruption and prostitution, particularly in Denpasar.

Police and government officials led the way in demanding money for services rendered or deeds overlooked, but the building trades became overrun with people stealing from major construction sites to sell materials on the black market. Prostitution had been a fact of life right through the Dutch colonial years, but in 1950s Denpasar, brothels proliferated. The pimps were often men struggling to make enough money to create the style of home the family had to have, while the whores were generally young girls who had married too young and then engaged in adulterous affairs with Bali's many 'lady killers'—older, married playboy types who were often also pimps.

One of the few journalists to document this period in Bali was Frenchman Jacques Chegaray, who had spent the postwar years hitching and tramp steaming around the world to write two long-forgotten books, *Going My Way Around the World* and *My Polynesia*. In 1952, Chegaray washed up in Bali and researched his third travel book, *Bliss in Bali*. Photos of the author reveal a rather daggy man in voluminous khaki work shorts and white business shirts, but his writing is conversational, not without humour and rich in detail.

'Access to Bali is not easily obtained,' he writes. 'Not everybody who wants to can land here, and visas other than for transit are rarely granted.' Chegaray may have been gilding the lily here, but Sukarno had certainly

Chapter 9 Our Mission in Bali

tightened up entry procedures, and even if you managed to get the papers, actually getting there was no picnic, even in the new age of airline travel. He reached Bali by way of plane hops through Basra, Daran, Karachi and Calcutta on KLM, then trains from Jakarta to Surabaya, and from there, steamer to Buleleng. The trip took more than a week.

Like so many Westerners before him, the first thing Chegaray noticed about Bali was its topless women, but any prurient interest he may have had was disguised through the old journalistic trick of pointing to the prurience of others.

> Exposing their breasts had for long been the privilege of Bali womanhood. After the proclamation of Indonesia's independence the Sukarno Government forbade this practice. Today, if the townsfolk have accepted the new law, village dwellers are reluctant to follow suit. Previously only prostitutes covered their bosoms ... I was assured this restrictive measure had been taken to stop the influx of over-inquisitive American tourists, said to have spent fortunes yearly crossing the Pacific merely to focus their cameras on the naked breasts of the Balinese women.

Chegaray was impressed by the quality of Balinese art but critical of its increasing mass production:

> The Balinese are born artists. Their skill in reproducing classical models is unsurpassed. Innovation, however, is more rare. Balinese art, which was dormant, has had a brilliant revival with the recent influx of tourists, mainly American ... It is fashionable to criticise the hurried tourists who, between planes, visit the whole island in three days; yet it is because of them and their constantly growing demand that thousands of Balinese wood carvers make a living.

The Frenchman's most potent observation, however, was this early glimpse of Sukarno's lurch towards totalitarianism, under the subheading, 'Is it the end of old Bali?'

> ... As a reaction against Dutch conservatism, the new government is trying to enforce an exaggerated modernism. It is now fashionable among officials and higher-ranking civil servants to despise the old Bali, but this is very natural in the circumstances. The students

of Singaradja [sic] and Den Pasar [sic] shrug their shoulders when one mentions the temple festivals, though these are unique in the world. On Aug 17, Independence Day, a ridiculous procession made its way through the streets of Den Pasar. To the music of a military band, all the little school-girls of the town marched past, three abreast. Amongst them were little half-Chinese girls of six, dressed in uniform and wearing the Mao Tse Tung cap ... It was the saddest sight you could imagine, and the Europeans who saw the parade were horror-stricken. 'We had eight years of that under Hitler,' the German chemist's wife whispered in my ear.

By the early 1960s, the Lewises (now five, following the birth of Richard in 1956) had joined the fast-growing ranks of motorists in Bali, becoming the proud owners of a Jeep Wagoneer. The vehicle was a necessity rather than a luxury—Rodger and Lelia had started the Bethel Children's Home in Klungkung to enable Christian children to be schooled safely, after a young Christian boy had been killed when students who were taunting him pushed him into a ravine, and they needed to go back and forth to remote mountain villages—but it also enabled them to take the children for visits to expat friends in Denpasar, Sanur and Kuta Beach.

In Sanur, they would often visit Wija and Judith Wawo-Runtu, an exotic couple with young children, who were just beginning to build a series of traditional bungalows along the beachfront that would eventually become the Tandjung Sari Hotel. Little Dick Lewis was great mates with Timi Wawo-Runtu, and the two would play at the edge of the lagoon while their parents took tea (or perhaps something a little stronger for Wija) on the terrace. In Kuta they would also call on beachfront friends, the English leprologist Dr Spencer Reed and his wife who lived where the Kokes' Hotel Kuta Beach had once stood.

'Klungkung was 40 kilometres of narrow road to town with very narrow bridges where a car could get stuck,' Lelia Lewis recalls with a laugh, 'but when the children were around we'd come in once a week and we'd go all the way to Kuta, which in those days was a long, long drive. But it was worth it, to play on that lovely beach, and, of course, to see the Reeds.'

The Lewises made no apologies for the fact that their mission in Bali was to save souls in the name of Jesus Christ, but the means to this end was, in Lelia's words, 'to show them God's love through good deeds'. In addition

Chapter 9 Our Mission in Bali

to the Bethel Children's Home, they had established a clean-water program, and were working with their next-door neighbour, the one doctor assigned to the regencies of Klungkung, Gianyar, Bangli and Nusa Penida, to try to control serious diseases in the villages.

In many ways, health care in Bali had progressed little from the nineteenth century, as Jacques Chegaray observed:

> When a serious case of illness occurs in a family, the house becomes taboo; the door is hung with pandanus leaves and no one is allowed to go near the patient unless he has previously rubbed his feet on the threshold in order to remove any evil influences. The rainy season, from November to May, is the time for epidemics. Infantile mortality increases and cases of malaria are legion. Malaria is treated with a salty decoction of dadap leaves to which aniseed, onion and some powdered charcoal have been added ... The most widespread complaints are skin diseases, so often encountered in tropical countries ... the dreaded leprosy, which is never referred to as anything else but 'the great sickness' is a scourge against which the Balinese are utterly helpless. Formerly, lepers were hounded out of their homes ... today they go on living in their villages ... but never did I come across one in a Balinese hospital. The system used in the detection of the disease among the villages is primitive in the extreme. With the exception of a few centres, Bali possesses no heath service, social workers or district nurses, and there is not a single chemist's shop in the whole island.

Spencer Reed arrived in Bali in 1956 determined to help turn around the island's dismal record in the treatment of lepers. Although her novel of the *puputan* of 1906 (*Love and Death in Bali*) was fiction, Vicki Baum had based her account of the fate of the high-caste, handsome dancer on the contemporary treatment of lepers. They were forced from the villages and made to live out their days by stagnant ponds and swamps at the beach, where their ablutions would be upriver of no one. Very little had changed in the fifty years leading up to Reed's arrival, yet within a few years he and a small team of volunteers had achieved miracles, thanks in large part to a new wonder drug called dapsone.

Like many groundbreaking drugs, the suspected side effects of dapsone opened up a ferocious debate within the medical community, and in

1960, Reed was forced to defend his field work with dapsone against attacks from his former medical mentor, Dr Hubert Cochrane:

> Here in Bali the contrast between the pre- and post-dapsone patients is most striking. All the former—300 of them—who were not lucky enough to heal spontaneously have now been gathered up to live in six leprosaria by the sea, clothed and fed by the government. Practically all of them have revolting and pathetic mutilations. In marked comparison are the 2000 out-patients who are making dramatic progress under dapsone. This they receive regularly ... every two weeks at one of 90 different places throughout the island ... Not only is ugly infiltration receding, but ... contractures and mutilations are now a thing of the past.

Although they were around disease all the time, the Lewises themselves were relatively fortunate. Lelia contracted tuberculosis and had to fly home to the US to have a lobe of her lung removed, but after six months in a sanitarium she returned to Bali, full of energy again. There were frequent rounds of dengue fever and Dick contracted malaria, but most of the time the family had little more to contend with than the regular bouts of 'Bali belly'. But in 1963 a sequence of events began that seemed to Lelia to be straight out of the Old Testament.

> Our landlord, the Dewa Agung, was head of the committee for the religious festival, Eka Dasa Rudra, held once every one hundred years, and when the first offerings went up to the Mother Temple, the mountain [Gunung Agung] started to erupt that very day. The trucks that were taking them up to Besakih just kept going as the eruptions got worse. Days and days went by and still it kept getting worse. Then finally it really erupted, and everything went dark from the ash fall-out. In Klungkung we got a lot of ash and sand, and our water supply was cut off because it was spring-fed. We had to go about 10 kilometres every day to a spring where we could bathe and do our laundry, but we couldn't go up to the higher villages near there because it was too dangerous. People were supposed to have evacuated, but a lot were killed because they simply went back to their villages and went into a trance.

Chapter 9 Our Mission in Bali

The eruptions of Gunung Agung in March 1963, the first in modern times, were catastrophic for Bali, with several thousand people killed and more than 100,000 left homeless. But many in Bali believed that this was only a small part of a terror or curse being unleashed by offended gods, a process that had begun the previous year with a plague of rats and a famine of biblical proportions. And what had offended the gods so? One theory that emerged was that the priests had got the dates wrong for the forty-day *Eka Dasa Rudra*, which would seem a bit extreme, but a theory with broader political ramifications had been circulating for more than a year. In this one, Bali was being punished for the affronts it had allowed President Sukarno to get away with in building a holiday mansion above the holy temple of Tampaksiring, and frequently summoning its priests to perform elaborate welcome ceremonies for his guests. It was also claimed that he 'staged nightlong parties that degenerated into orgies ... dispatching his aides to collect the prettiest young girls to be delivered to the palace, there to be debauched by himself and his party'.

Whether it was Sukarno's debauchery or something else to blame, Bali's curse continued. Lelia Lewis recalls:

> Right after [the eruptions and subsequent earthquakes and floods] all the bodies awaiting cremation had to be burned immediately, and we had a cholera plague. Then there was another rat plague, and the rice was all destroyed. It went on and on. People got boils and died.

And then, when it seemed things could not get any worse, they did.

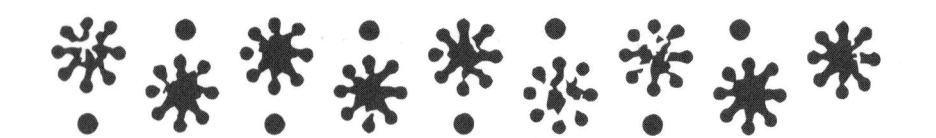

Chapter 10 The Year of Living Dangerously

The best-known references to the killings draw attention to the calm and dignified manner in which suspected communists allegedly allowed themselves to be executed, as if to suggest that a massacre was just another of the many mysteries of exotic Bali, or that if the Balinese were able to treat death with such resigned indifference, so might we.

Geoffrey Robinson, 1995

They met backstage at a fundraising show on a balmy, late-summer Saturday night in Palmerston North, New Zealand, where he was studying agriculture under the Colombo Plan and she was a journalist. He was also a Balinese dancer, she a ballerina. They ended up doing a routine in each other's arms that brought the house down. They were married within a year and Janice Babington became Mrs Djati Mantjika. She had no idea how much cultural change that involved.

Jan Mantjika is seventy-three at the time of our interview, a thoughtful, gentle woman with a ready smile. When she reflects on her fifty years in Bali, there is often a twinkle in her eyes, but there is also resignation and some sadness. It hasn't been an easy life, not even at the start.

Jan and Djati had their first child in 1963, and, Djati's studies finished, they moved to Bali in 1964 so that he could join the agriculture faculty of Udayana University. Deeply in love and preoccupied with the new baby in her arms and another on the way, Jan had given little thought to what life would be like in President Sukarno's Indonesian Republic, but cultural differences suddenly came into focus when they arrived at Jakarta's airport and were met by armed soldiers and marched off at bayonet point to be strip-searched. The hostile greeting was part of Sukarno's *Ganyang Malaysia* (Crush Malaysia) campaign, which was also aimed at the British and any of

Chapter 10 The Year of Living Dangerously

their outposts of empire, such as Australia and New Zealand. What's more, within the communist-controlled government there was increasing suspicion of academics who had graduated from 'imperialist' countries, rather than Russia or China.

In Bali Jan and Djati initially lived in Djati's family compound, where Jan felt safe and loved, but when they moved into an apartment on campus, 'I knew that everyone was very suspicious of me and a bit afraid to talk for fear of being branded capitalist imperialists. The communists were very powerful and there was a real culture of fear.'

When Djati became chairman of a lobbying group of academics advocating justice reforms, the Mantjikas found themselves targeted even more. Jan rarely left the campus now, spending her time looking after two young children and tending their small vegetable garden. As the Sukarno government became more warlike and less functional, Djati often went weeks without receiving a pay packet, forcing the young family to live on a handful of rice and their tiny garden plot. And in September 1965, Jan announced to her husband that they would soon have a third little mouth to feed.

Meanwhile, in Klungkung, Rodger and Lelia Lewis were also beginning to feel the increasing isolation of being 'imperialists'. Lelia recalls:

> We went on home leave [to the United States] in 1964, but I knew at the time that trouble was coming from the PKI, you could just feel it. When we came back at the end of the year, people we would normally visit began to say, oh please don't come see us anymore. Everywhere in the villages we would see the signs. They'd have parades right in front of our house. One time they had this guy handcuffed and in grubby clothes out in the street with a big sign on him, 'Imperialist Capitalist'. People that we knew were communists, true cadres, would spit at us, and there were spies in our midst. The governor at the time was also communist. One day a cadre we knew came to our house and went out back and dug a hole, six by six. We had no idea what it was for until much later. We knew that something was going to happen, but in God's hands we had no fear.

Almost twenty years after he had seized power, Sukarno was considered by many Indonesians to be a spent force—ever more corrupt, inefficient and lurching menacingly to the left, a position that even sections of his own military found untenable. It was conventional wisdom that the Father of the Republic had passed his use-by date and would get his comeuppance soon enough. On Bali, however, political unrest was being fuelled by more mundane issues, such as hunger. The 1964 famine had exacerbated resentment that while the Communist PKI was trying to break down the caste system, the party was doing nothing to help achieve a more equitable division of land ownership that might prevent many Balinese families from starving.

By 1965 there were political rallies on every street corner in Denpasar and Singaraja, but the event that brought the island closest to widespread violence was not a political rally but the cremation of the Lewis family's landlord and neighbour, the Dewa Agung of Klungkung. The highest level of cremation tower, eleven tiers, was built for the departure to the spirit world of this revered old man, and thousands of his subjects prepared for the elaborate ceremony. But the PKI massed its men outside the palace on the eve of the cremation, determined to crush this demonstration that the caste system was alive and well, even if the Dewa Agung was not. Klungkung was spared a bloodbath only when the police and PNI nationalists took the communists by surprise, and they fled after a brief skirmish.

A couple of weeks later, on the evening of 30 September 1965, rogue pro-communist army units, under the command of Lieutenant Colonel Untung, kidnapped and then killed six generals from the Army High Command, claiming them to be in league with the American CIA. Their corpses were flung down an unused well in the village of Lubang Buaya, near Jakarta's Halim Air Force base, and Untung announced the formation of a 'revolutionary council'. But the politically unknown head of the strategic reserve, Major General Suharto, had been left off the hit list, and within hours he had led a successful counter-coup, delivering power to the anti-communist nationalists. Retribution on the communists began almost immediately; wresting the presidency from Sukarno would take much longer.

The issues surrounding the twin coups that would become known by the bizarre acronym 'Gestapu' (derived from 'G30S/PKI' or the 30 September Movement) were quite complex, but the Suharto forces managed to dumb it down to this: the evil communists had been overthrown, now was the time to take revenge by exterminating them. The bloodbath began in Java, but by December it had spread to Bali.

Chapter 10 The Year of Living Dangerously

> A hot day in December, 1965. I was nine years old—a blond, sun-crisped Bali *bule* boy—and a Balinese man I'd never seen before hunched on the parlour sofa of my parents' house in Klungkung, east Bali. He reeked of fright: acrid, bitter, biting. He was silent, hands clasped between his knees. A former member of a communist community organisation, he was helpless, hopeless, marked for death … not by [his] gray-skinned pallor but by stink. I'll never forget that smell.

So begins Dick Lewis's written account of his homecoming that Christmas. Dick and his older sisters had just flown in from their missionary school in Bandung, Java, landing on the grass airstrip at Tuban where their father had been waiting to drive them home to the hills. Rodger Lewis said very little on the long drive. He seemed preoccupied. When they got home the children understood why.

All around them, innocent people were being dragged from their homes and slaughtered in the streets by their countrymen—shot, hacked to death or beheaded. Dick Lewis says:

> Klungkung had a large PKI presence, with many of the high caste Brahman families being party members. Kids I'd played with on the streets and fields and banyan trees simply disappeared. Thousands of corpses were tossed into estuary ravines by the seashore, and into the ocean itself. A journalist staying with us told of seeing a raft of bodies floating in the surf, sharks leisurely feeding off them.

The killings were carried out by the Red Berets, a nationalist troop, mainly Balinese, but the death lists were created by the *banjar*s and other community groups who simply had to imply some previous association with a socialist group, like a teacher's union, to write a death warrant for enemies, troublesome family members or creditors on land deals. In short, when Gestapu came to Bali, people used it as a time to get even, for anything and everything.

Dick Lewis says:

> My parents got word that two students from the high school down the road were going to be killed that afternoon because they were suspected of being members of some leftist organisation.

111

> The nationalists were going to kill them and the principal and some of the teachers had quietly drifted away to a coffee shop. My mom and dad heard this from another student who was staying with us, so they went down there and they stared that lynch mob down until the cops arrived. When no one else was brave enough to go visit the suspected communists in jail, my dad would go. He was the only one with the guts to do that.

Jan Mantjika remembers:

> Awful things were happening and not necessarily just to people thought to be communists. If someone had a grudge it was relatively easy to get your enemies put on a death list. I know of one person who was only five years old then, and they came for his father. The mother put him and his brother into the bedroom behind a bamboo wall, but he could peep through, and he saw his mother and father with their hands tied behind their backs and they were kneeling. Then a blade came down on the back of their necks and took both heads off at once. That poor person has had to live with that ever since.

But Jan also experienced the terror first-hand.

> Our accommodation at the university was at the far end of the road, quite close to the immigration office where they kept people they couldn't fit into the jail, and every now and then one would escape. This poor guy came running along and had to jump over a fence to get into the university. He tripped as he jumped and these men with knives caught up with him and started hacking bits off him. It was horrible, and it was in my yard! He ran around the back, thinking there would be an exit, but there wasn't and he had to come back through this gang of frenzied people.

Like many people who actually suffered the long-suppressed horrors of Gestapu, Jan Mantjika had to stop to compose herself this far into the story, and was never comfortable about continuing.

When Suharto's nationalists had taken control in Klungkung, the purpose of the hole that had been dug in the Lewises' backyard became

Chapter 10 The Year of Living Dangerously

frighteningly clear. 'The Red Beret commanders came in and they showed my father the [communist] list with our names on it. That was to be our [family] grave. We were to have been eliminated,' Dick Lewis says.

Lelia Lewis remembers that she and Rodger had been baffled by the fact that their family had been marked for murder by the communists.

> Well, we were imperialist capitalists, as they kept saying, but maybe it was also because we were Christian. But it didn't make any sense, and it didn't get any better when it was the communists who were being killed. You see, this is Bali, and even in the nicest little *banjar*, there are resentments. The Balinese are human, and this was a time to settle scores. We knew a guy who had been the head of the communist-controlled teachers' union, but he wasn't a communist. The Red Berets were the ones who would come in and do it, but it was the locals who were deciding who went on the lists. So one day this guy from the teachers union came in, and our kids were all there, and he said, 'I know I'm going to be killed.'

The death squads stalked the streets of Bali's villages and towns right through the wet season and into the dry. Everyone had stories, but few were told until much later. 'We had people stay with us, we took them in,' Lelia says. 'There was one guy who we knew they were after, and we told him to stay inside at all times, but he went out on the road one day and they were waiting, and he was killed. There were people killed every day, and it left terrible scars.'

One response to a blog about Gestapu on Dick Lewis's website states:

> A friend from Klungkung once told me of the [time] he walked all night along that coast, to search for his younger brother, a promising university student, a brilliant linguist. He found his body on Pantai Lebih ... murdered for his leftist views, for his intelligence, for his promise. Another friend told me about witnessing the executions in Petulu, as a nine-year-old, curious about all the strange goings-on in his neighbourhood. Why were all these trucks carrying people off? Why did their teacher disappear? Why did his mother tell him not to go out? So with a few friends, he followed the trucks and witnessed machine-gun executions from behind the trees. Everyone who lived through that time had to contend with the terrors and never talk about what they knew.

Bali: Heaven and Hell

By late 1966 the terror on Bali was over. While Indonesia prepared to oust the now powerless Sukarno (his PKI support base having been wiped out) and embark on Suharto's 'New Order', Bali mourned its dead and tried to rebuild its spirit. More than a million people had been massacred in Java, Sumatra and Bali, but nowhere was the pain felt more than in Bali, where 5 per cent of the population (80,000) had been slaughtered. Detailed reports of the Gestapu killings had been suppressed by the Suharto-controlled cabinet, but most Western media analysis focused not on the enormity of the disaster (nor on the fact that US President Lyndon Johnson and the CIA knew exactly what was going on and did nothing to stop it, presumably believing that the only good communist was a dead one), but on finding some 'cultural explanation' for what had happened. Using the precedent of the 1906 *puputan* in Denpasar, the analysts claimed that the communists had threatened Bali's cultural traditions to the point where 'these people of grace and charm' had become frenzied and run amok, as they did.

The basic premise of most of the published accounts was that the Balinese normally lived in harmony, and were tolerant and peaceful folk until pushed beyond some unstated boundary, at which point they would become the opposite. It wasn't much of an explanation for the savage slaughter of more than 80,000 people, but it seemed to satisfy most.

As historian Geoffrey Robinson noted:

> Within the community of Bali scholars, the events of 1965–66 have been treated as a kind of academic no-man's land … To the extent that it has been discussed at all by academics, the post-coup violence has generally been portrayed as a historical aberration, caused by the lamentable meddling of outsiders—communists, Sukarnoists, Javanese—thereby casting no doubt on prevailing views of a harmonious, apolitical Bali.

Writing an introduction to her collected works about peace and harmony in Bali between the wars, just four years after the massacres, anthropologist Jane Belo made no mention of the slaughter. Writing in 1973, historian and anthropologist Clifford Geertz gave it just one sentence: '… there followed several months of extraordinary popular savagery … directed against individuals considered to be followers of the Indonesian Communist Party.'

Writing in 1976, historian Willard A. Hanna comes right out and says it: 'The events of late 1965 and early 1966 in Bali have never been fully

Chapter 10 The Year of Living Dangerously

reported and perhaps need not and should not be.' An unabashed supporter of Suharto's New Order, Hanna seems to imply that any further examination of the Suharto-inspired killings might lead to the gods unleashing still more catastrophes on the island. But on the ground in Bali in 1966, most people just wanted to try to forget the horrors they had seen or experienced, and get on with normal life.

Jan and Djati Mantjika had a son in January 1966, born in the midst of the chaos that was Denpasar. By year's end Jan was desperate to take the new child home to New Zealand to meet his grandparents. Her parents sent the money for the tickets and they flew south. It was to be a relatively long stay, because Jan needed to work for Western wages for a while to put some money in the family coffers. It had always been a battle for the academics at Udayana University to get regular salaries in the Sukarno years, but as the New Order became established, many lecturers were fired on the grounds of their alleged association with 'counter-revolutionary elements', and others, like Djati, often went months without pay.

When Jan returned to Bali in 1967 she sensed that there was more stability and a degree of optimism in the air, although still no regular pay packet for Djati. Suharto, now president of the Republic, had formed crucial strategic alliances with the United States and Australia, both waging war in Vietnam, and was now ready to resume the Sukarno-era transition of the Balinese economy from agrarian-based to tourism-based. In 1963, just as Gunung Agung had erupted, famine had followed and people started dying all over the island, Sukarno had turned the first sod of a monstrous Western-style hotel on the Sanur beachfront, and at the same time announced a timetable for construction of an international airport on the site of the Tuban airfield. Due to famine, pestilence, plagues of rats, wholesale slaughter of innocents and other tourism-negative episodes, transition plans had been put on hold momentarily, but by 1967 tourists, mostly oblivious to the full extent of the recent carnage, began to arrive, many to stay at the Bali Beach Hotel, Sukarno's dream for Bali, opened by Suharto in 1966.

Jan Mantjika hadn't seen tourists in Bali for years, but now there was a trickle of Australian students arriving, and often they were billeted with the Mantjikas. Djati had a thriving vegetable garden now and they had a chicken run, so there was plenty to eat at last. As the flow of students and academics increased, Djati found that he was spending too much of his time driving them around in borrowed cars, often in the company of Ibu Gedong Bagus

Bali: Heaven and Hell

Oka, a distinguished student of Ghandi and an intellectual, simply because they were part of the small minority of local academics who spoke English.

One day Ibu Gedong suggested to Jan that she should start a little business, charging a small fee for introducing students and other tourists to the culture of Bali. Jan recalls:

> We didn't really think of it as a business, but we certainly needed money, and it seemed fair to be compensated for the time we spent showing people around. But it was a struggle. I remember it was my son's birthday, he must have been turning three, and we didn't have any money to buy him anything, so my husband suggested we take him to the beach. On the beach we met a couple of nuns from Australia, nurses at St Vincent's Hospital in Sydney. Djati translated for them so they could buy satay from a cart, and he suggested that we give them a short tour. Somehow we had managed to borrow money to buy a two-door car with terrible shock absorbers, but the nuns loved the tour and went back to their travel agent in Australia and mentioned our names, and the travel agents actually came up to Bali and visited us.

On her last trip to New Zealand, Jan had freighted back a refrigerator, but the compound still had no electricity, so she had traded it for a tiny block of land. The travel agents offered her a deal. 'They said they'd give us the money to build an office and house on that tiny block, and we could pay them back from the clients they sent us. It seemed unbelievable, but it happened. We were in business!'

Their partner in the endeavour was a company called Japan Tourist Bureau, although they were Australians who had nothing to do with Japan, other than sending people there. Clearly, the Bali office had to have a name of its own. Jan thought long and hard about this, and eventually came up with a name that seemed to cover everything. So began Jan's Tours, the first Western tourist agency of the modern era, still operating today.

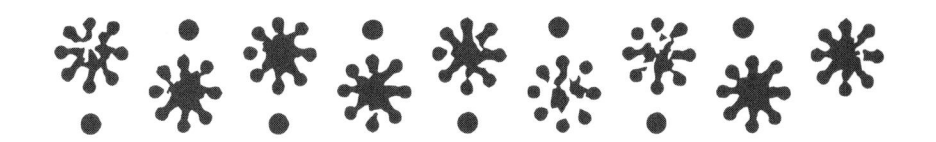

Chapter 11 Bali Style

Absolutely every aspect of life, whether it be the structure of buildings, designs for an offering, components of a painting or master plan of a village is viewed as a living organism, having a head, body and feet.

Barbara Walker, 1995

The slow rise above the palm trees of the 'international-style' eleven-storey, 300-room Bali Beach Hotel, on exactly the same stretch of beach where the Dutch invaders had landed sixty years earlier and provoked the 1906 *puputan*, occurred at precisely the same time as the Balinese were again running amok and slaughtering each other.

Many Balinese and long-term expats saw this as a very bad sign indeed, while others viewed Suharto's eventual realisation of his predecessor Sukarno's tourism dream as a major step towards securing the future of the fragile Balinese economy. With a world-class hotel delivered (thanks to Japanese war reparations) and an international airport well underway, prosperity must be just around the corner, they argued, once the blood of 80,000 people had been washed from the streets and cliff tops and beaches, and replaced with welcoming billboards. One thing most people agreed on was that Suharto had to do something to breathe new life into Bali tourism. In 1964 there were just under 36,000 tourists, but this figure dropped by 20 per cent during the Gestapu period and continued to decline as Suharto established his 'New Order'. In 1968 only 11,000 tourists visited the island of the gods. Bali needed a circuit-breaker and the double whammy of international airport and luxury Western-style hotel was it.

Among those who were appalled by this rapid transformation of the quiet and pleasant beach of Sanur were the artists, architects, designers and bon vivants who had, in the post-revolution years, picked up the pieces of the Walter Spies era and begun to create a modern Bali style, based upon respect for local tradition and a desire to live within the environment, rather than in a cocoon placed upon it. The Belgian painter Adrien-Jean Le Mayeur and his beautiful Balinese wife, Ni Polok, had presided over Sanur's leading cultural salon through the war years and the revolution, but by the mid-1950s, Jimmy Pandy, a half-Dutch, half-Indonesian art dealer who had taken up residence in Bali in the late 1940s as a tour guide for Thomas Cook, was the leader of the pack, entertaining the likes of composer Benjamin Britten and his partner, the tenor Peter Pears, at his beachside bungalow with attached guest houses.

Like Spies before him, Pandy was an amusing and attentive host to many of the movers and shakers who passed through Bali, but his three guest houses could accommodate only the happy few; other influential visitors stayed at the Segara Beach Hotel (established 1956), just along the beach from Pandy. The Segara was built by Ida Bagus Kompiang, a Balinese visionary who saw a future for tourism when life in Bali was catastrophic for most. Although there was only a trickle of visitors in those days, Pak (or 'Mr') Kompiang started 'Bali Night' once a week, with traditional food, music and dance, and it soon became a beachside institution. Although Sukarno later persuaded the Kompiangs to cede their land to make way for the Bali Beach Hotel, they answered back with the Segara Village Hotel in 1967 and remained a force in Sanur hospitality.

Frequent guests of Jimmy Pandy in the late 1950s were an exotic couple named Wija and Judith Wawo-Runtu. He was born in Holland in 1926, the product of a Dutch mother and Sulawesan father, and had grown up in Java. She was an English-born artist. They married in London in 1952, had the first of five children the following year, then moved to Jakarta to establish an antiques and interior design business. On buying trips to Bali, they soon connected with Jimmy Pandy.

While sailing along the coast with Pandy one day, Judith noticed a small coconut grove next to the Pura Tandjung Sari. 'I believe the owners are willing to sell,' Jimmy told her. The Wawo-Runtus built a primitive bamboo house with a grass roof and no electricity. On each trip, as their family grew, they extended the home, and by the 1960s they had surpassed Jimmy Pandy, with four bungalows available for friends to rent. Thus began Tandjung Sari, the first hotel to provide what would become known as 'Bali Style'.

Chapter 11 Bali Style

Interestingly, the Indonesian photojournalist Rio Helmi, who would later co-produce the seminal book *Bali Style*, was one of the first guests to stay at Tandjung Sari in 1963, arriving with his diplomat father for a few days when he was just eight years old. He told writer Diana Darling: '... we were amazed at how simple it was because the buildings were all bamboo and thatch. And there were all these Balinese doors. It was funky. Jakarta was already a world of concrete, so this made a big impression on us.'

Wija and Judith Wawo-Runtu ended their marriage in 1963 and, apparently seamlessly, he married Oemaiati Soesetio (always known as 'Tatie') the following year. They had met in the shadow of the eruption of Gunung Agung, and despite his growing reputation as an incorrigible playboy, Wija and Tatie, who brought another four young children to the marriage, settled down to make a go of their funky, chic beachfront hotel. Both people of style and charm, Tatie and Wija had soon attracted the world's A-list, from Dewi Sukarno, Margaret Mead and Mick Jagger, to various Asian princes and princesses, and Australian artist Donald Friend, who took up regular residence in the mid-1960s.

In 1969 Friend, a heavy drinker and smoker, took ill and was hospitalised in Sydney for several weeks, before being taken to Glenrock, the country estate of the distinguished Australian architect Peter Muller and his wife, Carole, to recuperate. Peter Muller recalled:

> While he was with us he suggested that we go back to Bali with him. I felt that he had an ulterior motive but we were very pleased to go because we'd heard a lot about Bali by this time, so we went and stayed in his house on the beach in Sanur. While we were there his partner and sponsor, Wija Wawo-Runtu got hold of a four-wheel drive vehicle and drove me all around the island to look at the architecture. It transpired that Wija, Donald, and another partner, Chris Carlisle (an English businessman who had become addicted to the Sanur lifestyle), had acquired a small parcel of land on the beachfront and they wanted me to design a hotel using only Balinese craftsmen and artisans from the villages and only local materials. They hated what the Bali Beach Hotel had done to their local environment. It had been built with Japanese reparations and not one single Balinese worked on it. We stayed about six weeks and then came back to Australia and I immediately began designing a hotel that we called 'Matahari'.

The concept of the Matahari was to design and build a major tourist hotel of 120 rooms that would 'set an example and standard for future hotels' in a way that Wija, Donald Friend and others believed the Bali Beach had not. Muller designed a traditional village-styled complex of gardens and walled courtyards, blending traditional Balinese architecture with Western standards and services. By June 1970, he had produced a thirty-page brochure that Chris Carlisle would use to sell the project to Australian investors, but between the time of Muller's first visit to Bali and Carlisle hitting the road with his Matahari prospectus, the mining giant Poseidon had crashed and taken the investment market with it.

The Matahari project on the stretch of beach known as Batujimbar did not proceed, but the concept of a high-end traditional hotel did, with Wija Wawo-Runtu and his partners selling their land to the promoters of a new development that would eventually become the Bali Hyatt, which described itself in now familiar terms as 'the first international hotel to use local materials and crafts as well as traditional building forms, such as pitched roofs, open courtyards and pavilions'.

Peter Muller filed away his Matahari plans for another day—a day that would be a long time coming—but Bali was now an ongoing part of his universe. He recalled: 'Carole had fallen madly in love with Bali and wanted us to go back and build a little house for ourselves, so in 1972 we did that. We found some land next to a friend's property in Campuhan, and on it was a dilapidated structure known as the Bonnet Studio.'

The studio of Rudolf Bonnet, one of the leading lights of the Spies set between the wars, had a colourful history. After being interned by the Japanese during the latter part of the war, Bonnet returned to Bali and entered a prolific period of his painting career, selling many of his best works to President Sukarno, who would visit the studio while in residence at his palace in Tampaksiring. An art lover with a keen eye for a deal, Sukarno beat the artist down on price time and time again, procuring fourteen of his best works, but following a dispute over the price of an oil painting in 1957, Bonnet found himself blacklisted. He returned to Holland and the studio sat abandoned for fifteen years.

Muller said:

> We took out a fifteen-year lease and I pretty well rebuilt it.
> The place was derelict, with deteriorating columns. I added

Chapter 11 Bali Style

> a kitchen and bathroom and put in a mezzanine floor as our bedroom, rebuilt the roof in bamboo and alangalang thatch. It was a very simple, modest house. It cost us $3000, complete with all the furniture we designed and had made locally. There was no running water or electricity. It was absolutely wonderful.

While the Mullers were putting the final touches onto their Campuhan studio they were visited by an American named Charles Osborn and his Scandinavian wife, who were enchanted by the restoration of the studio and asked Muller to design a house for them on beachfront land they had just leased at Seminyak, north of Kuta.

Peter Muller was not remotely interested in residential architecture projects for other people, but Osborn was a persuasive guy, and Muller and his wife, Carole, agreed to look at the property. He recalled:

> It was an absolutely magnificent piece of land. There was a wonderful little creek that ran near it and burst out onto the beach, it was just beautiful. So I designed them a house, and while I was designing it Charles came back to me and asked if I could add five guest villas for his friends—Princess Grace, Salvador Dali, people like that. I just smiled. Carole and I stayed on in Bali and built a prototype guest villa on his land using only Balinese materials and technology. It took six months just to do the prototype, entirely built by hand without electric tools. The builder had previously only built a restaurant, but he was brilliant and we lived in it until it was finished. There was an old well nearby so we bought a diesel pump and a generator that gave us our water supply. Charles wanted four more built straightaway. He would return to Europe and come back with suitcases of money. He had the ability to get people to invest in his projects without any security or even any shares!

Although they remained sceptical of Osborn's friends in high places, Carole discovered that the eccentric Spanish artist Dali was indeed a close friend, and Julian Moulton, the grandson of the founder of Chase Manhattan Bank, was one of the many investors. Another buddy was PepsiCo vice-president Herman A. Schaefer (chiefly famous for having secured the Mountain Dew soft drink company for the Pepsi group for just $2 million in 1964 after arm-wrestling the chairman), who pressured the corporation's Indonesian bankers, Citibank, to invest $780,000 in the growing project.

Peter Muller recalled:

> Charles kept wanting me to add more villas and he finally decided he wanted a mix of villas and guest rooms. Very quickly it grew to 75 rooms, including 12 villas. This was when it went from a private residence to the Kayu Aya Resort. His own house, the beginning of the project, I eventually needed to convert into the entrance and reception area. My idea with Matahari had been to build a beautiful walled Balinese village with austere pathways with lovely walls and doorways leading into the walled garden guest rooms. Charles' place in Seminyak didn't start out as a hotel so this never eventuated. It just grew.

Muller had been able to incorporate some of his traditional ideas into what was now the Kayu Aya, but he again shelved the Matahari plans for another time and continued working on turning Kayu Aya into a functioning hotel. He said:

> We had convinced a very successful chef from Australia, Patric Juillet (Juillet's, Le Café), to come to Bali with his wife and child and set up the kitchen. On the very day the project was finished and we were leaving to go back to Australia, the actual owner of the hotel—Pak Adi, the local businessman who Charles had used as his mandatory Balinese sponsor—moved in with all his henchmen. They just took the place over. Patric had to roll his family up in a carpet and smuggle them out in a *bemo*!

By this time—1974—there was a lot of investment money tied up in what was potentially Bali's most beautiful hotel, but the local owners seemed intent on driving it into the ground while Charles Osborn and other investors, eager to try to negotiate with the Balinese, found themselves 'blacklisted' (denied an entry visa). With no guests and no cash to pay them, the staff simply walked off. Luxurious rooms were looted for fittings like air-conditioning units, and the jungle began to claim back the manicured gardens. A string of

Chapter 11 Bali Style

fly-by-night operators took on 'management rights' and offered hippies and surfers five-star rooms for $5 a night.

This was the Kayu Aya as I remember it from my second trip to Bali in 1975. Full-moon parties in the still-beautiful gardens were legendary, with all kinds of drugs on offer, musicians jamming under half-finished pavilions and stunningly beautiful women from all over the world dancing near-naked in the moonlight. The party only lasted a couple of seasons, and I don't remember Tony Mathers being there, but having known him a little in his earlier years at a chic Sydney hang called Fantales, it doesn't surprise me that he was. He blogged:

> I offered [presumably the local owners, although he claims elsewhere to have struck a deal with Charles Osborn] a proposal of bringing the property up to a standard where it could accommodate paying guests. My payment would be free board initially, and, once funds were being generated, a percentage. I housed myself in the Presidential Suite and brought on board to help me another Australian, Terry Stanton, who was there with his wife, the actress Arna-Maria Winchester … Terry had worked for me at Fantales as a carpenter and was extremely creative and capable of leading a team to commence maintenance and repairs throughout the resort.

When Terry Stanton died in 2010, expat landscape gardener and social chronicler Made Wijaya (formerly Michael White) wrote in his obituary:

> The Kayu Aya was Emerald City for us shoe-string hippies: it had luxury villas for rent … an amazing Olympic size turtle-fed swimming pool on a vast beach front terrace and, most importantly, it had Terry Stanton and … Arna-Maria Winchester holding court as rogue GM and vixen consort. Stanton had wrangled the job as 'general manager' through guile—his only real talents were drawing, bullshitting and tying knots, but he was weapons-grade in those three disciplines.

With GM Stanton presumably holding the place together with knots, Mathers claims he then filled the habitable rooms with paying guests by pinning notices in the couple of tourist restaurants that had popped up in Kuta. It was a shabby act for what was potentially one of the great hotels of the world, and Mathers's fragile tenure soon came to an end. He blogged, leaving much to the imagination: 'A couple of scammer/surfers from Australia and California took a villa for a month which led to my undoing and leaving Bali.'

Meanwhile, Citibank was not amused that the VP of PepsiCo had pushed them over a cliff into a disastrous investment. Although it was not a huge amount of money in their terms, there was a principle at stake here, and they fought the Balinese owners in the Jakarta courts for almost three years, finally winning the case in 1977, and, as a foreign-owned company, they were obliged to immediately put the property up for auction.

According to Peter Muller, all Citibank wanted was their investment back, plus interest, which Muller estimated was approximately the cost of construction. With most of the other investors blacklisted or in jail, it was shaping up to be a very interesting auction. Enter stage right, sniffing a bargain, the world's savviest hotelier, Biki Oberoi. Oberoi soon ascertained that there were only two serious bidders, both local, and neither with the funds to meet the reserve price. He cut a deal with both of them. If they formed a partnership and gave him long-term management rights, he would finance them at better than market rates.

On Christmas Day 1977, Oberoi phoned Peter Muller in Australia and asked him to fly to New Delhi for a meeting. So began Muller's second stint restoring, expanding and finessing the hotel that would become the Bali Oberoi, still the benchmark for the island's coastal resorts. The job of refining the Oberoi would take Muller thirty years.

Another defining aspect of Bali's emerging modern/traditional style was the rise of the native restaurant tailored to Western sensibilities. The Dutch colonialists, who sponsored the first wave of tourism, had never really got it, believing that Balinese cuisine should be presented with silver service in starched dining rooms. The *rijsttaffel* tasting platter, still to be found in tourist hotels, was their answer to the desire of some adventurous tourists to chow down with the locals. I still remember marching home pissed off from the somewhat luxurious new Kartika Plaza in 1974, after a less-than-satisfactory and over-priced *rijsttaffel*, the most bland meal we had devoured in Bali after a week of eating at seafood markets and on the hard benches of depots and street-side *warung*s.

The next phase of tourism, reflecting independent Indonesia, was Sukarno's Western dream of generic hotel restaurants like the rest of the

Chapter 11 Bali Style

world had, exemplified by the rubbish served at the Bali Beach Hotel. But just as Wija Wawo-Runtu and Donald Friend had reacted against the internationalism of hotel architecture, so the first post–Ngurah Rai Airport tourists reacted against the dumbing down of cuisine by opting for cheap and legitimate roadside *warung* food. Ironically, in male-dominated Balinese small business, it was two young women who created the iconic restaurants that paved the way for Balinese fare as we know it today, and both started with nothing, selling food on the street.

Born in Kuta in 1949, Zenik Sukenny spent nine years with a foster family in Jakarta, getting a well-rounded education, before returning to her recently widowed mother in late 1969. Although her English is still patchy and sometimes difficult to understand, Zenik had learned life skills in her time away from Bali that made her ripe for conducting business in the early days of the tourism renaissance. But first she had to get a start.

In early 1970 Zenik began selling soft drinks on the beach at Kuta. Soon there were many drink sellers competing with her, but Zenik's point of difference was that her drinks were icy cold, because she would collect them from her supplier early in the morning and break up a block of ice to wedge between the bottles of Coke and Fanta. This, combined with her sunny nature and incredible ability to remember almost every customer's name, soon gave her a thriving business. She developed a regular following, including an expat teacher named Mike (no one had a surname in Bali back then) who urged her to use her people skills to start a food stall or *warung*.

With a little financial help from Mike, Zenik opened her first *warung* by the new lifeguard tower. It was promptly burned down by jealous rivals, but she moved under the trees, and then on to a position by the temple on Jalan Pantai. It was here that she started to make her name, using the same easygoing approach to business she had used on the beach, offering credit to people who had no money, even loaning regulars cash to fix their *losmen* bills before the Immigrasi revoked their visas. Zenik was open and friendly and trusting, and most people responded to her trust. Her English was still dreadful, but Mike taught her to put price tags on everything so that she could point if words failed her.

Having moved rapidly from drink selling to *warung* management, Zenik went to her mother and asked if she could sell a pig on her behalf. When her mother agreed, she grabbed a squealing piglet from the family compound and took it to the stepmother of a young friend, Made, who cooked and sold *babi guling* in a small *warung* near the crossroads that the tourists had nicknamed 'Bemo Corner'. At a time when the US dollar bought 210 rupiah, Made's stepmother offered 225 for the piglet. Zenik took the money back to her mother and asked her how much she wanted. Her mother looked her up and down and smiled. 'Why do you want money?' she asked.

'Because I want to start a proper business,' she replied.

'Give me the twenty-five and keep the 200,' her mother said, 'but make it a good business.'

Thus Zenik started her *warung* with less than one dollar in capital, but soon she had a name for the best pancakes and fruit salad in Kuta. She had the continued support of the growing band of expat surfers and hippies, although one, a vegetarian American named Michael Boyum who lived across the street, insisted that she supply him with a constant flow of durians at market price. When Boyum's parents visited from Hawaii, Zenik was rewarded for her trials. They bought her a motorbike.

By 1972 Zenik was fielding offers of partnerships and sponsorships from all sorts of dodgy blow-ins. But one offer rang true. Two Americans, Bob and George, (no surnames, no pack drill) offered the necessary funding to turn Zenik's *warung* into a proper restaurant, with no money coming out until the cash flow covered the Balinese staff wages. George had a momentary rush of blood to the head and got Zenik to sponsor and partner him in a land acquisition (where the Kopi Pot cafe sits today) for the new restaurant, but soon realised it was not central enough. Instead, the restaurant began to take shape in Zenik's family compound in a *gang* behind Jalan Pantai.

In June 1972, Zenik noticed a new customer at the *warung*, a tall Englishman named John. He was friendly enough and had a nice smile, but the relationship got off to a rocky start when he complained about her famous pancakes. 'At Dayu's I can get two large pancakes for 10 rp,' he protested. 'Here it's 50 rp for one small one.'

Zenik let fly: 'Well, go to Dayu then, if you don't want best quality, Mister, you go to Dayu. My food, their food, no comparison.'

John laughs at the memory of this first encounter more than forty years ago, as we sip tea in a garden pavilion of their boutique hotel, Zenik laughing as she shares that long ago moment, but still adamant that no one could touch her for quality, even though more than twenty restaurants had sprung up in Kuta since the new airport opened. John was a construction worker from England doing a slow working tour around the world, but he

Chapter 11 Bali Style

had dabbled in landscaping, building waterfalls and ponds, so he was put to work creating a new garden in the family compound, around which the new restaurant would operate.

The restaurant did not yet have a name, but Zenik's *warung* was already so well known that it appeared in John's guidebook, so it seemed pointless to change it. But one day another American came to the compound looking for George, and left his calling card, which stated he was the owner of Poppies Restaurant in La Jolla, California. Within a couple of days George revealed that he had sealed a deal to name their restaurant Poppies, too. John just scratched his head. He was not yet a partner.

Poppies Restaurant had its soft opening at Christmas 1972, made more difficult than it might have been by Zenik falling down the compound well the day before. She lay at the bottom with injuries to her back and stomach for several hours before Bob and John heard her moans and hauled her out. In hospital the doctors wanted to keep her in for observation, but Zenik explained she had a restaurant to open. Bob signed a disclaimer and reluctantly the doctors let her go.

The first menu was handwritten and Zenik had decorated it with drawings of flowers. She also put her own name at the bottom so that her *warung* customers would know it was her. It featured such traditional Balinese dishes as steak sandwich and cheese-and-tomato omelette, and the drinks list included 'large cold beer' at 150 rp (about 40 cents) and just one wine, Brem Bali. Within a couple of weeks, however, Zenik had added a seafood chowder that would remain one of the restaurant's most popular dishes for decades.

The big opening was 8 January 1973. John had already left to resume his travels, Bob and George made themselves scarce and all the hard work fell to Zenik, whose day began at 2 am with a visit to the Jimbaran fish markets and finished when the last reveller left after midnight. Zenik served fixed-price lobster to a packed house. Mick Jagger, about to start the Rolling Stones' Pacific Tour if the governments of Japan and Australia would let him in, came over from Tandjung Sari for the evening. Zenik recalls: 'I gave him Table One.' Poppies had arrived.

The American partners drifted off, John came back, joined the business and he and Zenik eventually married, built accommodations on family land, then bought more land and built more accommodations, expanded into Koh Samui, Thailand, opened the Kopi Pot and, in John's words, 'just rolled along'. The restaurant has evolved over the years, but I can still sit by one of John's ponds and channel 1974, when my friends and I would argue and laugh into the night, and Geoffrey, who's still the barman today, would fuel our excitement with double Black Russians. The brown door still leads into the small room where Zenik was born and her mother died.

Poppies, whose address has long been Poppies Lane I, is now surrounded by the detritus of Kuta, and yet it is an oasis of timeless style. More than that, it has continuity, and not much in Kuta can boast that.

When Zenik sold her mother's pig to finance her business, a pretty fifteen-year-old girl with hair down to her waist took the animal off into the family compound to be slaughtered while Ibu Gede counted out the rupiah. Made Masih had left school at thirteen to help out in the family business while her father took on extra work as a rice farmer in the paddies along the Denpasar road. The *warung* near Bemo Corner had been run for several years by Made's mother and her stepmother (her father's first wife), Nyoman Sadi, but by 1970 it had become known to the hippies and surfers who frequented it as 'Made's Warung', because the vivacious, laughing teenager gave the place its character.

Five years younger than Zenik, Made developed a bond with her rival when her older brother intervened to stop Zenik's family's house from being stoned.

> He helped her because sometimes in those early days, when you're a Balinese girl with a Westerner they stone your house, but my brother, he told them, no, you don't do that. And because Zenik is coming from Jakarta she's not wearing sarong like us, she more Western, but I like her and we become friends after that.

Made's fractured English (she says it hasn't improved much after forty years being front of the house in the restaurant game) belies the cunning business brain that has made Made's Warung the best-known restaurant brand in Bali.

By the time Zenik opened Poppies, Made had successfully converted her *warung* into a small restaurant. Her father sold a cow and they used the money to buy some tables and chairs and kerosene lamps, but they had no refrigeration. While Made opened up to serve breakfast each morning, her mother would walk the 6 kilometres into Denpasar markets and then walk back with the day's food on her head.

Chapter 11 Bali Style

In 1973 a young Dutch musician and antique dealer named Peter Steenbergen arrived in Bali at the end of a long journey along the so-called 'denim highway' from Europe. Seeing an opportunity to base himself in a tropical paradise and support his lifestyle by exporting antiques from Java, he rented a room behind Bemo Corner, strode down the dusty Jalan Pantai to eat at a *warung*, and immediately fell in love with the gorgeous young girl who served him.

Made's English was appalling and Peter's Indonesian even worse. They communicated by playfully throwing peanuts at each other. 'It was because we can't let people see what we feel, not even look in the eyes, you know, because then not nice for the parents,' Made recalls. 'I want to be good to make my parents happy, but I'm in love, you know?'

Peter started filling the restaurant with Dutch colonial antiques and tribal masks, and it soon developed the look and feel of an Amsterdam coffee house, which made it the 'it' place of Kuta. In those days you could sit in the front row at Made's for a few hours and the world would come to you. But Peter's growing involvement with the restaurant didn't disguise his growing involvement with Made. 'As the months passed by and the chemistry between us grew stronger, my relationship with Made became a relationship that was ruled by chaperones,' he says. 'Taking Made to the movies, for example, required that I buy a ticket for at least two relatives. And a day trip to Kintamani involved renting a mini-bus and loading in the entire family.'

Peter desperately wanted to marry Made but felt he could not ask her parents for fear that they would refuse and forbid her to see him again. 'At that time, to my knowledge, no foreigner had yet married a Kuta girl.' He sought the advice of Ketut, a Balinese friend from Denpasar, who had recently married Jean Lane, an American woman who had opened another new restaurant in Kuta, Kubu Krishna. Ketut advised him to seek forgiveness rather than approval. '*Kawin lari*,' he said. 'We do it all the time. Elope.'

Ketut helped draft a letter to Made's parents, which he then delivered a few hours after Peter had met up with Made at the markets and driven her in his Chevy Impala to the security-ringed Bali Hyatt hotel in Sanur. Made recalls that she was terrified of her parents' reaction throughout their five-day 'honeymoon' at the Hyatt, but she had Peter and the novelty of elevators, knives and forks and air conditioning to keep her mind off it. On the fifth day her cousin on her mother's side was sent to tell the lovers that the family had accepted the relationship and they could live in the cousin's compound.

Some months later they were allowed back into the family compound and she could resume working at the restaurant while the family planned the traditional wedding ceremony.

Made's Warung continued to boom.

Chapter 12 *Morning of the Earth*

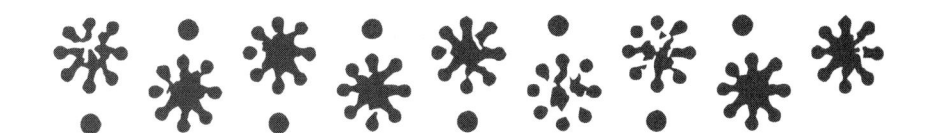

We are the measure of all things and the beauty of our creation, of our art, is proportional to the beauty of ourselves, of our souls.

Jonas Mekas, 1967

In the wake of the Gestapu genocide of 1965–66, Kuta Beach was a lonely stretch of yellow sand for years, unridden waves and fringing reef frequented only by the small population of local fishermen. Once there had been surfers, but they had long gone and were yet to return.

'Never saw another white person. Sand dollars and tumbleweeds on the beach, water perfectly clear.' These are the memories of Richard E. Lewis, born in Bali of American missionary parents in 1956, who first discovered the beach in the months following the horrors of the Gestapu.

> June 1966. My family's red Jeep Wagoneer trailed dust as it bumped down the dirt road leading through the coconuts to the beach … I was impatient to see the ocean … I had no idea about the sport of surfing, but even then I was praying for swell. I can't remember not being able to swim, and I can't remember when I first figured out how to body surf. But that's what I loved to do. I wasn't the only one. A bunch of local Kuta kids would also play in the surf, sometimes with driftwood, or broken bits of bamboo outrigger … Dr Spencer Reed, a British leprologist working with Balinese lepers, and his family lived in a bungalow on the beach, on the same property where the Kokes had built their hotel back in the 1930s, and where the Hard Rock Hotel is now. During our end of year and Christmas vacations from boarding school (in Java), we would visit them and go swimming.

These trips without parents required three changes of public transport. If the Reeds were not home, Dick Lewis and his brother would sneak into the Natour Beach Hotel to shower. The only other construction visible on Kuta Beach, the Natour was a ratty collection of falling down, thatched-roof bungalows on the other side of the sandy *pantai* track, past the boom gate that was meant to keep jeeps off the beach. The Natour had grown out of the remains of K'tut Tantri's Sound of the Sea guesthouse. By this time, it was owned by the national tourism authority and was about the only hotel in Kuta, but few tourists stayed there, preferring the staid Dutch-style comforts of Denpasar's Bali Hotel, or the luxury of the Tandjung Sari and the new Bali Beach Hotel in Sanur.

After body surfing, the Lewis boys would eat and drink from supplies they had brought in a knapsack, or make the long trek up the path to the airport road, where an untidy cluster of *warung*s offered cakes and tea. Dick remembers drinking cool water (never chilled in those days before refrigeration) from an earthenware jug with a long spout. 'It was rude to put your lips to the spout, so you kept the spout high and arced the stream straight into your mouth. The water was boiled over wood, and tasted smoky.'

Wayan 'Bobby' Radiasa, also born in 1956, was one of the village kids who played in the surf with the Lewis boys.

> We'd just pick up a piece of driftwood or whatever and use it as a hand plane for body surfing. It came very naturally. We just kind of knew what to do to ride a wave. There were no tourists at that time. My father was a fisherman and my grandfather too, so we played a lot on the beach. The beach was really our life, it used to be so nice.

By the late 1960s an emerging breed of knowledgeable surf adventurers was starting to peer at atlases and Admiralty charts and wonder where in the world uncrowded waves might be found. Sydney-based merchant skipper Captain Ron Ware was one of those, and having plied the waters of the Indonesian archipelago for many years, he was said to have surfed in Bali many times in the mid-1960s, telling very few about it.

But Sydney University graduates Geoff Watson and John Pratten were not part of the methodical few. It had been several years since the Bruce Brown film, *The Endless Summer*, had popularised the notion of discovering waves in exotic and unlikely locations, but most surfers still had no idea

Chapter 12 *Morning of the Earth*

where to look, other than to the established surf meccas of the Pacific. Aiming to stretch out their gap year to two, Watson and Pratten had been prowling the Australian east coast in a clapped-out Holden utility, surfing every day and living on the smell of an oily rag, as their parents frequently lamented. But a chance meeting with the development manager of a big engineering firm led Pratten into a conversation about his desire to discover an unspoilt and uncrowded surf location, preferably with palm trees and warm water.

'If you want unspoilt go to Bali before it's too late,' said the manager. 'I don't know good surf from bad but I've seen waves breaking there. An international airport is being built even as we speak and a year from now it will be ruined, so go now.'

The two young men sold their cars and whatever else they could get a price for, purchased round-the-world airline tickets worth several years' salary, and got to the airport with their 8-foot Keyo surfboards for the flight to Jakarta in early May 1969. The bustling Indonesian capital was full of militia with automatic weapons slung over their shoulders, and cab drivers who had never seen surfboards before. The Australians travelled to their hotel hanging out the back windows holding their boards along the sides of the battered American sedan.

When they finally made the ferry crossing to Bali after days spent sharing airless train carriages with people and poultry, they hitched a ride to Denpasar in a UNICEF kombi. Somewhere along the potholed road from Gilimanuk they spotted waves breaking along the shore. 'Yes!' cried Geoff Watson. 'There's surf!'

The only reason the two surfers ended up in Denpasar was because that's where the UNICEF kombi was going. They had no idea where to stay or how to start looking for surf, but they found a cheap *losmen* with a cesspit in the yard and immediately distinguished themselves by climbing into the traditional *mandi* (bath) and soaping themselves up, rather than ladling water from it over their heads in the normal manner. 'It was mentioned by our hosts,' said Watson, now seventy and still working as an architect and taking regular surf trips around the globe.

'In those days you couldn't find maps in Third World dictatorships,' he said. 'We found that right through the East. It seemed like they didn't want people to find things.' But after showing their surfboards to staff and other guests, they were finally told that they might be able to use them in the waves near the holy temple at Tanah Lot. Then they discovered they could rent a motor scooter for very little, so before attempting to find Tanah Lot, they rode out on a reconnaissance mission from the south coast to the north.

'We saw the new airport under construction and the still water of the bay beyond it,' said John Pratten, 'but we didn't know about Kuta and we certainly didn't know about Kuta Reef. To be honest, I don't think we were tuned into looking for waves on reefs.'

Having found no surf on their excursion, they turned their attention back to Tanah Lot and had a *bemo* take them to the temple. The rice farmers left their fields and gathered on the rocks to watch as they rode their first waves, cheering excitedly when they wiped out. Watson and Pratten came back and surfed for the next couple of days, but both developed chronic Bali belly, and after almost a week confined to their bunks, they began the long trek back across Java.

In August 1969, the Ngurah Rai International Airport opened on the site of the old Tuban airfield, on a narrow isthmus of land just south of Kuta, with Qantas immediately offering a direct service from Sydney and Melbourne.

One of the first surfers to use the new airport was Russell Hughes, an Australian champion surfer who had placed third in the world championships in Puerto Rico just nine months earlier. A handsome and rather dapper young man who had grown up in Brisbane and the Gold Coast but had been nomadic most of his life, Hughes also had a somewhat devious, shadowy side. His real name was Tony Wayne Snitcherling and his half-brother was Russell 'Mad Dog' Cox, a bank robber who was by 1969 well on his way to becoming Australia's most wanted. Why Tony Snitcherling took on the same first name as his half-brother is anyone's guess, but Hughes always danced to his own beat. Bob McTavish, one of his surfing mentors, wrote:

> Young Russ Hughes ... was brought up tough. A serious scar that cut across his left eyebrow was a gentle and permanent reminder of that. It gave his face a look of constant curiosity ... His quick wit, his devilish pranks and go-get-'em attitude meant that the fun always happened around Russell Hughes.

After the world titles, Hughes had made his way to California and then to Hawaii for the winter surf season, where he joined top American surfers Rusty Miller, Mike Doyle, Garth Murphy and Joey Cabell at their surf and

Chapter 12 *Morning of the Earth*

psychedelics hideout on the island of Kauai, where the favoured activity was surfing big Hanalei Bay at night while tripping on acid. After this sojourn he had apparently made his way to Europe and then Kabul, Afghanistan, which had become the major supply source of hashish oil. Whether he was carrying a trafficable quantity of the drug when he landed in Bali on the way home will never be known, but Hughes, who died of cancer in Canada in 2011, always lived the high life despite often having no visible means of support.

Hughes spent a couple of months in Bali in the latter part of 1969, and, being used to powerful waves and reefs, it seems likely he would have ventured further than Kuta's beach breaks to the reefs beyond the new airport runway and across the isthmus in front of the new Bali Beach Hotel. Around this time Dick Lewis, on vacation from school in Java, wandered down Jalan Pantai to the beach:

> I just came over the rise to check the surf and there was this guy, riding a board. My jaw dropped. When he came in I could tell he was an Australian by his accent. I was overwhelmed by this thing, surfing. I remember it very clearly because I had no idea that such a thing existed. It's possible that some of them [surfers] were there [earlier], but very few of them, or you would have heard about it. I wasn't there all the time because I was at school, but it's certainly possible that a few surfers came and went and I just didn't see them.

In that same dry season, Bobby Radiasa saw his first surfboard rider at Kuta.

> There were five of us who later became the first Indonesian surfers, and we lived in the village right at the beach. There was only one road and it wasn't really a road, just a track, and it passed right by our *banjar* so I think we would have seen people with surfboards if there had been one before. We just watched that first guy and were amazed. I couldn't speak any English so we didn't talk to him, didn't find out his name or where he came from.

When he got home to Australia, Russell Hughes was happy to share the knowledge that there was good surf in Bali, but he became evasive and annoyed when pressed for more detail, clearly planning a return to his new secret spots. He revealed enough, however, to excite the interest of several people in the inner sanctum of Australian surfing, amongst them filmmakers Bob Evans and Albert Falzon.

By the early months of 1970, being on the jet route had already started to make some differences in Bali. The trickle of hippies on the overland trail between Europe and Australia who managed to find their way to Bali had become a stream, and many of them gravitated towards the cheapest place where you could enjoy an idyllic beach life—Kuta. Within the travelling cognoscenti, the fun hubs of the East became known as the 'three Ks'—Kathmandu, Kabul and Kuta. To accommodate the hippies and cater to their desire for privacy (to roam naked and smoke pot) more of the outlying villagers started converting part of their compounds into *losmen*, and it became more common along the beachfront to see long-haired, butt-naked and skinny hippies wandering out of the jungle holding hands and passing reefers around.

After endless months dodging bullets in the frontlines while covering the Vietnam War for the *Honolulu Advertiser*, young photojournalist Leonard Lueras thought he'd died and gone to heaven when he pulled his battered Surfboards Hawaii log out of the back of a *bemo* and surveyed Kuta Beach for the first time. Lueras had lugged the heavy board overland from Jakarta, and he was ecstatic to wash the dust of the road off it and himself in the empty beach breaks. He checked into Losmen Kompiang and went off for dinner at a Chinese restaurant, where he immediately ran into the Australian surf adventurer Peter Troy.

Lueras recalls:

> Kuta was just this really nice little place, a sleepy fishing village, with lanes where you walked through coconut forests. No phones, no electricity. It was just kerosene lamps and these weird ceremonies at night and you'd just kind of wander around in disbelief. I ended up staying for three months.

In the village of Kuta another group of young people, mostly American but with a few Australians and Europeans in the mix, had started to take up residence on a semi-permanent basis. The young men would go away and come back regularly: the women were more transient. Often a man would come back with a different beautiful woman (frequently Thai) each time. Most of these men were surfers, and many went by a mysterious alias,

Chapter 12 *Morning of the Earth*

like twenty-two-year-old 'Abdul', who rocked into Kuta in late 1970 with $100,000 in cash burning a hole in his pocket.

Born Warren Anderson in Laguna Beach, California in 1948, Abdul had dropped out of school to become a stoner surfer, hanging out on the beaches of southern Orange County, subsisting by getting a stash of weed on credit from the Brotherhood of Eternal Love hippie crime syndicate up in Laguna Canyon, smoking half and selling the rest to his surfing buddies. Looking to improve his lot in life, he ramped up his selling and was soon in trouble with the law. Facing three to five years on marijuana charges, he invested some of his dope profit and had the Brotherhood set him up with a full set of false ID through the Weather Underground in Los Angeles. The Weathermen advocated ending the war in Vietnam by creating violent mayhem at home, so they were pretty good at getting wanted men out of the country. With a birth certificate from Ohio, a driver's licence from Nevada and a draft card, he presented himself at the Federal Building in LA and walked out with a passport bearing the name James Robert Monroe.

Abdul had enough money for a one-way ticket to India with $2000 left over. He knew people who were running scams with Nepalese hashish so he figured he'd do the same. He left Delhi and travelled to Nepal. He recalled:

> I used to make dog cages out of plywood and in the middle part of the ply I'd put the hash in. I could fit about 12 to 15 pounds in one cage. I'd send them off with little Lhasa Apso dogs [Tibetan terriers] by clipper cargo and they'd arrive in the States within 24 hours and friends would pick them up. It wasn't big money, maybe $20,000 a crate, and I'd have to pay people off out of that. But the dope was like $20 a kilo in the government shop in Kathmandu. I put together a few loads in a year or so, then came to Bali. I was a beach guy, not a mountain guy, and I wanted to get back to the waves. I'd made more than $100,000 in a year, man. I was ready to retire! I arrived in Bali with a couple of boards and a couple of tee shirts and pockets full of money.

There was a cool scene developing in Kuta and Abdul fit right into it. He was 'flamboyant, goofy and so bold', fellow scammer Mike Ritter recalled. 'With his long, wild hair and dark-olive skin, he stood out from the others. He was always teasing and cracking jokes.'

Bali: Heaven and Hell

The 'others' included Bob Jones, Ray Lee, Dick Marsh, 'Bogie', Bob Laverty, Bill 'Chops' Barron (an artist and friend of the legendary Malibu surfer and con man Miki Dora), Bruce Fitzgerald, Richard Jones, and an intense and bug-eyed young man named Mike Boyum. Abdul recalled:

> A lot of these people are dead now. We were just a bunch of young guys with very chequered pasts. No one had a job, no income that you could talk about, except Laverty who was an heir to the Thriftimart drug store chain. He was kind of the wayward kid and the family paid him $5000 a month to stay away. He was a loner, he liked to take pictures, always had a camera with him. He had epilepsy.

Laverty, who was to become a key player, albeit briefly, in the early years of Indonesian surf discovery, came from serious money. His father, Roger M. Laverty, had bought a small grocery store chain in Los Angeles in 1930 and later bought out the much bigger drug store chains of Thriftimart and Smart & Final. When he died in 1969, the business was worth more than $200 million. Roger Laverty II took charge of the empire, and, against his mother's wishes, banished his layabout kid brother to the far parts with a fat monthly remittance.

But the most intriguing of the Kuta cronies was Mike Boyum, a military brat who was born in Key West, Florida in 1946, but spent his childhood moving from base to base along the eastern seaboard as his father developed into one of the navy's top pilots. Boyum and his brother, Bill, five years younger, started surfing in the early 1960s, but Mike was more into sailing and soon dropped out of George Washington University to explore the Pacific and beyond.

California-born filmmaker Bill Leimbach met Boyum in Washington, DC when they were both students. He found something likeable in the intensity of the young, blond ball of muscle. He recalled:

> We'd do college breaks in Fort Lauderdale, get chicks and party on, standard stuff. We spent time in the Bahamas and the Caribbean together too, sailing and surfing. Then I went up to New York City with him for a while, before coming back to California, and eventually going to London to study film.

Chapter 12 *Morning of the Earth*

> We corresponded through that time, and when he moved to
> Bali he said I should come visit. It took a while but I did.

Mike Boyum had been living in Kuta for six months or more when Abdul arrived in 1970 and the two soon met. They surfed the beach breaks together, and sometimes Kuta Reef up near the airport, and hung out at Boyum's rented house on Jalan Pantai, where Boyum introduced him to his newfound passions, durian fruit and magic mushrooms. The foul-smelling, cheesy durian that he bought each morning at Zenik's *warung* was definitely an acquired taste, but its dietary properties were positive. Boyum claimed the same properties for the wild hallucinogenic mushrooms that popped up in cow turds all over South Bali every time it rained, and ingested them by the dozens, mainly as soup or as a smoothie. The benefit was a mind-bending stone that often lasted for days. Boyum rarely went a day without them, but unlike most users, he was energised by them to a frightening degree, often surfing huge waves way beyond his capabilities while off his head.

You would have expected the two men to have an immediate bond, but Abdul loathed Boyum from the outset.

> He was just an asshole from day one. Nobody outside of the few people he sucked up to really liked him. He wasn't cool. [In Kuta] we were all brothers and he wasn't. We were all doing something outside the law but Boyum was the most inept of us all. These days he has this image of some super smuggler, but he was a fucking idiot. He was the first guy here, that's true, but what a piece of shit he was. In the end he was playing both sides. If he didn't like you he called the DEA. He was the kind of guy who didn't know how to be civil. He was always trying to hold something over you that he could use to his own ends.

Perhaps one of the reasons for Abdul's animosity was the fact that when he decided to lease some land along the beachfront, Boyum insisted that he would not get a building permit unless Abdul loaned him $5000. Abdul paid up but soon discovered that Boyum's claim was bogus, and the 'loan' was never repaid.

Abdul recalled: 'When I first arrived in Kuta I met this Indonesian hippie guy, walking around playing a recorder, shit like that, and he goes, "If you like it here you should buy some land."'

Bali: Heaven and Hell

The thought of buying in Kuta had not occurred to Abdul. So far he loved everything about Bali except Boyum, but he wasn't a settling-down kind of guy. Nevertheless he found he enjoyed the company of this strange hippie (Javanese as it turned out), whose name was Pranoto and whose extended family seemed to control a lot of land. Pranoto was full of whacky ideas and one of them was to set up a small bar, or *warung*, selling sugarcane juice to the other hippies. Abdul leased some space in the village and ordered a battery-operated juicing machine from Singapore. Pranoto opened his juice bar and enticed people off the street by playing his recorder like a snake charmer.

Repaying the favour, Pranoto kept bringing unbeatable land deals to Abdul.

> One day I cracked. I told him I didn't want to live in Kuta but if he could find me somewhere a mile down the beach, maybe I'd be interested. A few days later he takes me way down the beach where there was just nothing and shows me this huge plot of beachfront land. I said it was way too big, I only wanted to build a little beach shack. And he goes, 'But it's very cheap.' It was. In fact it was probably the cheapest land on the island because the Balinese did not want to live facing the ocean. The village of Legian was up beyond the coconut groves and rice fields about half a mile back from the coast, but on the beach there was nothing, so I bought 35 *ares* [just under an acre] of beachfront land for one million rupiah, which was about $2500. The purchase was in Pranoto's name but we had an understanding that it was my land. That was enough.

In Australia the bush telegraph was sending out a cryptic message from Russell Hughes that something was going on in Bali. Only the cool could break the code, and the home of surf cool at the time was the Whale Beach house, at the far end of Sydney's northern beaches peninsula, where the surfing magazine *Tracks* began publication in October 1970. *Tracks* was the brainchild of perpetual architecture student and surfer John Witzig, surf photographer and designer Albert Falzon, and music entrepreneur David Elfick, who had co-founded the successful pop music publication, *Go-Set*. In rough tabloid newspaper format, *Tracks* mocked the surfing conventions of the day, railed against pollution, apartheid and the Establishment, and championed pot, sex and soul surfing. It was an instant hit, providing Falzon

Chapter 12 *Morning of the Earth*

and Elfick with a platform to raise enough money to produce a surf movie that similarly broke new ground.

Falzon had honed his camera skills working with pioneer filmmaker Bob Evans through the latter part of the 1960s, but he had developed very different ideas about how a surf movie should be presented. Whereas Evans favoured the conventional documentary approach with a narrator (usually himself) explaining the action, and dropping in laboured and often lame jokes as the viewer was taken from one surf location to the next (before inevitably reaching a climax with big-wave thrills and spills in Hawaii), Falzon wanted to produce a poetic vision of the idyllic surfing lifestyle: no crowds, no cityscapes, no contra payback shots of jetliners taking off and landing, and most importantly, no narration. An original soundtrack of Australian music, organised by Elfick, would set the mood.

After having shot late summer and early autumn on the north coast of New South Wales and on Queensland's Gold Coast (mostly Kirra where there were no visible high-rises) with the top surfers of the day, like Michael Peterson and Terry Fitzgerald, and at rural Lennox Head and Angourie with surfers like David Treloar who had embraced the 'country soul' movement, in May 1971 Falzon watched a rough edit and felt the movie was taking shape but somehow lacked the wow factor. At the end of the year he would have to take the mandatory trip to Hawaii for the big-wave finish, but some kind of exotic side trip would be the icing on the cake.

Elfick came up with an idea. Although he was not a surfer, he had spoken at some length to Russell Hughes about his adventures in Bali. Elfick's girlfriend, Lissa Coote, an overland trail adventurer herself, recalled the amazing stories her mother and grandmother had told of a cruise-ship voyage to Bali in 1939. More recently, Lissa's Sydney University friend, Geoff Watson, had told her of surfing solitary waves on the island in 1969. Elfick secured a deal exchanging *Tracks* advertising pages for airline tickets, and presented the case to Falzon.

'The last place I wanted to travel to was Asia,' Falzon recalled. 'Like a lot of surfers, I was pretty focused on heading out into the Pacific, but David was into the hippie trail.'

In fact, it was Coote who was in love with the hippie trail, but she had introduced Elfick to India and Nepal the previous year and he, too, was becoming enchanted. And, as far as Bali was concerned, Falzon didn't need much encouragement.

I didn't really question it because by then David had the airline tickets, we had no money and we were looking for ways to add some adventure to the film. We knew through Russell that winter was the time to go, but that was all the research we did. The decision was to go East. That was it, full stop.

Elfick had done a contra deal with Pan Am for enough tickets for him to take Coote and Falzon to take his girlfriend, Tanya Binning, but since they were not at all sure there were any surfers in Bali, they needed to also include talent, and Elfick had an idea about this, too. He knew that of all the surfers he had filmed over the past six months, Falzon saw special qualities in a fourteen-year-old kid from Narrabeen named Stephen Cooney. Cooney was an exceptionally talented surfer and he had a face that could be loveable little boy one moment and streetwise bad-boy surfer the next. Since they were going into the great unknown, Elfick felt the film needed a father figure to guide young Cooney through his boy's-own adventure.

It just so happened that the 1965 United States surfing champion, craggy-faced Rusty Miller, was living in Byron Bay and driving down to Sydney for one week every month to sell advertising in *Tracks*. Miller was only twenty-eight, but he'd had a wealth of surfing experience in all kinds of waves, and as a student he had travelled through the Far East for a semester on the University of the Seven Seas. Moreover, he was a thinker who sometimes smoked a pipe to underline his gravitas, and he was a free-thinking hippie who had just spent a season surfing Kauai on psychedelics with Russell Hughes, Mike Doyle and Joey Cabell. He was perfectly cast as the old man of the sea.

Because of the free ticketing, cast and crew had to fly into Jakarta in early June and do the overland trek to Bali before setting up a base at a *losmen* not far from the Kuta beach breaks. Strangely, they did not cross paths with Abdul, Boyum or any of the other shady expat surfers. In fact, Falzon does not recall seeing any other surfers until a near-naked hippie appeared on the path through the coconut groves one day with a recent model twin-fin surfboard. (Another Russell Hughes acquaintance—Brisbane rag trader Maurie Chagoury, who had grown up with Hughes at West End—surfed Kuta in June 1971 and reported seeing not one other surfer in three weeks.) Not that the isolation bothered the filmmakers. There was surf every day and Falzon was happy enough to film his stars wandering

Chapter 12 *Morning of the Earth*

down jungle tracks, eating rice dishes at roadside *warung*s and riding the sparkling beach breaks alone.

When they paddled out to distant Kuta Reef one day and sighted a shark too close for comfort, Miller was the calm voice of experience. 'Just keep paddling, easy does it.' Nervously juggling a heavy camera-housing on the front of his board, Falzon was fearful, but Miller's calm approach helped him through the crisis. The shark swam away.

And then the surf went flat. On a tight budget and an even tighter shooting schedule, Falzon and Binning took a *bemo* out beyond the airport and onto the dusty Bukit Peninsula to search for surf. They were dropped at Pura Luhur Uluwatu, one of the island's most important temples, at its extreme southernmost tip, and slowly worked their way back north along the cliff, more than 50 metres above the ocean. It was a long, difficult and exhausting hike in the heat of the day, but eventually Falzon saw what he'd been looking for. 'It was almost dead flat, but with a two-foot wave on the corner, crystal-clear water, perfect tide. We just sat there and watched and I started to think that with just a little more swell we'd have to come out and surf it.'

Two days later the swell rose enough for small waves to break at the end of Jalan Pantai and on the distant reefs. Falzon and his crew piled back into two *bemo*s. This time, being a larger group, they attracted attention at the temple and soon had a bunch of scruffy village kids following them and wanting to touch their hair and clothes. When the kids realised that they were heading back north, looking for an access point from which to reach the surf, they guided them across the rocky fields, past their village and down to a knoll above the waves. The village fishermen had built a rough bamboo ladder to enable them to climb through a small cave and reach the ocean. The kids were anxious to show this to the strange visitors with their long planks, but Falzon and his surfers had eyes only for the lines of swell marching down the point.

Falzon said:

> I had told them all there was a beautiful wave out there, not expecting it to be big. I had no idea of the intensity of the place, no reference point. When the swell came up to about shoulder high on the beach, I was thinking it would be shoulder high out there, too. I wasn't ready for what we saw.

Bali: Heaven and Hell

Miller and Cooney watched carefully for some time before easing themselves down into the cave and pushing out into the break. While Miller paddled way out to await a big set, as was his habit in Hawaii, Cooney paddled into a smaller wave halfway out with the exuberance of an excited kid. Miller, now seventy, smiles when asked if Cooney therefore caught the first wave at what would become one of the most famous surf breaks in the world. 'He may have.' They surfed the powerful left-hand break all afternoon while Falzon filmed from the bluff, and even as they clunked home down the potholed Bukit track, they were planning their return.

The swell escalated again, and this time the crew went out to the Bukit better prepared and planning to spend the night. As they passed by the pig pens of the village known by the name of the head man, Windro, the children took up chants and followed them down to the surf. The men threw down their machetes and scythes in the fields and followed, soon filling the vantage points along the cliffs.

The tide was low and the surf was huge. With no leashes to secure them to their boards (a luxury whose time had not yet come), Miller and Cooney, man and boy, stood on the platform of reef and waited for the waves crashing beyond them to subside so that they could paddle out. Shooting from a lower angle than the first day, Falzon saw an image of profound beauty that would stay with him forever, as it would with so many who later saw the film. The two silhouetted figures were bathed in an eerie yellow light as the high surf crashed around them in this remote and dangerous place. It was an image that captured at once the excitement and trepidation of surf exploration, and in the minds of the pioneer surf explorers, it was an image that would be forever Bali.

In contrasting styles, Miller and Cooney masterfully rode the big waves all day, and Falzon knew he had the segment he wanted. At sunset they set up camp at the foot of a cliff behind the cave, lit a fire and cooked fish and rice while their laughing fishermen hosts stood guard in the shadows. They passed a joint around and Miller got out his harmonica and softly played some songs.

Falzon remembers:

> It was a spectacular full moon, one of those moments that's sealed in the memory. This perfect place, good friends to enjoy it with, Rusty playing music while the moon lights up

Chapter 12 *Morning of the Earth*

sparkling waves breaking across the reef, two fishermen sitting watching us. It was too shadowy and we were too exhausted to film it, but I've never regretted that. I think some moments are just meant for you personally. I never once got anxious that I wasn't filming it, because I knew I was capturing it on another level. I think that indirectly that comes out in the film.

Miller says:

> Late that night the tide came up really high and we were pushed right up against the cliff. The water came up to the bottom of the knoll and it felt like it was closing in on us. We felt the spirits, that's for sure. We knew we'd got the waves and we knew that finding the spot was significant, but we could never have imagined what it would symbolise in the future. We were more interested in the magic of Bali. It was that era when we believed in the cosmic universality of the planet.

The cosmic universality of Planet Surf was about to undergo a seismic shift with the release of Falzon and Elfick's landmark film the following year. Falzon adapted his title from the famous 1950 Jawaharlal Nehru description of Bali as the 'morning of the world', calling it *Morning of the Earth*.

The filmmakers took as their philosophical positioning statement a quote by underground film guru Jonas Mekas: 'We are the measure of all things, and the beauty of our creation, of our art, is proportional to the beauty of ourselves, of our souls.'

Thousands of surfers wrote that down or memorised it as they made their way to travel agencies to book their tickets to surfing's new frontier.

Chapter 13 The Hippie Highway

Kuta also serves as the home of a few score international hippies, who have imported their ugly life style to the splendid sandy crescent of Kuta Beach. That these wan apostles of latter day savagery should have selected the same point of penetration as did the early merchants need not signify equally lasting impact. Fortunately they are not drivers but drifters.

Willard A. Hanna, 1976

At first it was a trickle but it soon became a stream. Abdul, Laverty, Boyum and the rest of the Kuta surf crew didn't know what to make of the skinny, wild-eyed guys and gals who popped out of the jungle and onto the beach with nothing much more than matted long hair and loincloths, or threadbare sarongs that they dropped onto the sand before dancing naked into the ocean.

The Balinese villagers seemed more tolerant of them, laughing at their stoned antics and their blissed-out mushroom raves, but the police and immigration authorities were less amused. These were not exactly the tourists the New Order had in mind for Bali's visitor-led economic recovery. There were hippies and hippies, of course. Some were just students on gap years who'd left their inhibitions in London or Berlin when they hit the Hippie Highway, loading up on drugs for the journey in Kathmandu or Kabul, and hitting Bali with Hans Hoefer's new guidebook under their arms. But some were seriously, seriously out there.

Around the middle of 1971 a lean, bearded American man in early middle age began raving at whoever he could find wandering along Kuta's sandy shore. His stream-of-consciousness ramble was hard to listen to, but some of the hippies found that if they persevered, Gridley Wright occasionally dropped a few pearls of wisdom. That wasn't all Gridley Wright had dropped since he'd opted out of stockbroking, left his wife and joined the

Chapter 13 The Hippie Highway

counterculture. A sometime associate of Timothy Leary and a graduate of Yale, Wright had founded the Strawberry Fields commune in Decker Canyon, California, where he and his followers practised yoga, free love and consumption of vast quantities of marijuana and LSD. When not otherwise occupied, Wright wrote free-form poetry and philosophised.

The party came to an abrupt halt, however, when Wright was arrested on drugs charges and served almost two years in a Californian penitentiary. When his parole was up Gridley left for the Far East and the Pacific, travelling through India, New Zealand and Australia before turning up in Bali, where he burned his American passport, explaining: 'I am not a tourist anymore. I am home. I do not need a passport when I am home.'

Much of what we know of Gridley Wright's bizarre behaviour in Bali is courtesy of a very strange website called *GridleyWright.com*, established by Chris Lorenz, whose father, Keith, travelled to Bali from Bangkok in 1971 to interview the wild hippies who were said to be taking over the island. The wildest hippie Lorenz could find was Wright.

Exactly what wisdom Wright imparted in their hard-earned interview is only hinted at on the website in nanosecond audio grabs that make no sense at all. A couple of months later Wright was deported from Bali. He returned to California where he established an LSD-based, child-worshipping cult called Shiva Lila, but when the cult's practices of collective parenting and group sex ran afoul of state laws, he and his followers moved to the Philippines, then, when chucked out of there, to Goa, India, where Wright died of pneumonia in 1979 after having been stabbed several times by a drug-crazed Australian man. His eighteen followers said they did not mourn him because he had simply grown tired of his body and was 're-transmissioning'.

Gridley Wright may have been an extreme case, but by the early 1970s, there were hundreds of lost souls and seekers after truth wandering around in the palm groves of Kuta and beyond. In the Western world the Summer of Love, with its perceptions of love, peace and drugs, had long passed; in Bali it was only getting started.

The London version of *Oz*, probably the most influential counter-culture publication in the world at that time, signalled that Bali was well and truly on the hip radar when it published a major feature article on the island in a summer 1972 issue. 'Hippie Fingers in Bali Sugar' was the result of associate editor Jim Anderson's early summer foray on his way back to London from Australia. Anderson, a well-known figure in the Gay Liberation movement, made no secret of the fact that his priorities in Bali were getting high and getting laid, but his report, steeped in self-deprecating humour, is an interesting snippet from the times.

Anderson opened his article with an increasingly familiar depiction of the Balinese character:

> Its beautiful, child-like people have a calm, harmonious way of life, quite remarkable in an area of the world with so tropical and violent a climate. Nevertheless the Bali people have a habit of running amuck at irregular intervals, the last time in 1965 when as many as 100,000 were massacred in a fortnight. The victims were almost all islanders associated in some way with Communism, but in Bali the killings were ritualised and trance-like, and the victims and the killers both so willing that commandoes were hurried from Java to restrain them.

The romantic notion of the Balinese turning on a dime from 'child-like' to homicidal and suicidal maniacs is perhaps an over-simplification of the shocking events of Gestapu, still fresh in many minds at the time of Anderson's visit.

Drugs played a predominant role in Anderson's Bali experience, as they did with most of the 'freak' tourists:

> There always seems to be a good supply of excellent grass from Sumatra, or Buddha grass from Thailand. Pipes, joints, chillums and bongs were filled with heady mixtures which often included dried mushrooms and opium. Pure acid from several sources, in particular an amiable Australian with a big bottle and an eye-dropper with which he would dose you as you wished, a taste or a mouthful ... a lot of spurious coke turned up and anaesthetised everyone's nose and mouth for a while. Groups of pot trail veterans from Penang, Goa, Pondicherry and so on, were arriving all the time, but there never seemed to be serious over crowding as there is in those places, and there wasn't anyone who could remotely be described as heavy.

Anderson would take any drugs available, but he reserved his greatest praise for the magic-mushroom experience: 'Psilocybin has none of the dark corners

Chapter 13 The Hippie Highway

of acid and I recommend the mushrooms as one of the very best ways of learning to love and know yourself, your fellow man and Bali.'

A gay man in an island paradise that had been a pleasure pit in previous eras, Anderson found sexual encounters hard to come by:

> Denpasar ... was, of course, full of sex for sale, and some guys made the trip as often as their pocket or their inclination decided them ... I found the freak lifestyle on the whole very chaste. Relationships flowered and died but indulgence seemed to be in dope rather than in bed ... The Balinese certainly don't treat each other as sex objects and were either offended or mystified if advances were made to them on that basis. On my first couple of blistering days out on the beach, I felt, as usual, duty bound to sample the local product ... but I found that the boys, who in every way were loving and affectionate and great fun to be with, did nothing but giggle and look amazed when I put my hand on their cocks ...

Although Australian himself, Anderson seemed to identify himself with the cool European hipsters, rather than his countrymen in Bali:

> Kuta was interesting because there were two distinct types of freaks—seasoned Europeans and Americans who had been on the road for years, and greenhorns from Australia and New Zealand for most of whom Bali was one of the first foreign countries they had been to ... Admittedly, Kuta was the good side of the freak coin—the physical and mental wrecks were still stranded in India or Kabul ... and there were no Satanists, psychedelic fascists or maniacs with guns. The people most ill at ease were the one or two short-haired Australian juice freaks who, in the absence of any Fosters, were reduced to defiantly drinking the really bad local beer or the even worse sweet rice wine.

Sometimes the lines between surf adventurers and hippies became blurred. Australian John Ogden was just nineteen and recently called up for National Service when he hitchhiked from Adelaide to Darwin carrying a homemade surfboard in 1972. After hanging out with overland hippies in a tree house at Lameroo Beach, he was so inspired by their travellers' tales that he jumped

Bali: Heaven and Hell

on the cheap *'bemo* of the sky' milk-run Zamrud DC-3 service through Timor and the lower archipelago to Bali.

He checked into a cheap *losmen* on Jalan Pantai, surfed at the end of the street and soon ran into Abdul and Mike Boyum, who took to the kid with attitude and let him hang out with them. Ogden recalled:

> With typical American ingenuity my new surf buddies had managed to determine the boiling point of psilocybin, and had distilled the creative juices out of Bali's famous mushrooms. Then Abdul returned to the compound one day with a surprise. He had been to an *apotik*, the Indonesian equivalent of a drug store, to get something for his toothache. The *sakit gigi* powder supplied was meant to be rubbed onto the gums and in the process of doing so Abdul realised it was pharmaceutical grade cocaine. Before long we had visited every *apotik* we could and had collected a large jar of this amazing toothache powder. It must have been a bit like Australia pre-1927 when it was still legal to buy cocaine from chemist shops.

Ogden later wrote:

> Fortified with a shot glass of concentrated psilocybin brew, a large joint of Sumatran weed ... and a dose of toothache powder, we would hit the surf. The touch of water was a whole new sensation and surfing was the realisation that we were riding waves of energy. It was on one of these surf sessions at an outer reef when the boys in our boat yelled out warnings of a large set coming. I started paddling quickly towards the horizon with Abdul just in front of me. We cleared the first wave but it was going to be a close call getting over the next. I was frantically scratching up the face ... when I saw Abdul ... swing his board around to take a perilously late takeoff. What happened to him was lost to me as I punched through the lip only to see another wave through the spray ... Inspired by Abdul's mad bravery I too swung my board around as the wave started to break ... I managed to get to the bottom of the wave but as I went to bottom turn my legs gave way ... I was swept up the face and pitched with the full force

Chapter 13 The Hippie Highway

of the breaking wave. My right eardrum burst when the side of my head hit the water, and the water pressure opened the tear.

Both men survived their stoned wipe-outs and popped up laughing, perhaps a little manically. After a few months Ogden had no money and no plan. An Australian friend advised him to go home and apply for a deferral from the army so he could study. Gough Whitlam was certain to be elected soon and he had promised to end the draft. Ogden took the night flight back down the archipelago to face his future, but he would be back. Bali had touched his soul.

Not all the Australian hippies arrived on the *bemo* in the sky. There were even cheaper ways to get there, and one of them was to crew on a fishing or cargo boat, or a yacht delivery. While most of this action happened in Darwin, some came from far ports in a reversal of the voyage of today's boat people, and often it was just as dangerous. In the early 1970s, Sydney yachtie, hippie and sometime surfer Mark Keatinge started doing boat deliveries along the Australian east coast. In 1973, while he was recovering from the blissful stone of the Nimbin Aquarius Festival, he received a request to deliver an English yacht to Bali, picking it up in the remote Western Australian Pilbara port of Onslow.

This was the kind of adventure that didn't get offered every day, and two of his Sydney friends who were still lounging around in Nimbin with him were keen to come along for the ride. Gary Maskell, from Bondi, was a beach guy, but he didn't know much about sailing. Michael White, an architecture student and promising tennis player, knew even less. One of the boat's new owners completed the unlikely ship's complement. When they eventually arrived in Onslow they found that the *Kimbala* was a wreck that had been sunk and refloated and had been mostly used as a floating brothel, servicing the men of the fishing fleet, who were somewhat reluctant to let her go. Keatinge knew nothing of the boat's provenance, but it seemed likely it had been used for drug loads, and that the repairs might have been done in a hurry. 'But we were young and stupid, and the owner was in a hurry,' Keatinge remembers. 'So we set sail.'

They sailed for ten tough days, with Keatinge at the wheel and navigating, while Michael White read pertinent passages from an ancient volume of *Celestial Navigation for Yachtsmen*. The *Kimbala*'s pilot was equally ancient, advising Keatinge to make landfall at Labuan Tereng on the other side of the Lombok Strait, where there was no customs office.

Bali: Heaven and Hell

Keatinge recalls:

We just had to tie up and go ashore because we were totally exhausted. We were very hungry and thirsty, because apart from the boat leaking, the water tanks had been leaking, too. Someone had to be pumping the boat for an hour and a quarter every two hours! We were hoping that the leaking would stop when the wood got wet and the boards took up, but it turned out that the keel bolts were just about corroded through and water was leaking through the bolt holes. We were lucky the keel didn't fall off, which it subsequently did. The only food we had was chapatis with Vegemite or honey, and brown rice with soy sauce. We had a tape deck and one cassette, Pink Floyd's *The Dark Side of the Moon*, which we played day and night. Close to Bali we got knocked back a whole day by the current. I told the other guys that we'd see the mountains of Bali the next morning and we spent all day nervously looking for them. Another night passed but the next morning we were still looking and Michael pointed up above the clouds and there was Mount Agung. We motored all day into Labuan Bay.

The crew went ashore with three dollars between them and exchanged it for a meal at a dockside cafe that had them heaving up on deck all night. At first light a posse of police, customs and immigration officers descended upon the boat. Keatinge remembers:

They got us all out on the dock and proceeded to search the boat. We were terribly wasted, but relaxed because there were no drugs on board. But they found some. They found a bottle of Emu Lager, and then they found a packet of alfalfa mint tea. We were arrested and taken to the Mataram lock-up and thrown in. We were questioned for ages and statements were taken. They claimed that tests had been done and the Emu Lager was liquid heroin and the alfalfa tea was ganja. I offered to drink the beer in one gulp to prove it was only beer, but they said no, that would be destroying evidence. So then they presented statements for signing that were all in Indonesian, so we refused to sign them because we couldn't read them. They'd taken our English statements

Chapter 13 The Hippie Highway

and had them translated, so they got a young policeman who spoke English and he started translating them back, and that's when it became apparent that we'd admitted to everything!

While the arguments flew back and forth, the crew of the *Kimbala* toughed it out in a filthy lock-up, until one evening in walked an Indonesian who chirped in a broad Aussie accent, 'G'day, mates, what's up?' He told them his name was Wayan Kaleanget Mona and he said he'd talked the police chief into allowing them to be kept under house arrest at his place.

Keatinge says:

> We looked at each other and didn't know what to think. Maybe he was Interpol. If the boat had been used for moving stuff previously, it was possible that someone might be interested in us. But we took this guy at his word and went with him. He said he'd picked up the accent in Long Bay jail in Sydney for eighteen months and he'd only just got out. Now it was getting really weird. He took us home to his estranged wife's house, rooted around in a desk and pulled out a Sydney newspaper with a story about an Indonesian being arrested in Kings Cross with a whole lot of marijuana. He'd smuggled it in cases of antiques, gone straight to the Cross and started selling.

Why Wayan had chosen to become a criminal was hard for the crew to understand, since he was from a highly respected family and was the *kupala desa* (head man) of a major Lombok trading town. Despite his criminal record in Australia, in his village he had been given the responsibility of looking after the *gamelan* and in the evenings the Australians would be serenaded by band practice while the women passed around *sate alit*.

The crew and the *Kimbala* were eventually released without a word of explanation, and they continued on to Bali. By the time they reached Benoa Harbour they were at each other's throats. Michael White went off to Surabaya to teach English and play tennis, Gary Maskell lost himself in the drug dens of Kuta, and Mark Keatinge and the boat's owner decided to careen the boat at Tanjung Benoa and try to repair it. They sold Mark's three pairs of Levi's for a month's food, then funded the repairs by stripping the copper off the hull and selling it. Eventually, they sold the *Kimbala* for enough to cover airline tickets home.

Bali: Heaven and Hell

On a full-moon night in a humble *warung* on Serangan Beach in Bali in late 2013, the surviving crew of the *Kimbala* were reunited in celebration of the fortieth anniversary of their unusual landing in Bali. It was a warm and wonderful evening, with a sultry *kronchong* string band providing the backdrop to time-honoured stories and the slurping of Bintang beer. Mark Keatinge, now a leading light of his *banjar* in Sanur, where he and his Balinese wife also run a restaurant and a highly successful international construction business, had flown Wayan Kaleanget Mona over from Lombok, where he is now a leading Hindu priest, to join the party. They were eager to light the candles and eat the *Kimbala*-shaped cake, but where was bloody Michael White!

Finally, accompanied by some consorts, the man who has been known as Made Wijaya since the 1970s made a dashing entrance, moving to the beat of the *kronchong*. Bali's leading social commentator and a landscape designer of international repute, he looked just a little uneasy at being reminded of how he got here all those years ago, but he was soon lost in the embrace of the other survivors.

✳ ✳ ✳ ✳ ✳ ✳

A couple of months after the *Kimbala* limped into Benoa Harbour, a tall Englishman of patrician good looks landed at Ngurah Rai International for the very first time and approvingly sniffed the frangipani and clove-scented air, despite himself. A self-described hippie, he and his brother had made a pact years before that they would avoid anywhere in the East that had an international airport and a high-rise hotel, and Bali now had both. And Lawrence Blair was here to join his brother, Lorne, and mother, Lydia, in what they had described as the paradise of Ubud.

Lawrence recalls:

> I rented a motorbike at the airport and rode it up towards
> Ubud and got hopelessly lost. There aren't many signs today,
> but back then it was dreadful. It was getting dark and I was a
> little worried that I'd have to camp out and get eaten alive, but
> then suddenly all these fireflies started to explode everywhere,
> in a moment of exquisite beauty that sadly you don't see
> anymore, and suddenly I didn't give a damn about being lost.

Chapter 13 The Hippie Highway

Dr Lawrence Blair was then aged thirty-one, and although he did not look, talk or even think like your average hippie, he had seen more, done more and investigated more of the intricacies of the cosmos and the complexity of cosmic consciousness than any given hundred of them. Born in London during the Blitz, he had been schooled briefly in the south of France, and later, when his mother remarried a pilot and adventurer, the family moved to Mexico City, where he and Lorne, three years his junior, attended the French Lycée and then the University of the Americas, where Lawrence completed his Bachelor of Arts in philosophy in Spanish, before being sent up to Bailleau College, Cambridge.

A brilliant scholar, Lawrence was above that, an adventurer. He recalls:

> I was fourteen, my brother was eleven when we arrived in Mexico. We became comfortable living in an alien culture from an early age. Lorne and I were the only kids, and we both shared the love of adventure. Everything was an expedition. Boys always look for hidden treasure, but when we got to Mexico, we discovered there really is such stuff.

In the mid-1960s, Lawrence and Lorne's stepfather died, and their mother, Lydia, long a devotee of meditation, became enchanted with a Javanese guru and began spending time at an ashram in Jakarta, which led to Lawrence's first trip to Indonesia in troubled 1965.

> I was a delegate to a spiritual conference, and we were told not to leave the ashram because we could hear gunfire outside all the time. But I did, of course, and got swept up in a demonstration where they burned the British and American embassies. I took some photos of tanks charging the crowd that got onto the front pages of the [Singapore] *Straits Times*.

Being exposed to the year of living dangerously in Jakarta only made Lawrence more eager to explore the mysteries of Indonesia, but he was locked into studies in Britain. 'After Bailleau, they sent me up to study in a new faculty at Lancaster University called comparative religion, which sounds incredibly dull, but isn't because you can stick your nose into everything from witchcraft to hallucinogenic drugs or any other altered state of consciousness.' Which is precisely what he did.

Lorne, meanwhile, quit his business degree a few weeks before graduation in Mexico to work with a leading documentary filmmaker, which led him back to London to work as an assistant director at the BBC. In different ways, the brothers were moving in the same direction. Lawrence was finishing his doctoral thesis in contemporary mysticism, while Lorne was researching ways he could make documentaries about Indonesia. When the Beatles created Apple Films in the late 1960s, they were looking for ideas about mysticism. It was Ringo Starr who made the connection with Lawrence, who explained that he understood the mystic realm, and that his brother was researching its practical application in a filming project involving Bugis pirates and the supernatural in the most remote parts of the Indonesian archipelago. 'Pirates and the supernatural, you got me,' the drummer is alleged to have said.

Apple Films financed the Blair brothers to the tune of 2000 pounds plus post-production costs, which enabled them to 'set sail with sixteen fierce Bugis tribesmen on a 2500-mile voyage through the Spice Islands in search of the Greater Bird of Paradise'. It wasn't much, but it was enough to give the brothers nine months, inspired by the book, *The Malay Archipelago*, by Alfred Russel Wallace, to trace his journey and become the first to film in colour the amazing bird that he had been the first Westerner to record. And it was enough to set in train an enormous body of work called the *Ring of Fire*. The only problem was that after the Blairs had produced two films, they couldn't find a buyer. They decided to meet at Lorne's new place in Bali and rethink their sales strategy.

After some years of commuting between Los Angeles (where he lectured) and his new home in Bali, Lawrence eventually settled full-time on the island while continuing to work on the *Ring of Fire* series. Eventually, it was picked up by PBS in America and the BBC in the United Kingdom in 1988, an accompanying book followed, and the work became a bestseller. Tragically, Lorne Blair fell down a manhole in Bali in 1995 and died of complications two days later.

'There's not a day goes by I don't miss him,' an older, still patrician, Lawrence Blair says as he finishes lunch at a terrace restaurant just a few hundred metres from his Legian home. His good eye sparkles. The other is hidden behind a patch. 'I'd like to say it was a poison dart, but in fact it was a

Chapter 13 The Hippie Highway

rare cancer, discovered just days after Lorne's death. Bali is a dangerous place to live when you're old. I shouldn't be here when I'm eighty, but I will be. Where would I go? It takes hold of your soul.'

With that, the septuagenarian psycho-anthropologist who made the world aware of, among other things, the 'hundredth monkey effect', and has visited more of Indonesia's 17,000 islands than possibly any other human, takes his leave, cycling up the laneway from the beach, his hair flopping in the breeze.

By the mid-1970s there were even more hippies in Bali, but their ranks had split into two camps, as noted by first-time visitor Vitek Czernuszyn, who later became a resident businessman:

> I actually felt quite alienated the first time because I wasn't a junkie. There were the junkies and there were the spiritual people. I didn't feel at home with either, but I chose the spiritual crowd because at least they didn't nod off when you were talking to them. There was this extraordinary moral compromise, and this was one of the defining things about early Bali. People just reinvented themselves as whatever they wanted to be.

The junkies gravitated to safely isolated outposts like Golden Village and the abandoned Kayu Aya in Seminyak, while in Kuta, hippie havens were springing up to cater for the more acceptable 'spiritual people'. One of the first was Kuba Krishna, just down the lane from Poppies, opened by American Jean Lane in 1975. A resident of Bali since 1970, Jean had built a basic kitchen in her *losmen* room and started cooking for herself during a cholera epidemic in Kuta. Later, when she married a Balinese man and had a child, she decided to open a restaurant on family-held land.

She recalls:

> I was a vegetarian but when I opened a restaurant I soon learned that not everyone was. On the other hand, a lot of the overland hippies wanted to eat vegetarian, so I started catering to them. I made an oven out of bricks and started making bread, but there was only white flour available here at the time, so the woman next door had a big mortar and pestle and she would pound rice and make cakes for the holidays. I talked her into pounding corn, soy

beans, mung beans and sesame seed. I'd toast them and she'd pound them, then I'd mix them up with white flour and make bread. It took a while but it started to get pretty good. Then someone brought me a yoghurt culture from Europe and I started making yoghurt. The place became very popular with the hippies, then later the surfers and the entrepreneurs, and I guess everyone else.

Jean's hippie hang would eventually become a Mexican taverna in a sign of the cosmopolitan times, and the hippies would become a lesser presence in Kuta and in Bali generally. But their influence would be felt in all aspects of Western life in Bali for many years to come.

Chapter 14 Bukit and Beyond

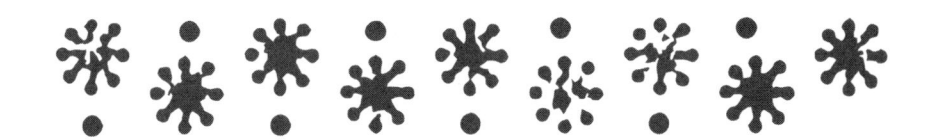

The consistency and quality of Bali's waves amazed me. At the time, surfing there was quite an adventure. Only a few guys surfed Uluwatu; instead of people, monkeys watched from the cliffs. One of the crew was a guy named Bob Laverty ... it was already apparent that Bob was nervous about staying much longer on Bali. Word was spreading fast about the great waves ... For Bob, the thrill was in getting off the beaten path, finding those isolated barrels of gold. So I listened up one day when he decided to include me on some privileged information—a secret he'd been holding on to for a while.

Bill Boyum, 1993

Surfers love to find the pot of gold at the end of the rainbow, and then swear others to secrecy to protect this private Valhalla, while at the same time embroidering the legend of the discovery to suit their own purposes. Surf adventurer Bill Boyum, the younger brother of Mike Boyum, wrote a fascinating account of the first overland mission to remote Grajagan in Eastern Java, which was published in the highly respected magazine *The Surfer's Journal* some twenty-one years after the discovery had been made, and four years after the mysterious death of Mike Boyum in the Philippines. In the years since, Boyum's account has been reprinted in surfing guidebooks and anthologies and has been widely accepted as the 'real story'.

And indeed, it is true that Bob Laverty, the black sheep heir to the Thriftimart fortune, and others in the Kuta cool crew did fear that Uluwatu would soon be overrun by surfers, and decided to explore the possibilities of another break they had seen from the air. But there is a considerable body of evidence that Bill Boyum wasn't involved. It is difficult to unravel the truth of an obscure adventure that happened more than forty years ago when many of the protagonists are either dead or career criminals to whom deceit is second nature, but the conflicted tale of the discovery of Grajagan's incredible surf break (G-Land, as it became known) is a fascinating part of Bali's surf lore, offering rare insights into the paranoia and obsessive secrecy of the surfer-scammers of the 1970s.

Most sources agree that it was Bob Laverty, the unassuming Californian remittance man, who first noticed the long crescent of reef that tapered along the edge of the Plengkung Forest Reserve at the south-eastern tip of Java while on a flight from Jakarta in late 1971 or early 1972. Laverty apparently saw trails of white water along the reef, indicating its surfing potential. At the time, fewer than a dozen of Bali's surfer expats were surfing at Uluwatu on a regular basis, and none of them had investigated any further along the Bukit Peninsula cliffs, where in later years another half-dozen world-class surf breaks would be discovered. But it was typical of the Kuta crew that they should seize on a secretive and potentially dangerous mission. For them, the grass was always greener somewhere else.

According to Bill Boyum, Laverty shared his secret one day and the two men set off on fat-tyred motorcycles to find the break, and were subsequently threatened by border guards at the Java ferry, taken by barge across the Grajagan lagoon by villagers, and finally walked long kilometres up the beach to the break when their bikes were defeated by crunchy coral. They slept, exhausted, on the sand and woke up at dawn to become the first to surf Grajagan's perfect waves. But according to at least two other accounts, Laverty made this journey alone and without a surfboard, took photos of the line-up and came straight back to Bali to mount a full expedition.

'Laverty made a solo recon trip to Java and returned with photographs of the most beautiful, perfect waves anyone had ever seen,' wrote Peter Maguire in his 2014 book, *Thai Stick*, based on interviews with Mike Ritter, who was one of the original Kuta crew, and was present when Laverty returned. Ritter made subsequent trips to Grajagan, although by his own account he was too stoned to get involved in the first expedition. Organising that fell to Warren 'Abdul' Anderson, who had a boat. Abdul says:

> Bill Boyum has about three or four different versions of how he discovered G-Land. I'll tell you what really happened. Bob Laverty rode over there and roughed it and got in there somehow and took pictures. When he came back and showed us, it became the place we had to go. I had all the Admiralty charts because

Chapter 14 Bukit and Beyond

> I'd brought a Hobie 16 in 1971. By this time I'd bought land on the beach in Legian and built a place, so when I sailed in I just hauled the Hobie up onto the beach and left it there. When we decided to do this G-Land trip, I looked after all the provisions and we just pushed out into the surf from Legian—me, Bob Jones and Ray Lee on the Hobie with three boards and two big bags of provisions. We had a stove and rice, potatoes, beans, water. There was barely enough room for us to sit on the trampoline.

According to Abdul, the rest of the crew set out overland at the same time, planning to rendezvous on the ocean side of the Grajagan lagoon in a couple of days. The land party included Mike Boyum, Bob Laverty, Bill Barron and Chris Lilley, but not Bill Boyum. The sea party got underway at around 2 am, aiming to make Grajagan by late afternoon.

Abdul recalls:

> I had a cigar box full of Thai sticks, so we started smoking doobs right away. By about 10 am we'd lost the wind and we were just bobbing around, baking in the sun. About three in the afternoon a land breeze picked up and we started making progress towards Java. We had no compass, we just aimed in the general direction. I didn't even know dead reckoning. We got in near the coast of Java, probably this side of G-Land. It was about 4 pm and I didn't want to try to get in over the reef at night, so we sat out there until we saw a little area where boats had been going in. We got to about 100 yards from the dry reef and I looked over my shoulder and saw a sneaker set, about eight feet faces, right behind. I came about and Bob and Ray were paddling oars and we just punched through the first wave as it feathered, then just got through the next two. As soon as they'd passed, I turned the boat around again and got in through the reef as fast as I could, hauled the boat up and spent the night on the beach.

The boat crew spent another night on the beach before the land party arrived, where they took on more water and began the long 20-kilometre walk up the beach while Abdul steered the Hobie back out beyond the break and tacked into the wind. By late afternoon of the third day, they were all looking at perfect waves peeling down the reef. The thrill of surf discovery trumped

* 161 *

exhaustion and they attached their homemade, sock-and-bungie-cord leashes and enjoyed their first perfect session at G-Land.

Abdul recalls:

> We were out in the line-up, sharing these perfect waves, and we looked into the beach and there were monkeys everywhere, raiding our campsite. They were into everything! So after that one guy had to stay in and mind the camp while the others surfed. Our camp was pretty basic, no tents or anything fancy. Because I owned the boat, I'd sleep on the trampoline and some would sleep underneath. The rest of the guys just slept on sarongs on the sand. It rained a bit and we'd collect the water in the sails. If it rained heavily I'd be sleeping in a couple of inches of water. We were there a week or 10 days and by the end we all had crotch rot. I don't think we even caught fish. I guess most of us were vegetarian.

On his reconnaissance trip, Bob Laverty had heard reports of tiger sightings and isolated attacks, so nobody went into the jungle. Abdul says:

> We had hermit crabs and monkeys on the beach. That was enough to deal with. One day I went maybe ten metres into the jungle and a clump of bamboo started shaking, so I got out of there real quick and never went back in. We had no weapons other than knives for cutting food, but nobody got hurt and there were no boards broken. We were just so lucky. We didn't leave anything or name anything. We just left the place like it was and headed for home one morning into 25 knots of wind, white caps all over the sea and a couple of metres of chop on the top. We had to tack into a headwind most of the way, soaking wet. It took us something like fifteen hours to get back and we arrived at two or three in the morning and just ran it straight in through the surf.

A week or so after they returned from Grajagan, Bob Laverty and some friends were surfing Uluwatu on a moderately big day when Laverty spied a large set approaching. Paddling seaward, he told his companions he was taking the wave, turned and dropped down the face out of sight. Sometime later one of the other surfers spotted Laverty's board floating inside the break,

Chapter 14 Bukit and Beyond

and when he tried to retrieve it he discovered Laverty's limp body attached to it by bungie cord.

Again, the circumstances surrounding Bob Laverty's death are shrouded in mystery. In Bill Boyum's written account, he, Laverty and Bob Jones were surfing alone that day, and it was Boyum who made the grisly discovery. Although he says that 'we worked on Bob for about an hour, trying to bring him back', he offers no further detail. Mike Ritter's account doesn't place Boyum at the scene and nor does Abdul's.

According to Abdul:

> I wasn't there but Ray Lee and Bob Jones were. There was at least one other, too, but it wasn't Bill Boyum. I went out later to help carry his body out, so I spoke to everybody involved, but I'm not sure who actually found the body floating in the tide pools. I do know they freaked out, man. No one had jobs, we were all doing illegal stuff so we could live the dream. Everybody had a little thing going on, whether it was smuggling hash oil out of Pakistan or Thai weed out of Bangkok. And fuck, man, Bob's dead and a lot of people are going to want to know what happened. So the guys came back here and told me the story and I said I'd go out there. Four of us went out to Uluwatu, taking a sleeping bag, some sheets and ropes. I took a flashlight, too, because it was about 4 pm. We got all this stuff together, jumped on our bikes and raced out there. We got down to the tide pool and grabbed the body and stuffed it head-first into a sleeping bag. We just left the board. He was a big guy and by now he was waterlogged, too, so his feet stuck out the bottom of the bag. This was about 100 metres down from the cave, so we all had to lift him up on our shoulders and carry him back up the reef, and coming through the cave we were chest-deep in water with waves smashing in on us. By now it was dark and the flashlight didn't work. It was creepy in the dark, but we got him into the cave and pulled him up the ladder and onto the ledge above the cave. We had about 100 feet of blue plastic rope so we tied that around the bag and then strung it up the cliff-side so that it wasn't going to go anywhere. This guy's family was friends of [President] Nixon's, you know? We really didn't want to get mixed up in all of this by going to the police.

Bali: Heaven and Hell

The next morning Abdul went to the public phone at the airport and called the US embassy anonymously and told them what had happened and where the body was. Embassy staff flew over from Jakarta and recovered Laverty's bloated body. There is no evidence of any investigation into the death by either American or Indonesian authorities, but even today, when old Bali surf hands gather, someone will trot out the story of 'what really happened' to Bob Laverty. And the legend keeps growing. In their book on the drug trade, Peter Maguire and Mike Ritter contend that, 'When Laverty's father arrived in Bali to claim his son's remains, he cut his long red hair, shaved his beard and dressed him in a tuxedo for the trip home.' Apart from the fact that Rodger Laverty Sr had been in his own grave for three years when his son drowned, no one ever claimed the body.

Over the summer of 1971–72, although Albert Falzon's *Morning of the Earth* was still a few weeks away from its theatrical release, the Australian surfing cognoscenti was fast becoming aware that it contained some revelations about the wave potential of Bali. One of the first centres of this growing intelligence was in the unlikely setting of an old boatshed at Palm Beach, on Sydney's northern beaches peninsula, where underground surfboard craftsmen Glynn Ritchie, David Chidgey and Mitchell Rae had set up Outer Island Surfboards. The rumours circulating about Falzon's discovery of a new break at the tip of the island consolidated what they'd previously heard from Russell Hughes, and they made plans to down tools and go after securing seventeen-year-old Rae a passport for his first overseas trip.

Before departure, Ritchie and Chidgey had a blow-up (not for the first time) so Chidgey made his way to Bali independently. Rae still remembers arriving in Bali for the first time:

> I will always have that vision. No traffic, no tourists, a raw coral track leading down to perfect waves. Three restaurants and a couple of *warung*s. I just walked round with a giant shit-eating grin on my face the whole time. It was a surfer's Disneyland, it had everything I treasured, in abundance. No crowds, offshore winds every day, consistent swell.

They settled into a cheap *losmen* near the beach and a routine of surfing Kuta Reef and the Kuta beach breaks all day, every day. 'We knew about Uluwatu, of course,' Rae says, 'But the swell was consistent and we had perfect waves

Chapter 14 Bukit and Beyond

to ourselves every day, so there was no need to explore.' They soon ran into Chidgey and he and Ritchie kissed and made up. The three amigos were surfing the reef alone one afternoon, high on Chidgey's acid, when 'this enormous canoe comes out from the beach at Kartika Plaza, with a figure all in white in the middle of it, wearing a panama hat, straight out of a Bogart movie. It was Miki Dora, of course.'

Random sightings of the legendary Malibu surfer and international con man were not that unusual in the early 1970s. He would show up out of nowhere and disappear just as mysteriously. Sometimes he would shun contact, other times he would ooze charm. Rae recalls the latter:

> He's slowly off with the white suit and the dark glasses while we watched between sets, and over the side with his board, wearing white boardshorts, of course. We surfed for a while and got him talking and he lived up to the legend. He told us we should come over and surf this perfect right-hander he was surfing alone in front of the Bali Beach Hotel at Sanur. He was friendly and fabulous, living large, having fun.

Chidgey had a plan to cover the expenses for the trip, as he always did. In their final days in Bali, he put Rae on the back of his bike and rode into Denpasar. They pulled up in front of the Adiasa Hotel and Mitchell followed Chidgey up a flight of stairs and into a shabby sitting room, where the teenager was somewhat shocked to be joined momentarily by a group of army officers.

'What's goin' on, Chidge?' he asked.

'Just smile, I'll handle it,' Chidge responded.

The soldiers seemed friendly enough. They slammed a 5-pound bag of Sumatran heads down on a table and sat around it while Chidgey counted out the rupiah. Back at the *losmen*, Chidgey pulled out his tool bag and some resin and they systematically chambered out their surfboards, packed the weed into the cavities and glassed over them.

Mitchell Rae had smoked his first joint at thirteen and had been surfing on acid for at least two years, so he was an old hand at recreational drugs. Still, he'd never crossed international borders as a mule before, so Chidgey sent him through the airport formalities first, so that he could keep an eye on him—or perhaps do a runner if things went pear-shaped. The happy-go-lucky kid just smiled and sauntered through at both ends, and they were soon ripping their boards apart in Chidgey's Avalon garage to uncover the booty.

So that was Bali. Too easy.

Falzon's *Morning of the Earth* premiered at the Manly Silver Screen on 25 February 1972, to rave reviews. 'Our most ambitious surfing movie,' said *The Sydney Morning Herald*. While it was an immediate cult success, *Morning* did not have mainstream distribution, so Falzon and his producer and partner, David Elfick, had to rely on the time-honoured surf-movie roadshow circuit to generate cash flow. For this they employed Steve Otton and Kim Bradley, two young peninsula surfers who hung out at the *Tracks* office in Whale Beach.

Bradley, or 'the Fly' as he was universally known, was a wisp of a kid with sensitive freckly skin who lived next door to the surfing Sumpter family in North Avalon. He was just a good-natured urchin with a dark streak a metre wide, but the kid could surf. The first ridden wave in Falzon's movie showed Fly's unique style, so he felt some ownership over the film, and took delight in touring it up and down the country halls of Eastern Australia. But Fly, like Mitch Rae, was connected to surfing's jungle telegraph, and he had heard the Russell Hughes stories of the reef breaks of Bali for years. As the roadshow tour continued, having sold the tickets, dimmed the lights and run the projector, he would watch Stephen Cooney (a grom his own age from down the road) and Rusty Miller pull into the huge, sparkling walls of Uluwatu and smoothly navigate down the line, and every night the pain of being here, not there, grew more intense.

At the end of 1972, after yet another sell-out show at a big coastal centre, Kim Bradley counted out the takings, put them in a paper bag and headed for the airport. More than forty years later, Albert Falzon, sipping herbal tea in the living room of his country home, paid for by the movie, throws back his long hair and laughs uproariously at the memory. 'I can't fuckin' believe he didn't do it sooner! It was the best review we could have had. Fly saw the movie and escaped to Bali and never came home. How good is that!'

Within weeks of his arrival in Bali, Kim Bradley had the place wired. He knew the breaks, he had transport to them, he could organise anything a new arrival needed, and he'd found teen love with a pretty drink seller on the beach. When the first influx of *Morning of the Earth* surf tourists began to arrive in 1973, Fly was there to help them.

Chapter 14 Bukit and Beyond

Photographers Dick Hoole and Jack McCoy and tyro filmmaker David 'Mexican' Sumpter were in the vanguard of first arrivals in the southern spring of 1973. Sumpter had somehow organised to liaise with hero surfers Wayne Lynch and Nat Young to shoot sequences for his first surf film, while Australian-born Hoole and American Jack McCoy from Hawaii were fooling around with a stills photography partnership called Propeller that they had just created. So nobody had a real job, but Sumpter had used his ski-season-instructing money to fly Wayne Lynch, free of the law since the abolition of military conscription in December 1972 by Gough Whitlam's new Labor Government, to join him in Bali.

Sumpter recalls:

> Jack McCoy suggested to me that I take Wayne Lynch to Bali because he'd been out of the picture for a couple of years through running from the draft thing, and there were plenty of lefts up there. I phoned Wayne and he was keen, so I bought him a ticket for $299 and we were off, no agreement, no nothing.

The 1966 world champion and then guru of 'soul surfing', Nat Young, was also acutely aware of the Bali possibilities. He later wrote:

> After the [1972] election results were announced it was a very jubilant Wayne Lynch who phoned me in Byron to confirm our plans for a surf trip to Bali that coming winter. David Mexican Sumpter was making a surf movie and would pay for Wayne's ticket ... Just like everyone else who'd seen the movie, *Morning of the Earth*, Wayne and I were totally over the top with the idea of riding the giant barrels of Uluwatu.

Unfortunately, the enigmatic Lynch, the most exciting Australian surfer to emerge on the world stage in the late 1960s, contracted malaria soon after arriving, had his stay cut short and was not to reappear in Bali for more than twenty years. But Sumpter got his ticket's worth, with some memorable footage of Lynch at Uluwatu, while Hoole captured a dramatic photograph of Lynch negotiating a foamy Ulu barrel that found its way into a prime position on the wall of the Summerhouse, a health-food restaurant that Jack McCoy and some friends were setting up in Torquay, Victoria.

Bali: Heaven and Hell

Before he had to leave, Lynch managed to spend some time seeing the sights with Nat Young, who wrote:

> There were quite a few hippie types in Bali at that time, pseudo surfers who paddled out and played around on a surfboard from time to time but never really got into it seriously. My favourite among them was Big Eddy, six feet six inches of muscular, bronzed American, with a heart of gold, who was totally dedicated to turning on everyone who visited Bali. Originally from New York, he'd spent years following the hippy trail ... The first time Wayne and I met him he was on his daily stroll along the beach at Kuta with a huge torpedo-shaped bundle of Thai sticks tucked firmly under his arm. We'd watched as he greeted a couple 50 metres down the beach, handing them his gift and treating them to his infectious smile.

Despite the fact that he was travelling with his then wife, Marilyn, and baby daughter, Naomi, Young also managed to slip away for a stoned dinner with Abdul at his Legian beach house:

> 'Fun in the sun and income too', was Abdul's motto, and he delighted in laying it on you at every chance he got ... Abdul had the first sixteen-foot Hobie Cat that I ever saw—a really neat toy that he handled very competently. One night after dinner he sold me on the idea of sailing straight off the beach in front of his house to go and ride some incredible lefts [in Java] ... It was a crazy idea but late that night we set sail, totally prepared to the tune of a hat, sunglasses, a pair of boardshorts and a tee shirt. For provisions we had only a bottle of water and some muesli bars ... Under the effects of liberal amounts of high-quality marijuana, the night seemed to pass quite quickly.

But in the morning common sense prevailed and with no provisions and facing a headwind, the adventurers gave up on their G-Land mission and returned to Bali.

The Australian surfers stayed in *losmen*s along Jalan Pantai, or in the network of sandy lanes behind. Kodja Inn, about halfway between Bemo Corner and the beach, was particularly popular. Dick Hoole says:

Chapter 14 Bukit and Beyond

> When Jack McCoy and I arrived from Singapore we just got in a *bemo* and asked him to take us somewhere to stay near the beach. He picked up on my Aussie accent and took us straight to Kodja Inn. They were just basic rooms but they suited us fine until the Americans came. They were getting 600 rupiah to the dollar and we only got 400, so they were a bit flasher than us and lashed out on bungalows.

The surfers ate at Poppies, the 'it' place in Kuta, although a lady called Kempu had started making good, wholesome food in a *warung* next to Lasi Erawati *losmen* just up the lane, and Big Eddy Gardner had opened a juice bar on Jalan Legian, using some battery-powered juicers and blenders he had imported from Singapore. And of course there was Abdul's sugarcane juice bar on Buni Sari.

Life was good in Kuta, but in the eyes of Bali's true surfing pioneers, it would be 'the last good season'. The following year the floodgates opened.

In 1974 Australia hosted the most lucrative season in pro surfing's brief history, with relatively big money on offer at the Rip Curl Pro at Bells Beach and the 2SM Coca Cola Bottlers Surfabout on Sydney's northern beaches. Among the international surf stars to arrive were Gavin Rudolph and Shaun Tomson from South Africa, Sam Hawk and Mike Purpus from California, and Gerry Lopez, Reno Abellira and Jeff Hakman from Hawaii. None of them were a match for Australia's Michael Peterson on home turf in the events, but the Hawaiians in particular impressed wherever they went, with their flowing surfing and breezy manner.

In Torquay, Victoria, for the Bells Beach event, they ate regularly at McCoy's Summerhouse. Lopez and Hakman (known respectively as 'Mr Pipeline' and 'Mr Sunset' for their prowess at those famous breaks) had gone to school with McCoy in Honolulu, and both Lopez and McCoy had been on the Hawaiian team at the 1970 world titles at Bells. Mr Pipeline had hurried home to a warmer clime, and McCoy had stayed and made a life in Australia.

On one of their first visits to the Summerhouse, Lopez got up from the table and examined a big photo tacked to the back wall. It showed Wayne Lynch on a threatening, foamy wall at Uluwatu, the shot that Dick Hoole had taken the previous season. 'That's some freakin' wave,' Lopez said.

'Like a machine, bra,' said McCoy. 'Day after day, overhead, double overhead, triple overhead, offshore and pumping, man, all season long.' Lopez and Hakman booked tickets the next day.

Bali: Heaven and Hell

The idea of surf exploration had been around for a decade, since Bruce Brown filmed Robert August and Mike Hynson sliding down deserted sand hills to get to Cape St Francis in *The Endless Summer*. Surfers then had been inspired to travel the world, and particularly South Africa, in search of the perfect wave, but there had been nothing like the invasion of Bali in 1974. In today's terms, the tourist numbers were miniscule. At the end of the 1960s Bali had little more than 10,000 tourists a year, in the 1970s the figure began to grow at 10 per cent and spiked to 12–14 per cent in 1974–77, but even so, in 1974 there would have been only around 20,000, compared with today's foreign arrivals (excluding domestics) of more than 3 million a year, and fewer than a thousand of them would have been surfers. Still, if you'd been surfing Kuta Reef alone for three or four years, it seemed like a hell of a lot.

One of the reasons for this was the fact that international airline travel was getting easier and cheaper. You could now fly direct to Bali on the Flying Kangaroo (although Indonesia's Garuda was much cheaper) and prescient travel agent Jack De Lissa had established Bali Easy Rider Travel Service in 1973, offering three- and five-week packages that included a cheap *losmen* and a motorbike. Other agents soon followed suit.

But the main reason for the surfer invasion was *Morning of the Earth*. While Mexican Sumpter and I were further fuelling the fire by road-showing his slightly derivative *On Any Morning* in Australia, *Morning* had opened in California and Hawaii, with full-house patrons gobsmacked to see big, high-quality waves somewhere other than in Hawaii. In surf communities all over both states, atlases were being pulled down off bookshelves, globes were being spun and airline tickets were being booked.

Lopez and Hakman soon fell into the web of Mike Boyum, and Lopez into his lifestyle program of yoga at dawn, followed by a huge magic-mushroom smoothie, a *bemo* ride to Uluwatu, a fast jog into the break and an all-day surf session. Abdul says: 'Boyum was a star-fucker. When those guys were in town, he wouldn't give you the time of day.'

Soon there were more stars. Lopez's Pipeline partner, Rory Russell, showed up with his own film crew, funded by a big-time dope dealer from Maui and headed by a clever young cameraman named Spyder Wills. Lopez's filmmaker friend, Yuri Farrant, followed, and the two big American surf magazines, *Surfer* and *Surfing*, sent their gun photographers, Jeff Divine and Dan Merkel. Hoole and McCoy shot photos for *Tracks* and a tyro surf

Chapter 14 Bukit and Beyond

journalist named Jarratt contributed a humorous take on the invasion called 'Uluwatu You, Sport'.

As a sideline to his photography, Hoole, who had committed to spend the whole six-month season in Bali, punctuated by a visa run to Singapore, began selling counterfeit student cards.

> There was no discount air travel in those days, but these student cards would get you a cheaper fare, so we started forging them. They were being used right along the denim trail (another name for the hippie highway). We had blank cards and then we'd take the picture and put the fake stamps on top. They were very cheap, maybe $20, and they usually worked.

Through the family connections of his girlfriend, Made Ringin, Fly Bradley had established himself shaping surfboards and fixing dings at a hole in the wall next to Lasi Erawati. He was the first of the Australian surfers to establish real links with the villagers, but others soon followed. Dick Hoole says:

> We got to know the main families of Kuta and they were all interconnected. The younger generation were learning English very quickly. It wasn't taught in school yet, but they knew they had to pick it up to sell us stuff, and it seemed to come quite naturally to them. The other side of getting to know the locals was that we were starting to think about getting involved in property deals with them, and then the story of the Kayu Aya came out, with the owners being denied visas and the locals just taking it over and trashing it. We started to think that investing in Bali was maybe not such a great idea.

Hoole, McCoy, Bradley, Boyum and other regulars at Uluwatu also began to develop a strong relationship with the dirt-poor peasant farmers of the small village midway between the temple road and the surf break whose proper name was Sibilan, but had become known to the surfers by the name of the temple along the cliffs. Likewise, the surfers came to know the village not by its real name but by the name of its head man, Windro.

The dusty, arid Bukit Peninsula had once been home to teak forests where the raja of Badung would hunt deer on horseback, then it became a dumping ground for the detritus of society in Badung. They were taken up onto the limestone plateau by ox-cart and left to fend for themselves. Many of them were true survivors who tilled the stony land and eked out a living. Windro's people were the direct descendants. For a brief decade or two before the roads became clogged, it took only forty minutes to drive from Kuta out to Uluwatu, but culturally you might have been a few centuries away.

When the first surfers came to Uluwatu, they picked their way along the cliffs from the temple, but it took only a short time for Windro and his villagers to realise that these intruders could provide income, or at least an opportunity to barter. Often led by Windro himself, they would wait in the bushes by the road and wave down *bemo*s half a mile before the temple. For cigarettes for the men and perhaps a coin for the kids, the villagers would guide surfers along a much quicker trail down to the sea, through the stiles of their fields and past their thatched-roof compounds and pig sties. The men would carry the boards, the girls offered buckets of warm soft drinks from their *warung*, and the boys kept up a happy chorus of: 'What you name? Where you come prom?' The mothers and older sisters would wave shyly as visitors passed the village, feigning disinterest as they gracefully drifted between the buildings, carrying water or food on their heads.

Mexican Sumpter recalls: 'It started out at 50 rupiah to carry your board or your cameras, but every time the Americans went out there, the price doubled because they wouldn't bargain.'

Hoole says:

> We began to get very close to the people there after a while, because we could see how little they had and yet they were so giving and willing to let us become part of their family. They had nothing, and yet they were happy to share it. At first it was just building the trust to where we'd leave boards and equipment out there overnight, then they fixed up a couple of rooms in the compound where we could sleep overnight, and soon we were helping them build a little *warung* on the cliff so they could sell us drinks and food and there was some shade. They were the golden years at Uluwatu, a very special time.

Grajagan was back on the radar in 1974, with Abdul skippering another mission, this time on a trimaran that had been abandoned after a bungled drug run. Abdul recalls:

Chapter 14 Bukit and Beyond

One of the guys, Bogie, was from a wealthy New York family and he brought a trimaran here. He was going to do a load to Australia, a couple hundred pound of Sumatran rag weed. He was rich, he didn't need to do a load to anywhere, but he wanted to be one of the guys, I guess. He looked like Jesus, with long hair and a beard, and he was on some weird diet of dried fruit. He took off for Australia with this other guy and he just snapped, lost his mind, maybe from eating all that dried fruit. They turned around and came back, throwing all the weed overboard. Bogie was a basket case after that, he'd sit there with a blanket over him and you'd have to feed him. So his family came and got him and he left the trimaran here, just abandoned it. We thought we may as well use it, so off we went back to G-Land.

This time there was no parallel land-based expedition. The yacht was big enough to take eight of them with surfboards, a small gas stove and a Zodiac tied behind. Abdul says:

We were still roughing it, but we could stay on the boat the whole time.
We anchored in the channel and watched it get bigger and bigger.
I caught the biggest waves of my life and nearly drowned a couple of times. It got so big we nearly lost the Zodiac, dragged under in the surge.

As the swell dropped the surfers on that trip—Mike Boyum, Bob Jones, Ray Lee and Mike Ritter among them—began to realise the full potential of this amazing wave park, with its different sections of reef providing waves of completely different character but equal quality. Boyum, in particular, although by no means a good surfer ('no style and even less grace' was how Jeff Hakman described him), by now had learned enough to realise what G-Land would mean to surfers who were skilled enough to handle it. Sitting on the trimaran, Boyum looked at the section they called Speedy's and imagined Gerry Lopez streaking across it, deep in the barrel. High on psilocybin, as he almost always was, he looked at the waves, and back at the jungle, and back at the waves again. He had seen the future. He would build a surf camp right there, at the edge of the jungle.

But this surf camp would not be for the faint-hearted. It would be for the toughest of the tough, the surf commandos. It would be for him and for Gerry.

Chapter 15 The Traders

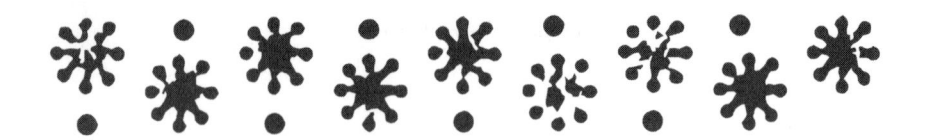

The expats who made their lives and businesses in Bali were the unsung heroes really. The star surfers got all the publicity, but guys like Steve and Robert and Tim and Fly just stayed here and learnt how to live with the locals, speak the language, run a business. They flew under the radar, their reward was the lifestyle.

Dick Hoole, 2013

Stephen Palmer was a sweet guy. Bit of a dreamer, but always thinking about others. So when his best mate, Robert Wilson, was turning twenty in 1974, Stephen organised one hell of a party.

Since early schooldays in Sydney's western suburbs, Stephen and Robert had been best friends, and when they became surfers, they'd catch the train down to Cronulla on the weekends, surf their brains out and catch it home again, sunburnt and stoked. 'Westies' had a bad reputation along the beach suburbs, were sneered at and heckled as they made their way between the station and the beach, but often the disadvantage of living so far from the surf bred the most resilient and serious watermen, straight shooters who just got on with the job.

Robert had left school in 1970 and apprenticed as a plumber, while Stephen enrolled at a technical college to study engineering. Stephen got a kombi and they started taking surf trips together whenever they could, down south to Bells or up north to Noosa. In Noosa in 1973 Stephen smashed himself up while surfing the Boiling Pot, and, dripping blood as he made his way back to the car park, he was accosted by an American hippie who was selling alfalfa-sprout sandwiches from a tray. 'Hey, man, let me take a look at that. You need some patchin' up, fella.'

Chapter 15 The Traders

That was how they met Wally and Lily. He was from California, she was from Hawaii, and they'd arrived in Noosa via just about everywhere. They shared a meal and Robert and Stephen listened intently to every word about the far-out places they'd seen in the East, the beautiful beaches, the perfect waves. 'The one place you guys have to go to is Bali,' Wally declared. The two westies filed that in the memory bank.

Almost a year had gone by but Stephen still remembered Wally's advice when he planned Robert's party. First he organised the beer and the dope, then he phoned *Tracks* and rented a private screening of *Morning of the Earth*. A guy called Steve Otton would come out with the movie and a projector and all Stephen Palmer had to do was supply a screen. He borrowed a giant bedsheet and strung it up from the second floor of their apartment block. Then he put a few chairs around the courtyard, popped a can of beer and waited for the guests to arrive.

Robert was expecting a small gathering of friends, but when he arrived he was guided to the back of the block by the sweet aroma of hashish and a billowing cloud of blue smoke. The opposing youth cultures of Guildford and beyond had gathered that night—bikers and landlocked surfers side by side, hundreds of them wedged in a small courtyard next to the Hills Hoist, watching the greatest Australian surf movie of all time. Robert remembers being spellbound when the Bali sequence began, and everyone—bikers included—began to hoot and holler as the two surfers rode majestically across backlit, big Uluwatu. He knew he had to go there.

Sydney surfer and advertising cadet Peter Neely was a gate-crasher that night. He recalls: 'I'd heard a rumour that *Morning of the Earth* was going to be screened at a private party, so, like a lot of others, I got the address and just turned up. It wasn't hard to find, just follow the mushroom cloud.' Within the year Neely, like Robert Wilson, was following his dream to Bali.

The next day Robert booked his tickets, flying TAA to Darwin, then joining the '*bemo* of the sky' to Bali via Kupang. At least that was the plan. When he presented himself at the Merpati desk they asked him to show his traveller's cheques. Robert proudly produced his new 'black light' Commonwealth Bank book. 'You can withdraw money anywhere,' he explained. They sent him away, telling him he needed real money to enter Indonesia and that he'd have to take the next plane. It was a weekly flight. 'I felt like a dumb westie,' Robert recalls. 'I tried never to let that happen again.'

Bali: Heaven and Hell

Killing time at a flophouse in Darwin, he reread the letter that Wally and Lily had sent him after hearing of his travel plans:

May 23, 1974

Dear Robert,

Here is a last-minute message that will help you on this tremendous adventure that you are about to embark on.

Money and passport—these are your entire security, always be aware of their whereabouts. Except in Bali, keep them both close to your skin, never in your bag. It would be a good idea to have your bank write out a letter saying you have so much money in the account to flash to questioning border officials. Always study the local currency and know how to count in the language—be able to calculate quickly the price of items in Australian money. Try to find out the current rate of everything (food, taxi, hotel, bus etc) before entering a country. Example: price of *bemo* from airport to Kuta is 25 rps.

Keep a small notepad on hand to jot down info from other travellers who you'll be talking to all the time. Never accept the first, second or third price on anything. Bargain, bargain, bargain. Sometimes we would take two or three days to finally agree on a price for something. Send things home by sea mail—cheap and slow, nothing very valuable. Remember when you get ripped off or over-charged, you are rich, they are poor.

Borders—never cross borders with dope—too big a risk. Look clean and straight and don't hang with hippie types. Don't always believe what the officials tell you. Be aware of each country's requirements, eg Ceylon you must change your traveller cheques at the bank and stamp it in paper they give you. Keep track of your injection expiration dates. Know how long it will take you to get out of the country and how much you have left on your visa. Stretch your money—make it go forever. Get a student card.

Carry small items from your home country for gifts, such as coins, used stamps, postcards. Carry pictures (or postcards) that will help explain what your country is like—surfing, kangaroos etc. Words will never explain those.

Chapter 15 The Traders

> Travelling the way you are is the best learning experience there is. It is like being in a far out movie that goes on and on and never stops. You will learn how most of the world lives and what they hold as important—it's usually not money.
>
> Try to keep a journal of the things that happen to you 'cause you'll never remember all the unbelievable things you will go through.

When he did finally fly to Bali he sat next to a Californian surfer who had been before, so they took a *bemo* straight to Lasi Erawati in Poppies Lane, beginning what would become a long association with Kempu and her family. His new friend, Chris, then took him to a restaurant on Jalan Buni Sari for a mushroom omelette. 'I used to love Mum's mushroom omelettes, so I tucked in,' Robert remembers. Walking back to the *losmen* he began to feel strange. He walked straight past Lasi Erawati and kept going to the beach, where he sat all night watching the advance and retreat of the tide.

Robert Wilson spent about six weeks in Bali on that first trip, finishing up by going overland to Jakarta, then hitching rides on tramp steamers through Sumatra to Kuala Lumpur, where he flew home and started saving for the next trip. When Stephen Palmer finished his engineering course at the end of 1974, he did the same thing, and by the middle of 1975, the two friends had worked out a routine to keep themselves in Bali much of the year. They would buy floral-print rayon shirts for a dollar, roll fifty or sixty tightly and hide them amongst dirty tees in their bags, then sell them for eight dollars at home. This turned $60 into almost $500, more than enough for the next ticket.

Stephen Palmer recalls that their small enterprise leapt to a new level when they started exporting shantung silk shirts under the Santosha label. The brightly patterned, heavier-weight shirts were a smash hit along their coastal network of surf and 'head' shops. 'I could never get past Crescent Head before I sold out!' An even bigger break came later that year when they secured an advance order for $5000 of clothing from Wakefield Surfboards in the western suburbs, where Robert had once moonlighted, cutting fins and glassing boards.

Stephen recalls:

> It was our big break and we totally stuffed it up. We had to scrounge the money together for the order, and then we sized

it all wrong. The Balinese had this idea in their heads that all Westerners were huge monsters, so a small size was enormous, and it went up from there. When we got the stuff back to Sydney, Robert's mum had to take everything in. I'd done production engineering and I began to realise that if we were going to do larger quantities, I needed to get involved with the process and introduce some standards and controls. So I actually moved into the factory of our supplier on Jalan Sulawesi in Denpasar, and started introducing patterns and sizing grids. That really started to give us an advantage over the other surf trader start-ups.

Within one year, Stephen Palmer's Bali dream had gone from palm trees and reef breaks to living in a factory much like the ones back home in Guildford. Robert Wilson's life had also taken another detour after he became obsessed with the idea of becoming a commercial diver and finished up working a season in the freezing North Sea off Aberdeen. *Morning of the Earth* it wasn't.

The partners got back on track when Robert realised that what Stephen was starting to do with manufacturing and design in Bali was just as exciting as the world of diving. Stephen had started a brand he called Om Bali Clothing Company. He says: 'I called it Om to remind me that there was a higher purpose in what we were doing. It wasn't just about the money, at least not at first.' He had sold his kombivan back in Australia to fund improvements in production, and now the two men put in $10,000 in cash to get a serious production cycle happening.

Stephen had focused on producing high-quality batik prints for women's clothing, and had become such a perfectionist that he had begun importing bales of rayon thread from China and getting it woven to a specific tension so that the batik would be perfect. Robert came up with the idea of avoiding prohibitive sales tax by combining lacework with batik so that their garments could be classified as 'handicrafts' and attract minimal tax. From a westie who didn't know about traveller's cheques, he'd come a long way.

Robert took charge of the lacework business, branded Firefly, while Stephen and new partner Michael Chahine looked after general production. They passed $1 million in sales in 1979 and kept heading north, with 3000 employees across Indonesia, 600 of them in Bali, mostly packing and freighting to fulfil the growing orders from around the world. Robert still tried to

Chapter 15 The Traders

surf every day. For Stephen, it had become a low priority. The business was the challenge.

In 1974 two surfing mates from the NSW Central Coast flew to Bali with an adventurous business plan. Both Dave Wyllie and David Thomas were only in their early twenties but were already seasoned travellers. Thomas had been travelling the world since leaving school in the 1960s and had lived in Europe and Canada. Wyllie was a couple of years younger than his friend, but the previous year he had come to Bali alone, and at a time when Kuta was considered a remote outpost, he had ventured to Medewi on the west coast, where he stayed in the family compound of the Islamic village head man and snake catcher, and surfed the reefs in solitude. Seeking out the beach too far was to become his lifelong passion.

Now, along with Thomas's wife, Janine, they were coming to Bali to live. Soon after getting married, the Thomases had shared a house in Sydney's Newport Beach with an artist couple who had studied batik in Yogyakarta in the late 1960s and founded the Australian Batik Association. David Thomas was fascinated by their collection of unusual textiles and *ikat* weaving from the island of Sumba and other parts of the eastern Indonesian archipelago, and sensed a commercial opportunity.

Thomas recalls: 'From what our housemates had told us, we thought we'd be able to buy the textiles in Bali from Chinese traders, but there were none, so we had to look further afield. We decided to go to Sumba.'

Their investigations revealed that the colourful owner and chief pilot of Zamrud Airlines, Captain Jack Rife, often brought textiles back from his 'milk run' flights, and had a substantial private collection. Thomas says:

> We were so naïve that we went to see him to ask if he would mind if we tried to do some business in textiles. We had ethics, we didn't know Bali was full of outlaws. Jack just poured us a long drink, grinned and told us to go right ahead, he'd even fly us there. So we flew down to Waingapu, the main town of Sumba. It was like the wild west, but we were taken in by an Arab family that had a little hotel, and we started to make connections.

In 1975, with the war in neighbouring Timor making headlines all over Australia, the two Daves rented a Honda 125 motorbike in Kuta and took it to Sumba in the belly of Jack Rife's DC-3. Although their stated mission was to travel further in search of rugs, the two surfers were also looking for remote surf breaks, since they figured they would be spending considerable buying time on Sumba. With a war happening just across the strait, all the islands of the east had special security measures in place. On Sumba, if you left the main town you were required to report to the police at every village you travelled through so that your passport could be stamped. But when the two men on the small bike reached Melolo, they decided they would strike out for the coast but return to spend the night, so there was no need to report in.

At the edge of an exquisite bay, the two men found a makeshift lean-to, spread out their camp blankets and settled back to watch the sun set. Wyllie produced two tabs of high-quality LSD and soon the golden hues of the sunset had blended into the rich green canopy of a non-existent jungle. As it got dark, the trip got even better. Thomas saw flashes of light in the bushes behind them. Suddenly, screaming tribesmen armed with spears and machetes surrounded them, betel-nut patterns smeared across their angry faces.

Thomas remembers:

> We jumped up and this old white-haired guy started yelling at the others to kill us, or so it seemed. I looked at Dave and said something ridiculous like, it's a good night to die. Dave shouted, 'Fuck that!' One of the younger men started telling them that we were okay, not spies. But still they weren't sure. They marched us to their village, right on the beach, just around the bay. They were Savunese fishermen, not from Sumba, and the head man was just sitting there in the moonlight, looking at us as if to say, what are you doing here? But he was an educated man who spoke Indonesian and we sat up and talked to him all night. He became a lifelong friend.

The partners leased space in Kuta, opened a gallery and filled it with textiles. It was soon followed by a second, near the Kuta markets. They started mounting exhibitions, the first at the Bali Hyatt Resort, then at the Bali Beach Hotel. By 1977 they were exhibiting in New York and Archipelago Textiles had an international reputation as the world's foremost collection of *ikats*.

The two Daves kept returning to their secret bay, where they were made to feel like locals and allowed to build a house where they stayed and

Chapter 15 The Traders

stored surfboards and equipment. Over time, Dave Wyllie ended up living there, and married the head man's daughter.

Young English businessman Richard Flax arrived in Bali in early 1975, and, like so many others in that time, will always remember his first experiences of the island through a stony psilocybin haze. He recalls:

> I went straight to Poppies Lane, checked into a *losmen* for 300 rupiah a night, blew out the oil lamp and lay down to sleep, got up the next morning and walked down the lane towards the beach. Hungry, I pulled into a place where there were a few young people, and asked what was good for breakfast. A girl said, 'I can only eat half my mushroom omelette, would you like the other half?' Bugger me, four days off my scone! I've never forgotten that introduction because I think I saw Bali the way the Balinese saw it. A light went on in my head and I said to myself, you are home.

Born and educated in London, Flax then went to work at Christie's, the world's largest fine arts auction house, where he moved through all of the departments before settling on antique jewellery, and then trading in pre-Christian antiques. But in 1970 he fell in love with an Australian girl and followed her to Sydney, landing a job with Percy Marks Jewellers. Flax and the girlfriend, Louise, married, but she was then accepted by the Australian Opera Company and went on the road for six months. Flax also dabbled in the arts, joining the Hayes Gordon drama class at the Ensemble Theatre, but separation was hard on the young marriage, and Flax finally flew to Louise in Melbourne and laid his cards on the table. The marriage was over.

Feeling the need to ponder his future on a beach somewhere, Flax remembered the excitement on board the plane from England when, on a clear morning over the Indonesian archipelago, the captain had announced that passengers on the left could see the island of Bali. Peering down at a sun-sparkled sea and rugged coastline, he'd felt a strong urge to be there. Now was his chance.

Flax immediately began to identify with Bali's magical and spiritual aspects.

> I'd been in a lot of weird and inaccessible places around the world already in the course of my work at Christie's, so I didn't think

twice about renting one of the ubiquitous Honda 125s and taking off. I ended up in Klungkung market and this priest walked up to me and said, 'Hello, Richard.' This was a reality that I knew existed, and it still exists here, but if you don't see it, you just don't see it. I do, and many of my Bali stories are related to this. Because the Balinese live on many different levels that are not open to most Westerners, and because there are three million people here who believe in these levels and have categorised them, they are actual realities. We've learned to place restraints on our reality, they haven't, and they therefore have the ability to communicate at different levels. They don't talk to Westerners about this, of course, because they know it would be regarded as mumbo jumbo.

In Kuta in 1975, Flax soon became part of the expat group who was becoming accepted into the local community.

When we talk about community we all know what it is in an esoteric sense, but this was a real, functioning community where everyone had a role. Each community of 300 or 400 people was an independent, cohesive unit that made up the whole. As Westerners, we were able to perch on the edge of it and see how it works, because the Balinese are inclusive. Each of these *banjar*s, and there are seventeen in greater Kuta, takes care of its own in every respect. One of the first ways we became involved was through entertainment, because there wasn't any, apart from the dances and ceremonies in the banjar, so we'd go along to all of them. We had to change the way we were about a lot of things, and let go of who we were. I didn't come to Bali as a surfer, for example, but I soon became one.

Having decided he would live in Bali, Flax paid a visit home to London. He recalls:

I took some sankit sarongs back with me. They were those marvellous woven sarongs with silk stripes. I gave one to my sister and her eyes popped out. She suggested we cut the end off and make a bikini, then wrap it in the sarong. She had her own public relations company, so she said she'd make introductions at Harrod's.

Chapter 15 The Traders

> We walked out of there with a 25,000-pound order. I didn't have the money to fulfil it so I took it into Barclay's Bank and said here's my order from Harrod's, will you lend me some money? They agreed, and I came back to Bali and went into production. I remember filling boxes with these bikinis and sarongs and taking them out to the plane myself because there were no customs agents. There were seven tailors in Denpasar and they were all working for people like us.

Flax says that he didn't particularly enjoy making clothes and wasn't much good at it, so he looked for trading alternatives.

> I went back into my past and started working with jewellery, eighteen-karat gold from the village of Celuk, making three-coloured gold jewellery with precious stones in it, and sending a box a month to contacts in France. And then we went into wood, doing carved banana palms and other big pieces. There were probably 100 Westerners [at that time] who had recognised the skills of the Balinese and were taking them to world markets. We'd realised how good the wood carvers were and we got heavily into it, doing containers full of everything from frogs to furniture.

Among the traders doing good business in the late 1970s was the Shearer family from Perth, 'trippies' as they were known, who exported containers of clothing and handicrafts back to their home state and sold through their own wholesale and retail network. Oldest child Peter was now focused on developing the American export market, while triplets Judy, Jan and Graham ran the Australian exports. Graham was starting to concentrate on a fast-developing photographic career, but his place in the family business was quickly filled by Jan's boyfriend, Kevin Lovett, an Australian surf adventurer who had been one of the first to surf Lagundri Bay, Nias, in 1975.

After spending a day with her at Uluwatu, Richard Flax began dating Judy Shearer, and soon they were inseparable. He joined the family business, bringing some new ideas to the table. He recalls:

> I had some good friends who were doing batik on rayon, and I was particularly interested in a process called *pagi sore*, which in this case involved putting the batik into light

jersey tee shirts, so I made some samples and showed Judy and Jan and Kevin, who were amazed. This was the way it was going, this innovative Balinese/Western fusion in fabric design. I went into the business making these tee shirts.

The Shearers' business continued to thrive into the 1980s, and at one point they had five shops in Perth and Fremantle in addition to the wholesale business, but Flax soon drifted back to his growing jewellery business. He also began to look at other opportunities for an entrepreneur in Bali, and discovered they were everywhere.

Rex Patten, a young engineer from New Zealand, was another surfer who found his way to Bali in 1975 via the lucrative reconstruction projects of post-cyclone Darwin. As soon as he arrived in Kuta he knew he'd found home, and began looking for ways to support himself. A happy-go-lucky knockabout with the gift of the gab, he snooped around the artisan markets in the hills and looked at what people were exporting and to where.

He says:

I'd always been interested in jewellery, and they had great silver here but no stones, so I went to India and Sri Lanka and bought a bunch, came back here and swapped a few of them for the work I wanted done, then sold them back in Australia and New Zealand. Our big seller was a design of small flowers with a beautiful little stone in the middle. Sold thousands of them. I'd go home for Christmas and sell some things, sell some more in Sydney or Melbourne, then come back to Bali via a couple of months' work in Darwin.

But as the number of Bali traders increased, Patten looked for a market that wasn't being serviced. He found it in South Africa, having flown there on spec with a couple of suitcases of jewellery. In Jeffreys Bay he offered the jewellery on consignment to feisty Cheron Kraak, who had a few surf stores under the name Country Feeling. Within days of returning to Bali, Patten found that Cheron had paid for her stock and re-ordered. As the South African business flourished, Patten travelled regularly to Jeffreys Bay, he and Cheron became firm friends and he built the first house on the point overlooking the famed surf break for her. When Cheron took on the licence for surf giant Billabong in 1984, Patten supplied jewellery for both companies.

Chapter 15 The Traders

Tim Watts got the lowdown on Bali from a girl he'd dated through high school on California's Monterey Peninsula.

> She'd lived with me on Kauai one season so she knew what good waves looked like, and she came home from taking a round-the-world trip with her mother and was just raving about this place called Bali. She said she went out to Uluwatu and Gerry Lopez and Jeff Hakman were there, and they were raving about it too! I'm thinking, I am there.

It took Watts another couple of years to finish university (with a degree in sculpture), get some money together and come up with a pretext for spending a long season in Bali. He worked out of an arts foundry on Monterey's famous Cannery Row and was starting to produce commercial sculpture that sold well, so in Bali he would learn how to make *gamelan* instruments while his girlfriend studied Balinese dance: except the surf was so good that they did nothing but. Watts recalls:

> By '76 Kuta Reef was getting a little crowded, but nowhere else was. We hadn't figured out tides or swell direction yet, so we'd just jump in a *bemo* and head out to Ulu and surf all day. We knew about Padang Padang [the spectacular break down the line from Uluwatu] by then, but it had been kept pretty quiet.

Watts also surfed the reef breaks of Sanur and sailed over to neighbouring Nusa Lembongan for perfect waves in solitude, but the buzz in surfing circles was about Grajagan. The few who had been there swore others to secrecy before showing trophy photos of massive lefts peeling down the reef. Watts had some Californian friends who had made the G-Land trip with Dave Michel, a young Australian surf explorer who, like Kim Bradley, was developing into a legendary figure. Watts started drooling. He had to go, any way he could.

> We managed to hire a turtle boat with no motor, and it took us a full day to get over there, just me with some Aussies, Californians and a friend from France named Francois Lartigau. We got it good, not great, but it was enough to see the potential. My claim

Bali: Heaven and Hell

> from that trip is that I named a clump of mangroves on the reef 'Money Trees' because it marked the take-off point in the line-up. The mangroves got washed out in 1980, but the name stuck.

It took them two days to sail and drift back to Benoa, but as soon as they were on dry land, Watts began plotting to go back to G-Land before his money ran out.

> By October a friend and I were just desperate to get there before the wet season, so when I ran into an Australian down at the harbour who was looking for crew to help him take his trimaran to Sri Lanka, we signed on. We arrived at G-Land in time for a giant south swell, anchored in the channel and surfed it for a week, then surfed our way up the Java coast, and on up the Sumatra coast to Bengkulu.

There was still a long way to go to Sri Lanka, and there were some tensions on the boat. Watts didn't trust the skipper's dead-reckoning navigation, nor was he impressed with the integrity of the boat, which was severely overloaded. Feeling terrible about it, they decided to jump ship in Bengkulu. From there Watts left Indonesia and spent the southern summer surfing and odd-jobbing in New Zealand and Australia, before ending up in Darwin where work was plentiful in the wake of Cyclone Tracy. He worked for four months as a labourer on construction sites and headed back to Bali with a bag of cash, just in time for the winter trade winds to kick in for the season.

Having made the decision to try to make a living in Bali, Watts cast his eye around the trader community and saw that there were still opportunities in exporting clothing to the US. Despite the failure of his one previous attempt to export garments home (when the package went missing), he partnered with his former college roommate in a venture they called 'Little Dogs of Bali', after the numerous scrappy canines that ran wild in the *gang*s and alleys. Watts says:

> It was kind of a joke; you don't call anything a dog in the rag trade, right? But we started sending stuff back and while I ran the design and production in Bali, my friend was quadrupling our money at the flea market in Encinitas. All of a sudden we had a company.

Chapter 15 The Traders

Little Dogs developed a reputation for its stylish threads but never made enough money to really break through internationally. While the California sales end was relatively profitable, on the supply side, Watts was using most of his cash flow to fund the next production run. But he had an enviable lifestyle. After marrying a local girl in 1979 and fathering a son, he found himself living and working in Sanur, where most working days began with a long surf on the reef, and ended mid-afternoon with a fast bike ride out to Uluwatu, where he kept a stash of boards at Leter's *warung*.

> Surfing is what made doing business here okay otherwise the frustrations would just nail you. I don't think I could have done it without the surf. I never took my eye off the prize. I was hardcore, surfing thirty hours a week for years and years. I just couldn't stop.

Watts's first marriage didn't work out, and by the end of the 1980s he had two more sons and another failed relationship behind him. He also called a halt to Little Dogs. 'It had given me a lot of knowledge but no real financial reward, so my partner and I decided to pull the pin and we both moved on to other things.'

Watts used his knowledge of the fabric world to establish a new business in handmade batik for the lucrative home decorative market. It was difficult to break into but eventually Walter and Philip 'Flippy' Hoffman, the canny old surfers who ran Hoffman California Fabrics, the supply house founded by their father in 1935, took on Watts's range and began to sell it around the world.

About the same time, a Balinese friend of his first wife came to his office in Sanur and dropped a gunnysack full of beans onto the floor. 'Can you help me sell it?' he asked. Watts responded, 'Depends. What is it? It stinks like a forest fire!'

The sack was filled with 10,000 vanilla beans, still smoky from the curing process—*Vanilla planifolia*, or the Andrews Orchid, a fruit of Mexican origin that had first been imported to Indonesia by the Dutch in the 1800s, and was mainly used in Western countries as flavouring in products like ice cream and soft drinks. As Little Dogs wound down, Watts had taken on some work with the United States Agency for Internal Development (USAID), helping to develop locally run small agricultural and garment businesses, so he knew a little about the potential for export profit in some areas of agriculture. He did more research and discovered that one cartel controlled 85 per cent of the world market and fixed prices. He also found that many big vanilla consumers were tired of the cartel selling them inferior beans at inflated prices. Watts worked out that he could upgrade the curing process and still deliver refined vanilla to market at little more than half the cartel price. He decided to take them on.

He sent out a form letter to one hundred buyers and got ten responses. He had a foot in the door. 'It took five years to break the cartel and make a profit,' he says, 'but after that the business did very well.' By 2003, Watts and his partners owned the fifth largest vanilla-exportation operation in Indonesia, but the business was peaking. New food regulations allowing higher percentages of artificial flavouring devalued the market, while climate change was affecting the regularity of the crop. Watts, getting older now, found himself jumping in and out of light planes too often for too little profit. 'Vanilla's a young man's game,' he laughs. 'It was time to move on.'

He withdrew from the industry to focus, once again, on fabric.

By the middle of the 1980s, Bali had become an epicentre of cool, and the fashion factory of the world, according to Australian-based entrepreneur Vitek Czernuszyn, who would soon reflect just that when he started Bali's first colour magazine.

> Bali was the place where a lot of world trends started, like the rat's tail, for example. [Italian fashion designer] Milo did it to his hair one day, and other people around Seminyak started to copy it. Soon the style was all over the world. The 'Jakpak' [multi-coloured patched jacket] came out of Bali, the creation of a couple of young designers, and went ballistic all over, appearing on the cover of Time. There were factories in Java churning out thousands upon thousands of Jakpaks for the world market, but Keo and Stephen, who designed it, never made any real money out of it. That was the story of those times, and yet the fashion industry was really driving Bali's economy in the early and mid-eighties. You could just arrive with a suitcase full of clothes and have them all copied exactly, and everyone was doing it. Paul Ropp [who went on to become one of Bali's most distinctive and successful designers] was one of those people who used to arrive with a bag of samples and have them manufactured. One day he arrived and hung up his samples in the showroom,

Chapter 15 The Traders

and someone who was working there wore one of the shirts that night and burnt a big hole in it while smoking a joint. This was in the days when nearly everything had a Japanese shredded look. So the person then put the item back in the showroom, hoping no one would notice. Thousands of those shirts were made, all with a burn hole in them, painstakingly created by teams of tailors using crackling kretek cigarettes. The Balinese manufacturers would go to any length to do the right thing, even if they didn't understand it.

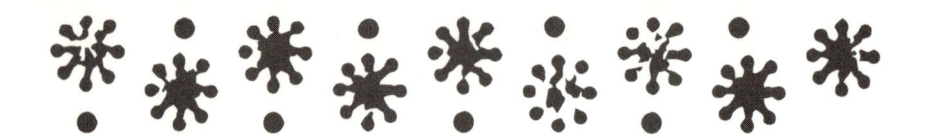

Chapter 16 *Balinese Surfer*

Some of the most precious memories of my life are of surfing into the sunset at Halfway Kuta after work most days, watching the locals smiling broadly as they zoomed across the golden walls of water ... It's a whole different world out there, looking back at palm trees and volcanoes.

Peter Neely, 2013

In 1969 Australian publisher Kevin Weldon visited Bali for the first time, spending an enjoyable couple of weeks in the company of Wija and Tatie Wawo-Runtu at the Tandjung Sari in Sanur. While he liked swimming in the placid waters inside the reef at Sanur, Weldon had been a surf lifesaver all his life and wanted to bodysurf in real waves, so he had a driver take him to Kuta, where the waves were pounding the shore at the end of Jalan Pantai. Within minutes of swimming into the break, Weldon had pulled a young French girl out of the waves, nearly drowned.

When he returned to Kuta two years later he met a fit young Balinese man named Gde Berata who told him there had been many more drownings. While the American expat Mike Boyum, who lived adjacent to the beach on Jalan Pantai, had helped organise and train a few Balinese men to act as part-time lifeguards, his interest was sporadic and it was an inefficient and totally inadequate service. 'I told [Gde] that if he got 100 Balinese together, I would send four international lifeguard instructors to train them,' Weldon later wrote. 'He did, I did, and the Balinese lifeguards were formed.'

Wawo-Runtu arranged the management of the major hotels to contribute to a fund to help pay the wages of the qualified lifeguards, and the service flourished. (Weldon was on hand in 2012 to help celebrate its fortieth anniversary.) But the major achievement of Weldon (and Boyum before him) was in getting the Balinese to overcome their fear of the ocean.

Chapter 16 *Balinese Surfer*

The Kutarese had been a fishing culture for many generations, but their working proximity to the waves had done nothing to diminish their morbid fear of the evil spirits said to reside in the watery *angker* (spiritually charged place). While greater exposure to foreign cultures since independence had begun to break down their own traditions, fear of the ocean had proven remarkably resilient, until youngsters like Nyoman 'Bobby' Radiasa and his friends started playing in the shallows. Later, when the first surfers began to appear, they got even braver, paddling the big boards close to the shore and mimicking the moves of the *bule*s.

When filmmaker Bill Leimbach arrived in Kuta in 1972 to stay with his college friend, Boyum, one of the many things he found appealing about Bali was the tribe of cute kids who would follow Boyum and his friends as they left the surf, then grab their boards and try to ride the shore break.

> I found it incredibly interesting that these Balinese kids were becoming surfers when their whole Hindu culture told them not to. The ocean was the home of demons and evil spirits, but these kids of coconut farmers were borrowing boards, or sometimes getting the boards that Australian and American surfers left behind in lieu of paying their *losmen* bills, and learning to surf. They would often surf naked because they had no shorts. This was happening right along Kuta and Legian but also out at Uluwatu. I took a trip out there with Michael and was amazed to see these kids learning to surf in one of the best waves in the world.

When his vacation was over, Leimbach went back to London where he was finishing a documentary on the Asmat people of New Guinea—formerly head-hunters and cannibals—for the BBC.

> As the film neared completion, they asked me what else I had, so I told them about the kids learning to surf, that there's this great story of cultural change, and a new way of looking at Bali. At the time the BBC was interested in the intellectual story of Hinduism and here was a way to tell it from a sporting perspective. They bought the idea, but I had another project ahead of it in the queue, and it took me until 1976 to get around to making *Balinese Surfer*.

Bali: Heaven and Hell

Over those four years, Balinese surfing went ahead in leaps and bounds, and the anonymous kids in the Kuta shore break became competent surfers who travelled in a pack (as *bule* surfers tended to do) and gave each other Western nicknames. In addition to 'Bobby' Radiasa, Nyoman Suardana became 'Godfrey', Ketut Jadi was 'Big Froggy', Gus Gina 'Ripper', and Made Darsana 'Joe'. Also part of the original gang were Gde Narmada, Agung Adi, Wayan Sudirka and young Wayan Suwenda. Most of the boys were from the Kuta *banjar*s of Pande Mas, Buni and Segara, but Gde Narmada had drifted in from Gianyar, via Denpasar, where his parents had sent him to school, but instead he sold cakes door to door. A born entrepreneur, Gde moved to Kuta in 1973, aged eighteen, and became a tour guide for hippies.

'I was shocked to see that they swam with nothing on,' he recalled. 'But they seemed peaceful and they loved nature, and Kuta was all trees, fields and streams back then.' When the surfers started to arrive in numbers, Gde was quick to adapt his guide services to suit, showing new arrivals where the best breaks were long before he really knew. But his friend, Joe Darsana, soon got him into surfing. 'Joe used to lend me his board. The two of us would go to the beach with one board and take it in turns to surf. We wore ordinary short pants, not board shorts. We surfers were all good friends back then, and it was easy to get waves because there were so few of us.'

Joe was quickly becoming a master of the sport the Bali boys called *serup* (to slip) or *nyosor ombak* (ride the edge of the wave), and used what little money he had to relieve visiting surfers of their dinged boards as they flew out. By 1974 he had enough to open a surfboard hire shop on Jalan Pantai that he called Joe's Surf Shop. It was the first Balinese-owned surf shop. Gde opened the second, Ulu's.

Australian surfer Peter Neely arrived in 1975 and surfed every day at the beach break a couple of hundred metres north of Kuta that was becoming known as 'Halfway' (to Legian).

> I remember the Balinese who surfed being very strong and fit, with the standouts being Big Froggy, Wayan Suwenda, who laughed and chatted all the time, and Wayan Sudirka who had the most flowing powerful style. Sudirka won the first Bali surf contest in 1975, and Suwenda won the second in 1976. I was good mates with all three, visited their houses, knew their families—especially Froggy, who I lived next door to for a year and went to Java with in 1981. I got

Chapter 16 *Balinese Surfer*

to surf some beautiful, uncrowded waves with all the original Bali surfing pioneers. They were incredible to surf with because they have a lot of fun in the water, always joking and laughing. You have to understand that these guys were rebels, breaking with centuries of Balinese tradition, venturing into the 'evil waters'. So their joy at discovering the fun of surfing was inspiring.

It is difficult to imagine how much the rising tide of tourism (and specifically, surf tourism) changed the lives of these young men. Before 1970, greater Kuta had a population of 9000, the vast majority of families eking out a living from farming and fishing. There was no irrigation in Kuta, so their dry crops consisted of coconut, soybeans and cassava, while they grazed a few cattle on surrounding paddocks and tended pigs in the family compounds. Fish sales at market were sporadic until a processing plant was built in the 1970s, and outboard motors were also very scarce. The end result was that until the economy began to move significantly from agrarian to tourism based, most families existed on the 1968 level of per capita income of between $40 and $70 a year. By the mid-1970s, the smartest of the Kuta teenagers were making that much a month.

Despite his many flaws, Mike Boyum became a real mentor to the young Kuta surfers. Bobby Radiasa recalls:

> We met Mike in about 1973 and he started to take us surfing to different places, out to Bukit and the other [Sanur] side. He was a friend to me and I respect him very much. He had a lot to do with establishing surfing in Bali. Other people think in their different ways, but to me he's a hero. He taught us a lot, not just surfing. He taught us to enjoy ourselves.

When Bill Leimbach returned in 1976 to make his documentary, he had his then-wife, Claire, young daughter, Carly, and the film's financial backer in tow, so the first thing he did was to hire Bobby Radiasa, whom he'd met the first time as production assistant—a role that sometimes encompassed fixing and minding as well. The financial backer, who was supposed to double as sound man, was a 'pasty-faced Pom' who couldn't handle the tropics and fled for home. Enter Richard Flax, an Englishman who *could* handle the tropics. 'He had a background in stage production and he already knew Bali better than most, so he was perfect for the role, and we hit it off from the start,' Leimbach says.

But the shoot itself got off to a disastrous start when thieves sliced through a canvas wall in their *losmen* and stole the Nagra sound recorder. While Leimbach worked out the costs of flying to Singapore and buying another one, Claire Leimbach drew a picture of the equipment on a piece of paper with the offer of a reward above it. She got it photocopied at Bali Easy Rider Travel Service and had them tacked up all over town. Leimbach says:

> I got a knock on the door the next day from the police to say they thought they'd found it. I had to go to the station in Denpasar and there it was on the desk, but there was still a negotiation to go through to get it back. I was fearful that we wouldn't have enough to pay the bribe, so I just kept telling them what a relief it was to get the sound recorder back so that now we could make our very important film for the BBC. Eventually, they just gave it to me.

Once they started filming, *Balinese Surfer* proved to be a set piece. Leimbach knew what he wanted and Flax knew where to find it, whether it was an appropriate backdrop for an interview or the right mouthpiece to bring to life the ongoing cultural transition that underpinned the film. The dramatic centrepiece, however, proved to be a nightmare for both cast and crew. Possibly influenced by Boyum's commercial agenda—to get a licence to run a surf camp—it was decided that the conclusion of the film would be a boat trip to the wilds of Grajagan—as it turned out perhaps more dramatic than they intended.

Leimbach recalls:

> There were only about three boats in Bali you could charter and we chose this trimaran owned by a French guy. It was only a one-night sail but we sailed for two nights and then we ran out of fuel. Mike Boyum had gone overland to bring the governor and the tourism minister over. It was a big thing to have the BBC doing a show on these kids. The French skipper was out of it on hashish the whole time, he only had a rope anchor line and we were just all over the place. The kids were seasick and

Chapter 16 *Balinese Surfer*

wanted to go home. By the time we eventually got to G-Land the officials had gone but Michael was still there, fuming.

As well as Bobby Radiasa, the surfers included Big Froggy, Little Froggy and Wayan Suwenda. Bobby had already been to G-Land once with Boyum, to help him talk to the villagers about his camp-site plan, but the trip had been nothing like this:

> We left from Benoa Harbour and we were very happy, drinking coconut milk and orange juice. Maybe not so good! The Frenchman was a bit crazy and we went in the wrong direction. Instead of one o'clock, we went 11 o'clock and we got further and further away from where we should be. I liked to be on boats, but my friends didn't like it so much, and it took us a couple of days to get there and we'd nearly run out of supplies. Finally we saw the land, but we anchored in the wrong spot. In the middle of the night the boat dragged anchor and we were very, very close to the waves. Everyone was sick and panicking. We tried to get the motor started and it wouldn't. Then it would and we got lucky. God was kind to us.

Bill Leimbach recalls:

> We wanted to film the kids surfing but they were all too sick and weak and hungry, and they just didn't want to go out. Little Froggy was probably the best surfer, but he was just so tiny and fragile. They all took off down the beach, thinking they could walk back to the road and get a ride home. They couldn't of course, and the next day they were back, in worse shape than before.

Tim Watts had been hired by Boyum to assist with the camera equipment and help wrangle the young surfers. He remembers:

> This was just after Boyum had started to set up the [surf] camp in April [1977] and the surf was pretty much flat. Boyum was building the tree houses with local guys from Grajagan. It was raining and the fresh water was building up just behind the beach. All the guys working for him had malaria. The Balinese kids were

very uncomfortable with this and with the short food and water supplies. They attempted to walk to Grajagan but turned back after they got a few hours past [surf spot] Tiger Tracks. They were in tears. We eventually got them down across the bay [in the boat] and they got out. Ten days later we all came down with malaria.

Leimbach says:

We got everyone home safe, but it certainly didn't go to plan. There hadn't been many documentaries made on Bali, so it wasn't like we were yet another film crew coming through. For me as a filmmaker it was one of the best times in my life, and the BBC loved it. It showed on *The World Around Us* at 7.30 pm on a Sunday in London and rated well.

Despite the fact that he had 'a real job in a restaurant', Bobby Radiasa heard the clarion call from Mike Boyum more often as the surf camp came closer to completion. 'I worked at La Barong, then Lenny, then Casablanca,' he recalls. 'I liked those jobs, meeting new people, but I also liked to go surfing. I would work for Mike on those trips and get my food for nothing, get to go surfing, eat mushroom.'

Radiasa's main role at G-Land was to smooth the way for Boyum, greasing the palms of Grajagan's head men and ensuring that the village got its fair share of the work. He also signed the permit that enabled Boyum to build his first bamboo tree house on the beach, in the name of the Bali Surfing Club, which had just been formed, and the Grajagan Surfing Club, which existed in name only. But he had to defer to Soejarno, the district chief from Banyuwangi, as construction boss. When it opened for business the camp consisted of a 5-metre-square tree-house sleeping loft with thatched roof and bamboo walls, and a mess hall below it with a couple of trestle tables, two single-burner gas stoves, a big ice chest and a few big sacks of rice. It was rough and ready, but it was luxurious compared with what the pioneers had put up with. The only problem was that the dozens of surfers wanting to come were told the camp was booked out until further notice.

As he'd always imagined it, Boyum's G-Land surf camp began life as a private club for himself and a few friends, like Gerry Lopez, Rory Russell and the dynamic Australian goofy-foot surfer from Newcastle,

Chapter 16 Balinese Surfer

Peter McCabe. Understandably, this did not delight the surf adventurers with lesser names who had been waiting for the camp to provide a better base for their G-Land adventures. After being refused a permit when he arrived with two Australians on a boat called the *Queen of Oz*, Rex Patten built his own boat and started sailing east, rather than west. Tim Watts had decided he didn't want to know about the land camp after his bout of malaria, but he got mad when Boyum wouldn't let him sell $750 in camping credits he'd taken for his work in helping set up the camp. Nor did Boyum's private club please the Indonesian officials who had been convinced that the camp would bring a steady flow of tourists to the poverty-stricken eastern tip of Java.

For its second season, Boyum had to compromise, holding the camp for his private expeditions during May and June, then opening it for the public under Radiasa's management through July and August, taking week-long bookings for up to ten surfers at $200 a head, plus transport from Bali. As if to underline his new commercial intent (or perhaps his reputation as a groupie), Boyum in 1980 hosted ABC's *American Sportsman* when they filmed a documentary on New York touring pro Rick Rasmussen during a phenomenal swell. Tim Watts remembers: 'They had Dan Merkel filming [TV star] Trapper John, MD, out in the water with Ras at all-time Speedy's Reef, and he thought he was going to fall off a cliff and die.'

According to Watts, the Trapper John fiasco signalled the beginning of the end for Boyum at G-Land. The Indonesians were beginning to lose faith in his management of the camp and his wild, stoned mood swings made it difficult to negotiate with him. Bobby Radiasa was under increasing pressure to use the fact that his name was on the permit and take over.

> By that time the other boys were having troubles with Mike and they asked me to take it over. I said I'd try. I still wasn't thinking about the future, I wasn't a businessman, but I'd been going there for five years and I had to start looking after myself. I was getting old. I already had a wife and child. So I tried to make peace, not war, but Mike was pissed off now and he just wanted to burn it down.

This was precisely what Boyum did one night in a fit of rage, dumping a drum of gasoline around the perimeter of the small camp and lighting it, then watching from the shadows as smoke billowed into the salt air and his G-Land dream disappeared.

Bali: Heaven and Hell

Radiasa recalls:

I didn't mind, he spent the money and got it built, fair enough. At the time there was no national park, it was just jungle belonging to the district. When it got burned there were really only two huts there. So when I started my business it was sleeping bags on the sand again. It was a camping trip, but everyone was happy, and they paid good money. They weren't surf stars, just normal guys who wanted to surf. That was the way G-Land should be.

Back in Bali, the idea of the Bali Surfing Club, mooted since 1975 to help foster Balinese talent, was beginning to gain some traction. Mike Boyum had been the early driver, organising a couple of small contests, but this role had been taken up next by Kim 'Fly' Bradley, who had settled in Kuta with wife Made Ringan, started a family and established PT Bali Design in Poppies Lane. Bradley felt that competition among the young Balinese surfers would bring about rapid development, so he organised a proper surfing contest for them in 1979.

Bradley, like many surfers in Bali in the 1970s, frequently ate and hung out at Kempu's *warung* at Lasi Erawati in Poppies Lane. Kempu's husband, Rizani Ida Karnanda, was not a surfer, but he admired what they did, and he was an educated man and an effective local politician with connections in the highest circles in Bali. Bradley recalls that after weeks of pestering 'Riz' about different issues concerning the establishment of the club, he said: 'Okay. You handle the day-to-day running of the thing and I'll take care of the Department of Sport and everything else, and we'll set this thing up properly for Indonesia.' On 8 April 1979 the club was officially formed with Rizani as coordinator and over seventy Balinese surfers (thirty from Kuta, twenty-one from Legian, ten from Sanur, and five each from Uluwatu and Canggu) as members. Its committee included Bobby Radiasa, Wayan Sudirka, Gde Narmada and Ketut 'Big Froggy' Jadi.

The club held its first contest at Legian Beach, and the presentation ceremony at the Pande Mas *banjar* attracted a large crowd, among them the Governor of Bali, Ida Bagus Mantra, and the national Minister of Sport. 'To see surfing get that kind of recognition by the government gave our sport and our lifestyle credibility in the eyes of the Indonesian people,' Bradley said.

Chapter 16 *Balinese Surfer*

In running the day-to-day affairs of the club, Fly Bradley had plenty of assistance from within the ranks of the expat surfers, including Dave Wyllie, David Thomas and Jeff Doig, but when bigger events loomed, the stalwart turned out to be a former rock musician named Paul 'Gringo' Anderson, who had arrived in Kuta in 1975. Anderson had been in bands since the 1960s, and music had somewhat sidetracked him from surfing, but he had grown up in Victoria and had spent every summer camping at Torquay and hanging out at the surf club, watching the antics of famous old-school surfers like 'Mumbles' Walker of the Boot Hill Gang. So surfing was in his blood, but it got a little diluted when rock stardom beckoned.

He recalls:

> I played in a band called The Moods, and they went on to be the opening act for the Rolling Stones' tour, but by then I'd moved on to the Town Criers, who had a hit with the first version of 'Love Is in the Air'. When I moved to Queensland in 1967, I started the Capital Showband and we had some success, too.

By 1975, however, music wasn't paying the bills and Gringo was working in a menswear store until a friend walked in one day and gave him a detailed account of the perfect waves he had just surfed on the reefs at the end of the Bali airport. Gringo resigned the next day.

Staying at a *losmen* on Buni Sari, Gringo soon hooked up with some adventurous mates and travelled overland through Java, taking in the sights and the business opportunities, as well as the surfing potential. He says:

> I was a bit inspired by the adventure of it all, so I came back to Australia and started to put a business together with some clothing, combining it with a little shoe business I had—Gringo's Handmade Leather, shoes, belts and so on. A partner and I opened Adventures in Paradise, the first hippie/Bali shop in the Centre Arcade in Surfers. It was an amazing shop for the time, with antique jewellery and leather and clothing and textiles, and it did very well, setting me up to live mostly in Bali for the next seven years.

Kim Bradley was a great delegator, and although he was initially sceptical of Gringo's motives, once he discovered that he had quickly learned Indonesian and had administrative experience, he became the go-to guy for the Bali Surfing Club. Anderson says:

> Fly never actually did much himself, but he was a great ideas man and he inspired people to get on board. He and Dave Wyllie were trying to get the Om Bali guys to sponsor an international contest, and when he finally got their attention, he hand-balled it straight to me.

Om Bali and its sister company, Firefly, were flying high in the fashion game by this time, and were unlikely starters to fund Bali's first international surfing competition, except that Stephen Palmer needed to reconnect with surfing. He remembers:

> I'd given up a lot of surf time for work. Robert [Wilson] would come and try to get me to go for a morning session at Sanur and most times I just couldn't. But one morning Fly came and dragged me over to Sanur for a six- to eight-foot, super-glassy barrel session with only him and his Japanese mate. For the next twenty-five years we would laugh about how good that session was.

Between sets, Bradley told Stephen Palmer about his very big idea. Palmer was immediately receptive, even though it didn't make a lot of business sense for Om.

> It was really all about the idea we had that we wanted the Balinese to see excellent surfing. The whole thing had just started here and we thought, wouldn't it be great if we brought the world's best here and we could sit on the cliff and watch them go for it. We were selling ladies fashion, so there wasn't much commercial advantage, we just wanted to do it.

The Om Bali Pro Am 1980 was meant to be a small affair, but Rizani got the Balinese officials excited about it. Gringo Anderson recalls:

> Some of the stuff we did was huge, big opening and closing ceremonies, a lot of people coming and going. It was logistically wild. We did what everyone thought was impossible in Bali.

Chapter 16 *Balinese Surfer*

You had to deal with something like thirty-two government departments—the navy, the army, intelligence, narcotics division, diplomats, you name it. Sport, religion and tourism were all in the one department back then, so that was a lucky break.

One of the first problems was that everyone wanted in, including some people who were better off staying out of Bali. New York pro Ricky Rasmussen was in all kinds of trouble, having bribed his way out of jail in Bali and being on the run from gangsters he had ripped off in a drug deal at home, but he phoned from New York wanting a start in the contest. 'I put his name down,' Gringo says. 'Then I got a call from the head of Indonesian intelligence wanting to know what was going on. I just handed the phone to Rizani. This was the kind of stuff going on in the background.'

The view from the sponsor's tent, had there actually been one, was quite different. Stephen Palmer remembers:

I was amazed at how easy it all was. In the Suharto era there were some things that worked really well, and this was one example. The tourism minister got behind it immediately, hotel rooms were supplied without any negotiation, transport was organised, official welcome and farewell functions were all done for us. Once the government decided to back it, they were fantastic at every level. We wanted to run it all at Uluwatu without building any infrastructure, and that's pretty much what we did, but the one regret I have is that after the success of the first one, they built a road into the break. I used to love walking in along the track—this narrow goat track with cactus either side, and stiles you had to climb over. I always regretted that we inadvertently caused that.

To this day, there are jaded old surf adventurers in Bali who date the beginning of the end of surfing's golden era on the Bukit to the building of that road, and the subsequent bridge to Padang Padang. But the Suharto-led development push on the peninsula was already on the drawing board and nothing was going to stop it. It was just a shame that the surfers had to open the door.

But the Om Bali Pro succeeded in bringing the highest level of pro surfing to Bali, with some of the best free-surf performers in Bali in that era and beyond, winning the title: Terry Fitzgerald in 1980, Jim Banks in 1981 and Terry Richardson in 1982. By 1982, however, Om was starting to fall apart and so was the Pro. Om had fallen victim to growing too fast: it simply had too many cooks in the kitchen, and no new sponsor waiting in the wings. Gringo Anderson and Dave Wyllie quit the organising committee, and Fly Bradley stayed on and did the best he could, but he, too, was starting to fall apart.

Bali's first foray into pro surfing was over, but under Pak Rizani's watchful eye, the Bali Surfing Club went from strength to strength.

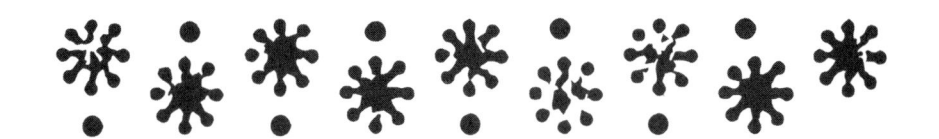

Chapter 17 Rhonda and Ketut

'I mix special drink for you today, Rhonda.'
'Thank you, Ketut.'
'You look so hot today, Rhonda, like a sunrise.'
'Thank you, Ketut.'
Australian television commercial, 2013

The wiry little man in the white singlet limped around to the other side of the massage table, sized up my back between the second and third ribs and began gouging into me with his elbow.

'This not hurt a bit, very good for you,' he lied. I was prepared to do anything to be rid of the back pain I'd suffered for the past couple of weeks, following a fall down a flight of wet, wooden stairs, but this was excruciating. A cagey old physio, Ketut Gede Putrawan, Dip. Sp. Th. engaged me in conversation to take my mind off what he was doing.

'When you first come to Bali, Phil?'

'Nineteen seventy-four.'

'Oh, then you probably heard of me back then. Everyone in Kuta and Legian knew me. I was "Ketut Funky", remember?'

I didn't, but Ketut had soon slipped into the story of his life anyway, and it was fascinating. Born in Denpasar in 1952, by the early 1970s he was working part-time on the local radio station as DJ Ketut Funky. He also became part of the first generation of 'Kuta cowboys', hooning around town on a motorbike, long straggly hair flying in the breeze, a cheeky grin revealing a set of glittering white teeth as he hit on tourist chicks, with a high success rate. Although we admired their audacious style, we *bule* boys hated these guys, because at this stage of Bali's cultural development, there was virtually no reciprocal arrangement with their sisters. Ketut Funky played guitar in a local band, he had a slick patter and a ready joke to tell in passable English. He seldom went home alone.

In 1977 Ketut Funky met Frances Mourant outside the Three Sisters cafe on Jalan Legian. She was a year younger than him, a strong-willed girl from Jersey who had been travelling the world and was now making her way home from Australia overland on the denim trail. She was delayed in Bali waiting for a girlfriend to catch up to her, and had temporarily run out of money, so Ketut invited her to move into his family compound in Denpasar. She was uncertain. 'But I want to marry you, Frances,' he teased. She knew he meant nothing by it, but after a few days in the compound, she began to see that he had a serious side, and she liked him a lot.

In due course Frances's girlfriend showed up and Frances kissed Ketut goodbye and got on the bus for Yogyakarta. She had plenty of time to think on the seventeen-hour trip, wedged between a young family and a wicker basket of chickens. When they arrived in Yogya she told her girlfriend that she was going back. The bus let her off at the top of Jalan Padma, and Ketut, sitting on his bike, chatting to the pretty new arrivals, saw her alight and hoist her backpack over her shoulder.

'I nearly crapped myself,' he recalls. 'She'd come back to marry me!' They were married in a Hindu ceremony in Denpasar two months and two days after having met.

While this was by no means the first mixed marriage of the new tourism era, it was still rare, and the brave girls like Frances who married Kuta cowboys generally wanted to see them leave the playing ground completely for a decent interval, rather than just sit it out on the bench. But Frances could not see Ketut being happy in faraway Jersey or in England—in fact, she was in no hurry to return to her family either—so they moved to Australia, where she had a work visa, secured Ketut's status by marrying again at Penrith Court House, and settled in Sydney's western suburbs. Ketut got work as a dogman at a timber yard while Frances worked part-time giving riding lessons at a stable. Their first son was born in 1978. In 1980 Ketut quit smoking and cut his long hair. Theoretically, it should have been safe to go back to Kuta now, with Ketut's cowboy days long past, but life had taken them in a different direction.

They bought the stables, moved it to five acres at the edge of the metropolitan sprawl and opened for business, doing trail rides at three dollars an hour. Within five years they had 250 acres and 120 horses in work.

Chapter 17 Rhonda and Ketut

Meanwhile Ketut, who had learned several skills over the years, studied sports physiotherapy and opened a small practice. It soon became his passion.

Ketut and Frances and their two sons returned to Bali many times—although the first time Ketut went alone, in 1986, he hated what it had become and fled after five days. In 2001, after their two grown-up boys had moved out, they decided to sell up and move to Bali for good.

Ketut ground his elbow into my back and talked over the top of my pronounced groan. Then he flicked a gym towel at my butt and said, 'Good as gold now, champ,' laughing at the ocker patois that still comes easily to him. He limped around to the other end of the bed (a motorbike accident had cost him about an inch off one leg) and sat where he could eyeball me. 'So that's my story. You want to hear more about Bali, you come to my place and we'll have a cuppa.'

While not many Western girls married the more outrageous Kuta cowboys, several found romance with quieter Balinese men, and a few married and started families. American Jean Lane was one of the first, marrying a Denpasar man named Ketut in 1973. Their son, Wayan Krishna, born in 1975 in a back room of their new restaurant, Kubu Krishna, was the first of Kuta's 'international kids'.

The new mixed marriages seemed to be a recipe for business success. Made's Warung and Poppies were both run by strong local women with supportive Western husbands in the wings, and as Robert Wilson and Stephen Palmer built up their garment-export business, they, too, were in long-term relationships with local girls who gave them roots in the community. But Kim 'Fly' Bradley was the first of the surfers to really lay his cards on the table.

Soon after he met Made Ringan, Fly told his friends he was going to marry 'the most beautiful girl in Kuta'. He was barely out of his teens, a high-school dropout with a good heart but a dubious work ethic and some sloppy personal habits. She was even younger, a drink seller on Kuta Beach with no life experience beyond working out the miniscule commission she made on sales after a day of lugging a heavy bucket up and down the sand, pleading, 'You want cold drink?' But her parents had no objections to the marriage as long as the scruffy Australian surfer met his family responsibilities, so Fly became a Hindu and they were married in a traditional ceremony.

'When Fly fell in love with Bali, he fell in love with the whole package,' says a friend, 'and that included Made. Unfortunately, he wasn't always as good to her as he might have been.'

Bali: Heaven and Hell

In the very early days, Fly once invited my wife and I to his humble home for sunset drinks. Made appeared to greet us when we arrived, but she then disappeared into a back room, and only emerged when her husband yelled for another round of Bintang tallies. Despite his embarrassing lack of social graces, Fly and Made seemed genuinely happy together much of the time, they soon had two beautiful children, Dewi and Ardi, and Made turned out to be a business powerhouse. Together they established Surfaris Inn and a chain of about a dozen Bali Design stores.

Dick Hoole says: 'Made turned out to be the Gordon Merchant [Billabong founder] of Bali. She was behind their amazing success, but the whole family worked in the business and contributed, and in that sense it was a traditional Balinese business.'

Fly Bradley was a fearless charger in the biggest waves Bali could produce, a stand-out performer at Nusa Dua and all over the secret spots of the Bukit, 'A perennial grommet who would catch the bomb sets everyone else would paddle over,' said friend Peter Neely. But years of exposure of his fair and freckled skin to the sun eventually resulted in skin cancers so severe that he had to give up surfing and cover up from neck to ankles. Always an enthusiastic drinker, Fly now sought serious solace in the bottle. Inevitably, his marriage broke up, although he remained close to his children and he and Made maintained a friendship and a business association.

✳ ✳ ✳ ✳ ✳ ✳

Jero Asri Kerthyasa, the royal princess of Ubud, throws back her head and roars with laughter in a most un-royal manner, causing first-time patrons of the chic tea house in Petitenget to look up from their china cups and peer at our small table towards the back of the room, beyond the ceiling fans. The regulars don't even notice. It's just Asri being Asri. She's the proprietor of the best tea house in Bali, give her some space!

Born Jane Gillespie in Singapore in 1954, Asri was brought up on Sydney's North Shore, attending the exclusive Abbottsleigh Girls' School, where most students have a clear path in life laid out through family expectations. In Asri's case it was a little different. Her father had served twenty years with British Army intelligence in different parts of the Far East, and he instilled in his children a love of things Asian. So when Asri was nineteen,

Chapter 17 Rhonda and Ketut

she took a long Christmas break with a couple of university friends and flew to South-East Asia. They started their holiday in Bali.

She recalls:

> I hated the food. Everything was cooked in rancid coconut oil. I just couldn't find any food I liked. They were trying to do Western food, but they did these weird fried egg things, or turtle fried in coconut oil. It was hard to find genuine Indonesian food. I went from Bali to Yogya and loved the food there. We did Bali, Java, Singapore and Malaysia over a couple of months, and I loved everywhere else, but Bali not much at all. It might have had something to do with where we stayed—Adi Yasa in Denpasar, behind Gajah Mada, then somewhere in Kuta, but I don't remember where. All I remember is the noise of the motorbikes. In those days the transport we used was mostly *bemo*s. If you got a taxi it would be one of those huge American cars. They always had plastic-covered seats and every time you took a corner you'd go flying.

So Bali was not Asri's preferred destination when her mother suggested a girls' trip four years later.

> I suggested Singapore, because Mum hadn't been there for twenty years or so, and I thought she would enjoy seeing it again, but she'd heard about this man called John Foster who did fabulous tours in Bali. What sold me was the news that he took his own disinfectant and his own cooking oil, which I thought might get rid of the coconut taste in everything. We were based in Ubud and this time I fell in love with Bali. When we arrived at a restaurant John would hand his oil to the kitchen staff and they'd cook with it. They didn't mind at all. Everyone was so obliging, the dancers were wonderful, the people, the whole village of Ubud, absolutely wonderful.

Asri and her mother spent two weeks in Ubud in 1977, a fortnight that would change her life forever. They were staying at Puri Saraswati, soon to become Cafe Lotus (a landmark Ubud restaurant) and on the third night she met Tjokorda Raka Kerthyasa, prince of Ubud, grandson of the Dewa Agung, the last official king of Bali. She recalls: 'He was a bit of a playboy really, or so I thought, but his brother's second wife was running the place, so he was around all the time, and we warmed to each other.'

At the end of the vacation, Asri had made up her mind. She would go home, quit her job as a preschool teacher, ditch her Aussie boyfriend and come back to Ubud to be with Raka and write a children's book. She was working towards that goal when she received a letter from the prince, asking her to cool off, to just be friends for a while. Asri recalls: 'That was okay. I handled that. I hooked up with another boy and he was going to come to Bali with me, but I left before him and by the time he arrived in Bali I'd gotten back with Raka. I always felt a little guilty about that.'

Our conversation is interrupted briefly while Asri barks out a few orders to the Indonesian staff of Biku, one of the most popular cafes in the greater Seminyak area. A frequent customer, I am always astounded by the fact that every time I go there, the princess of Ubud is working the floor, or sitting in a corner doing the books, or meeting with suppliers, always quietly in charge, exuding control but not power. Throughout her life in the public eye in Bali, Asri has been pulled and pushed every which way, and yet she maintains a dignified, almost regal, bearing in public, while being warm, friendly and funny in private.

But back in 1977 she had no idea what she was getting herself into.

> Cultural differences? I didn't know anything about the culture, so I didn't notice any differences! I fell in love and our cultures didn't come into it. I had a three-month visa and by the time that expired we had decided to get married. Raka had a normal job, working at the museum [in Ubud] and studying art at the university. I just didn't think about his family and what marrying into it would mean. I guess I knew, but the royal family back then was pretty basic, pretty much like everyone else except they had a car! The palace was nothing special.

But they did have royal conventions, and the prince marrying a Western commoner was not one of them.

> Usually, they had arranged marriages within their own caste, but fortunately nothing had been arranged for Raka,

Chapter 17 Rhonda and Ketut

> but that didn't mean the family was in favour. The brothers didn't accept me very well at first, and some other family members in the government had me checked out by Interpol. They asked me for my passport so they could run checks. I had nothing to hide so I didn't think twice about it.

According to Asri, the royal wedding at the Ubud palace was 'quite a simple affair, really'. The *Australian Women's Weekly* thought it was a bit more impressive than that, putting the dazzling young couple on the cover with the headline, 'Meet Australia's Newest Princess'.

Asri's parents both attended the wedding, her father delighted that she was becoming a Hindu, a religion he had long admired. The Gillespies gave them some start-up money as a wedding gift, and Asri and Raka used it to open a small *losmen* on land Raka owned at Campuhan. They named it the Tjetjak Inn. They rented out a few rooms and lived in the least attractive one, serving their handful of guests the obligatory thermos of tea and bananas for breakfast. There was no restaurant, but Raka's mother would cook meals on request. The prince and princess had no electricity, running water, phone or refrigeration, until they finally bought a kerosene fridge.

The couple's first child, Tjokorda (TjokDe for short), was born in Bali, but life was tough for mother and son, and second child Max was born back in Sydney. The family decided to remain there while the children were young, returning to Bali for six weeks over Christmas. Asri went back to teaching and Raka took a job at the Australian Museum, working on their Indonesian Collection.

Asri says:

> We ended up living in Australia for ten years, then in 1993 we came back to Bali for a year, and decided to knock down our *losmen* and build a hotel. We went from one extreme to the other; the architect got a bit carried away, ten villas, very high end. We had to get new bank loans, but suddenly we had this luxury hotel. We called it Ibah.

Everyone loved the new hotel, with its plush villas tucked away above the river, but under a succession of managers, it failed to make any money. Asri got tutors for the children still in school (Max finishing high school, and daughter Maya in kindergarten) and moved into the manager's office herself.

She knew very little about hotel management, but she soon turned around Ibah's fortunes.

Meanwhile, Raka had assumed more responsibilities in Ubud as his older brother began to ail, and he had become a legislative member of Bali's House of Representatives. Although the royal families of Bali had had no power since independence, the ceremonial and advisory role in the regency, combined with his life in national politics, kept Raka busy and the family in the spotlight. Asri put her foot down early, as she had done decades before, over the issue of multiple wives. 'I told him then he'd have to divorce me first, and I told him later that I wouldn't be a politician's wife. They were both tough decisions, but love got us through. It's a strong marriage.'

✳ ✳ ✳ ✳ ✳ ✳

The writer, editor and former sculptor Diana Darling and I are sitting in the garden pavilion of the Warwick Ibah's spacious restaurant, directly above the Kerthyasa family temple, enjoying a leisurely lunch. She sips her wine and says: 'My Bali story is really a series of love stories, which is perhaps why I've never talked much about it before.'

She is right. Despite almost half a century involved in arts and literature, including some considerable successes and associations with many of the leading lights in both, Darling has for the most part flown under the radar, for many years now living quietly in the family compound of her Balinese husband, Agung. And yet there are many, this writer included, who regard her 1992 novel, *The Painted Alphabet*, as the best work of fiction about Bali, and impatiently await her next, a whimsical satire on the effects of tourism.

American-born Darling (then Diana Pugh) first came to Bali in 1980 with Australian painter Brett Whiteley, his wife, Wendy, and Joel Elenberg, the man she was in love with. Both sculptors, Diana and Joel had met the previous year in Carrara, Italy, and after a passionate summer affair, he returned to Australia to leave his wife. In autumn, Diana received a letter from him, asking her to come to Australia to join him, but it was not the joyous communication she had hoped for. He had been diagnosed with an aggressive cancer and the prognosis was not good.

Diana flew to Sydney and she and Joel moved into the Lavender Bay house of artist Peter Kingston, next door to the Whiteleys. While she nursed Joel through chemotherapy, they planned a return to Carrara, once he was

Chapter 17 Rhonda and Ketut

better, but as the months passed, they both knew that would never happen. A friend who had just returned suggested that some time in Bali would be good for their souls. Together with the Whiteleys, they checked into the Bali Oberoi in Seminyak at the beginning of June.

Architect Peter Muller was in residence with wife Carole while he restored the hotel he had designed eight years earlier. Diana also met Made Wijaya (formerly Michael White), photographer Rio Helmi and John Darling, a tall, red-headed Australian who had just made a landmark film on Balinese culture, *Lempad of Bali*. Wherever she went, the vivacious Diana seemed to land in the thick of the action, but there was no joy in her situation. Joel's condition was becoming graver by the day.

They moved to a small bungalow at Yasa Samudra on the beach at Kuta, then to a quiet little hotel in Sanur. Aware that Joel was nearing death, his friends and family began to gather, including his estranged wife and daughter, and a month after the couple's arrival in Bali, Joel Elenberg died in that small hotel room, surrounded by love.

Diana decided to remain in Bali, staying with John Darling first, then with Made Wijaya. She recalls: 'Bali made a huge impact on me. I was raw, and after spending months in and out of hospital with Joel in Sydney I'd missed being outdoors, out in nature. All of Bali was outdoors in those days, and it seemed to be alive with spirits. I wanted to be here.'

She stayed three months, but had obligations to return to in Carrara. John Darling asked her to join him in Amsterdam, they enjoyed a romantic interlude in Paris, and decided to marry when they returned to Bali, tying the knot at a government office in Gianyar in July 1981, on the same day as Prince Charles and Diana.

She says:

> It's possible that I fell in love with John because I'd fallen in love with something in Bali. In any case, when we came back to Bali, I got besotted with the culture and started soaking up John's library. We were married for six years, but somehow marriage was not right for us, because we got on fine before and after it. I wasn't a very good wife and he wasn't a very good husband, and unfortunately we had no children.

Although the marriage failed, Diana came to understand Bali under John's tuition.

Bali: Heaven and Hell

> He was a very romantic person and he had a very romantic view of Bali and the Balinese, and I was educated about Bali through his eyes. We thought the Balinese were a bit super-human, with uncanny powers of intuition, dexterity—anyone who could think up their music is not a normal person. Our *pondok*, our tiny house between the rice fields and a river gorge, was so close to the earth. It was an intense way of living. You had to get home before dark, and you followed the cycle of the moon. No electricity, and the water came up on the head of a nice woman from the village, or at least it did until I appeared on the scene. Then we had a young man who captained a small family who brought up the water and split the firewood and did the offerings.

While the Darlings were still married, they came to know Agung, the village masseuse. Diana says:

> After John and I split up, I was living in the Hotel Ubud and Agung lived up the street. Agung and I would run into each other at a *warung* and talk and play chess. It turned out that he'd just split up with his wife as well. I was building a little house up in the mountains then. I wanted to re-create a *pondok* situation on my own. I couldn't afford to buy land in Ubud, so I found some land in Tegalsuci, a mountain village eight kilometres before Kintamani. Sometimes in the evenings back in Ubud I would run into Agung and I'd bore him with my building stories and he'd bore me with his dieting stories. One evening Agung and I fell in love. He was Bali Lite, he was knowable. It was like being hit on the head with a fairy stick. It just happened, and we've been in love ever since.

When the house at Tegalsuci was ready to move into, Diana made an alarming discovery:

> I got cold feet. What I didn't realise at the time was that I was building a house in the real Bali, nothing like Ubud. I had a sudden realisation of how much on a different planet this village was. The idea of actually living there overwhelmed me ... It's on one of the main roads to Kintamani, but it's quite isolated, with no experience

Chapter 17 Rhonda and Ketut

of foreigners. The people were very nice to me, but I felt like such an oddity among them that I just chickened out. So instead of moving into my house, Agung and I moved in together at the Hotel Ubud.

The following year they reconsidered.

By this time our relationship had become firm enough to think of such a thing. After a year or two the village authorities asked us very politely if we would please get married, because it was against their *adat* [moral code] for unmarried couples to spend more than three consecutive nights together. I ummed and ahhed about that because I didn't like the idea of being told to get married. Besides, neither of us was formally divorced yet and it would involve a lot of paperwork. But finally we did get married, in 1992, and we lived in Tegalsuci for another thirteen years. That was where I wrote *The Painted Alphabet*. We had a wonderful life there.

✳ ✳ ✳ ✶ ✳ ✳

In my early years in Bali, I remember walking through villages and experiencing the most extraordinary sensation of feeling totally separated from what I was seeing. It was as if the Balinese were behind glass, or I was watching an old movie on a huge screen. They were so absorbed in their daily activities that it gave me the impression I was invisible, and in a way maybe I was.

So begins Janet DeNeefe's fascinating memoir with recipes, *Fragrant Rice*. The restaurateur and founder of the Ubud Writers and Readers Festival has not been invisible in Bali for a long, long time, but her wonder continues, some forty years after her first taste of the island.

Born and raised in Melbourne, Janet came to Bali on a family holiday in 1974, at the age of fifteen. Bali was not really on the family vacation radar in Australia at this point, but her father had been influenced by his eccentric artist father and his cronies. She recalls:

The family home was like a drop-in centre, a piano in the living room, aunts and uncles popping in, people being brought home

from the pub for dinner. My grandfather knocked around with
a lot of other artists, and some of them used to come to Bali in
the late 1960s. So Dad had heard all these stories about Bali and
when he had a bit of money in his pocket, he decided to bring
the family here. My sister was in art school, so she loved the idea,
and we'd just seen *Morning of the Earth* and been blown away
by the Bali segment, so we were all ready for an adventure.

The De Neefes spent a few days in Kuta but their main base was Ubud, then little more than a market and a few streets of artists' studios. Janet loved it from the start, but it took her a decade to get back. 'I had to finish school for starters, and then I was working and not happy in my job so my sister said, "Come back to Bali!" So I did. That was only a short trip, too, three weeks, but I met Ketut on the second day.'

Janet travelled with a college friend and stayed at the Hotel Tjampuhan. As they drank in the bar, she noticed two handsome Balinese men sitting on a sofa, chatting as they smoked clove cigarettes. 'One was the prince of Ubud, Tjokorda Gede Putra Sukawati [Raka's brother], the other was Ketut.'

By the time she returned to Melbourne, Janet and Ketut were in love. They exchanged passionate letters every few days, but to keep the flame alive she wanted to cook Balinese food, and have the cooking smells transport her back to Ubud. When she could find nothing in Melbourne's bookshops, an idea began to form. 'I'd been fascinated with Balinese food since the first trip, but also just the general subject of food had fascinated me all my life. I was determined to learn to make the dishes I'd experienced there, and write a cookbook.'

Janet returned to Bali in January 1985 and moved into Ketut's family *losmen* in Monkey Forest Road, Ubud.

> I had a daily routine where I'd go to the market in the morning
> with Ketut's sister or the family helper, and then I'd hang
> around in the kitchen for the morning and watch lunch being
> cooked. So my whole morning program was really research
> for the cookbook. Then I would take a *bemo* to Ketut's
> wood-carving gallery in Mas and watch and help him.

Chapter 17 Rhonda and Ketut

Janet returned to Melbourne after eight months, but she was soon back, and in 1987 she persuaded Ketut to fly to Melbourne with her to meet the family. Ketut formed a bond with her dad, but Janet soon realised that her dream of living with Ketut in Melbourne and making a life together was never going to work. She later wrote: 'During the months that followed, I thought seriously about our cross-cultural relationship. Ketut's visit to Melbourne exposed differences between us that I was oblivious to in Bali, but I couldn't imagine life without him.'

Five years after their first meeting, Janet and Ketut were married, with ceremonies in Australia and in Bali. Four children and many businesses later, they are a formidable power couple in the Bali business community, although Ketut prefers to stay in the background. More importantly, says Janet, they are still very much in love.

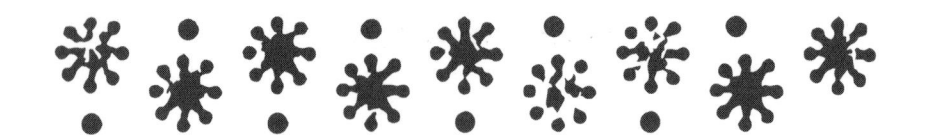

Chapter 18 Into the Mystic

Cokorda Nawang lived in the local palace, with old-fashioned courtyards full of pretty pavilions and gardens. He was a jovial man who delighted in explaining to foreigners the mysteries of Bali—its dances, calendars, and rituals, and the mystical laws that governed its architecture. He told amazing stories of witchcraft. 'You see that tree?' he'd say. 'It was once my great-great-grandmother, a very brilliant sorcerer. But she crossed a powerful witch from Sanur and he turned her into a sapling. On the full moon it sheds holy water.'

Diana Darling, 2012

Novelist Diana Darling first read her hilarious short satire of spirituality to a rapt audience at the Ubud Writers and Readers Festival in October 2012. It was a preview of an eagerly awaited novel-in-progress that will take aim at various aspects of what Darling calls the 'mystery of tourism' in Bali, including the island's frequently misunderstood and easily ridiculed attraction for those seeking the inner life, or spiritual path. She took it as a promising sign that the reading was received with so much mirth and a tremendous ovation at its conclusion, because Bali's spiritually enlightened (or those who imagine they are) have not always been able to poke fun at themselves, even though in the early days the path to enlightenment was often trod naked and lit by psychedelic flashes.

The Western search for enlightenment through Eastern philosophy has been around for as long as the spice trade and the silk road, but its modern form can probably be dated from the beatniks (Kerouac's dharma bums were definitely looking for something mystical, albeit through the bottom of a liquor bottle) and may be considered to have reached its peak when the Beatles trooped off to India with the giggling Maharishi in 1967. In Bali by the early 1970s there was a ranting, raving Gridley Wright in every coconut grove, but the island really hit the global guru radar later in the decade, with a fleeting visit from Baba Ram Dass.

Born in Boston in 1931, Ram Dass found both fame and notoriety as Dr Richard Alpert long before he met his guru, Neem Karoli Baba, in India in 1967. While completing his doctoral studies at Harvard in 1961, Alpert began 'explorations of human consciousness' in collaboration with Timothy Leary, Ralph Metzner, Aldous Huxley and Allen Ginsberg, using psilocybin, LSD-25 and other psychedelic chemicals. The group produced several books on the subject of psychedelic enlightenment, but Leary and Alpert found themselves unceremoniously run out of Harvard in 1963 for unspecified irregularities. They went to Mexico and continued their studies using copious quantities of magic mushrooms. Interviewed by a Canadian television crew in 1966, Alpert said he had taken more than 300 acid trips and they had done him nothing but good. By the time he left for India, like Leary he was a countercultural icon.

According to the Ram Dass website, Alpert's transformation to Ram Dass ushered in a new life of selflessness and meditation. According to Bali pioneer Kevin Lovett, Ram Dass was still tripping when he landed in Kuta almost a decade later. Lovett won't talk about it now, but in 2005 he wrote:

> ... he arrived with a large travelling stash of Sandoz grade LSD-25, an unattached group of bule goddesses, and three guardians ... What transpired is the stuff of legend ... When Alpert arrived in Bali ... he had a reputation for not travelling lightly, always carrying a large quantity of his laboratory standard acid which was probably sufficient to turn on the whole planet at any one time. In any man's language Baba's stash was marked 'rocket fuel, industrial strength, handle with care', and subsequently an impromptu party formed at a local restaurant where the aforementioned group of nymphs dived into Baba's 'sugar bag' (with some of them keeling over almost immediately after take-off).

Lovett recalled that the three local *bule* guardians wisely played a supporting role from the sidelines and were thus able to report seeing 'a vast number of varied physical reactions from Baba's out-of-control group of handmaidens, including intra-uterine contractions, core body temperature increases ... nausea, lack of bowel control ... muscle tension ...' The guardians worked 'tirelessly through the evening, providing TLC and ferrying the single white female passengers on Baba's runaway intergalactic express down to the abandoned Kayu Aya'.

According to Lovett, there is no record of what happened to the 'handmaidens' at the abandoned hotel, which was notorious for impromptu bacchanalian frivolity, but Ram Dass is alleged to have made a dash for the airport as he saw the potential disaster unfolding.

Guru outrages aside, many of the people who have come to Bali over the last fifty years, to live or for extended travels, have arrived with some sort of transformative expectation, a vague notion that experience of this mysterious and magical island would change their lives in some substantial way. Many already had the beginnings of a spiritual core within them, although they may not have identified it. Some would embrace the Eastern religions, others would simply become fellow travellers. Still others would claim they found their own path to enlightenment in psilocybin or in riding the perfect wave.

I like anthropologist and author Fred Eiseman's description of his personal journey, because it tallies with the experience of so many I have interviewed for this book:

> I have adopted Balinese Hinduism. I was not converted to Hinduism. Quite the contrary, I was like the character in Moliere's *Le Bourgeois Gentilhomme* who realised that he had been speaking prose all his life and didn't know it. I had been practising a philosophical form of Hinduism since adolescence and never realised that my beliefs were consistent with a large organised body of religion.

Filmmaker Albert Falzon had no idea what he was stepping into when he arrived in Bali to shoot scenes for his film in 1971, but the raw spirituality of the people immediately made a lasting impression:

> When you step into Asia from a Western country, you see these people walking around so harmoniously, so connected to all their kingdoms, the women still bare-breasted and with so much beauty and dignity. I just felt at home with it all, much more so than with the brutality of Western religious systems. I'm Catholic, my family comes from Malta, a whole line of religious

Chapter 18 Into the Mystic

belief. My father was an altar boy at St Mary's Cathedral! Going to Bali and seeing these people so connected with their spirituality through everyday life was a real awakening.

Although his surfer's instincts were to stay close to the Bukit and the Kuta reefs, when Falzon returned to Bali with a new girlfriend for an extended stay in 1976, he found himself in deepest Seminyak with the hippies.

> We were based around Blue Ocean and Golden Village, and in the beginning I used to think, how could anyone live up here for an extended time! My mindset wasn't on that at all, but Hannah Satz, this six-foot-tall, lanky Jewish nomad woman from Melbourne, turned my life around. She was definitely focused on the East and I got drawn into it. Bali was a real stepping stone for me on that level. The people who had been attracted there were hippies from all over, a free-spirited, international group who really appreciated the Balinese.

Falzon says he hadn't been seeking a spiritual path:

> I don't think you really have to go looking for it, it permeates the air whether you're spiritually aware or not. You can't be there without being affected by those people. It was a profound experience for all of us. It changed my thinking and I spent much of the next ten years in Asia.

David Thomas was already a spiritualist when he arrived in Bali in 1974, and his experiences with Dave Wyllie in Sumba only reaffirmed his belief in the 'subtle realm'. He met Falzon in the late 1970s, when he was combining his work as a textile trader with surfing, golf, and assisting in 'the global movement of spiritual information'. He and Falzon became spirit brothers and subsequently worked together on a series of films about Eastern spirituality, including a trek to Tibet for the world's largest spiritual festival in 1985. He says: 'My years in Bali equipped me for doing all of that.'

Although Thomas says that at certain times he has embraced Buddhism ('You have to at some stage, because if you don't practise harmlessness you can't work with forces, you simply can't move forward'), he now describes both himself and Falzon as Agni yogis, followers of the 'Teaching of Light'. He is one of a growing number of people who believe that many of Bali's social and environmental problems are related to the dilution of the subtle realm in the face of Western materialism.

He says:

> I do a lot of work in Bali with magnetic energies. I can help locate underground running water or magnetic earth lines where the *prana* [energy] runs over the planet. They're either in a healthy or unhealthy condition. When people first started moving out to the Bukit to live, an American woman, who had some particularly barren land, asked me to come out and see what the energy lines were like, and activate them if necessary. I went out there and met the man she leased the land from, who owned all the land around there. He was a *pemangku* [low-caste priest] and he asked me to come and have a look at the temple he had just built. He told me he'd built the new temple because he'd had a dream that there was going to be a calamity with the old one. So they built a new temple, further back from the cliff, and not long after, the cliff under the old temple fell into the sea.

Thomas cites this as an example of the spirit world informing a material decision, but he fears that many people who have built on the peninsula's high cliffs, his own friends included, will not be able to hear or heed such signals.

Richard Flax, now an insurance entrepreneur and still a practising Buddhist, believes that the Balinese have long been resigned to the fact that the coastal tourist strip from Petitenget to Uluwatu would have the worst of Western materialism's destructive forces hurled at it, and still survive.

He says:

> It's where the Balinese black energy source is most powerful, and it's been that way for hundreds of years. Before we came along, this place was where the negative forces, which are as essential as the positive forces, were centred. Anything that might be negative for Bali would be allowed only there, under this ethereal grid that the Balinese understand. This strip exists because of the expectations of tourists of any resort around the world. Bali doesn't need what

Chapter 18 Into the Mystic

it's got, and if you simply took it away, Bali would still be Bali. This process began in 1963 when the volcano went off and they knew they had to gird themselves for hard times and sacrifice ahead. In a way it's like the Australian government preparing to sacrifice the north of the country in 1942 as the Japanese made ready to invade. Here they have been prepared to sacrifice this small strip in the south. To a degree, this is why they tolerate changes that we might not. My Balinese family in Legian is exactly the same now as when I first came here in 1975. Sure, they've got computers and Nintendos and so on, but their lives are consumed by the needs of their tradition, religion and their village community. That's their focus. We're just the *orang jawa*, not too much to worry about.

But Flax himself worries about the communities in Bali that have 'sold their soul' and turned their backs on their *adat* (traditional culture). He says:

Legian, where I live, is still a *desa adat*, a traditional village, and several of the seventeen *banjar*s within the Kuta/Legian area are still the same, allowing the people who live there to retain their focus on what matters. All we see is the clubs and the noise and the pollution, but the Balinese don't say a word about any of that. Their psyche is on a higher level. They don't get annoyed about things like that. They are possibly the most tolerant people I have ever met, but don't cross them, because they're like a sleeping tiger.

Om Bali Clothing Company founder Stephen Palmer was one of the first of the expat traders to acknowledge the spiritual side of Bali:

We had some very spiritual, esoteric experiences in the early days, particularly down at the Petitenget temple, which is where La Lucciola is now. That's an intensely magical area. When I was living down there I'd get up before sunrise and go and sit in the temple and meditate as the sun rose. I did that pretty much every day for six months, and some interesting things happened. I was in my room one night, two of us sharing, each with a narrow bed under a wooden window. When the window was shut it was very dark and the only light you could see was fireflies. We were talking about how

> belief could make things happen, in particular the *barong*. Then suddenly this feeling came over the room, and I felt massive legs walking over my chest, first the front legs, then the back. I was too freaked out to look at the middle of the room, and then it happened again. Finally, it went quiet, the feeling left the room. We just lay there in the dark thinking, did that really happen? We weren't smoking. That's why Bali is Bali, because that sort of thing happens.

Mish Pulling (now Saraswati Mish, and a Bali resident for more than twenty-five years) was nineteen years old when she arrived in Bali alone in early 1976, on her first overseas trip. She took a *bemo* into Kuta and found a quiet *losmen* where she made friends with the Balinese family who owned it. She recalls:

> They took me in as part of their family. There was a scout hall in Kuta where they showed kung fu movies, and we'd go along as a little group, me and the Balinese. They were my entertainment. I never felt the need to mix with other tourists. I'd go exploring all over the place by myself and never felt afraid.

She started hanging out on the beach at Kedonganan, making friends with the old fishermen who worked on their boats and mended their nets under the trees. One of them started to teach her Indonesian and she put together a small but useful vocabulary. In Singaraja she stayed in an old house with a fabulous library of old books about Bali, and there she experienced her first encounter with the supernatural.

> I'm not sure if that's how I should describe it, but it was certainly from another realm. I saw a shadow on the wall that took on the shape of a butterfly as I watched it. Later on I would experience many such things, but only ever in Bali. I would dream of a snake, wake up and walk outside and there would be a snake. Funny things happened. There was this access to another dimension, something going on that was out of my experience, but I liked it. There was a mixture of this strong energy and the gentleness of the Balinese. That first trip changed my life, and I was never the same. I cried and cried when I left. I later went to India and travelled around, and saw many things, but I always had Bali in my mind.

Top left: Gerry Lopez flying down the line, Uluwatu, 1974. Photo Dick Hoole.

Top right: Lopez (background) and filmmaker Yuri Farrant, Kuta, 1974. Photo Dick Hoole.

Left and above: Albe Falzon on the *Morning of the Earth* shoot, 1971. Photos courtesy Albert Falzon.

Top left: Jalan Legian, Kuta, looking towards Legian, 1975. Photo Peter Neely (*Indo Surf and Lingo*, indosurf.com.au).

Top right: Cruising Legian beach, 1978. Photo Dick Hoole.

Above: Jalan Pantai, Kuta, 1980. Contrast this with the same photo taken eight years earlier on back jacket. Photo Chris Hazzard.

Right: The crew of the Kimbala reunited in Bali after 40 years. Photo Phil Jarratt.

Above: Mike Boyum negotiates board and camera carriers for his team, Uluwatu, 1974. Left: The author at Windro Village, Uluwatu, 1974. Below: Kim 'Fly' Bradley sports a reef bounce trophy, Uluwatu, 1974. Bottom right: Mike Boyum boot camp at G-Land, Java, 1978. All photos Dick Hoole.

Bottom left: Cub reporters Jack McCoy and Dick Hoole, 1973. Photo courtesy Dick Hoole.

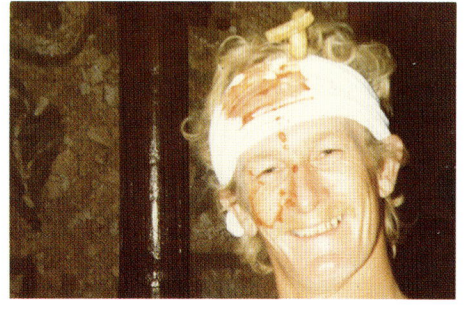

Top: Fly Bradley, fiancée Made and friend model the first Bali Design clothing range, Poppies Lane, Kuta, 1975. Photo Peter Neely (*Indo Surf and Lingo*, indosurf.com.au).

Above left: Robert Wilson learns to cook in Kempu's kitchen, 1976. Above right: Steve Palmer and groms, 1976. Photos courtesy Robert Wilson.

Right: David Thomas in Sumba, 1977. Photo courtesy David Thomas.

Top: Bali Surf Club *bule*s and Balos, 1980s.

Above left: Local legends Made Kasim and Wayan Suwenda, 1990. Above right: Om Bali pro contest site at Uluwatu, 1980.

Left: Om Bali judging panel, Gringo Anderson right front. All photos Dick Hoole.

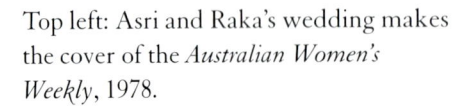

Top left: Asri and Raka's wedding makes the cover of the *Australian Women's Weekly*, 1978.

Top right: Ketut Funky and Frances, 40 years on. Photo Phil Jarratt.

Above right: Diana Darling addresses the Ubud Writers and Readers Festival, 2012. Photo courtesy UWRF.

Above: Mr Fixit, Richard Flax. Photo courtesy Flax Archive.

Right: Wayan Agus Parwita makes an offering with son Putu and wife Made, Pererenan, 2013. Photo Phil Jarratt.

Top left: Jalan Legian afternoon gridlock, 2011. Photo Dick Hoole.

Top right: A tsunami of trash on Kuta Beach. Photo Jason Childs.

Above: Fishermen on a sunset sea of tranquility, oblivious to traffic and pollution. Photo Dick Hoole.

Left: Weed farmer in the Lembongan tide shallows. Photo Dick Hoole.

Australian expat photographer Jason Childs captures two moments of exquisite beauty in modern times on the Balinese south coast. A perfect wave goes unridden on the Bukit; surfer and priest Made Kasim takes his offering to the sea gods.

Chapter 18 Into the Mystic

Mark Keatinge, who arrived in Bali on a leaky boat with Made Wijaya in 1974, is now a respected member of Banjar Dangin Peken in Sanur, the biggest *banjar* in Bali, representing some 350 families, and once famous worldwide for its *gamelan* orchestra, which toured extensively in the 1950s. When Keatinge married his wife, Ketut, in the 1990s, he married into a leading family of the *banjar*, but as Ketut had no brothers, when her father passed away Keatinge was invited to become the family representative.

One of a small number of Westerners who have *banjar* membership, Keatinge is quite proud of his role in the community and takes his ceremonial duties very seriously. He says:

> From the beginning I was very interested in the culture, and that was the real reason I kept coming back. I think with a lot of people of our generation [he is sixty-five] it's not the surf or the beaches, it's the culture. From early days I was always heading off to temples and I was very interested in the magical side. Since I joined the *banjar*, if someone dies I turn up with a knife on my hip and start stripping bamboo and making twine and doing all these ceremonial things they do. I'm in the *banjar* now until I die, and if someone else dies, I must turn up. If I don't, when I die no one will turn up to look after me. Within the family I have to go to weddings and tooth filings, that sort of thing, but within the *banjar* I must go to funerals. It might seem a bit odd to an outsider, but I like being part of that.

Keatinge's largely secular role in an organisation that has come under fire in recent years for its alleged failure to protect *adat*, has ironically brought him closer to his Balinese family and given him greater understanding of their beliefs and traditions. Although they were first married in a Sydney registry office, Ketut and Keatinge could only be married in a full Hindu ceremony in Bali after he had studied to become a Hindu and been interviewed at length by the head cleric. He recalls: 'The Balinese are usually quite free and easy about their religion, but this was not long after the introduction of the so-called "Mick Jagger law", and things had tightened up a lot.'

When the Rolling Stones' singer married former model Jerry Hall (his partner for thirteen years at that stage and the mother of four of his children) in a lavish Hindu ceremony in Bali in 1990, photographs and film of the event were broadcast around the world. But in the eyes of the Balinese, it was a sham wedding, the couple having observed none of the requirements for a Hindu marriage and paying off anyone who presented an obstacle. For the Balinese this was an unforgiveable example of the commercialisation of their religion. They had bristled when a hotel corporation used the Hindu daily offering in an advertising campaign; now they went ballistic.

The Balinese authorities had no problems with people promoting their traditions and beliefs, as long as they did so with due respect. When filmmaker Bill Leimbach made a television series called *Quest for Healing* in the late 1980s, he filmed an episode in Bali, using Westerners John Darling and Lawrence and Lorne Blair to open the door to the island's religious and psychic healers. Lawrence Blair, a born entertainer with a degree in comparative mysticism, turned a difficult subject into a delight, and the Balinese loved it. Twenty years later, their acceptance of the Western portrayal of their spirituality would be tested in a much more significant manner.

When New Yorker Elizabeth Gilbert published a travelogue/self-realisation manual/love story called *Eat, Pray, Love* in 2006, she tapped into a huge market of dissatisfied women of a certain age who'd spent too much time working or raising a family and not enough time fulfilling their dreams. The book went straight to the top of the *New York Times* bestseller list and stayed there for a very long time. And since a third of her book was devoted to Gilbert finding inner peace and hot romance in Ubud, it didn't hurt Bali's spiritual capital in its slow revival after the 2005 bombings either.

But Ubud had seen nothing yet. After several reconnaissance trips, about one hundred cast and crew, headlined by Oscar winners Julia Roberts and Javier Bardem, rocked into the once-quiet hill station in 2009 for a six-week shoot that would employ more than 300 domestic technicians and actors, and contribute an estimated US$12.5 million to the local economy. By the time the movie premiered at the Balinale film festival in 2010, an *EPL* industry providing packaged healing, yoga and personal growth experiences had sprung up in the expectation that the movie would inspire a tourist boom. They were not disappointed. Despite mostly negative reviews ('Eat, Pray, Hurl' was one headline, 'as profound as perfume' another comment), the movie was the second-most watched in US and Canadian theatres on its debut weekend, grossing US$23.7 million.

'Ubud has become a haven for middle-aged, single Australian women waiting for Javier to jump out from behind the bamboo,' photographer Rio Helmi lamented in 2013. 'In Ubud these days there are a lot more women

Chapter 18 Into the Mystic

with yoga mats over their shoulders,' said princess of Ubud, Jero Asri Kerthyasa. 'And they love their bicycles. The healers are making a fortune.'

Diana Darling told the *Asia Times*:

> Ubud's gridlock, horrible sidewalks and inflated prices might mean that none of the hundreds of tourists who come here every day will ever come back, but there are still several billion people on earth who haven't been to Ubud yet, and tour agencies will keep trying to capture them and send them up the hill.

For all their many faults, the book and film of *Eat, Pray, Love* did very little to damage Bali's spiritual dimension, other than to trivialise it and turn it into a commodity. Still, the Balinese could at least reap some direct financial benefits as cashed-up Western women abandoned the big hotels in search of an 'authentic' experience. Much more offensive have been the subsequent attempts by entrepreneurs to co-opt the tawdry *EPL* phenomenon for their own even more tawdry schemes.

Consider Morgana Rae, an American woman of a certain age and as fine an advertisement for cosmetic surgery as you'll find anywhere. Ms Rae defines herself as a 'life coach, financial alchemist and money goddess'. She sells a message of 'making money by putting love first', by which she means paying her a very large sum to attend the 'Ultimate Money Goddess Bali Retreat' in, where else, Ubud. Staying behind secure villa walls, goddesses in waiting will use yoga to 'invoke the Divine Feminine' over 'six days of pampering, mentoring, shopping and adventure in an exotic paradise', which is, by the way, 'the ideal incubator for your transformation into a Money Goddess', and 'a location fit for a Goddess'.

Rae continues, leaving no cliché unturned:

> I selected Bali for this amazing retreat because I wanted to create an UNFORGETTABLE and POWERFUL EXPERIENCE. The land itself is MAGICAL. We will be based in Ubud, the SPIRITUAL and ARTISTIC center of the island. The massages, the pampering, the temple visits ... all of these activities are designed to give you the kinesthetic experience of being a Goddess and taking extraordinary care of your mind, body and soul. Bali is a land of beautiful beaches, rich rice terraces, a plethora of vibrant-hued flowers—it's truly

> a feast for the senses. In fact, Bali is the land of Lakshmi, the
> Hindu goddess of wealth, abundance, beauty, and courage ...

Rae stops short of invoking a fairly recent addition to the Balinese Hindu deity—the *dewa uang*, god of money. Perhaps that was too crass, even for a Money Goddess, but interestingly, the modern, two-car, no-rice-fields Balinese see nothing conflicting at all in worshipping a god of money.

So has modern materialism and Bali's phenomenal growth spurt fundamentally altered its spirituality? Diana Darling, who has spent half her life in Bali, says:

> I'll always be a foreigner. I've learned that many of my assumptions come from way back in my life, from America, as little as I have to do with that anymore. So yes, culturally I'm a tourist. The closer I live to Balinese society the more I realise that while I feel welcomed in it I do not feel identified by it. I don't feel Balinese.

Darling believes it is important that old expats recognise that there is still an appeal.

> I try to imagine what it's like for people to come and experience Bali now. The aesthetic has changed so much. I remember a lovely man at the Ubud Writers Festival a few years ago, on his first trip to Bali. It was a panel session they seem to hold every year about whether Bali is being ruined. All the cool people were saying that it was, and this man stood up and talked about how beautiful Bali was. Then he burst into tears, because he was so moved by a temple festival he'd been to the night before. We have to remember that Bali is still there to be discovered.

Like the coastal expats, Darling believes that traditions in Ubud continue under the gloss.

> The appearance of Ubud has changed very much, but I don't think the ritual culture has changed. But things are changing socially. When we lived in the rice fields, in the evenings we'd get together in the village and people would read from the old books, keeping the embers

Chapter 18 Into the Mystic

of this old magic and culture alive. Now in our family compound, which isn't particularly rich, we have five families and each has its own television, and each family stays in its corner watching it. We don't all get together unless there's a religious ceremony.

David Thomas says:

Bali is not what it was in terms of the spiritual world. When materialism starts it creates a vacuum and the spiritual aspects get pushed aside and dark forces get sucked into the vortex. That's what has happened and there's only one way out of that—to evolve, and that takes a long time. Bali used to be a planetary ashram where you were protected from the outside world while you developed yourself. It's no longer so.

Diana Darling has a more positive view:

The magic is still there. It just takes getting out of one's room to find it. The first thing that springs to mind is during a tooth-filing ceremony in our compound, just a little epiphany. Suddenly the *gamelan* started to play and it was so startlingly beautiful that it gave me shivers. Another time during a ceremony at the house, a child of about four months in the arms of his grandmother kept looking at me with this incredibly benign smile, not like a little baby, but like a deity. Bali's magic doesn't smash you in the face the way it used to, but it's still there. I think the gods in Ubud have become a bit shy. You have to be quieter perhaps, or stoned, or newly arrived, to find the magical and the supernatural, whereas once it was everywhere.

Chapter 19 Expatria

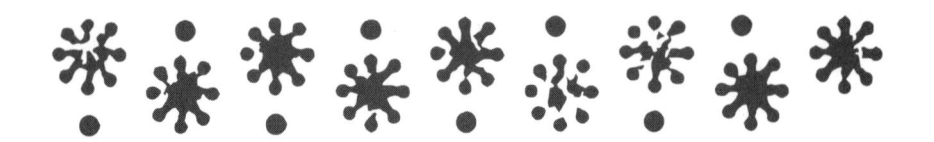

Bali today is you buy the largest piece of land you can afford, build the highest fence you can get away with and create your own Bali.

Stuart Membrey, 2013

Expat businessman and mystic Stephen Palmer is showing us his palatial home, overlooking the beautiful beach and legendary surf break of Padang Padang on the Bukit Badung Peninsula. It may or may not be on the market for US$8 or 10 million, Palmer is not sure. He may put it on the high-end vacation rental market at a ridiculous price, but he's not sure about that either.

Palmer saw this cliff-top land for the first time in 1979 and fell in love with the idea of building the ultimate beach shack on it, but ownership of cliff-top land on the Bukit in those days was a verbal tradition and, there being no paperwork, it was almost impossible to negotiate a lease. Besides, it was the dry and dusty Bukit where nothing would grow and no one had any money. Why would anyone want to live there?

In the 1990s, following the Tommy Suharto–led investment plunge in Nusa Dua and other parts of the lower Bukit, land certificates were issued for large plots running along the cliffs to the temple at Uluwatu. Palmer teamed up with expat businessman Michael Little and rising night-club mogul Kadek Wirinatha, and together they bought more than 100 *ares* (1 hectare) with staggering ocean views and direct access to the beach via fishermen's tracks down the cliffs. Wirinatha sold out before they started building (cashing up to fund his airline start-up, Air Paradise), but Little and Palmer took on new partners, and, through Wirinatha, engaged the award-winning French-born resort architect Fredo Taffin, who had just designed a club called Ku De Ta in Seminyak for Kadek. Taffin's brief was to create a compound of three beach houses that would complement each

Chapter 19 Expatria

other while each retained a distinctive look. Palmer's house was the last to be built, starting in 2005.

He says:

> I have to tell you, if I'd designed this place it would be nothing like this. It would have adobe walls, thatched roofs, recycled timber, lots of gardens growing fruit, lots of things I feel strongly about. But the overall plan was already well-established, so when this place was a basic shell, I had to decide how I was going to make it work within the overall design. I kind of went, okay, I guess we're into luxury, let's go!
>
> I wanted as much nature surrounding me as possible, so I created this driveway with a canopy of trees on top so that from above, all you see is trees.
>
> The Bukit is known to be very dry, although it does have a good, short rainy season. So I went for big-volume rainwater tanks. Under the driveway I have swimming pools lined with ceramic tiles rather than concrete so we don't get any leaching into the water. These are 3.5 metres deep the whole length and width of the drive. I can store enough water here to get through the dry season if I'm very careful—500,000 litres, which is the equivalent of 100 water trucks. They go from the top of the drive to the end of the garage. People thought I was crazy, but if I could do it again, I'd dig eight metres deep and have over a million litres. You cannot get enough water.

Finally we get to the banyan tree.

> It's where the spirits reside. Normally, people here don't put banyans in their houses because spirits will come and stay. Well, I wanted them to have a place to hang out. The seers who have been here have verified that they're here. We have banana trees here, 80 to 100 pieces of fruit per tree, and a monkey sitting on that wall will not come into this space because of the spirits.

We enter the building, pausing at the door so Palmer can caress the walls. 'The skin of the building is granite and every corner, every edge has been ground back so there are no sharp edges, for both the aesthetics and a good tactile feel. And it's good feng shui to have a really heavy, good front door.' We push inside, where meditation music drifts out of unseen speakers. Palmer fiddles with his iPad, adjusting the volume.

We move on, admiring the museum-quality, old Sumba rugs on the walls of the office, the subtle aroma of the cinnamon bark laminated onto the plywood of the toilet, the paintings on the walls—mostly originals by friends who have made a splash in the art world—the Afghani woven fabrics. In the master bedroom we are commanded to look up.

> The ceiling is ironwood on the outside, and then underneath it has five-centimetres-thick refrigeration foam with aluminium either side of it, and then bamboo flooring on the inside. At night I light it with directional lighting and it looks beautiful. The insulation stops the radiant heat.

We walk onto the terrace overlooking the sea. 'All the doors came from Italy but the glass is local. The door handles I saw in *Miami Vice 2*, took a screen shot and had them copied in China.' We move back inside. 'The LED reading lights are in the middle so one person can sleep while the other reads, no intrusion. Then there's the panic button.'

Palmer gets very animated and jumps onto the bed and assumes a foetal position while reaching beside the bed for a buzzer. 'Should you have a heart attack or think there's an intruder in the room, you hit the button and six seconds later the desk light goes on.'

There's more, much more—we haven't touched on the gym, spa and steam room, or the home cinema, or the pool area … but two hours have passed in the blink of an eye, and we both have appointments. 'Don't worry,' says Stephen, 'We can finish the tour another day.'

Palmer's magnificent obsession is an exquisite piece of real estate in which he has probably invested far too much time, money and emotional commitment. But like most of what he has done over his nearly forty years in Bali, it is from the heart, and it is beautiful. There are many other expat palaces, traditional and modern, of which you could say the same. But for every one of them, there are a hundred or more 'McMansions' hidden behind high security walls that make Kerobokan Prison look like a cubby house, and they reflect the exclusion mentality of many of the modern expats, the ones who want to be 'in' Bali for its cost of living and its climate, but not 'part of' a

Chapter 19 Expatria

place where there are so many compounding social, structural, bureaucratic and environmental problems.

The first expats of the modern (post-revolution) era were artists, designers and traders, mostly clustered around the peaceful waters of Sanur. Here Jimmy Pandy held court for European visitors, while the Australian painter Donald Friend, newly arrived from Sri Lanka, worked in a beachside bungalow and drank at the beach bar of the Tandjung Sari with pals like the American art collector Bruce Carpenter.

But by the 1970s the surfer-scammers had begun to set up another expat enclave around Kuta, the hippies with the wherewithal were building jungle shacks in deepest Legian and Seminyak, and a new generation of *bule*s was discovering Ubud. Australian architect Peter Muller was among the first, taking a lease on artist Rudolf Bonnet's old Campuhan studio and rebuilding it as a country escape. Publisher Kevin Weldon followed soon after, building a traditional house with magnificent views over the Sayan Ridge.

There were many other places in Bali just as beautiful, with much cheaper real estate (even in those years, when long leases could be had for very little), but the expats tended to cluster for companionship and, more importantly, for creature comforts. Sanur, closest to Denpasar's commercial hub and the diplomatic residences of Renon, was best served with electricity and phones. Kuta and Ubud had neither, but by the early 1970s progress was on the march in both places.

In 1971, in response to the 1969 opening of the Ngurah Rai International Airport and the sudden surge of tourism the 'Master Plan for the Development of Tourism in Bali' was drawn up by the Indonesian government as part of an aid program financed by the United Nations and carried out by the World Bank. Indonesian public servants worked with a French consulting firm to plan the expected growth resulting from identifying Bali as the 'showcase of Indonesian tourism'. The plan called for consolidation of the Sanur, Kuta and Ubud corridor as the tourist hub and limiting development elsewhere, the philosophy being that in this way most of the island would remain unspoiled and culturally pure, and tourists could be bussed from their dormitories to gaze in awe and wonder on day trips.

Three years later the Indonesian government sponsored a convention of the international tourist industry association, PATA, an event originally planned for 1963 and cancelled at the last minute due to the disastrous eruption of Gunung Agung. Back in 1963, it was to have been President

Bali: Heaven and Hell

Sukarno's grand presentation of Bali to the world market; a decade later President Suharto claimed it as his own, political evidence that his transition of Bali's economy from failed agrarian to successful tourism services was working.

And there was clear evidence that this was true. In Kuta alone, tourist numbers had increased from 6000 in 1972 to 18,000 in 1974, while over the same period a handful of locally owned hotels and *losmen*s grew to more than a hundred, and restaurants from two to twenty-seven. But growth was uneven, and in all the wrong places. The Suharto government wanted to target upmarket, wealthy tourists; instead they were getting the riffraff youth culture, vacationing criminals and sexual misfits. So at PATA for the first time a bold plan was presented to develop a purpose-built, upmarket resort village well away from the surfies, the hippies and the arty-farty deviates, at the fishing village of Nusa Dua on the lower end of the Bukit Peninsula, not far from the airport.

No one took the slightest notice of the Nusa Dua plan—in fact, none of the expats, except for surf explorers like Fly Bradley, David Thomas, Dave Wyllie, Robert Wilson, Tim Watts and a few others, even knew it existed, much less that it had one of the best reef breaks on the island. Nusa Dua sat dormant for years while Bali's unplanned growth went berserk in Kuta and northwards along Jalan Legian. It didn't take much to make the Kuta cool surf crew edgy about the number of people suddenly surrounding them at Made's and Zenik's *warung*s. Just about everyone had something to hide, and why risk it when there was endless deserted beach to the north? Abdul had already cut and run for Legian, and when the abandoned Kayu Aya and the Golden Village bungalows at the edge of the Seminyak *sawah*s (rice fields) became available to rent, the move was on. By the late 1970s, the stretch of black-sand beach in front of the villages of Legian and Seminyak had become the hip centre of Bali.

Italian fashion designer Milo Migliavacca and Irish-Australian designer Linda Garland both built houses on the beach, Garland's circular house becoming a famous early expat architectural statement. But New Zealander Rex Patten claims to have built the first 'real house' in Seminyak, in between boatbuilding and clothing runs. 'There was Golden Village of course, and Dave Wyllie had set up this sort of Indonesian thing,' he says, 'but mine was the first house in Seminyak built by and for a Westerner. Still got it too, and I'd still have an ocean view if bloody Paul Ropp hadn't built in front of me.'

Chapter 19 Expatria

In 1978 Melbourne party boy and sometime rag-trade retailer Malcolm Williams finished a relationship, sold up his house and shop and came to Bali to think about his future. He'd been before, in 1970, staying in Segara Village in Sanur, when he and a friend who owned a head shop called Magic Mushroom in Melbourne rode bikes over to Kuta and tried the real thing, barely making it back to catch the night flight home. This time he stayed in Kuta, but immediately hired a motorbike and went exploring. He recalls:

> I found a dirt track heading down to the ocean and just followed it until I came to a *losmen* and *warung* called Blue Ocean. It was very basic but it was right on a wide expanse of beach and it was beautiful and quiet. Abdul's house was on one side and a place called Evergreen on the other, then there was nothing in either direction. I checked into a room and stayed there.

Williams met one of the owners, a Balinese called Yasin, and over a few days he started to hatch a plot. He could set up a beach bar here for next to nothing. He had contacts in Melbourne, people would come. As it turned out, there was a deal to be done. Yasin seemed keen, but one day a Westerner came and sat in the *warung* and Yasin ran a mile. Malcolm learned too late that it was David Bailey, who had been the most recent former partner in the Blue Ocean. But Williams wasn't really looking for negatives. He had a little Bali dream in play, but when he roughly costed what replacing the *warung* with a proper restaurant was going to cost, he realised he was going to need a partner. He flew back to Melbourne and put the word out. Ian White was the first to put his hand up. Williams didn't know a lot about Ian, other than that he was a party animal, and seemed like a good bloke. They shook on it.

'To be honest, we really didn't have a clue. But we knew the kind of place that would appeal to us, so that's what we tried to create,' Williams says.

The Blue Ocean was just a concrete slab with a thatched roof and a couple of bamboo walls, a few rough tables, a limited menu, a fridge full of cold beer, a record player and some backgammon sets. None of that mattered. The sign out front was an exotic image of a biplane flying over a tropical island that Williams had adapted from a cigarette tin he'd bought in London. It was like a beacon. Williams looked like the young Mick Jagger, Ian White like Rod Stewart. They hung around the bar in loosely draped sarongs and nothing else.

Bali: Heaven and Hell

Williams recalls:

It was a big scene with the Europeans, with backgammon and racquetball on the beach, guys playing bongos. The European women were much hotter and more approachable than the Aussies. We didn't set out to appeal to the Euros, but the backgammon scene was happening, and the fact that no one ever wore any clothes on the beach, and half the time chicks would walk into the restaurant naked, that was a pretty big draw.

For a few years, Blue Ocean rocked. It was the 'it' place of Seminyak. One day in 1984, a large shark got caught in the shallows in front of the restaurant. I wrote in my diary:

The lifeguard grabbed the swimming flag and used it as a harpoon. The crowd of Balinese thought it was great sport as the shark in its death throes sent showers of bloody water over the front row. Then someone produced a machete and the fin was gone. Suddenly there were flashing blades everywhere and we retreated, watching an old man dance happily up the beach with his dinner ... Later, when I went down to the bar for a drink and to book the Blue Ocean Jeep for the next day, Ian had stuck the shark's head on a spike at the entrance and it was starting to stink. Malcolm sat down heavily opposite me. 'Sometimes I don't know what Ian does for a fucking brain,' he muttered, but the shark's head remained.

There were a few management issues on which they did not see eye to eye, but on one thing they were agreed: the police security patrol was useless. Williams recalls:

Drunk local guys would come in and break bottles and cause fights, and the police couldn't control it. They'd approach these guys and they'd tell them their father's name and the cops would just back off for fear of reprisals. So we got rid of the cops and cut a deal with the army. The army guys would take them out on the beach out of sight and talk to them, then you'd hear a gunshot and the guy would never come back. They didn't shoot them, but they'd fire one past their ears to give them a strong warning.

Chapter 19 Expatria

The Melbourne partners were having too much fun for it to last. White went to Amsterdam and got into all kinds of trouble. Williams found that his nominee, Yasin, was a creature of habit. He learned from his army contacts that Yasin was shopping him to Immigration for visa infringements. Hauled in for a blacklisting, Williams was given forty-eight hours to show cause why he should not be deported. Outside the government offices, a Balinese man engaged him in conversation and gave him the address of another man who could help. Within the allotted time, Williams had become legal and swapped his part-ownership of the Blue Ocean for a better deal at the Bruna Beach Bar. That was the way Bali worked. You didn't ask questions.

As the number of Westerners living full-time or part-time along the Kuta/Legian/Seminyak strip grew, they started to need services that didn't exist. Part-timers were always trying to run businesses from afar using sketchy communications, or organise the export of statuary or furniture that would make them feel like they were in Bali for the long months when they weren't. Often, these 'pieces of Bali' were in fact the recent inventions of other expats, like the coconut-palm carvings and the massive bamboo lounges designed by Linda Garland and her Indonesian husband, Amir, that became a smash hit in the mid-1980s. But that didn't seem to matter.

In the early days part-timers did most of their business at Bali Easy Rider Travel Service, at the Melasti Beach Bungalows in Kuta, where you could rent a car or bike, send a telex, pick up mail and organise freight. Later, in the fax era, Krakatoa Business Centre in Seminyak became the place. 'Get out of the heat and into the air conditioning,' trumpeted their advertising. 'Local and International Phone Facilities—unsurpassed fax service—translation service—computer, typing and word processing facilities.' All of this and the Mont Blanc French Café adjoining.

Vitek Czernuszyn recalls:

> There was a very strong bond between the thousand or so expats, and it was bound up through Krakatoa, which was our message service and the place you'd go every day. You could send a fax and go have a nasi goreng next door while you waited for a response. They had about six girls working their butts off round the clock.

Although German graphic designer Hans Hoefer and writer Starr Black had produced the first Bali guidebook in 1970, the somewhat accidental

Bali: Heaven and Hell

publication of *Indonesia: A Traveller's Notes* by American Bill Dalton in 1973 gave young, hip travellers more of the kind of information they were after, including how to freeload island to island ("You can sail all over Kalimantan and Sulawesi without bread if you go to ferry captain and say you haven't any, he will more than likely take you") and directions to recommended brothels and where to score dope.

Dalton, who still lives in Bali today, had been on the overland trail from Europe and knocking about South East Asia for more than three years, keeping copious travel notes in a spiral-bound folder, when he was asked for some tips by a couple of German students he met at a youth hostel in Cairns, Queensland. Happy to assist, he pulled out his notes and started giving them information, but a New Zealand journalist and fellow guest rushed over and grabbed him by the arm. "Mate, that information is worth money. I wouldn't be giving it away."

He told Dalton about a hippie arts festival about to be held in the New South Wales town of Nimbin the following week, and offered to give him a ride half the length of Australia on the back of his motorbike. Dalton chatted up a girl at the public library and snuck in at night to "mimeograph" 800 copies of the four-sheet notes. Over three days at the landmark Aquarius Festival, Dalton sold out at 50 cents a copy and a publishing company was born. By the end of the year his notes had expanded into a primitive handbook which he explained in his introduction as a guide for "prospective overlanders of shortcuts, money saving ploys, off the wall adventures, items to buy and sell, working oportunities, cheap places to sleep, eat and get high—a general Manual of the Gypsy."

By the mid-1970s Dalton's renamed *Indonesian Handbook* was a strong seller for the company he had founded, Moon Publications, but it was soon overtaken by Tony and Maureen Wheeler's *South East Asia on a Shoe String*, first published in 1975. However, in the decade that followed, there was still no print media information for the fast-growing expat and tourist market, until Bali's only daily newspaper, *Bali Post*, added an English-language page to its Sunday edition in 1979. New Zealander Sarita Newson, who had married a Balinese man in 1975 and begun a family, was hired to gather expat news and translate relevant articles written by Indonesian journalists. She in turn hired Made Wijaya, the flamboyant Australian expat who was making a name for himself as a landscape designer. Wijaya's column was not everyone's cup of tea, but it developed a readership, and the English section

Chapter 19 Expatria

expanded to two pages. It was later taken over by photojournalist Rio Helmi, with even more success.

Vitek Czernuszyn recalls:

> I went back to Bali and saw how many bars, nightclubs and new tourist ventures there were, and really no information about them. I saw the need, but I had no money, so I put a dummy issue of a magazine together—just cutting and pasting on the floor of my *losmen*—and went out looking for money. There was no shortage of it in Bali, and I soon had a backer.

Vitek's *Bali Echo* was a colour broadsheet a little reminiscent of *Tracks* magazine, which was perhaps not surprising since its founder, Albert Falzon, had been persuaded to interrupt a long vacation in Seminyak to design the first issue. As well as entertaining editorial features, the *Echo* included an exhaustive information index and listings of restaurants, bars and accommodations. The ads were not easily won in the beginning. 'I'd often have to go and explain the concept of advertising,' Vitek says. 'Unfortunately, my simplistic explanation—if you buy a photo of your bar to put in my magazine, people will come and spend money—didn't always work because if no one came they wouldn't pay, or they wanted their money back.'

Vitek convinced visiting supermodel Elle Macpherson to pose for the cover of the second issue, then sold Indonesia's national airline, Garuda, a back-cover package for a year in a deal that included all his air-ticketing needs and air freight of the magazine to key feeder cities, like Amsterdam. Bali's first *bule* magazine was up and running.

In late April 1985 I found myself back in Bali, covering for the Australian news magazine *The Bulletin* the first-ever visit of US President Ronald Reagan for the ASEAN Summit. Arriving a week ahead of the event to sneak in some surfing, I was astounded to see road workers rolling bitumen day and night, frantically trying to meet the deadline for completion of the new Nusa Dua road, which had to be wider than any other road in Bali in order to accommodate the outriders for the presidential motorcade. At long last, Nusa Dua was coming of age as the new centre of high-end tourism.

The only problem was—and this became apparent when we jackals of the press descended on the hotel precinct—that the first hotels of the development were aimed at the mass market and did not reflect the luxury hype that had preceded the opening. Made Wijaya wrote later:

> With the construction of the first hotels on the Bukit in the early 1980s—the Nusa Dua Beach, The Grand Hyatt and The Hilton, all in the Nusa Dua Tourist Development Zone—the southern-most reaches of the Bukit became popular, if not exactly fashionable. These new hotels were sparkling but commercially so; purpose-built for the mass tourist trade. The more discerning tourists still went to hotels and home stays near less-gated and more cultured communities.

The deregulation of the Indonesian banking system in 1987 created an immediate investment boom and a rush to develop new hotels. Some of these were luxury boutique hotels, scattered around the island—like Peter Muller and Adrian Zecha's Amandari in Ubud, where Muller was finally able to employ his Matahari traditional village concept, as well as introducing the infinity pool—but the greatest concentration was in Nusa Dua, and points beyond on the once-unwanted Bukit Peninsula. The 1992–93 construction of the Four Seasons all-villa resort at Jimbaran Bay at the foot of the Bukit plateau was a clear signal to the new Chinese investors swarming in from Hong Kong and Java that the Bukit was open for business.

For the surfers, this had been the case for the better part of a decade. The discovery of high-quality surf breaks right along the Bukit cliffs in the 1980s led to more and more *losmen*s and *warung*s popping up, but once the surfer/traders started to make money, they began to dream about leasing land and building dream homes above the perfect waves. When land certificates became available in the early 1990s, they were right there at the front of the queue with the Chinese developers.

But it was to be an Indonesian, rather than a Chinese, whose name would become synonymous with the good, the bad and the ugly aspects of development on the Bukit. President Suharto's youngest son, Hutomo 'Tommy' Mandala Putra Suharto, was born in 1962 and grew up in the lap of luxury, wanting for nothing as his father creamed off personal billions from the national interest. In the early 1990s President Suharto gave Tommy the national monopoly on the lucrative distribution of cloves, a key ingredient in Indonesia's popular kretek cigarettes. Later he was also given control of the Indonesian national car project, the Timor—an enterprise condemned by

Chapter 19 Expatria

critics as doing little more than lining the pockets of the Suharto family at the state's expense.

None of this was enough for Tommy, who saw the potential for enormous profits on the Bukit and used corrupt divisions of the Indonesian Army to force landowners at Pecatu and Dreamland Beach to sell land at cheap prices to a company he controlled. According to Made Wijaya, 'The one protest by the peanut farmers of Pecatu was quashed when Tommy Suharto arrived in a Rolls Royce with a phalanx of lawyers.'

At the height of their arrogant powers, Suharto and his playboy cronies seemed to believe that no rules applied to them, not even at the golf club. David Thomas had added golf-course design to his portfolio of skills and had worked on setting up the championship course at the Nusa Dua club. Playing off a handicap of four, he was frequently invited to play with the club's leading lights, including high-ranking police and army officers, judges, lawyers and immigration officials. The only people who ever gave him any trouble were Tommy's henchmen, who refused to pay for anything. When Thomas demanded to see a greens-fee receipt before they took a golf cart, he was abused. A week later he was refused entry coming back in from Singapore. He had been blacklisted.

Thomas flew back to Singapore, then snuck into Indonesia via Bintan Island. He called the henchmen's bluff and used his police and immigration contacts to have the matter investigated. His blacklisting was dropped and a policeman and immigration officer were subsequently charged.

Tommy lost the clove monopoly and the car company when his father was thrown out of office in 1998 and the International Monetary Fund had to bail Indonesia out of its financial mess, and in 1999 he was found guilty of major land-fraud charges related to Bukit transactions. But, through a complex trail of trust funds and offshore companies, he is said to still control landholdings on the peninsula and lease to such hotel groups as Starwood, Accor and Hilton.

As Tommy Suharto and other unscrupulous developers ransacked the Bukit, the normally conservative *Bali Post* started reporting on a range of environmentally irresponsible and illegal events on the peninsula, including:

> unregulated mining of limestone and coral, salination of underground aquifers, diversion of water from farms to hotels and golf courses, the conversion of productive land—often forcibly expropriated

> ... and the complicity of the army and government officials in facilitating projects in breach of regional planning regulations.

While this was happening illegally, the Suharto government and the governor of Bali combined forces to legally increase the number of tourist-development zones from three to fifteen, and then to twenty-one. Bali land expert and academic Carol Warren wrote:

> National development policy had become almost entirely geared towards gross maximisation of the number of tourists visiting the island and the income they might generate. Provincial and regional government authorities for their part demonstrated an insatiable appetite for tourism growth. Eager to increase their revenue base—not to mention the opportunities for graft—they played midwife to enormous quantities of outside capital seeking a literal and figurative 'home' ... Later in the 1990s, the modern lifestyle desires and capital accumulation interests of the Jakarta elite fused to produce a scramble for property in Bali. Luxury residences with resort facilities are intended to service the New Rich (*Orang Kaya Baru*) among the Indonesian elite, who seek to escape the traffic and pollution of Jakarta.

Although they had their own minor-league plans for developing the Bukit, the expat surfers were incensed by Tommy Suharto's arrogant push. Peter Neely recalls:

> Fly [Bradley] came to me in a frenzy in the mid-1990s when he discovered Tommy wanted to build a 1000-yacht marina on top of the coral reef at Balangan. Fly showed me the plans he had secretly photocopied, with a waterslide carved into the cliff to add insult to injury. He was solely responsible for bravely fronting Tommy's men with a copy of my book [*Indo Surf and Lingo*] to show them how big the surf gets over that reef ... they soon realised how futile it would be to build anything ... and focused back on the golf course at Dreamland and filling in Benoa Harbour.

The Bukit really came of age (or hammered a final nail in its coffin, depending on your point of view) with the opening of the swank Bulgari Hotel

Chapter 19 Expatria

in 2006. 'Who would ever have thought that the Bukit and the venerable jewellery house of Bulgari would ever be joined in holy matrimony?' gushed Made Wijaya. 'For the resort, the famous design team of Antonio Citterio and Partners from Milano created a sumptuous village-scape and drop-dead gorgeous interiors, which attracted a steady stream of super-rich Russians and Arabs.'

Now the floodgates were opened for the luxury villa developers. Wijaya said:

> 'The Bukit is a stupid place for smart villas,' one pundit commented recently, after viewing a full-page ad in *The Bali Times*; the ad featured a row of microwave oven–like terrace houses—all slam-dunked on a once gorgeous cliff. On the flat roofs, rows of Buddha statues (in square ponds) act as lightning rods. It must be said that the Bukit villa boom has not managed to attract many responsible architects, or good designers for that matter: most of the New Age Bali-besotted build formulaic ultra-minimalist, split-level dream homes, with a token smattering of Balinese-ness.

Wijaya concluded by asking: 'Will the Bukit boom continue once the traffic has backed up and the water run out?' Perhaps Stephen Palmer has the answer.

While all this was happening on the Bukit, more and more Westerners were leasing plots of land with local nominees and building houses or villas for their own use and for holiday rentals. We joined the push in 1992 when our close friend Rennie Ellis was offered a half-share in just under an acre of land bordering a river in the village of Umalas. We'd never heard of Umalas, but he explained that it was close to the beach, beautiful and quiet, yet just a few minutes on a motorbike from the new social hub of Seminyak. There were no Western houses in Umalas but the villagers were keen to emulate what was happening in nearby Seminyak, and create income opportunities. Since we would be buying out an existing partner a few years into a twenty-year lease, costs were relatively low, and the cost of building a house to share was estimated to be about $25,000. We were in!

Rennie flew over from Melbourne to close the deal, arranging for an old friend, Su Alit of Alit's Beach Bungalows, to be our nominee on the contract, and consulting with expat housing guru Alistair Stewart. We planned to build within two years, but that went by in a flash, and we were still planning when we made our payment in advance for the third year. In our absence, Mrs Alit was informed that the payment had arrived two days late, and that our failure to build put us in breach of our lease anyway, and it had been revoked.

We were in shock, as were our expat friends, and we started planning retaliatory action, but the more we investigated our options in fighting a case in an Indonesian court, the more hopeless it seemed. People who understood Bali land deals told us that the only explanation for the owners not accepting our lease payment was that they had been looking for an out so they could sell for a higher price. That was all anyone knew. Sadder but wiser, we walked away from the dream of our own house in Bali.

Twenty years later my wife and I went looking for our lost land in the urban sprawl of Umalas. Surprisingly, given the amount of development that had taken place, we eventually found it untouched (apart from a soccer field where we had planned to build a house) on a bend in the river just above the narrow bridge that leads from Batu Belig to Brawa. Our friend Wayan Agus found a workman clearing some brambles from the property on the other side of the water and asked him if he knew why it had not been built on.

Wayan came racing back to the car with exciting news. 'Now I understand what happened,' he said. He explained that the estate across the river was owned by Kadek Wirinatha, the Balinese entrepreneur with a finger in every pie. When Kadek had built his mansion twenty years ago, he had bought the property across the river as a buffer against being built out.

We had been gazumped by the richest man in Bali. It made me mad all over again.

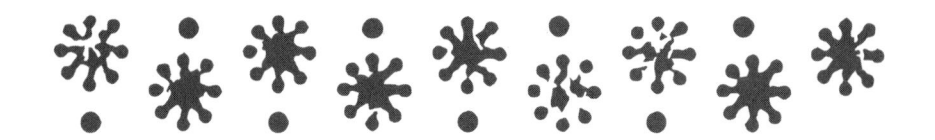

Chapter 20 The Day After

I couldn't believe, it could not happen in Bali. The phones were not working so I couldn't phone my boss... When the phones came back on in the late afternoon, I started to get phone calls from my friends. 'Wayan, you still alive?' By night-time our boss had called us back to the restaurant, not to open it but to make sure everybody was okay and had somewhere safe to stay. It was very dark in Kuta that night, and quiet. No cars, no people. Everyone was crying. I sat in the dark and cried, too.

Wayan Agus Parwita, 2013

Sunday 13 October 2002

It was after midnight when Richard Flax drove home through the quiet streets of Seminyak, and everything seemed completely normal. While his wife, Judy, had played nervously with her mobile phone on the way home from Ubud, trying to get a signal, Flax had come up with a plan. He would go home, drop Judy and daughter Lara, then drive into Kuta, because it seemed logical that this would be where something had happened. He would see if his help was needed.

But Flax didn't get that far. As he pulled into the Legian compound and opened the gate into the courtyard, one of his landlines was ringing, then another. Unusually for Bali, the Flax compound had four landlines to accommodate Flax's various businesses. For more than twenty years, Flax had been the go-to guy for emergency evacuations of expats needing medical care they couldn't get in Bali. It was a role that had grown out of the fact that from his earliest surfing days in Bali, riding his kneeboard on the Bukit, Flax had always carried an extensive medical kit, a legacy of the days he'd spent on the road in Third World countries looking for artefacts for Christie's.

Flax recalls:

> People would knock on the door and say, oh, mate, I've got a surfboard up the arse. There was very little care available locally at that time, so I just started doing patch-up jobs with my kit, stitches and so on, and as a consequence, if it needed further treatment, I was the guy who helped get them on planes and out of here. In serious cases, I was the guy ringing up mates, saying give me a grand, we have to get this guy out of here or he'll die. Slowly, it developed into a system, and I think it saved quite a few lives.

One time Flax helped fly a wounded man from Borneo to Singapore, and after calculating the enormous costs that someone would have to bear, he sat in a hotel room in Singapore and phoned insurance companies.

> At that time there really was no international health insurance, but I explained what I wanted and they sold me a policy. From then on, when people complained about how much medical treatment was costing them, I told them about my policy. After about six months the company asked me to represent them in Indonesia with a product called Expatcare.

In Legian in the early hours, Flax flicked on a light and picked up the ringing phone in his home office. It was a colleague at one of Bali's bigger private clinics. She told him there had been a bombing and they had people being brought in with horrific injuries and they couldn't cope. They needed someone to help organise immediate care in other places, and they had nowhere to turn. Flax sat down at his desk and started dialling numbers. The medivac guy became a one-man, four-phone clearing house.

Flax's medivac work had given him a strong network of contacts in medical circles in Bali, but his other businesses had also given him access to high levels of government in Denpasar and Jakarta.

Flax managed to get through to a high-ranking connection at Sanglah Hospital. The man was distraught. The hospital was in chaos as victims arrived in *bemo*s and propped on the back of motorbikes. No one knew the full story, just that the roads out of Kuta were in gridlock as people with transport tried to flee the area or get to hospitals. At the scene, people who could were helping burns victims into holding areas until some form of

Chapter 20 The Day After

transport arrived. Flax choked back his emotion and worked the phones, knowing that until mobile services were switched back on, there would not be many alternatives.

He recalls:

> I finally got on to the Australian consul, I asked him what he had on the ground, and he said nothing. Resources? None. I told him we were in deep shit, that we had between twenty and forty seriously injured people in Sanglah who would die if we didn't do something. At that stage we didn't know nationalities but we knew there were Australians among them. Bali couldn't cope with this, and Australia was the only real evacuation option.

Flax told the consul he could use his evacuation contacts in Jakarta to get a BAC-111 in the air within the hour. All he needed was $75,000. The consul called back with an approval. Flax started phoning contacts at Royal Perth Hospital, four hours from Bali, where Dr Fiona Woods had the best burns unit in the country.

The sun was coming up in Legian. Friends started arriving at the Flax compound, bringing computers, whiteboards, anything that might help. The mobile network was back up and expats all over Bali were waking up to the terrible news, and many were going straight to the hospitals and clinics to volunteer. Flax says: 'Sanglah's immediate reaction was typically Balinese. They let people come into the wards and adopt a victim. People were lying on the floor all over the place, seriously injured or dying, and volunteers would just come in and nurse them.'

✳ ✳ ✳ ✳ ✳ ✳

Unable to sleep, Alison Chester sat up through the early-morning hours, flicking between the BBC and CNN, hoping for snatches of information. CNN was reporting a massive explosion in Bali, but they had no details. At about 4 am she phoned a friend who was a nurse and asked if she knew anything. Yes, said the friend, Sanglah was calling for volunteers. Alison decided to go in at first light with her daughter, Rachel.

At Sanglah they were given loose instructions to move through the wards, just checking on people, making them as comfortable as possible.

Bali: Heaven and Hell

Alison attached herself to two Indian doctors, a married couple on holiday from Perth. She recalls:

> We got to one corner of a ward where three beds had been partitioned off with a screen. I had no medical experience but I could see that their injuries were horrific. The doctors told me to stay there, and do what I could to help them. I sat down next to a young girl, held her hand and offered some soft words of encouragement, and it changed my life.

Alison Chester had come to Bali in 1983, an Englishwoman running away from a failed marriage in Australia. She started doing suitcase runs between Denpasar and Australia selling clothing she had designed, and in 1984 she met Yanto, a handsome young man from Yogyakarta. They were married in 1987, created a label called Yanto's Collection and opened a small shop on Jalan Padma. The business had its ups and downs over the years, but the financial crisis of 1998 played into their hands, with big payments in US dollars arriving just as the rupiah crashed, enabling them to pay off their local business debts. By 2002, Alison was running a successful private label business, selling to the United States and Germany.

In the corner of the ward at Sanglah, Alison did what she could for a woman from Perth and a man who occupied the other beds, but her focus was on the young woman from Sydney whose name she discovered was Jodie O'Shea. From about 7 am until late afternoon when the orderlies took the girl to the plane, Alison talked to her, fanned her, helped her sip water and kept her from lapsing into a coma. She says:

> I couldn't see how burnt her body was, but her face was terribly swollen, which didn't stop her from talking a bit and even trying to smile. She told me about her dog-grooming business and she talked about the bomb. She said her friend, Michelle, was gone, and I said not necessarily. She gave me her mum's phone number so I called her about three times during the day. Each time I asked Jodie if she wanted to talk, and she said, 'Oh no, it will only upset her.' She was so selfless and considerate. We got painkillers about one in the afternoon and she said, and I'll never forget this, 'Give them to the other girl, she needs them more than I do.' Late in the day they got her on the stretcher and she looked up at me and said, 'Thank you for being with me all this time.'

Chapter 20 The Day After

Alison Chester clears her throat and looks away, until a small child commands her attention. We are sitting in the simple dining room of the orphanage she and Yanto now run on the outskirts of Denpasar. When she has tended to the little boy's needs she turns back to the conversation and smiles slightly.

> There's a reason for everything in life, isn't there? The three people in that room all died, even though Jodie was on the first plane out. The Indian couple got put before a tribunal in Australia and were told they shouldn't have put those people on the first plane because they were never going to make it. I met them at the one-year anniversary and they said they'd do the same thing again. I left the hospital that night and collapsed. I remember getting out onto the street and running into a girlfriend and she said, 'How could you do that?' I said I didn't know. It's amazing where you find strength. You think you're a weak person, but you do what you have to do. I went home and I couldn't get rid of the smell on my clothes. I thought it would stay with me forever.

Saraswati Mish Pulling was woken with a start in her Kerobokan home when her phone rang. Richard, the father of her daughter, Ruby, was calling from Melbourne and his voice was full of dread. 'Are you all right?'

'Of course. Why?'

He gave her the news of the Kuta bombings. She put down the phone and cried for a very long time, then she reflected on the strange incidents of the previous evening.

> We were at Bingin, up on the Bukit with some friends, my boyfriend and I, and they wanted us to stay the night but I wanted to go home. We started for home and I began to see weird things, like Western people in a crowd with things crashing into them. A voice kept saying to me, there's going to be an accident but you won't get hurt. I drove really slowly because things like that don't happen to me often, and when they do they usually mean something. At the bottom of the hill I didn't know which way to go, I was confused by all that was going on in my head, but my boyfriend yelled at me to turn right. If I'd gone left I would have ended up in Kuta. At home I felt shaken by this strange experience and sat upstairs with my back against the wooden wall and had a cup of tea. Suddenly, I felt something shake

the wall behind my back and I heard a loud noise. I thought it must have been a gas explosion. I went to bed but slept very uneasily.

When she had recovered from the shock, Pulling phoned friends to exchange information about the disaster, then drove to Sanglah to offer her assistance. She immediately ran into Kevin Lovett, an expat friend, who advised her to go from bed to bed with a jug of water. Then she was given the job of helping set up an emergency response room, with the names of the missing on a huge whiteboard across one wall. She stayed until the third day, when the police came and removed all the Western volunteers.

Her reaction was similar to many of the volunteers: 'When you're in the moment you just do what you have to, but we were going to Italy a few days later, and I just got on the plane and started bawling my eyes out. I felt so bad about abandoning the Balinese when they needed us most.'

※ ※ ※ ※ ※ ※

Hung-over and emotionally drained, surfers Tony 'Doris' Eltherington and Kim 'Fly' Bradley spent Sunday morning going around the Benoa marina bumming money off the surfers, yachties and adventurers to buy ice. Doris recalls:

> We filled Fly's truck with ice and went off to Sanglah Hospital. I knew the chaplain, Colonel Agar, and he said, 'Thanks, guys, ice for the doctors' drinks!' It was good to see he could muster a bit of humour under the circumstances. Then he told us to bring the truck around the back of the hospital. We backed up beside a big blue tarp that was covering up a stack of bodies. He said, 'There you go, just pile the ice on top.' Fly and I started shovelling the ice out and I noticed this black hand with a watch on it hanging out from under the tarp. It was just charred black and I couldn't take my eyes off it for a while. Then I turned away and puked.

Within forty-eight hours of the Kuta bombings, Richard Flax's unofficial command centre in Legian had been relieved of it duties when an Australian team of medical-emergency experts arrived on the Monday afternoon. Flax recalls:

Chapter 20 The Day After

> I still hadn't been to bed at this point, and they told me to put my head down and have a rest. I went to bed as instructed, but it only lasted three hours because the response team couldn't work with the local hospitals. What they were doing was well-meaning, but just not the right way to go about it. You don't walk into an Indonesian hospital and tell a doctor he's not doing things the right way, even if you are right. There were a lot of issues like that, and I had to come back on deck and spend the next day resolving cultural difficulties.

By this time the chartered BAC-111 had arrived in Perth with six survivors on stretcher beds, but Flax had realised there were so many victims whose lives were in the balance that a much larger aircraft was needed.

> I told them I could get a DC-10 out of Jakarta and strip the seats out and put in beds. It was going to cost about a quarter of a million but it was ready to go. It was authorised at our end and we were about to get it happening when [Prime Minister] John Howard decided to utilise an evacuation plan they already had in place for troops in Timor, involving Caribous, much smaller planes.

Sitting behind a big desk in his insurance-company headquarters in Legian a dozen years later, Flax struggles to control his frustration at what he sees as a series of bungles that seriously endangered the Australian relief effort, including the government decision to make Darwin the evacuation base, despite having far greater capacity at Royal Perth, as well as the best burns unit, and his personal battle to have gravely injured Indonesians evacuated despite President Megawati's insistence that 'we will take care of our own'.

On the other hand, Flax has nothing but praise for the 403 acknowledged volunteers, including his own group in Legian, who continued to work around the clock relaying information to families from communications centres, long after they had been kicked out of the hospitals, police chief Pastika, later to become governor, who Flax says was 'a pure joy' to work with, and the vast majority of the Balinese officials involved in the effort. He even saw a higher power at work in the midst of the disaster: 'It was Bali magic. Something happened, things came together to create positive outcomes in a very Balinese way. I was very much aware of a Balinese energy running through the chaos, even as I was in the middle of it.'

Flax later wrote:

> Compassion blended with tragedy and brought an intriguing dimension to the disaster ... Just as when lava parted and flowed around Besakih in 1963, subtle positive energies diverted negative energies and played a major part in the unfolding drama in Kuta ... As everyone struggled to cope in the days and weeks that followed the bombing, traditional Balinese ways of dealing with tragedy provided strength to all. Families and friends ... were immersed in a field of love and protection.

Saraswati Mish Pulling says:

> The Balinese took responsibility for a terrible thing. There was no blame, no talk of revenge. They took responsibility, they moved forward. They have a very good understanding of good and evil, lightness and dark, but their acceptance blew me away.

When the medals and awards were handed around much later, Flax was not among the recipients. He says:

> You know, with all of this, you have to work out whether you want to tell the truth or protect people's feelings, and sometimes you have to make that choice. But at the end of the day, I don't give a flying fuck. If it happened again I'd do the same thing.

In 2009 Flax was invited to address the third annual National Security Officers' Conference in Singapore, to give an insider's perspective on the 'spontaneous community-led response' to the 2002 Bali bombing as head of the newly formed Emergency Response Service Indonesia.

The bombings of October 2002, which ultimately claimed 202 lives, had an immediate and devastating impact on the economy of Bali. People simply stopped coming. Asri Kerthyasa, who was then running the Ibah Hotel in Ubud, recalls:

> *60 Minutes* [television program] came up to do a story and I was interviewed for it standing in the middle of Monkey Forest Road,

Chapter 20 The Day After

and for the entire interview nothing came by ... no cars, no people. And walking down Jalan Legian, it was the same. This was a time when Bali was in its tourism heyday, absolutely pumping. We were fully booked, and by then we had a lot of villas. And then nothing. Empty. It was unbelievable. The year before, 9/11 had had an impact, and East Timor and the financial crisis, too, but we got through all that. This was on a different scale.

Businessman Stephen Palmer recalls:

The entire island went into shock. People stopped moving around, and they started to wilt away. I used to always eat at Aromas [on Jalan Legian] and I knew the waitresses like family. One day one of them was crying. When she came to take my order I asked her what was wrong. She said she was having some stress with her husband because their family and his two brothers were all living in a one-room shanty because no one had a job. She was supporting everyone on a half-wage, which is what Aromas, like a lot of places, had done to stay open. I knew something had to be done to get the place back in gear, and from that encounter came the idea to do the Kuta Carnival.

The Kuta Carnival, which made its debut eight months after the bombings, in July 2003, was an attempt to show the world that the global capital of beachside excess was still capable of having fun. Moreover, it was an affirmation for both Balinese and expat residents that Kuta had the spirit to survive. For many Balinese families, directly or indirectly dependent on the tourist dollar, however, it was going to be a long battle.

Tourism and hotel management graduate Wayan Agus Parwita, who found himself out of a job within days of the bombing, having been the most recently hired at the Coral Reef, came from a family whose fundamental change in livelihood over the previous generation was typical of South Bali.

When Wayan's grandfather died unexpectedly in the mid-1960s, his dad, I Nyoman Suwita, was just fourteen. He and his older brother had to fish for eels in the rice paddies at night, then sell them in the markets each morning before school to put rice on the table for the family. Wayan's uncle went to work in a neighbour's field after elementary school, giving his younger brother, Nyoman Suwita, the opportunity to continue through high school. It was a huge sacrifice, but it enabled Nyoman to complete nine years of school, and study wood carving for the final three. He was training to be a temple carver, but while still at school he sold a few pieces at the markets to help support the compound.

Nyoman was a good carver and he found plenty of work locally, before being hired to work on major temple constructions in Java. When he returned he had enough money to buy some more land to expand the compound, marry his neighbour, Ni Luh Suji, and start a family. In 1984, when Wayan Agus was five, the family moved into a new two-room house with an external bamboo kitchen at the Cepaka compound. The family was upwardly mobile, there was no doubt about that, but Nyoman was still a little envious when he saw that a friend, also a carver, had made enough money selling his carvings at a tourist hotel in Sanur to afford a second-hand motorbike.

Wayan Agus says:

> He told my father he should try to sell his wood carvings to foreigners, because there were more tourists every year in Sanur and Kuta. So my father started to ride his pushbike to a hotel in Legian where he would sell his carvings. He didn't speak any English, but his friend told him to buy a calculator so he could show the tourists how much he wanted for each piece.

The hotel provided Nyoman with some storage space for his pieces and allowed him to sit on a mat in a corner of the lobby and demonstrate his skills, taking a small commission on his sales.

> My father was very surprised, very happy, because the tourists would come and pick up his carvings and he would show them the price on the calculator and they would take out their money and pay him. Soon he had enough money to buy a ten-year-old Yamaha PH-70 motorbike.

Although Ni Luh Suji, who only had two years' schooling, never worked, the family prospered as Nyoman sold more and more carvings. By the time Wayan was old enough to learn the art himself, his father had moved to a big new hotel in Seminyak, and set up Wayan in another hotel every afternoon after school.

Chapter 20 The Day After

I liked it because I would meet tourists and learn English from them and make some money. My father had three different hotels now, with my cousin working the third one. I would come home from school at 1 pm, have a rest for two hours then go to the hotel at 4 pm, taking my books so I could do my homework when there were no customers. That was my start in business.

Nyoman invested his savings in motorbikes that he could rent to tourists, and by the time Wayan went to university, he had worked out that he would need to buy two more bikes and get them working in order to put Wayan's younger brother, I Made Dwipayana, through chefs' school. The family still tended pigs and lived at the edge of a rice field, but in the space of a generation they had successfully made the transition from subsistence agriculture to tourism entrepreneurs.

Then the bombs went off in Kuta.

Nyoman's three hotels were near-empty and he stopped showing his carvings. He started to sell the motorbikes one by one to keep food on the table. The important thing was to keep Made in college. Wayan eventually found work on the Carnival Cruise Line, doing seven-month stints without a break in the Caribbean. He was paid US$70 a fortnight and had to buy his own airline tickets to and from the departure port. The cabin boys worked six hours every morning, then four or five at night, seven days a week, but they received free meals and a bed, and the passengers were generous tippers. Soon Wayan was regularly sending money home to the compound.

Between his fourth and fifth contracts with Carnival Cruises, Wayan fell in love, and missed the girl so much that he jumped ship when the cruiser docked, quit his job and flew home. Fortunately, the tourist economy at home had finally picked up, and then terrorists struck again.

While the bombings at Kuta Square and Jimbaran Bay in October 2005 resulted in a much smaller death toll (twenty-three), they underlined the dreadful and mostly unspoken fear that this might become a regular occurrence. People who had slowly come back to Bali now swore off it for life. Asri Kerthyasa says:

> After the first one everyone wanted to show solidarity, and they slowly started to come back. But after the second one, so many people just went, enough, we give up on Bali. At Ibah, we never

Bali: Heaven and Hell

really recovered from that. As an independent, family-run hotel, we just didn't have the PR machinery behind us. It got too hard.

Australian expat photographer Jason Childs was having a barbeque at his new house in Jimbaran. He'd just been back in Australia to see the Swans win the AFL grand final and was hosting a party for friends to drink beers and watch the replay. He recalls:

> It was a great day and no one seemed to want to leave. Then we heard the bombs. My wife, Michelle, grabbed some towels and we ran down the street. People were running towards us, away from the bombs. I shot photos and Michelle held a woman until she died. There were people in need of attention everywhere. I guess I was kind of immune to the horror, doing my thing and taking pictures. I got back to the house and sent the pictures around the world and never looked at them again, until about a month ago. I hadn't been able to.

Paul 'Gringo' Anderson had a regular Saturday-night date with a local girl. He'd usually pick her up at McDonald's at Jimbaran and they'd drive down to a favourite *warung* at the beach and have dinner. On Saturday 1 October, he'd been surfing Middle Reef at Kuta all afternoon and the boat driver had forgotten to pick him up. When he finally made it home he phoned the girl and told her he was too tired and couldn't make it. He says:

> She wasn't real happy about it but I was too tired to care. I fell asleep in front of the TV at 6.30 pm. A few hours later the girl calls back and she's crying and sobbing and thanking me for saving her life. I was on the phone to people most of the night, and at first light I went down to Jimbaran and saw the devastation. The warung was completely gone. Our table blown up, our mate, the waiter, dead.

Gringo stood at the bomb site, unable to move, trembling and crying. 'I just kept saying over and over again, the cunts, the fucking cunts! I should have been dead. Fuck these cunts. It still affects me today.'

A grizzled old surf explorer who's seen it all, Gringo removes his glasses, wipes his eyes and stares at a surfing photo on the wall for a very long time.

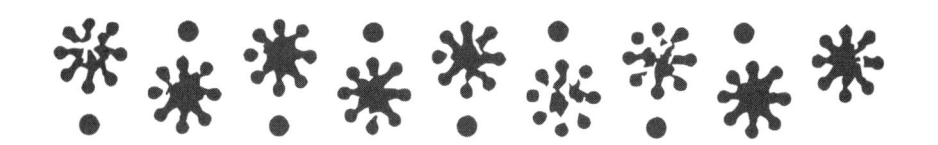

Chapter 21 Tipping Point

Police say the scant security measures put in place at many villas by their owners are partly to blame for the recent increase in criminality. Many villas stand alone and separated in rice fields, located at a distance from the more populous and secure residential areas. Both the police and the governor have in the past urged the installation of CCTV cameras, higher walls and additional security staff. Unfortunately, in many cases owners, more intent on preserving views than building tall fortifications, have ignored these recommendations.

www.balidiscovery.com

First, the good news. Since 1970, tourism and its related industries have transformed Bali from one of Indonesia's poorest provinces to one of its richest, with only 4.2 per cent of its people considered 'poor' compared with almost 20 per cent in the other islands of the section of the Indonesian archipelago known as West Nusa Tenggara. From being well below the Indonesian average in indicators such as education, infant mortality and nutrition prior to 1970, Bali is now well above the national average.

Now the bad news. The price of the economic turnaround has been huge and devastating in terms of its social, structural and environmental impact. It's frequently said that we are 'loving Bali to death', but photographer and social commentator Rio Helmi says: 'I'm a Buddhist, and we make a big distinction between attachment and love. Loving is caring, attachment is just wanting it for yourself.'

There is blame on both sides. We Westerners want more and more of Bali and the Balinese have been prepared to sell it to us. Now there are too many hotels, too many villas, too many cars, too much trash, and not enough water or rice fields.

Even some of the solutions are part of the problem. Faced with worsening traffic chaos in central Kuta, the provincial government built a looping, raised toll road between the airport, Nusa Dua and Benoa. Opened in 2013, the fly-over is the most ambitious transport project ever undertaken in Bali, and there is little doubt that it has eased the traffic flow through Kuta. But the concrete pillars built on limestone beds that support the raised road, and the limestone access tracks used during construction, now pose a serious environmental threat to the Benoa Basin mangrove forests and to the integrity of the entire waterway. The once-pristine basin has been progressively compromised since the development of the Benoa boat harbour in the 1980s, but now it has to also deal with toxic pollution from Denpasar's huge garbage dump on its shoreline and polluted sedimentation as a result of the reclaiming of Serangan Island.

Meanwhile, the island's other major traffic issue, the deadly dangerous and frequently gridlocked highway between Gilimanuk and Denpasar, continues to worsen as more trucks are needed to freight in more goods for more people who live on an island that has no deep-water port. The Gilimanuk road, where hundreds of Indonesians die in horrific accidents every year, has been little improved over the decades as Bali's official population has grown to 3.5 million—a figure most experts say is actually more like 4.5 million when you factor in illegal workers from other islands. When you also add in Bali's more than 3 million tourists each year, it is clear that the island's basic infrastructure is totally inadequate.

But people keep coming and the Balinese keep building. Or rather, they allow big Chinese money to fund construction of completely unnecessary buildings that illegal Javanese construction workers will erect.

'The carrying capacity of the island has hit critical mass,' writes Rio Helmi. 'Every high school kid in Bali knows [about] tensions over water shortage (in five-star hotels, each room consumes around five times a whole Balinese family's average of 200 liters a day) and disappearing agricultural land (more than 1000 hectares are 'converted' or urbanised annually).'

Bali already has too much of just about everything a tourist might need. According to a 2010 report compiled by Udayana University and the Bali provincial tourist authority (Diparda), projecting an expected 6.6 million tourists in 2015, Bali had more than enough hotel rooms, buses and rental cars. Considering that real tourist projections for 2015 are nowhere near that figure, the excess is ridiculous—more than 60,000 rooms where 40,000 would

Chapter 21 Tipping Point

have been more than adequate. In January 2014, *Bisnis Bali* website reported that the room count had been understated, and that there were about 85,000, which accounted for the fact that over the previous twelve months, while foreign arrivals grew by 13.5 per cent, hotel occupancy fell from 60 per cent to 55 per cent, and many mid-range, locally owned hotels closed. The glut of hotel rooms can be partly explained by developers finding a way around the provincial government's moratorium on hotel construction by inventing the 'condotel' whose rooms qualified as apartments. These continue to spring up around shopping complexes, catering mainly for domestic-market shopping holidays.

The 2010 report also noted that Bali had 676 buses with more than eighteen seats (about one hundred more than needed) and that there were already enough rental cars to satisfy demand well into the 2020s.

Too much of everything, everywhere, but the most controversial aspect of Bali's uncontrolled growth in recent years has been not the proliferation of mediocre, unused hotels, but the spread of the gated, high-walled villa. It's easy enough to find a quorum of old Bali hands who will rant for hours on the 'visual pollution' caused by whole new suburbs of 'McMansions', but the real concerns about the villa phenomenon go much deeper, right to the heart of Bali's cultural crisis and its sacrifice of *adat* or traditional land.

Rio Helmi reported in 2011:

> The head of the Bali chapter of the Indonesian business association APINDO, Panundiana Khun, stated early this year that land in Bali was no longer economically suitable for agrarian use and should rather be used for the tourism industry, and that Balinese farmers were better off transmigrating ... What caused the uproar in response to Khun's apparent gaffe is a long smoldering resentment in the Balinese community towards the excesses of the tourism industry and foreign investment, especially since government approval for Bakrie Nirwana Resort on land considered within the spiritual buffer zone of one of Bali's holiest sites, Tanah Lot, was rammed through during the Suharto era despite island-wide protests.

One of the most astute explanations of the seriousness of loss of *adat* is contained in a thesis written by Gusti Ayu Made Suartika in 2005, just as the villa explosion was beginning to create a new urban sprawl across rice fields and other agricultural land:

> In the most highly developed economies, greater regulation takes place than in those of the developing world. In principle, this situation applies directly to Bali, where the relative absence of regulation appears to offer greater advantages and a more open system to commercial capital, whereby local government can do deals in the absence of any legally sanctioned social controls. This, as one would expect, results in an administrative environment which is ... open to abuse, and unable to plan effectively for future development. At the same time the traditional system of land tenure managed over centuries by the *desa adat* institution, which resulted in Bali being one of the richest agricultural environments on earth, is being destroyed.

Suartika concluded that the loss of *adat* showed 'the state's incapacity to manage diverse demands for land by the various development sectors', and 'the absence of regulation favours tourism over *adat* land, which is the traditional territorial basis for the preservation of the culture'. Put simply, the state, through its greed, was selling out the culture. But others argue that the *banjar*s, supposedly the keepers of the flame, were equally culpable.

Rio Helmi writes:

> The most bitter feuds in Bali revolve around land. The passion the current ongoing debate on Bali's zoning stirs up indicates that this is something of a symbolic last stand for Balinese culture as a living, breathing entity. An ongoing real estate boom has meant more and more rice fields are replaced by luxury villas for expats. The other day when I remarked that the days of the Balinese farmer seem to be over, a Balinese journalist friend ... commented: 'No, actually they will remain farmers, but they will be tenant farmers. The Japanese and Taiwanese have been buying up land, not to build villas but as an investment in agriculture.' While the government fails the all-important agricultural sector in Bali, foreign investors are injecting capital into it, meaning the Balinese will no longer own their inheritance.

Chapter 21 Tipping Point

I've known Helmi for more than thirty years and, although we've never been more than acquaintances, I admire him immensely as Bali's savviest and most courageous media commentator, always prepared to put his balls on the line. The son of a diplomat, he is anything but, and he uses his birthright (half-Turkish, half-Sumatran, born in Europe) and his Western education to lash out, verbally and in his blogs, in both directions. I asked him for his opinion of the modern expats. It's a loaded question. Because of his mixed race and his perfect English diction, he is often mistaken for one.

> The situation that they are taking advantage of has been set up by others, but I can't stand Canggu [the new villa frontier]. It reminds me of an Australian suburb. My beef with most of those people is simply that they're ignorant [of Bali], they don't even know where they're living. But there's not much you can do about them, that door has been opened. There are expats who have accepted the responsibilities of living here and they deserve to be part of the community. For the people who come here on a tourist visa and don't pay tax and just want to suck what they can out of it, I'm sorry, no sympathy. If they want to contribute something worthwhile, great, but I just planted a tree, woohoo! Or, I helped Wayan put his son through kindergarten, give me a break.

Even-handed as always, Helmi turns the spray in the direction of his countrymen, and the breakdown of *adat*:

> In Indonesia it's relatively easy to get a law passed, but you need the political will to implement it ... Effectively, this is a one-industry island and it happens to be an industry that demands you adapt your lifestyle to it. You have to learn English, you have to understand how the tourists think ... and none of these are bad things, but it is more intrusive to your life and culture than going off to work in a factory.

Another forthright Bali commentator reinforces Helmi's view about the lack of political will. 'We have a regional, provincial, spatial plan to try to conserve rice fields and manage Bali as an organic island,' says I Made Suanatha, of the Wisnu Foundation, 'but it's not enforced ... the system is not strong enough to make people not corrupt it. We have a lot of regulations but very little compliance.'

Everyone is to blame: the national government in Jakarta for creating a culture of corruption and facilitating land grabs; the provincial government in Denpasar for failing to create sensible development checks and balances; the *banjar*s for looking after themselves at the expense of their culture; the rice farmers for seeing dollar signs instead of a future of penury; and the tourists and expats for coming. It's refreshing, therefore, when the bandy-legged little man kneading his elbow into your buggered back advises you to roll over and listen to his heartfelt defence of the common man.

Ketut Putrawan says:

> I thought of Bali every day of the twenty-five years I lived in Australia, but it wasn't always good things. There is much that is wrong with the attitudes of the Balinese, and only those who leave and learn about other places really move ahead. Balinese are not taught how to think at school. They are very conscious of status symbols and keeping up with the neighbours, and they are prepared to lose everything to do so.
>
> For example, fifty years ago when I was a child, if there was a death in the family, the body was wrapped in pandanus leaf and buried, and there would be a mass cremation every five to ten years. Then some wealthy Balinese started doing individual cremations and everyone followed. Now it is the norm and can cost as much as 80 million rupiah [$8000] when a middle-range public servant earns only 3 million rupiah [$300] a month. Many people are selling their land to pay for cremations, or putting themselves in debt for life. The do-gooders all say how terrible it is that Balinese families are selling their rice fields to expats to build their villas on, but these are the facts. Please listen.
>
> An *are* [100 square metres] of rice field will return about 2.4 million rupiah [$240] a year. If the land was leased for development it would fetch about 150 million rupiah [$15,000] which should return interest of about $750 per year. That's an income of more than $60 a month as opposed to $20 from the rice crop. But in addition, the leasehold will provide at least three jobs for the family (driver, maid, cook) at $50 a month for each. That's a total income of more than $200 a month as opposed to $20 for tilling the field. That's why my people are selling their rice fields to your people.

Chapter 21 Tipping Point

For the past couple of years, while doing the research for this book, I have based myself at a friend's villa in Pererenan, which adjoins Canggu in the heart of 'Villa World'. This is the land of the affordable villa—not the luxury cliff-top retreat on the Bukit, or the trendy glass-and-concrete hideaway in downtown Seminyak. There are half a dozen restaurants within walking distance and I can ride a pushbike down to one of three good surf breaks inside five minutes. It's not quite old Bali, as we knew and loved it, but it's mellow enough, and certainly a million miles removed from the nightmares of Villa World that seem to attract Australian media attention on a regular basis.

In January 2013, a major feature in *The Australian*'s *Weekend Magazine* reported:

> On the surface, the foreign enclave of Canggu offers a tropical idyll with backyard barbies and leisurely chats that until recently conjured up images of carefree 1950s Australian suburbia—minus the chores. But Canggu has become, in the past year, the focus of violent crime against increasing numbers of foreign residents who … live in grand villas that are slowly engulfing what was once a sleepy coastal strip of rice paddies and coconut groves. The expats came to Bali looking for paradise on a budget. But the realities of life in the developing world have quickly caught up with them. With each passing month this lush and easygoing tropical paradise risks losing something of its allure, even as the price tags for its outsized western-style homes continue to rise.

When I read this I'd just come back from a busy but enjoyable stay in Canggu. I wondered if we were talking about the same Canggu. The article went on to describe nightmare ordeals of armed home invasions, assaults and brutal stabbings and, most disturbing of all, the mysterious death of nightclub worker Denni North, an attractive thirty-three-year-old Queenslander who had been found dead beside the pool of her Canggu villa, and the brutal murder of thirty-four-year-old Sydney woman Heidi Murphy at her Canggu villa in 2008. 'Stabbed 37 times by an Indonesian man, the fashion designer had reportedly been asleep when the killer tried to steal the laptop next to her bed,' the writer noted. 'Murphy, who had no security guards, had said she felt safe in the isolated villa set among rice fields.'

Bali: Heaven and Hell

'In Canggu,' the report continued, 'twenty-four-hour security guards are the norm.' In the case of my friend's villa, this is almost true, but the shifts are based more on an obligation to employ the patron family than a response to a perceived threat. On the rare occasions I've come home late the security guards have been sound asleep in front of a blaring television. Is there a crime wave, and are the Javanese itinerant workers to blame? In the forty years that I've been coming to Bali, anything bad that has happened has been the fault of the Javanese, just as when I lived on the Atlantic coast border of France and Spain, any pollution in the water or trash on the beach was always said to have drifted north from Spain.

The article continued:

> Michael Risakotta, former police chief for the Kuta Utara district, which includes Canggu, says that unbridled development has lured Javanese organised crime syndicates to the area ... Admitting the crime wave is defeating police, Risakotta says construction workers who are required to provide ID to police typically give false identities, outwitting the severely under-resourced system. Foreigners are helping thieves by leaving houses unlocked, he adds, a practice harking back to the relaxed island paradise it once was.

Rio Helmi, who has spent time with the work gangs, finds this a bit rough on the Javanese:

> They work their butts off and maybe one in fifty is a thief. They come here for three months, go home for a few days and come back for the same period again. They make less than $10 a day and they live in shanties. The workers who stick with it, usually the older ones with families, can save about 4.5 million rupiah [$450] over three months, and that can go a good way. Then you have the more permanent work force who basically live here but go back to Java once or twice a year, usually with all their luggage on a motorcycle. They get a week off and it takes them two days to get to Yogya. And some of them get killed on the way. They don't pay tax but most are under the tax threshold anyway, and they do the work that the Balinese will not do. Who is going to tell me that these people don't contribute to the economy?

Chapter 21 Tipping Point

Helmi is one of a small number of commentators and academics who are frequently called upon to debate the prospects for Bali's future, usually for the benefit of groups of Westerners. Although Westerners have been claiming the ruination of Bali for the best part of a century, there is considerably more urgency about it now, since many opinion makers have decided that Bali has reached a 'tipping point'. Opinions vary as to what the tipping point actually is, but there is common consensus that Bali will know when it has passed because people will stop coming, and the economy will fall into a huge hole and people will have to revert to growing their own food and barter between villages, which sounds rather idyllic, and vaguely reminiscent of when we came in.

In the meantime, the Balinese worry about the loss of *adat* and their cultural identity while buying SUVs with their rice-field money, and *bules* worry about home invasion and the fact that it can take an hour to drive from Canggu to Seminyak, and all of this goes on while the island is being buried in discarded plastic, and, most importantly of all, is running out of water.

According to a report by the Japan International Cooperation Agency (JICA), Bali will face a major water crisis from 2015, with most of the blame resting on the tourism industry. According to JICA, one room in a star-rated hotel consumes 3300 litres of water per day whereas the average person in Denpasar consumes only 220 litres. (Some sources say a Balinese family will use less than 200 litres a day.) Bali's water resources are not coping with this kind of demand, and the problem is exacerbated by the significance of water in Balinese Hindu culture.

Bali's sophisticated communal irrigation system, known as *subak*, involves water flowing from channel to field and back to channel among multiple farms, but *subak* is much more than an agricultural tool. It is the backbone of religion and culture in Bali, and disruption of the system is tantamount to disruption of the culture. *Subak* has been virtually destroyed in South Bali by the demands of the tourism industry and the ongoing villa-land grab, and a similar course seems likely in the north as land is claimed for Bali's second airport.

Most of the hotel water comes from artesian wells and bores, but these are so over-taxed that they are now beginning to leach saltwater, causing the quality of water in South Bali to have degraded radically in recent years. Compounding the problem, mountain spring water that flowed in and out of rice fields as part of the *subak* system is now being sold to private companies to put into plastic bottles for tourists to buy.

Bali: Heaven and Hell

According to some experts, Bali's water deficit could be as high as 27,000 gigalitres in 2015. The power grid is also a problem, with 1000 megawatts of local power needed by 2018 to keep the lights on and the beer cold. Bali currently receives 700 megawatts via marine cable from Java and other islands, and self-generation programs are years behind schedule.

So yes, it's a 'dysfunctional urban mess', as one former expat describes it.

> The mess is so bad that it's almost beyond fixing, and the *banjar*s just don't care. When they started talking about building a peripheral road around Bali, the brahmans [high caste] said no, it couldn't be done because it would be above their heads. So someone suggested a tunnel, and they said no, because then all the bad spirits would come up out of the ground. How can you combine that thinking with life in the twenty-first century? At the end of the day, I don't think it's the tourists or the expats who will kill Bali—it's the Indonesians.

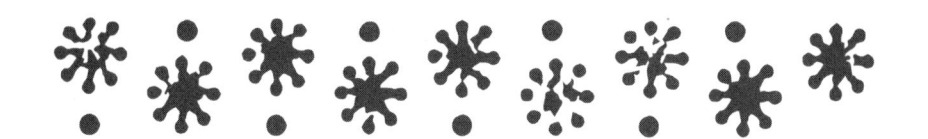

Chapter 22 *Kertha Yuga*: Hope

Some of the footage is almost hard to believe with the show's cameras capturing serious accidents and injuries as they happen. It's edge-of-the-seat real-life drama.

    Dan Meenan, Channel Seven's Head of Factual Programming

Bali brings out the best and the worst of Aussies abroad, from honeymooners to death-row prisoners to long-term expats. Like the island itself, this series offers something for everyone.

    John McAvoy, Managing Director, Eye-works Australia

Bali bashing is not a new sport for the Australian media. It was pioneered by George Negus and *60 Minutes* about thirty years ago when it suddenly occurred to the people whose lives are driven by the ratings chase that huge numbers of young Australians were flocking to the island in search of cheap thrills, and that their parents would be glued to their television sets for the duration of a shock-and-horror exposé of this evil place.

Negus used a series of motorbike accidents involving Australians as a platform for a scathing attack on the allegedly cavalier attitude of Balinese authorities towards issues of health and safety. It was a fairly one-sided report, with little to say about the increasingly appalling behaviour of many of the Australian tourists, whose rude, crude, drunken and disrespectful antics were not only putting themselves at risk, but were beginning to trouble the Kutarese. There were a few angry rumbles about the biased coverage from Suharto's tourism department, but the more entrepreneurial Balinese turned their revenge to financial advantage, creating a bestselling T-shirt that bore the legend, FUCK GEORGE NEGUS.

Bali: Heaven and Hell

The Bali exposé has been a hardy perennial of Australian television ever since, particularly in the wake of the Bali bombings, the Bali Nine and Schapelle Corby. The Nine Network's 2013 effort, a one-hour documentary called *The Dark Side of Paradise*, hung its promotion around the catchy tagline, 'An Australian dies in Bali every nine days'. This was based on figures from the Australian Department of Foreign Affairs for 2011–12 showing that thirty-nine Australians had died in Bali that year. This was perhaps shocking, but not as shocking as Thailand, where an Australian dies every three days, or the Philippines, where an Australian dies every five days, or Greece, every six days, or Vietnam, every seven days, or even the United States, also every seven days. Bali, which attracts close to a million Australian tourists a year, was only in sixth place on the deaths register, prompting this writer to wonder if the Nine Network was planning a series that might include other potentially lethal tourist destinations. *The Dark Side of Disneyland*, perhaps?

You could argue that Australian travellers, young and old, should be made aware that almost 1000 Australians die abroad each year, a significant minority of them in circumstances that might have been prevented. Ageing sex tourists in Thailand and the Philippines, for example, should be warned that alcohol, Viagra and hyperactivity can be a lethal combination. Young Aussie backpackers everywhere should be warned that riding a motorbike without a helmet is just plain stupid.

When it comes to Bali's specific life-threatening dangers, as outlined on the program—bad drugs, gangland bashings and black witchcraft—while much more interesting for a TV crew on a mission to shock, these are in fact minuscule contributing factors compared with traffic accidents, natural causes and existing conditions. And in Bali traffic-accident deaths are in decline while natural causes and existing conditions are growing. There is a simple explanation for this, although you won't find it in programs like *Dark Side of Paradise*. Bali's pathetic road system is in gridlock for most of every day: it's getting more and more difficult to get up enough speed to kill yourself. At the same time, ageing baby boomers are living longer and choosing to see out their golden years in Bali, where the air is warm and the beer is cheap. The term 'bucket list' was never more appropriate.

Channel Seven's 2014 Bali-bash series, *What Really Happens in Bali* had so much hype surrounding it that it provoked a hostile reaction from within Bali months ahead of its screening. The *Balidiscovery.com* expat news

Chapter 22 *Kertha Yuga*: Hope

website was particularly scathing in a home-page editorial calling for Seven to give Bali 'a fair go':

> The Balinese have a decades-long relationship with Australia's Channel Seven coverage of their island, having come to expect the very worst in biased Indonesian-bashing. What rubbish Channel Seven can't dig up against Bali, they manufacture or attempt to purchase from convicted felons as recently witnessed in the case of Schapelle Corby. Channel Seven does a terrible injustice to both Bali and to its many Australian viewers by continuing to adopt a sensational and highly biased approach to its coverage of Bali. If there is a 'real story' about Bali to be told you won't hear it on Channel Seven.

The website concluded its editorial by calling on the Seven management to tell the stories of 'Australians living relatively sedate and normal lives, making meaningful contributions to their adopted island home'. While that was unlikely to fit the remit of a commercial television network, there are in fact dozens of wonderfully positive stories to tell about expats—not just Australians but from all over the world—who are, in Rio Helmi's words, 'accepting the responsibility of living here'. Here are just a few.

Sydney dog groomer Jodie O'Shea died soon after landing in Perth on the first medivac flight in the wake of the 2002 bombings. It took days for the news to filter back to Bali and Alison Chester, who had nursed her through that dreadful long day of waiting for help at Sanglah Hospital. The delay made the news devastating for Alison, who was clinging to the belief that no news might have been good news, that miraculously this brave young girl had survived. From the tears and emotional turmoil of the days that followed, Alison can only remember one thing. She could not, would not, let Jodie's spirit die.

Drawn together in sadness and comfort, the bombing volunteers formed a loose network and support system for each other, and a broader network of friends and acquaintances started sending money to them to pass on to the most needy. Alison didn't know what to do with it until she received a phone call from a friend.

> She said there was a kid who needed a steel pin put in his leg.
> He was from an orphanage and had no money. The orphanage

had been affected by all the attention going to the bombing victims and they weren't getting their normal donations. So I paid for the operation with the money and we started helping that orphanage on a regular basis. That's when I found out about what goes on in most Bali orphanages, and it shocked me into action.

More than half of the children in the orphanage in Denpasar had been mentally and physically abused. Further research showed that of about seventy orphanages in Bali with as many as 5000 children in their guardianship, only half a dozen were performing their duty of care, the rest existing to get paltry government hand-outs—1 million rupiah ($100) per child per year—and to plunder donated funds.

In 2010 the *Bali Advertiser* newspaper reported:

> Many [orphanages] solicit donations in cash or kind from sympathetic tourists and expats which go directly into the pockets of the owners or to benefit their families. Some orphanages use the children as slave labour, forcing them to work on construction sites and beg in the street instead of sending them to school. Most of the orphanages here operate under religious banners; sadly, even a clerical collar is no guarantee that donations will not be misappropriated.

As soon as she realised the extent of the problem, Alison Chester knew what she had to do in Jodie O'Shea's name. She would set up an orphanage to take genuine care of needy children. There was a small problem. She had no real idea what to do first. She did not have a registered charity that could receive donations; she already had rescued twenty malnourished children from the island of Sumba and nowhere to put them. She phoned Richard Flax, the Bali expats' 'Mr Fix-it'. Flax had his own charitable foundation and he had extensive business contacts in Sumba. He immediately agreed to help Alison set up her Care For Kids Bali Foundation, and Alison started canvassing her business clients for start-up funds while husband Yanto looked for a building to rent to house the Jodie O'Shea Orphanage.

After long hard years of battling bureaucracy and scrabbling for cash, Alison Chester clearly takes great delight in the orphanage in Jadi Pesona estate, between Denpasar and Benoa, where needy kids play happily between the organic garden and the art and music studios while we chat in the mess

Chapter 22 *Kertha Yuga*: Hope

hall. It seems a happy place, despite the sadness in the lives of so many of its young residents.

The Jodie O'Shea receives no government funding—Alison did not want to be exposed to the corruption in that system—and is totally reliant on donations, which ebb and flow depending on media exposure. The day I interviewed her there was a constant stream of visiting tourists, the result of a recent television segment—European, not Australian.

While the vast majority of the sixty-eight children at Jodie O'Shea are not technically orphans, they all have stories of horrific domestic situations, abject poverty or abuse. A little girl who came to Alison for a cuddle while we talked had seen her father slit her mother's throat with a machete, then drink a bottle of poison in front of her. A spirited little boy called Agus had the saddest story of all. When his parents saw that his fingers had been jammed in a car door while in the care of neighbours, they apparently took this as evidence of habitual abuse, and went to the house and killed the entire family. In 2013 they were awaiting death sentences. Against all the advice of friends, Alison went to death row at Kerobokan prison to tell the parents that Agus was safe. The meeting drained her for weeks.

Care For Kids has its hands full running the Jodie O'Shea, but somehow Alison and Yanto also found time to join other NGOs in the relief work in Yogyakarta after a 2006 earthquake devastated some of the poorest villages in Java. Care For Kids has now been instrumental in building or rebuilding some sixty kindergartens across Java.

Alison says:

> At one point I thought I'd gone too far because I was so focused on getting money for Java and the orphanage was being a little neglected. But I couldn't walk away, and every time I go back and the teachers come running out and start hugging me ... How can you stop when you're giving a kid a better chance in life?

John Fawcett, now in his eighties, had to be dragged, kicking and screaming, onto the plane for Bali the first time in 1972. He was a high-flying Perth academic who had seen places like Colombo and Bombay on ocean voyages to Europe. Bali would be the same, he figured—dirty and smelly. But his wife, Sue, also an academic, had taken a group of gifted students there for a holiday and fallen in love with the island.

He recalls:

It was a household of three women and me, and I didn't always get my own way. I got off the plane in a huff and immediately started trying to find fault in everything. But that proved rather difficult because I love creativity, and I was lobbed in the middle of the most amazingly creative people I'd ever seen. In those days we would live in a cheap hotel ... We'd come up a couple of times a year and we eventually got a house in Jalan Mertasari that we shared with another family. Everything went great guns until 6 May 1981.

As a result of ongoing spinal problems, Fawcett went into hospital for an epidural. It was wrongly located and a powerful cocktail of drugs went straight into his bloodstream and to his brain. A healthy, energetic man in the prime of life, he suddenly found his body shutting down. Before the day was out he had been clinically dead twice. He was rushed to St Johns Hospital in Perth where he spent several weeks in intensive care, his life on the line. When he eventually stabilised, Fawcett was transferred to the Queen Elizabeth II Medical Centre to begin the long process of rehabilitation.

He says:

I'd lost my memory, had no coordination, my blood pressure was all over the place. It was a disaster of monumental proportions. I was forty-eight at the time and I was deputy director of Perth Technical College, I had everything going for me but it was all over. I spent two years and ten months in rehab, where the specialists took a great deal of interest in me because they likened my case to an alcoholic who wipes his brain out with drink. They believed that both could recover, so they worked very hard on me to prove that this was the case.

Fawcett had no memory of his wife, Sue, but they sat together day after day and reconstructed their history. But he didn't see his children for fear that it would confuse him, and he was not aware that his doctors were telling Sue that they did not believe he would recover. 'I'm no pushover,' Fawcett says with a wink. 'I always knew I would recover.'

And he did, although the marriage did not. Still heavily medicated but having regained much of his coordination, in 1983 Fawcett told his doctors he

Chapter 22 *Kertha Yuga*: Hope

was going to Bali to begin the next phase of his recovery. Sue did not want to give up her career, so he went back to the house on Mertasari alone.

Fawcett's damages case had been settled out of court for a large sum of money, so he had no real need to work, but through his knowledge and interest in Chinese ceramics, he became friendly with the governor of Bali, Ida Bagus Mantra.

> He was a lovely man and we would meet for breakfast a couple of times a week and talk for hours. Through him I was able to extend my visas and eventually become a permanent resident, but early in the piece, he said to me, 'You know, John, you can't stay here and do nothing. It's not healthy for you and it's certainly not helping Bali. You need to take on a project.'

The governor suggested Fawcett get involved with some form of medical technology that might help alleviate Bali's abundant health problems. Cleft lip and palate, for example, was a huge issue in the villages. Fawcett contacted Interplast, an American NGO that specialised in providing free plastic surgery in Third World countries, and discovered that they had recently established an Australian base, mostly funded by Rotary, to service the Asia Pacific. Through Interplast, Fawcett was able to have Bali's first plastic surgeon trained in Australia, and in 1989 he began a cleft-lip-and-palate program throughout the island.

On his many visits to remote villages, Fawcett had begun to notice the overwhelming incidence of blindness. When he looked into it, he discovered that many of the cases were cataract blindness, treatable by a simple operation that could be performed in the field in about fifteen minutes, provided the equipment and the surgeons were available. Now he really had a mission in life. He went to India to see eye-treatment camps in remote locations, then he went back to Rotary and put his cards on the table. 'I told them, why don't you bastards do something useful for once!'

An honorary Rotarian and a Paul Harris Fellow (the highest award the organisation has), Fawcett knows only too well how much his programs owe to Rotary, but he is a self-confessed 'stirrer' and he laughs long and hard at the memory of his cheekiness. Rotary came good with the funding and the Bali Eye cataract program began in 1991. A bus was converted into a mobile surgery and theatre and flown up from Perth by the Australian Air

Force. Within four years the program had successfully treated more than 4000 people.

The key to the field program was a new incision technique that replaced the more complex and potentially dangerous operations that were being used in Indonesia. According to Fawcett, 65 per cent of all blindness in Bali is curable cataract, and with blindness affecting 1.7 per cent of the population, and Bali's population having grown from 2 million to 3 million since the Bali Eye program began, there is not a moment to lose.

While Bali Eye's field team heads out into the villages of Bali or other parts of the Eastern Archipelago, screening about 800 people a day and treating cataracts as they find them in the back of the bus on that same day, John Fawcett is more likely to be sitting in the garden of his home and the offices of the John Fawcett Foundation in Sanur, selling social-responsibility packages to the big corporations, such as tourist hotels. (In 2013, the luxury Aman Group became one of Bali Eye's biggest supporters.) But there is still nothing he enjoys more than watching the miracle of sight restored. He says:

> How many ways can you change someone's life forever, and make them a friend forever, in twenty minutes in complete safety at low cost? It's a strange way to look at it, but that is what is so attractive to people who want to help us. It's not exactly the way I see it, but there's no denying it's been a rich experience for me ... I've never regretted a single day of being in Bali.

Fawcett, however, is not pleased with every aspect of modern Bali. In fact, he feels saddened by much of what the expats have brought to the island. He says:

> I have a view about expats and it's this: we're not Balinese and we never can be. We're just fooling ourselves if we think we can. The best we can be is good guests. That idea is not now being followed, and I think that's a big mistake for Bali and its culture. I feel we've disturbed the economic balance here. Land prices now are nonsense and it's such a temptation for the Balinese to sell their land for things like cars. They lose their heritage, and I find that very disturbing.
>
> Expats have to realise that their presence here can be valuable, and I think this is something the Western governments should be looking at. Rather than just giving aid money, they could provide

Chapter 22 *Kertha Yuga*: Hope

consultants in areas where expertise is needed, older people who are acclaimed in their fields. Yes, I'm talking about utilising grey power to make Bali a better place, and I'm the living proof that it can be done.

Matt George is pacing up and down in his shabby little office in a Kuta back street, pointing out the broken windows and peeling paint, not with anger but with pride and passion. These are his badges of honour. After his years of up-and-down surf stardom and flirtations with Hollywood, he is playing out the role of his life. It is 1965 and he is Guy Hamilton, the Mel Gibson character in the film, *The Year of Living Dangerously*.

Matt George, originally from California, is bald, brash and quite frightening when in full flight. Some people find his overblown theatrics difficult to handle, but he makes you pay attention, and since he realised that helping people in Indonesia was his calling, he has used the tactic to good effect.

Matt and his brother, Sam, arrived in Bali chasing surf in 1984. He says:

> We were ten years late, we knew that, we weren't with Hillary and Tensing Norgay, but we could still summit Everest. It was still satisfying, it was a culture of smiles, easy to integrate. I became a regular, every year or two. The most powerful impression I carried with me, and more than anything, kept bringing me back, was the smell. The scent of Bali really got inside me … Every time I came here was like getting a new tattoo. The experience stayed with you. I think Bali makes you love yourself. People with low self-esteem shouldn't go to a shrink, they should go to Bali.

George, who grew up on military bases, made a name for himself as a surfer, writer and photographer before making a surf-themed Hollywood movie, *In God's Hands*, that tanked. Somewhat burned by the experience, he returned to his military roots, training as a Navy Seal and joining various quasi-military organisations, but by 2004, he was in a bad place. He says:

> My life was a mess. I was in San Francisco, my girlfriend had left me and I'd fallen into very bad behaviour … [one] December morning I heard the news [of the devastating Asian

tsunami]. A thought came to me in a rush. The answer to the question of my life was Indonesia, always had been. I had to get back. I was medically certified and I'd already done all kinds of relief work. I was on a plane within twenty-four hours.

Although the effects of the Boxing Day tsunami were felt across a broad section of South-East Asia, for surfers whose Indonesian experience had grown out of Bali to encompass many remote parts of the archipelago, the devastation of the island groups off the west coast of Sumatra was intensely personal. These were villages they knew. George had quickly arranged a commission from *Surfer Magazine* to cover the story from a surfer's perspective, but his real agenda was completely different. 'By the time I arrived, I'd found my real calling. Nothing was being done right, so I said fuck it, I'll do it myself.'

There were many threads to the Sumatran relief efforts, and not everyone involved shares George's view, but no one can dispute the fact that he and Bill Sharp, from the surf-wear giant Billabong, did take matters into their own hands, chartering a boat in Padang and filling it with supplies and volunteers, reaching remote island communities while some aid organisations were still back in port making plans.

> Bill raised the initial money from Billabong and we raced around, filled the boat with the stuff we knew people would really need. We had live goats and chickens and seed fruit that could be replanted. I got a bunch of medical students to come with us and we were out of there in a matter of hours. It was a military procedure, like a Special Forces cadre, and we went out there and got the fucking job done.

George named his team Last Mile Operations, because they were prepared to go the last mile. With Billabong funding, they ran donated supplies to the islands for nine months, before George took Last Mile to Pakistan for relief work, then on to New Orleans in the wake of Hurricane Katrina. He came back to Indonesia after the Java earthquakes and Last Mile went to work again. Exhausted and almost broke, he was offered a relaxing break, a yacht trip from Langkawi in Malaysia to New Zealand. He recalls:

> When we reached Bali at dawn my heart just skipped a beat, because I'd forgotten about this place. I stood on the bow and

Chapter 22 *Kertha Yuga*: Hope

watched it grow on the horizon as we approached Benoa Harbour, and when I stepped off that boat, I knew I wasn't going to New Zealand. I wasn't going to leave this island ever again.

That was in 2009. George now edits *Surf Time* magazine in Kuta, teaches creative writing and keeps Last Mile Operations permanently on standby. He lives in a rented house on the Bukit and surfs there frequently. He says he loves living in Bali but worries that the 'tide of avarice' that was halted by the bombings has begun to rise again, fuelled by the influx of tourists and expats, himself included.

> I fear that tide is unstoppable because of the expats. Bali's modern economy was built on our surfboards because we've all been evangelists for it, so we all have to accept some responsibility. I've seen places wiped clean by the gods, and every day I pray that doesn't happen here.

George believes that only money can solve Bali's pollution problem, either through fines for littering or cash rewards for recycling. He cites an example of how this can work: 'I'm proud to say that the beach at Padang Padang is spotless because I pay for it. I give the head woman there a million rupiah ($100) a month and I tell her that as long as I see a clean beach every time I walk on it, she will get that money.'

Half a dozen years ago, veteran Noosa (Queensland) waiter Johnny Blundstone felt the urge to completely change his lifestyle. After decades spent front of house in some of the best establishments in town, he was ready for new challenges.

One day, with wife Cath and young son Huey, he trucked off to the Outback for as long as it might take for a new life plan to emerge. Under the stars at Kakadu one night, the family found themselves sharing a campfire with Norm and Linda vant Hoff, Australians of Russian and Dutch extraction who had started a small resort, based on sustainable living, in the wet mountain jungle of central Bali. If the Blundstones were looking for a radical lifestyle change, said Norm, here was one that might be of interest.

They flew over for a look, spent a month travelling around without finding anything terribly inspiring, then headed back up to Norm and Linda's Sarinbuana Lodge, in the shadow of Mount Batukaru, to pack their bags and head home. Over a final meal, Johnny told Norm that while he immensely admired what he and Linda were doing at Sarinbuana, it had now been done. 'But that's not the point,' Norm responded. 'The more people running sustainable business on this mountain, the better it will be for all of us.'

Mini, the lodge's smiling chef, said that she and her husband, Agung, had a large plot of family land down the valley just a few kilometres away, if Johnny and Cath were interested. Even as he tells this story, Johnny acknowledges with a whimsical grin that this might have been a scam of Nigerian proportions, but his outlook on life has always been serendipitous, and they shook hands on a deal that evening.

In 2010 they opened for business with a restaurant, a small office and four one- and two-bedroom cottages scattered along the rice terraces, with pristine spring water streaming under the entire property to feed the land and grow the crops to feed the guests. The biggest single investment in this resort was not an infinity pool or home theatre in every room, but a Pelton wheel hydro-electric generator to enable the Blundstones to power most of the resort from the adjacent waterfall. Bali Eco Stay became the first resort in Bali to generate its own power, and by mid-2015, the Blundstones were only a couple of vegetables and one storage solar panel away from being totally 'off the grid'.

My wife and I visited Bali Eco Stay for the first time in 2011 and found the Blundstones happily ensconced in paradise. Looking out over the hill station vista from our 'Rice Water' bungalow, my first question was, couldn't they have come up with a more romantic name for the resort? 'Google-friendly,' said Johnny. It's a long way up a very rough road to the resort, and there is no passing trade. People sympathetic to the aims of eco-tourism seek them out online, and there are thankfully enough of them for Bali Eco Stay to have achieved an average 60 per cent occupancy after just a couple of years.

When the rains tumbled down soon after our arrival, we took the opportunity to spend a productive, if indulgent, afternoon in Mini's Kupe Kupe Restaurant (yes, they stole her from Sarinbuana with Norm's blessing), which offers sensational organic food from the property's 'food forest', incorporating coconut, mangosteen, cacao and other local exotics, and Cath's permaculture garden, with sweet potato, beans, tomato, eggplant, corn, lettuce, ginger, chilli, papaya, bananas, durian and organic red and white rice. More than 70 per cent of their food is homegrown, and is cooked in their

Chapter 22 *Kertha Yuga*: Hope

own unrefined coconut oil. Local farmers supply chicken, duck and eggs, while the resort's water garden will soon supply several species of freshwater fish. Mini's food was superb—in two days we never had a dish we didn't devour, with special mentions going to the black rice pudding, and pear and parmesan salad.

The water supply for the resort is from an underground spring twice as pure as Bali bottled water. The spring comes above ground near the edge of the property and creates a natural swimming pool, below which the waterfall provides the power. There is no television, and the only music is the gurgling of the water below and the distant sounds of *gamelan* music from nearby villages. Spartan? Well, a little, until you slow your metabolism to the pace of your surroundings and realise you have everything you need.

One of the guiding principles of eco-tourism is interaction with local communities, and the Blundstones have already introduced permaculture to surrounding villages, set up a free lending library and offer village kids English lessons. Resort guide Alit took us on a fascinating two-hour hike through the rice fields and surrounding food forests, popping out in tiny villages where he proudly pointed out initiatives such as recycling stations, all introduced since the opening of the resort.

I'm a bit of a cynic when it comes to tourism interfering with traditional ways, but in the land of the plastic bag, projects like Bali Eco Stay are leading people back to their own cultures while offering them new opportunities in ours. I applaud the energy and enthusiasm of the Blundstones and so many others who are attempting to reverse the trend, to offer sustainable regionalism as an alternative to destructive globalism.

It's the kind of game-changer Bali needs, and it needs it now.

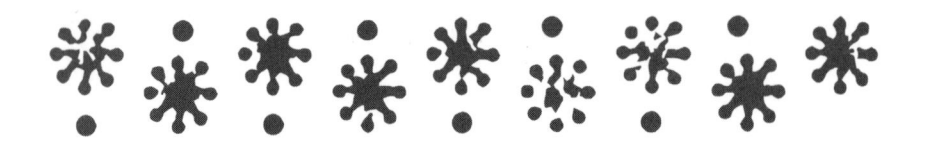

Chapter 23 Be Here Now

It should be clear by now that the oft-repeated question 'Can Balinese culture survive the impact of tourism?' is not a relevant one. Tourism is not an external force striking Bali from outside, like a missile hitting a target, but it is a process transforming Balinese society from inside.

Michel Picard

It's my last day in Bali. Last days are always hectic, but this one more so than many others because I am trying to filter the information I have gathered for this book, from observations, research and more than sixty interviews. I probably haven't got time to come back again before the deadline for my manuscript, so I need to have the book structured in my head so that I can pick up any last-minute information before I leave that might help plug the gaps later. Of course, the internet is a wonderful tool for connecting you with all kinds of random information, but it is always that minor detail that means so much that you can never find. It might be the wording of a road sign, it might be the colour of someone's hair, or the design of a tattoo. Inevitably, these are the things I find too late, usually scribbled in the margin of one of my many notebooks. 'Check!' it will advise. Today I must check my checks.

So these are the thoughts that fill my head as I wake at first light, as I always do in Bali, and quietly steal out of Umah Kembar, our friend Sue Cummings's villa in Pererenan, slip my surfboard into its rack on my motor scooter, and ride up the *gang* past the Wira family compound and onwards to the beach. Depending on tide and swell, I will ride to one or the other of my two favourite local surf spots, the river mouth left at the bottom of Jalan Pantai Pererenan, or Old Man's at Batu Bolong, right in front of the Tugu

Chapter 23 Be Here Now

Hotel. This morning it looks like an Old Man's day in the making, so I turn left out of the *gang* and ride through the rice fields, across the bridge at Echo Beach and up behind an extensive new hotel development that will eventually claim the cheap-and-cheerful beachfront cafes at Echo, then along the beach to Tugu and park behind the front *warung*.

There are already twenty bikes parked on the grass and even more surfers in the water, but the sets are regular, and I know I will get my quota of waves without too much trouble. This has been my Bali neighbourhood for a few years now, and I exchange good mornings with several of the regulars, most of whom perform some sort of unclear role at the Deus Ex Machina Temple of Enthusiasm just up the road from the beach. I also nod politely to the Brazilians, the Germans, the Russians and Japanese who have just learned to surf, and sadly, feel ready to tackle the forgiving waves of Old Man's.

Out in the line-up, my friend Monty snags a good one and tries to throw spray over me as he cuts across the wave's face. Steve 'Monty' Montell and wife Jennine left Noosa for Bali a handful of years ago to experiment with raising their boys as expats. The boys, both now in their teens, seem to be thriving on the free and easy lifestyle, but, in order to provide it, their parents confess that they have never worked harder. They have a small shop, Bomba, in Seminyak, and manufacture tee shirts and other gift lines. Monty does some hosting gigs at the Deus Temple, Jennine teaches expat ladies aquarobics, and they both manage villa rentals for absentee landlords, one of them Dare Jennings, the Mambo founder who has in recent years turned his obsession with motorbikes and surfboards into an intriguing lifestyle concept with Deus.

Jennine says:

To be honest, we don't know how long we'll last up here. After having spent a lot of pressure years working in the airlines as cabin crew, we didn't really want to work our arses off in Bali, but we are. But that's not the biggest problem. The biggest problem—and it's one I think about often—is that if one of the boys gets caught experimenting with drugs, doing what we did, what a lot of kids do, then he could be in prison for twenty years or even executed, or we could face financial ruin to buy him out of trouble. I can't speak for all expats, but that's the greatest fear the families that we know have.

Bali: Heaven and Hell

At Old Man's, Monty is back in the line-up, telling lies about how good his wave was. We share a few more and then repair to the *warung* for a good cup of coffee. The expats come and go, exchanging pleasantries and jokes, occasionally even a little malicious gossip, but mostly there's a good feel out here in the world of villas that Made Wijaya has labelled 'Expatria'. It's not the Bali we once knew, but it has its moments, and it makes a sensible base away from the traffic snarls and the worst of the pollution. I never ride my scooter beyond the immediate neighbourhood, but I can walk along the beach to Seminyak in under an hour, and catch a cab back in the relative calm of the evening.

I ride back up the road to Deus, where I have a meeting with Arly, a young Javanese designer whose work on some animation cells I had admired, and has been loaned to me by Deus Indonesia boss Dustin Humphrey to come up with a tee shirt design for an upcoming event. I meet Humphrey in the bike lot and we agree that there is time for a second coffee in the Temple's restaurant and bar before the day's work officially begins. In Bali there is always time.

Humphrey, a photographer and filmmaker from California with some serious credits in the surf world, met Dare Jennings on a flight just when he was getting a little tired being a Bali-based photographer. Jennings told him about his concept for the Temple of Enthusiasm, Humphrey signed on, and now he presides over a wonderfully mad creative stew within the cluster of traditional Javanese *joglo*s and *gladak*s (buildings) that make up the Deus compound. While motorbikes are being customised and surfboards shaped out back, a new local band might be rehearsing, a photoshoot might be taking place in the studio, a new show might be being hung in the art gallery and an exquisite new addition to the restaurant's Thai menu might be taking shape in the kitchen. And upfront on the shop floor the odd tee shirt will be sold to help pay for it all.

Sitting in a field that once fed many families, the Deus Temple might seem like the last word in expat indulgence, but in fact it is building a bridge between the expat and local communities, with exchanges of information on creative projects taking place every day.

Back at Umah Kembar in the afternoon, I go over Arly's design roughs, email him my choices and think about packing a bag. Then I take my notepads and sit by the pool with a glass of Plaga sauvignon blanc (the local wine blended from Margaret River grapes that is the answer to the Bali

Chapter 23 Be Here Now

expat's prayers—a good quaffing wine at an affordable price) and reflect on how I'm going to summarise my feelings about this place and finish on a note that trivialises neither the very real fears that people have for Bali's future nor its enduring appeal that continues to enchant new visitors.

By the time the Plaga has gone and the sun has dropped behind the wall of the Spanish villa next door, I have a vague notion that the stories of two of Bali's 'international children', pioneer expat kids who have grown up immersed in the good, the bad and the ugly aspects of Bali, sum up my feelings much better than some kind of highly subjective ticking of the boxes on a Bali report card.

Lorca Lueras was just four years old when his father, the journalist and photographer Leonard Lueras, brought him and his sister to live in Bali for a year while he produced a book called *Bali: The Ultimate Island*. 'I came through customs with a kid on each shoulder,' Leonard recalls. 'Came for a year and now it's been thirty. It was great for me because I'd just become a single parent and here I had a lot of friends and an incredible support system. But there were some tough times, too, for me and the kids.'

Lorca's earliest memories of life in Bali are of temple ceremonies and dances. He says: 'I was so little and I didn't get the cultural significance of any of it, but I loved the costumes and the spectacle. Like, when you're four years old and you're sitting right there on the floor while guys are ramming *kris* swords into their chests, it's kind of exciting.'

Later Leonard had a house built on a huge plot of shared land at Mertasari, and with plenty of room for a baseball diamond, he and Lorca shared their American heritage. Lorca says: 'Baseball was my first sporting love. We used to pitch balls a lot, and I got into the cards, the culture, the whole deal. But no one played it here, not even when I went to the Bali International School. I was really bummed, but then surfing came along.'

Leonard's pal, Tim Watts, taught Lorca to surf, pushing him into waves at Kuta Halfway, then Lorca graduated to the Sanur reefs, where he became one of the better surfers before heading back to the United States to attend college in San Diego, where he completed a degree in communications. Born in Hawaii, educated in Bali and California, it was anyone's guess where Lorca might end up, but for him there was never any real choice. 'I had a great life in San Diego—good friends, good lifestyle, living right at the beach—but I knew, almost from the start, that I would have to come back to Bali. It's what I know, it's what I love.'

Bali: Heaven and Hell

Back in Bali, Lorca, now in his early thirties, has carved out a name for himself in the surf media, producing videos and a magazine called *Lines*, as well as working on book projects with his father. But his passion is to use his communication skills to help solve Bali's many problems, and whether it's sustainability, pollution or financial management, the solutions start in the schoolyard. Lorca says:

> We're using our surf brand to do a lot of green programs with schools, trying to educate them about litter, but it's a difficult problem because a lot of the pollution comes from upriver towns where they don't have the same surf orientation as the beach communities. But you know, slowly, slowly, we're making some progress.
>
> Bali today? Traffic and pollution, but I love the waves and the lifestyle, so you have to take the bad with the good. But you don't have to accept the bad stuff. You can help make changes.

Many of Bali's international children have had to deal with issues of identity, none more so than Ketut Luca de Coney, who was ten before he realised he wasn't Balinese, and it nearly broke his heart. Today Luca is a likeable young man in his early twenties, self-possessed and at ease with the world. It wasn't always the case. When we spoke he had recently married his Slovenian girlfriend and their first child was on the way. 'I've created a family at a very young age,' he explains, 'maybe because I needed to.'

Luca was born in Bali in 1991 but he never knew his mother, an Italian painter named Marta Eloso, because she hanged herself when he was eighteen months old. He was taken in by a Balinese family and his new mother even breastfed him. Their tiny house was so crowded that the father slept outside.

Marta was evidently a troubled soul, pushed to suicide over the departure of Luca's father, a notorious rake, to resume a relationship with a previous girlfriend. John de Coney, once memorably described as 'a New Yorker with a karate mouth', was one of Bali's legendary characters, a one-time hairdresser to the stars who could turn his artistic talents to just about anything, including the design of beautiful houses, but he also had a self-destructive bent, and was a serial philanderer and a very ugly drunk. When de Coney died in 2001, blogger Made Wijaya noted that 'he left a tribe of gorgeous widows and spirited children'. Before cancer, the bottle or evil

Chapter 23 Be Here Now

spirits (depending on who you talk to) claimed him, de Coney had had four children by different partners, each of them a different nationality.

Luca went to a Balinese school with his Balinese brothers, and when he came home at 1 pm each day and went off with his mother to a *bule* house round the corner that she cleaned, he was only vaguely aware that the Western man who sat in a corner smoking kretek cigarettes and drinking beer had some kind of connection to him. Luca recalls:

> The two houses were in Legian, just a few minutes' walk between them, but I couldn't speak English, so when I was young I had virtually no communication with this guy, my father. And how could he be my father? He was a white guy. It was weird. I thought of him as more of a tourist.

Although he says he was never treated differently at school, Luca soon became aware that his skin was lighter. His mother was an enthusiastic coffee drinker, so he started to drink lots of black coffee, despite its bitter taste, in the hope that it might turn his skin a darker colour.

Just before John's death, the relationship between father and son became clearer when his father started talking about sending Luca to the Bali International School so that he could learn English. Although Luca couldn't understand why he had to go to a school that none of friends could go to, he started to learn English and converse a little with his father. Then John died. Luca was ten and extremely conflicted.

He says now that he didn't really begin to work out who he was until his older sister, Made (now a famous fashion designer with her own Lily Jean brand), became his legal guardian. Eleven years older than Luca and just starting her business, Made was sometimes a strict authority figure for a kid who'd grown up in the complete freedom of a Balinese compound, but she gave her little brother a sense of order and belonging. It didn't last however, and she fell out with the rebellious teenager, who hitch-hiked around Australia and worked as a surf coach before settling down to an arts course in Sydney.

Now he is back in Bali, working in his sister's business while he develops his own creative photography and a shoe label called LCD. Luca says that he is happy, but he is still trying to work out who he is.

Bali: Heaven and Hell

I visit my friends at their family homes and I see how they've got this little bit from their mums and this from their dads, but I don't know where my stuff comes from. After my father died I visited my real mother's family in Italy and discovered something about her as an artist, and that helped me a lot. And I found out a lot about my father, too, not all of it good. Some conversations would start out with, 'fuck your father, man', and stuff like that. But most of the old hippies say the same thing: that he was a dickhead sometimes, but he was also a great man. That's nice to hear. He could be rude, and I have that sometimes, too. I have his DNA, I know that, but I'm not him. How could I be? In every way that matters, I'm Balinese, and always will be.

Epilogue The Guns of Midnight

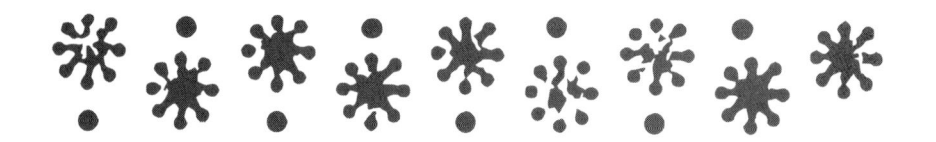

The Australian government deeply regrets the executions of Andrew Chan and Myuran Sukumaran. The government had hoped that Indonesia would show mercy to these young men, who have worked hard since their arrests to rehabilitate themselves and improve the lives of other prisoners. They committed a serious crime. Lengthy prison terms would have been an appropriate punishment. In jail, Andrew Chan brought comfort and hope to others and Myuran Sukumaran shared his skills to give prisoners the chance of a better life.

Australian Prime Minister Tony Abbott and Foreign Affairs
Minister Julie Bishop, joint statement, 29 April 2015

After a decade of waiting and hoping, and long months of government sabre-rattling, backroom bully-boy tactics and even threatened 'shirt-fronting', it all came down to tears and hymns in the hot jungle night, followed soon after midnight by the sharp crack of a volley of gunfire, heard across Nusakambangan ('execution island' to the breathless Australian media) as two Australian citizens and six other veterans of death row were shot dead.

These were the shots heard around Australia, if not the world. Having hounded the families of the convicted Bali Nine ringleaders Chan and Sukumaran as the prison officials callously forced them to walk the camera gauntlet to say their final farewells before the executions, over-excited news crews now reported for the breakfast shows every coming and going as the bodies were handed over for the long journey home. Strangely, however, no one seemed very interested in the back story of this supposedly forlorn place off the southern coast of Java, where relations between Australia and its nearest neighbour, the biggest Islamic country in the world, had hit a new low.

A prison island created by the Dutch colonialists more than a century ago, the 'Alcatraz of Indonesia' was soon regarded as the harshest penal

Epilogue The Guns of Midnight

institution in South East Asia, its maximum security prisons housing mass murderers, terrorists and drug traffickers, and an isolated stretch of jungle becoming Java's principal execution venue. During the mid-1960s Gestapu violence, President Suharto used the island to house hundreds of political dissidents—the lucky ones who were not slaughtered in the streets, but often died of disease and starvation—and ironically it was also briefly home to the president's bent son Tommy after his conviction for conspiracy to murder a judge.

But far from being a forlorn place, Nusakambangan is actually quite beautiful (if you can overlook the occasional ravages of illegal logging) and is home to seventy-one different bird species, fourteen reptile species and various mammal species, including the rare black-spotted leopard and Javan mouse deer. Towards the end of the Suharto regime, Javanese tourist authorities actually tried to turn the island into a wildlife resort, with tourist groups escorted around the perimeter of the prisons by armed guards. By the turn of the twenty-first century, however, it had become better known for its role as a refugee holding centre.

There were few objections from Australia when in November 2008 the convicted Bali bombers, Imam Samudra, Amrozi, and Ali Ghufron, were executed by firing squad on the island after their appeals for clemency were rejected. Then, in late 2014, newly elected President Joko Widodo announced that the execution of drug offenders would be resumed as part of his new war on drugs, and on Sunday 18 January 2015, five were executed.

As Indonesia's monsoon season grew in intensity, so did the outcry from Australia as Chan and Sukumaran were transported from Bali's Kerobokan Prison to Nusakambangan to await their as yet unscheduled execution. All but one of the prisoners awaiting the next round of executions were foreigners, and their respective governments made impassioned pleas for clemency, but the howls of protest that rang loudest were from Australia, where two convicted and self-confessed drug traffickers, albeit men who had found redemption, suddenly became mythical figures on the road to martyrdom.

Prime Minister Tony Abbott made embarrassing overtures to President Widodo that Australia was somehow owed a favour for his predecessor's generous contribution to Indonesian tsunami relief, while Foreign Minister Julie Bishop, usually more diplomatic than her boss, suggested that Australians should retaliate by not taking their holidays in Bali. But Indonesia didn't invent the death penalty, nor was it alone in still applying it. Within South East Asia, Malaysia, Vietnam, Thailand and Singapore all have capital punishment, and according to Amnesty International, China leads the world with the biggest number of the 682 executions carried out worldwide in 2012, the last year for which we have figures. Indonesia is not even in the top ten, but the good old United States of America, where thirty-two states still have the death penalty on their statutes, certainly is, with forty-three executions in 2012 and more than 3000 waiting on death row. So it seemed a bit rich for Abbott and Bishop to single out Indonesia for accusations of barbarism. In my view, legalised killing should be despised and deplored wherever it exists, not just selectively for political purposes.

In Indonesia, where Jokowi's reintroduction of the death penalty had overwhelming popular support, people were simply baffled by the hostility. 'Canberra really needs to contemplate whether it has the sufficient intellectual and cultural competence to understand, communicate and respectfully engage with Indonesian sensibilities and preferences on a wide range of international issues,' wrote academic Pierre Marthinus in the *Jakarta Post*.

> The issue is important because it carries significant implications for Australia's future dealings with Indonesia in particular and Asia in general.
> The Australian barrage of cringe-worthy diplomatic blunders concerning the latest round of executions might not have happened had Australian intellectuals provided their politicians with sufficient context-rich and timely advice.

Even in Bali, where few decisions made in Jakarta are ever seen as good ones, many people were confused and troubled by the attacks that were reported in their media. For Balinese whose entire economy is built on the tourist dollar, the threats of retribution seemed unfair and unwarranted, because in their simple logic, no matter what your views about the death penalty, these two Australians had knowingly broken a law of their country for which the penalty was death. End of story.

On the morning after that dark night on Nusakambangan, an Australian government representative whose presence before, during and after the executions had been quietly and solemnly dignified, in stark contrast to the shrieking from Canberra, accompanied a fleet of casket-bearing

Epilogue The Guns of Midnight

ambulances on the ferry to the port of Cilacap on the Javanese mainland, the first stop on the long journey home for burials. Majell Hind, the Australian Consul-General to Bali since early 2014, had been a support system for the condemned men and their families for months, a frequent visitor to Kerobokan and, since their transfer to Nusakambangan, she had also made the long trek there many times.

An Australian expat who is a close friend of the consul told me that Hind had become very close to the Chan and Sukumaran families and had been deeply moved by the courage the men had displayed in their final weeks, as every avenue of appeal faded away. Now, hiding the depth of her emotion behind a familiar sombre façade, it was her awful duty to drive with the bodies to the hotel where both families were staying some twenty minutes away, to officially inform them that the executions had taken place. Hind then joined the families to comfort them during the ten-hour drive to Jakarta for the flight home.

In every aspect of performing her official duties, Hind presented a human face of the Australian government that gained far more respect from Indonesians than Abbott's heavy-handed buffoonery. But in her short time on Bali, the consul had already built a reputation for the kind of quiet authority needed to get the job done while working effectively with all levels of the confusing and often conflicting provincial government. I met her briefly when she came to one of the launches in Bali for the first edition of this book, and was immediately impressed by her friendly, graceful manner. If the executions are to create ongoing tensions in Bali, then she is the perfect person to help diffuse them.

While Indonesians were scratching their heads about Tony Abbott, many of them were also beginning to wonder about their own President Joko 'Jokowi' Widodo, just months after his election had promised them a 'people's presidency'. The inhumane delays and general bungling of the executions had brought into sharp focus Jokowi's seeming inability to act decisively, and at the same time his subservience to the boss of his Indonesian Democratic Party of Struggle (PDI-P), former president Megawati Sukarnoputri, had been demonstrated at a conference in Bali at which she lectured him from the podium and denied him the opportunity to speak.

A few weeks before Jokowi took office, the highly regarded Australian think tank the Lowy Institute had published a paper on the new regime's likely impact on foreign policy, noting perceptively:

Epilogue The Guns of Midnight

There is widespread debate within Jakarta regarding the level of influence that Megawati and other PDI-P stalwarts will wield in Jokowi's administration. During the election campaign, she and her daughter Puan Maharani, who leads PDI-P's caucus in the legislature, sought to minimise Jokowi's role in decision-making. Megawati told a press conference on the eve of the campaign that Jokowi was merely an official of the party tasked with carrying out its ideology, a statement that contributed to widespread concerns among the electorate that Jokowi was a 'puppet candidate'.

This was the same man whose election *Time* magazine had heralded as 'A New Hope' in a front-cover headline. Clearly, Jokowi felt that his strong line on the executions would reinforce his strength as a leader that Megawati seemed determined to crush, but in several quarters of the Indonesian media, they had the opposite effect. Commentator Julia Suryakusuma wrote in the *Jakarta Post*:

> One thing that Western nations fail to understand is that the more you pressure a Javanese (Jokowi is Javanese), the more they will stonewall, especially if the manner is a judgmental, condemnatory and moral posturing way, like Australia's and France's. I sincerely think Jokowi is an idealist and that at heart he truly is populist. But when he got thrown into the arena of Indonesian realpolitik, ruled by ruthless, power-hungry wolves and lions, the former popular small town mayor got much more than he bargained for.
> So perhaps it's true what many of us had feared, that Jokowi as President of Indonesia is way over his head and has committed many misguided acts that are at odds with his idealism. He's failed several tests miserably and the executions are just the latest of many. For the executed, it's one failure too many.

I flew back to Bali just a week after the Nusakambangan executions and found that disillusionment with Jokowi amongst both expats and Balinese was rampant, but it had very little to do with his treatment of the Bali Nine. Many Balinese felt that the international focus on Jokowi's war on drugs had derailed one of his most important election promises, which was to fund new transport infrastructure projects to get the country moving again. The major spending was to be in clogged Java, of course, but there were also hopes that Bali, with no deep sea port or rail system and one hopelessly inadequate road link from Java (along which almost all of its food supplies now come since rice fields have become villa sites), would see some improvements, too.

The expats were more concerned about the proposed government 'inventory' of foreign-held land, though everyone was worried about the rumoured ban on beer, following pressure from the two Muslim parties represented in the Indonesian parliament. While the issue was being debated in Java, tourism authorities were quick to point out that the hedonistic island of Bali would be exempted in any case. Beer sales across Indonesia have increased by more than 50 per cent over the last decade, but research has shown that very little of it is drunk by Indonesians, with the vast majority being consumed by beer-swilling expats and tourists, most of them on Bali. In the end, the only impact felt in Bali was the disappearance of the ubiquitous Bintang beer from the shelves of mini-marts, although it was still readily available at every tumble-down *warung* on every street.

A few weeks before the executions of Chan and Sukumaran, a function room at the Best Western Heritage Hotel on Seminyak's rather unattractive Sunset Road was filled to the brim with more than 300 frowning *bule*s for a 'workshop and public forum' designed to quell rising fears amongst Bali's expat community that the Indonesian government was planning a crackdown on foreign landholdings. The forum was promoted as offering a 'path forward' from the 'nominee crisis', but since no representatives of the Jokowi government spoke or even attended, the expats who paid ten dollars to be present had to make do with advice from a human rights lawyer and an academic, and hear the alarming story of a *bule* who is battling in court with a Balinese nominee who has allegedly threatened her with gang violence if she pursues the case.

None of this is new. Had I been there I could have regaled them with the story of how my twenty-year leasehold was ripped up on a dodgy technicality in the early 1990s, only a few years into it. But I'm sure there were plenty with stories like that amongst the attendees. Then and now, if you think you hold land in Bali (or anywhere in Indonesia) through a local nominee, you'd better make sure you stay on the right side of the local, because you can't win in court.

According to my fly on the wall at the Heritage Hotel, various speakers estimated that there was currently $US8.4 billion of foreign investment in Bali through the various forms of legal and quasi-legal leasehold, with 140 active cases of disputed land before the courts. 'We were reminded that the nominee certificate is invalid,' my source said, 'and that when these arrangements come to their attention, the National Lands Office is required to strike out the name of the nominee and the land goes to the state. Both parties lose. Quite a few of the people at the forum were quite frightened by this prospect.'

Indonesia's fairly stringent foreign investment laws have been in place since independence in 1945, an obvious reaction to centuries of Dutch colonial control, and framed in law by the Basic Agrarian Law of 1960. It's a complex set of laws designed to keep Indonesia for the Indonesians, and as such has been subject to corruption since day one, but current or intending foreign 'landholders' need to know only this: there are three types of domestic land title for individuals in Indonesia—*Hak Milik*, *Hak Pakai* and *Hak Sewa*.

Hak Milik is basically freehold, and despite what estate agents and dodgy middlemen might tell you, foreigners cannot own land under this title, a subject we'll get back to. *Hak Pakai* is a secure leasehold of twenty-five years, usually renewable for another twenty-five years. Although there is a common misconception that it is a contract between the buyer and the government, in fact it is better described as 'conditional ownership' with conditions imposed by the government which include that the owner must be a resident, that the property is a residence, that a nominal tax must be paid on the declared value of the property, and that you can only have one of them. But the most common form of legal leasehold for *bule*s is *Hak Sewa*, negotiated directly between the owner and the lessor. This is normally for twenty-five years, too, but frequently such deals are complicated by technicalities such as who in the village really owns the land.

For this reason, the most popular Bali land deal construct for decades now has been through securing power of attorney over the person you believe to be the landowner. Dodgy to say the least, because Indonesian law does not recognise full power of attorney, and in recent years ageing baby-boomer hippies and surfers have been thrown onto the streets as their nominees die and the next generation claims the property or demands double the money.

While so far there has been no indication of a fundamental change to the land laws—and according to one expat with legal qualifications, 'They're just getting their ducks in a row, and trying to close the gaps made by "tolerated abuses of law" which allow all kinds of nefarious operators to wreak havoc, and damage the investment climate here, as well as the sovereignty of the nation'—what had stirred the *bule*s into a lather of righteous indignation was an interview with Ferry Mursyidan Baldan, Indonesia's Minister for Agrarian Affairs and head of the National Land Agency, who told news website *Kompas.com* that his office was about to begin an inventory of land 'owned' by foreigners. 'It is absolutely not allowed for a foreigner to own a single inch of land in Indonesia,' he was quoted as saying.

Baldan drew attention to foreigners using 'legally questionable powers of attorney' and 'fictive mortgage agreements' to control land, but when asked what sanctions might be imposed on foreign nationals found to illegally hold land, he replied, 'There is no need for sanctions, we will just divert possession of the land.'

With alarm bells going off all over Expatria, Baldan quickly added: 'We are doing an inventory, not conducting raids. There is no need for anyone to be frightened.'

Trying to hose down the hysteria, *Balidiscovery.com* went to their go-to notary, Rainy Hendriany, who is known as one of the more level-headed people in the emotional minefield of property title. Hendriany confirmed what many expats have heard in recent months—that the Jokowi government is seeking to clean up the mess before reviewing and perhaps relaxing legal *Hak Sewa* title and extending it to as much as seventy years.

Hendriany also ruled out legal foreign freehold: 'In my opinion, the political will does not exist to amend higher laws solely for the purpose of allowing foreigners to own property in Indonesia.' She concluded by telling *Balidiscovery.com* that in the meantime, inventory or no, it would be business as usual, at least in Bali:

> Bali is a small island and the recent abuse of zoning regulations, height restrictions and setback regulations has been in the best interests of nobody in the longer term, especially the Balinese themselves. That villa built today in the middle of nowhere with beautiful views over the *sawah* [rice fields], results in unaffordable higher land taxes for the adjacent subsistence farmers, which in turn results in the land being sold to new investors and the *sawah* views are soon gone. If this sounds all too familiar to some of your readers, perhaps it is because they live in parts of South Bali where it is already too late.

Epilogue The Guns of Midnight

As a result of the Heritage Hotel meeting, a group calling itself Kalompek Karja Krisis Nominee Indonesia (K3ni) has been formed to lobby the government for a fair deal for foreign landholders, and by mid-2015 a clearer picture of the Jokowi government's approach was beginning to emerge, with Minister Baldan clarifying that the land inventory would give all landholders at least eighteen months to put their leasing affairs in legal order before any action would be taken. While this caused massive sighs of relief across South Bali, the property columnist of the *Bali Advertiser* noted:

> These are strange days in Bali. While increasing tracts of the fabled island are given over to runaway property development of questionable provenance and merit, traffic congestion reaches epic Bangkok and Jakarta proportions, with foreign residents increasingly victimised, even killed as a result of property disputes, unable to obtain protection under the law from the courts or the police—despite all this and more, foreigners still want to come here, and stranger yet, want to invest in a home or property here.

Strange days indeed. Having acquainted myself with the fear and loathing in Expatria, I took myself off to the quietest, most serene place that I know in Bali, halfway up a mountain road that only a goat (or a dirt biker) could love, rented a cabin in the cool, moist jungle, with a view over terraced rice fields that will not become villas anytime soon, and began to contemplate what, if anything, had changed in Bali since I put the finishing touches on the first edition of this book, a little over a year ago.

Well, the urban creep along Bali's southern coast had moved a street or two further north, with the quiet *gang* in semi-rural Pererenan where I spend a lot of my time in Bali a little more built up, the surf breaks a little more crowded. And at the other end of the tourist strip on the Bukit, some pioneer expats were cashing up with Asian money, selling their cliff-top mansions for millions of dollars. However, overall the tourism and development boom of the past five years seemed to have slowed a bit, perhaps just taking a breather before the next round of money starts to pour in.

But did I detect any fundamental changes to Bali in the age of Jokowi? No, and it occurred to me that this may be because in the three years of intimate involvement with this book—researching, writing, promoting and now revising it—I had changed much more than Bali had. Advancing age

Epilogue The Guns of Midnight

and some health issues had slowed me down, and while I still surf frequently and am physically active in other ways, intimations of mortality had definitely changed my approach to how I viewed the things around me, and nowhere more so than in my beloved, bruised and battered Bali.

Here I pay more attention to the laughter of children, the small dramas that play out all around you, the simple offerings smouldering in family temples everywhere, the night sounds of the *gamelan* and the omnipresent smells of frangipani and kretek. And up in the hills, alone in the middle of the night, I even saw the dance of the fireflies above the *sawah*, for the first time in perhaps forty years.

It excited me much more now than it did the young man I was then, and lying back on my bed, I prayed to some unknown god that if I have another twenty Bali years left in me, I will see the fireflies dance again.

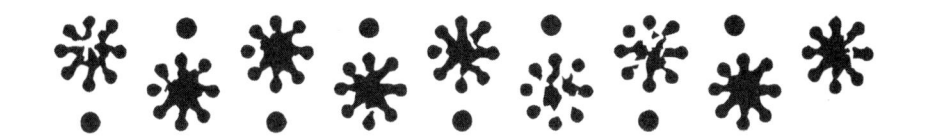

A final word about some of the major characters in this history

Paul 'Gringo' Anderson divides his time between homes in Kuta and a village on the east coast, with regular trips back to Australia. He works as a consultant for surf brand Billabong, surfs regularly and enjoys playing music with his friends.

Warren 'Abdul' Anderson lives on the same plot of land he leased in 1970, where his commercial concerns include the Seaside Restaurant and Seaside Villas. He works out a lot and plays golf.

Kim 'The Fly' Bradley: After years of suffering from skin cancers and self-medicating with alcohol, Kim Bradley's body finally gave up on him. *Baliwaves.com* website reported: '… The Fly peacefully passed away at his Bukit home in Bali on 26 March 2009. He was 53 years old. One of the original surfing pioneers of Bali, he will be sadly missed and his absence definitely felt by those who knew him. Growing up on the northern beaches of Sydney, Kim first travelled to Bali at the age of 17 where [*sic*] he has called home ever since. He contributed significantly to the surfing world in Bali over the years. He is survived … by his daughter Dewi, and two sons Adi and "Genghis". His untimely death comes as no great surprise to all that knew him well.' A long-time *banjar* member, he was given the rare honour of a full Balinese cremation, with the expat surfing community joining the Balinese for the procession through Kuta's streets to the beach. Kim's former wife, Made, took in Genghis, his son with a new partner, and raised him as her own. She continues to run Bali Design.

Diana Darling lives a quiet, happy life in Ubud with husband, Agung, goes to a gym twice a week, and is still working on her tourism novel.

A final word about some of the major characters in this history

Janet DeNeefe is the busiest woman in Bali, juggling hotels, restaurants, cooking schools and her brainchild, the Ubud Writers and Readers Festival.

Tony 'Doris' Eltherington is back doing what he loves, running surfing boat charters out of Padang, Sumatra, and spending his free weeks at home at Jimbaran, Bali. In early 2013, he made world headlines when he led the search for a man overboard in the Mentawai Islands off Sumatra. Long after everyone else had given up on the South African surfer, Doris studied the currents and searched a triangular circuit until the man was found, alive and clutching a piece of driftwood.

Albert Falzon lives quietly at his farm on the Mid-North Coast of NSW, Australia, and surfs every day. His spiritual take on life is documented on his *Daily Lama* website. He doubts he will return to Bali in this lifetime, but you never know.

Richard Flax lives in the same Legian compound he has had for more than thirty years, and runs his insurance business and charitable foundations from a nearby office block. He is an avid collector of rare books on Bali, still rides a kneeboard, and still helps tourists in trouble.

Rio Helmi blogs for *The Huffington Post*, runs a website about Ubud, and is still the most dynamic commentator about Bali affairs.

Lelia and Richard Lewis both live in Sanur. Lelia has slowed down a lot, but still takes God's love to Kerobokan Prison once or twice a week. Dick is a successful novelist who has recently branched out from young adult fiction to mainstream. He blogs at www.balisurfstories.com.

Leonard Lueras lives and works in his compound at Sanur, producing high-quality, limited edition books of art, history and photography. He produced a stunning album for US President Barack Obama, documenting the president's Indonesian family.

Jan Mantjika still runs Jan's Tours in Bali but spends most of her time working for her church and for children's charities.

A final word about some of the major characters in this history

Stephen Palmer is an active partner in the Surfer Girl retail chain, still lives in his Bukit mansion, which may or may not be for sale, and spends as much time snowboarding as he possibly can.

Wayan Agus Parwita is much in demand as a site manager for *bule* villa developments, but always tries to make himself available for investigative assignments.

Bobby Radiasa is still running the G-Land surf camp but is now trying to scale back work in favour of fishing.

David Thomas keeps a house in the mountains in Bali but now lives in New South Wales, near his friend, Albert Falzon. He still plays golf off a low handicap.

Made Wijaya continues to be Bali's most prolific social commentator, through his *Stranger in Paradise* website. He refused to be interviewed for this book but gave permission for use of quotes from his published works.

Malcolm Williams is a landscape gardener. In his spare time he flies drones over his property in Pererenan.

Robert Wilson divides his time between homes on the Bukit peninsula and Noosa, and enjoys taking long back country motorcycle trips with his wife, Fauzia.

Kadek Wirinatha lost a lot of money when Air Paradise went down, but he is still on Bali's rich list and owns hotels, clubs, restaurants and Bali's major wine distribution company.

Endnotes

Introduction
The distractions of Western capitalism have reached critical mass: Matt George interview with Stephen Palmer, *The Surfers Journal*, vol. 21, no. 4, 2012, p. 91.

Chapter 1
If we hate our brothers and sisters: From 'Now We Move Forward! (Sekarang Kita Maju!)', a speech delivered in English by Asana Viebeke L, of the Parum Sangita think tank, on Friday 25 October 2002 at a post-bombing press conference for the Indonesian media.

Wayan Agus Parwita, twenty-three, a recent graduate: Interview with Wayan Agus Parwita, Umah Kembar, Pererenan, 28 October 2013.

On the Sayan Ridge, high above the Ayung River: Interview with Richard Flax, Nakula Plaza, Legian, 21 and 22 May 2013.

Charter-boat skipper Tony 'Doris' Eltherington: Interview with Tony Eltherington, Padang Padang, 14 May 2013.

Rag trader Alison Chester was having a ball: Interview with Alison Chester, Jodie O'Shea Orphanage, Benoa, 3 October 2013.

The Sari Club was just starting to warm up: 'Victims recount the horrors ...', Keith Moor, *Herald Sun*, Melbourne, 8 October 2012.

In his apartment at the Aromas complex: Interview with Stephen Palmer, Bukit Peninsula, 2 May 2013.

'Bali's darkest hour' quickly became a tagline: BBC, 8 October 2003.

Endnotes

Chapter 2

The King of Bali sends the King of Holland his greetings: Letter supposedly written in Balinese by the Dewa Agung of Klungkung, translated into Dutch and presented to Captain Jacob van Heemskerck for his monarch, along with a beautiful slave girl, 1601. *Bali Chronicles*, Willard A. Hanna, Periplus Editions, 2004, p. 42.

Bali Aga villages are so designated: *Bali Aga Villages*, Carole Muller, Walsh Bay Press, 2012, pp. 4–5.

In the 1960s archaeologists discovered: *Fresh Light on the Morning of the World*, Jonathan Copeland with Ni Wayan Murni, Orchid Press, 2010, p. 3.

This was the first time: 'Wallace's Line in the Light of Recent Zoogeographic Studies', Ernst Mayr, *The Quarterly Review of Biology*, vol. 19, no. 1, 1944.

The artist and Bali scholar: *Island of Bali*, Miguel Covarrubias, Alfred Knopf, 1937, p. 4.

Covarrubias, of whom much more later: ibid.

Although the God-Kings of Bali: Hanna, p. 27.

Although they differ on exactly who did what: *Under the Volcano*, Cameron Forbes, Black Inc, 2007, p. 24.

Gelgel, in the verdant foothills of the east coast: *Bali, A Paradise Created*, Adrian Vickers, Tuttle, 2012, pp. 66–71.

The spice trade had become: Hanna, p. 35.

When the Houtman fleet left Bali: *The Longest Voyage*, R. Silverberg, Ohio University Press, 1997, p. 393.

These Dutch adventures signalled the beginning: The Rijks Museum Library, Amsterdam, www.rijksmuseum.nl.

While the board of the VOC in Holland: *The First Modern Economy: Success, Failure, and Perseverance of the Dutch Economy, 1500–1815*, Jan de Vries and Ad van der Woude, Cambridge University Press, 1997, p. 383.

As it happened, the best source of slaves: Vickers, pp. 29–31.

The Balinese had been slave trading: Hanna, pp. 44–45.

Endnotes

At the same time the Dutch began to see: Hanna, pp. 46–47.

Meanwhile, Balinese male slaves: Vickers, pp. 34–35.

Raffles was only in the East Indies for five years: *History of Java*, Sir Thomas Stamford Raffles, John Murray, London, 1830 (1817), vol. 2, Appendix, p. cxxxix.

Elsewhere, Raffles noted that: Raffles, p. cxli.

Raffles had championed the notion: Hanna, pp. 55–56.

While the Dutch kept their distance: Vickers, pp. 46–49.

Chapter 3

Ever since the Crusades of the early Middle Ages: *The White Rajahs of Sarawak: A Borneo Dynasty*, Bob Reece, Archipelago Press, 2004, p. 13.

Lange was born in the port of Rudkobing: *Mads Lange: The Bali Trader and Peacemaker*, Peter Bloch and Leonard Lueras, Bali Purnati, 2007, p. 21.

In the Far East their first base was: Bloch and Lueras, pp. 23–23.

Although Lange's youngest brother: Bloch and Lueras, pp. 44–45.

At that time Lombok was ruled jointly: ibid.

Lange and his brothers were well on the way: *Leven En Avonturen van een Oostinjevaarder*, Aage Krarup Nielsen, Querido, Amsterdam, 1928, pp. 17–40.

The Mataram forces sacked the fortress at Chakra Negara: Bloch and Lueras, p. 52.

The most vivid description of Kuta: Bloch and Lueras, pp. 60–61.

Dubois reiterated the widely held view: ibid.

Aage Krarup Nielsen, writing nearly a century later: Nielsen, pp. 17–40.

And then, of course, there were the opium wars: *Bali's Early Days: Widow Sacrifice, Slavery & Opium*, Dr A.A. Gde Putra Agung, Saritaksu Editions, Bali, 2000, p. 34.

Traders, merchants, sea captains, botanists: *Pioneering in the Far East*, Ludvig Verner Helms, W.H. Allen, London, 1882, pp. 12–14.

Endnotes

Thus began a two-year stint in Lange's employ: ibid.

Throughout the 1840s Bali became the granary: *Bali Chronicles*, Willard A. Hanna, Periplus Editions, Singapore, 2004 (1976), pp. 121–22.

The following day, however, the powder keg almost went up again: Bloch and Lueras, pp. 78–80.

As it turned out, there was not much: Hanna, pp. 82–83.

It was not to last. The Balinese did not pay: Hanna, pp. 108–11.

The Dewa Agung vowed to fight on to the death: ibid.

Lange was the official Dutch agent at last: Bloch and Lueras, pp. 153–59.

Chapter 4

Happy the warrior to whom the just fight comes unsought: *Love and Death in Bali*, Vicki Baum, Tuttle, 2007 (1937), p. 307. Baum is paraphrasing Krishna's lecture to Arjuna, who is about to lead his family into battle, in the *Bhagavad Gita*.

The main agreement to come out of the 1849 'peace': *Priests and Programmers*, J. Stephen Lansing, Princeton University Press, 2007 (1991), p. 20.

The first resident controleur, Bloemen Waanders: *Bali, A Paradise Created*, Adrian Vickers, Tuttle, 2012 (1989), p. 101.

Opium imports were taxed considerably by the rajas: *Bali Chronicles*, Willard A. Hanna, Periplus, 2004 (1976), pp. 208–9.

Some in the colonial government of the Dutch East Indies: 'On the determinants of opium consumption', paper by Eric W. van Luijk and Jan C. van Ours, 1998.

It's difficult to comprehend now: *The Quest for Life, Violence and Order in 19th Century Bali*, Henk Schulte Nordholt, published in *Masyarakat Indonesia*, 1989, vol. 16, pp. 197–212.

Under the opiumregie the government assumed: *Bali's Early Days: Widow Sacrifice, Slavery & Opium*, Dr A.A. Gde Putra Agung, Saritaksu Editions, Bali, 2000, p. 34.

In 1914 Dutch administrator: *Weg met het Opium!*, H. van Kol, Masereeuw and Bouten, Rotterdam, 1913.

Endnotes

By the early years of the new century the eight kingdoms: Hanna, pp. 155–56.

At dawn the Dutch marched on Denpasar: Hanna, p. 157.

Having received damaging international press: Bataviaasch Nieuwsblad, 4 May 1908, quoted in Lansing, p. 23.

The defeat of the Balinese kingdoms: Lansing, p. 22.

The Dutch humanitarian and clergyman Wolter Robert van Hoëvell: Vickers, pp. 114–18.

If van Hoëvell's friendship with Lange: ibid.

Jacobs, a doctor who came to Bali: Eenigen Tijd, Julius Jacobs, quoted in Vickers, pp. 124–27.

The Ethical Policy got a further boost in 1902: Hanna, pp. 175–91.

Chapter 5

Although I was in Bali only a few hours, it seemed I had always lived there: 'A Comedian Sees the World', Part V, *Woman's Home Companion*, January 1934.

KPM had been running steamships down the archipelago: 'Cultural Tourism in Bali', Michel Picard, *Indonesia*, no. 49 (April 1990), pp. 37–74.

This was not the first time KPM had engaged in marketing: Guide to the Dutch East Indies, Dr J.F. van Bemmelen and Colonel J.B. Hooyer, G. Kolff, London and Batavia, 1897, quoted in *Visual and Textual Images of Women: 1930s Representations of Colonial Bali as Produced by Men and Women Travellers*, Jojor Ria Sitompul, University of Warwick, 2008.

According to turn-of-the-century travel writer: Java—The Garden of the East, E.R. Scidmore, The Century, New York, 1899.

Between 1912 and 1914 Krause took more: Bali 1912, Gregor Krause, Folkwang-Verlag, Germany, 1988 (1922), p. 55.

When in 1928 KPM replaced the Denpasar: Brisbane Courier, 22 July 1930, p. 6.

Arriving at Buleleng in early 1930, the Mexican artist: Island of Bali, Miguel Covarrubias, Alfred A. Knopf, 1937, p. xvii.

Endnotes

After an hour or two spent with Powell: *The Last Paradise*, Hickman Powell, Jonathon Cape, 1930, from Andre Roosevelt's introduction, p. ix.

Although he has sometimes been described: *Bali, A Paradise Created*, Adrian Vickers, Tuttle, 2012 (1990), p. 138.

In 1928 Powell was set up with a family in the village: Powell, p. 3.

Powell's guide to village life was a man named Kumis: Powell, p. 198.

Powell, like so many bules *before and after*: Powell, p. 52.

When it was published in the United States: *The Saturday Review of Literature*, 11 October 1930.

Attempting to explain his campaign: Roosevelt, p. xiv.

Roosevelt's 'friend Spies' was the artist and musician Walter Spies: *Walter Spies, A life in Art*, John Stowell, Afterhours Books, 2011, p. 2.

In a letter written years later, Spies told of his early years: Stowell, p. 7, from a Spies letter written in May 1939.

In Bali Spies focused on his art: ibid.

While they did not have a lot in common: Vickers, pp. 148–49.

Roosevelt and Spies began working on a film: Stowell, p. 117.

In 1932 in Los Angeles, California: *Revolt in Paradise*, K'tut Tantri, Griffin, 1960, p. 5.

Although Island of the Demons *was well received*: Michelle Chin blog, 2009.

Chaplin's entourage in Europe was burdened: 'A Comedian Sees the World', Part V, *Woman's Home Companion*, January, 1934.

In later scenes Charlie is shown sitting: 'The Travel Narrative As Spin: Mitigating Charlie Chaplin's Public Persona in "My Trip Abroad" and "A Comedian Sees the World"', Lisa K. Stein, 2005, dissertation published by University of Ohio. In this fascinating work, Ms Stein ponders the effect of celebrity on travel reportage.

Inevitably, Chaplin also met Walter Spies: Stowell, p. 153.

Endnotes

Chapter 6

With my own eyes I saw how one of the best-known Europeans in Bali: *Walter Spies, A life in Art*, John Stowell, Afterhours Books, 2011, p. 219.

In a 1908 series of articles about the Indies: *Across the Equator*, Thomas H. Reid, first published as a series of articles in *The Straits Times*, 1908.

When she returned in 1912, having experienced downright hostility: *Java—The Garden of the East*, E.R. Scidmore, The Century, New York, 1899, p. 22.

Born in Amsterdam in 1874, Wijnand Nieuwenkamp: www.northbali.org.

Having witnessed the turmoil of the puputan *and its aftermath*: *Bali en Lombok*, W.O.J. Nieuwenkamp, Album 1, 1906; Album 2, 1909; Albums 1, 2, 3, Elsevier, Amsterdam, 1910.

Although Covarrubias and his wife had been impressed: *Island of Bali*, Miguel Covarrubias, Alfred E. Knopf, New York, 1937, pp. xviii–xix.

The Covarrubiases saw snatches of beauty: ibid.

The Covarrubiases found the 'real Bali' soon enough: *A House in Bali*, Colin McPhee, Victor Gollancz, London, 1947, pp. 14–15.

At a party in the New York apartment of photographer: *Colin McPhee: Composer in Two Worlds*, Carol J. Oja, University of Illinois Press, 1990, pp. 57–64.

Born in Texas to wealthy parents, Belo was typical: ibid.

The reef-fringed, white-sand beach of Sanur had seen a lot of trouble: *Tandjung Sari, A Magical Door to Bali*, Diana Darling, Editions Didier Millet, Singapore, 2012, pp. 14–17. Description of the Mershon home from *Our Hotel in Bali*, Louise Koke, January Books, Wellington, 1987, p. 21.

A tall young woman came sedately towards us: Koke, p. 124.

In Ubud Rudolf Bonnet, now ensconced at the Water Palace: Stowell, p. 158.

The second initiative was the establishment of Pita Maha: *Bali, A Paradise Created*, Adrian Vickers, Tuttle, 2012 (1990), pp. 160–62.

Spies was busy with numerous other projects, too: *The Island of Bali: Its Religion and Ceremonies*, R. Goris and Walter Spies, KPM, Batavia, 1931.

Endnotes

As well as having established herself as: Vickers, p. 168.

Mead and Bateson went straight to Campuhan: Mead/Bateson, *Bulletin*, vol. 28, October 1936, pp. 3–4, Library of Congress.

If the gathering together of this incredible creative stew: Stowell, p. 161.

I have been told that no country girl of decent Balinese family: In the East My Pleasure Lies, Theodora Benson, William Heinemann, London, 1938, pp. 163–207.

Another travel writer of the day, Mrs Larz Anderson: Eastern Seas, Isabel Anderson, Bruce Humphries, Boston, 1934, p. 212.

Soon after his arrival Colin McPhee was told: McPhee, p. 34.

Such attitudes were hardly rare in the colonial East: Bali and Angkor, A 1930s Pleasure Trip Looking at Life and Death, Geoffrey Gorer, Oxford University Press, 1936, p. 61.

Gorer was a Cambridge graduate who published: Understanding Blackness through Performance, Anne Cremieux, Xavier Lemoine, Jean-Paul Rocchi, Palgrave Macmillan, 2013, p. 207.

In 1936, Gorer spent several months travelling: Gorer, p. 116.

Gorer didn't find them particularly sexy either: ibid.

Perhaps the Orientals of Ubud only despised bule *men*: Bali's Silent Crisis: Desire, Tragedy and Transition, Jeff and Belinda Lewis, Lexington, 2009, p. 113.

The visiting Dutch journalist Mary Pos was not: Stowell, p. 206.

Michel Picard wrote: 'Cultural Tourism in Bali', *Indonesia*, Michel Picard, no. 49 (April 1990), pp. 37–74.

Chapter 7

'I will tell you what we will do,' Wyjan replied calmly: Revolt in Paradise, K'tut Tantri, Harper, New York, 1960, p. 75. Tantri is quoting the comforting words of her servant, in what seems an unlikely exchange.

As the Western world began to move out of the Great Depression: Bali Chronicles, Willard A. Hanna, Periplus Editions, Hong Kong, 2004 (1976), p. 227.

Endnotes

The mysterious K'tut Tantri (or Mrs Muriel Pearsen if you prefer): Tantri, p. 18.

Around this time direct air travel to Bali also became possible, although: Hanna, p. 227.

The new airport drew attention to the nearest village: Tantri, p. 65.

Apparently, the hotel in Bangli did not cover her living costs: The Romance of K'tut Tantri and Indonesia, Timothy Lindsey, Equinox Publishing, 2008, pp. 36–40.

Koke was a tall, slim, very fit man who had been: ibid.

But first they had to find a builder: Our Hotel in Bali, Louise Koke, January Books, Wellington, 1987, p. 50.

Before construction had finished, the Kokes: Lindsey, p. 43.

The Kokes had all kinds of takers for surfing lessons: Koke, p. 215.

According to Louise Koke, Lady Hartelby lived: Lindsey, p. 45.

By the end of 1937 the Kokes and Tantri were at war: ibid.

According to Tantri's account: Tantri, p. 74.

Although Tantri paints the hotel: Lindsey, p. 46; Koke, pp. 226–28.

Had Bob Koke become confused in old age: Lindsey, p. 47.

We are given an idea of what Tantri's hospitality: Walter Spies, A life in Art, John Stowell, Afterhours Books, 2011, p. 205.

It seems clear that Tantri was deluded: Lindsey, p. 51.

But Koke can't be trusted on this either: ibid.

Tantri claimed that KPM and the Dutch: Tantri, p. 83. Trumpets from the Steep, Lady Diana Cooper, Houghton Mifflin, 1960, p. 98.

Tourists stopped coming, and the Kokes realised: Koke, p. 267.

For the Kokes, however: Lindsey, p. 51.

Chapter 8

It is impossible at present to give further particulars: The West Australian, 24 February 1942, p. 5.

Endnotes

The attack on Pearl Harbor was a starter's gun: 'The Invasion of Bali', *World War II Magazine*, by Tom Womack, February 1996. Womack's excellent and incredibly detailed account forms the basis of my description of the invasion.

According to military historians: Womack, page unknown.

In the eyes of the propaganda-driven Western media: *The West Australian*, 24 February 1942, p. 5.

The Indonesian residents of Bali Island are enjoying a peaceful life: *The Dark Side of Paradise: Political Violence in Bali*, Geoffrey Robinson, Cornell University, 1995, p. 72.

The Japanese divided the East Indies into three jurisdictions: *Labour Relations in Japanese Occupied Indonesia*, Shigeru Sato, University of Newcastle, 2000, p. 18.

Perhaps the worst thing about this was that: Sato, p. 11.

The Japanese occupation was a watershed in Indonesian history: 'The History of Independence', www.mongabay.com.

The Japanese occupiers soon saw the value in Sukarno: *The Blue-Eyed Enemy: Japan Against the West in Java and Luzon 1942–1945*, Theodore Friend, Princeton University Press, 1988 pp. 82–84.

In July 1942, Sukarno was sent back to Batavia: Friend, p. 29.

It was a very different story on Bali: *Bali Chronicles*, Willard A. Hanna, Periplus, 2004 (1976), pp. 232–33.

During the second half of 1945, twenty-nine-year-old Colonel: Bill Dalton, 'Bali at War: The Struggle for Independence', *Bali Advertiser*, 2012.

Bali became part of the Dutch-controlled: Robinson, pp. 12–14.

In March 1946, just as the Dutch landings began on Bali: *Our Hotel in Bali*, Louise G. Koke, January Books, 1987, p. 272.

Chapter 9

In the name of the Lord Jesus, I deliberately set my feet on the soil of Bali: Dr Robert A. Jaffray, 1928, quoted in Richard E. Lewis's 'A Place to Call Home', *CMA Magazine*, 2008.

Endnotes

Although we are well and truly into the dry season: Interview with the author, Sanur, 25 May 2013.

In 1830 the Dutch tolerated the mission of a Reverend Ennis: *Bali Chronicles*, Willard A. Hanna, Periplus, 2004 (1976), pp. 144–46.

This shocking case aroused strong emotions: *Bliss in Bali: The Island of Taboos*, Jacques Chegaray, Arthur Barker, London, 1955, first published in France in 1953, p. 192.

This directive was an impossibility for a missionary: www.cmalliance.org, 'About Us'.

The Jaffrays made several largely unsuccessful attempts: 'Harper the Evangelical', *The Canadian Charger*, 14 April 2011.

Eight years after his death, little remained: Interview with Lelia Lewis, Sanur, 25 May 2013.

Lelia Lewis's memories of Bali in the early 1950s: *To Change Bali: Essays in Honour of I Gusti Ngurah Bagus*, edited by Adrian Vickers and I Nyoman Darma Putra with Michele Ford, *Bali Post*, 2000, and '1950s Lifestyles in Denpasar', by I Nyoman Wijaya, pp. 113–30.

Access to Bali is not easily obtained: Chegaray, p. 10.

Like so many Westerners before him: Chegaray, p. 34.

Chegaray was impressed by the quality: Chegaray, p. 133.

As a reaction against Dutch conservatism: Chegaray, p. 195.

In many ways, health care in Bali had progressed little: Chegaray, p. 102.

Spencer Reed arrived in Bali in 1956: *Love and Death in Bali*, Vicki Baum, Tuttle, 1999 (1937), p. 262.

Like many ground-breaking drugs, the suspected side effects: *British Medical Journal 2*, (1960), p. 1672, letter from Dr Spencer Reed.

Our landlord, the Dewa Agung, was head: Interview with Lelia Lewis.

The eruptions of Gunung Agung in March 1963: Hanna, pp. 238–43.

Endnotes

Chapter 10

The best-known references to the killings: *The Dark Side of Paradise: Political Violence in Bali*, Geoffrey Robinson, Cornell University, 1995, pp. 1–19.

They met backstage at a fundraising show on a balmy, late summer: Interview with Jan Mantjika, Kayu Api, Sanur, 26 May 2013.

Almost twenty years since he had seized power: *Bali, A Paradise Created*, Adrian Vickers, Tuttle, 2012 (1989), pp. 232–35.

By 1965 there were political rallies on every street corner: ibid.

A hot day in December, 1965. I was nine years old: 'The mass killings of 1965, or, why I don't like surfing east Bali's beaches', Richard E. Lewis, www.balisurfstories.com, posted 25 October 2010.

All around them, innocent people were being dragged: ibid.

Dick Lewis says: 'My parents got word: Interview with Richard E. Lewis, Café Kalimantan, Sanur, 14 May 2013.

Jan Mantjika remembers: 'Awful things were happening: Interview with Jan Mantjika, Kayu Api, Sanur, 25 May 2013.

Like many people who actually suffered: www.balisurfstories.com, posted 4 September 2012.

Lelia Lewis remembers that she and Rodger: Interview with Lelia Lewis, Sanur, 25 May 2013.

One response to a blog about Gestapu on Dick Lewis's website: Barbara J. Anello-Adnani, www.balisurfstories.com, posted 4 September 2012.

By late 1966 the terror on Bali was over: Robinson, pp. 1–19.

As historian Geoffrey Robinson noted: ibid.

Writing an introduction to her collected works: Belo's *Traditional Balinese Culture* and *Geertz's Interpretation of Cultures*, referenced in Robinson, pp. 1–19.

Writing in 1976, historian Willard A. Hanna: *Bali Chronicles*, Willard A. Hanna, Periplus, 2004 (1976), p. 244.

Jan and Djati Mantjika had a son in January, 1966: Interview with Jan Mantjika.

Endnotes

Chapter 11

Absolutely every aspect of life, whether it be the structure of buildings: *Bali Style*, Barbara Walker and Rio Helmi, Thames and Hudson, 1995, p. 32.

Among those who were appalled: *Tandjung Sari, A Magical Door to Bali*, Diana Darling, Editions Didier Millet, 2012, pp. 39–42.

But his three guest houses could accommodate: ibid.

While sailing along the coast with Pandy: ibid.

Interestingly, the Indonesian photojournalist Rio Helmi: Darling, pp. 44–45.

In 1969 Friend, a heavy drinker and smoker: Interview with Peter and Carole Muller, Darling Harbour, Sydney, 25 March 2013.

The concept of the Matahari was to design and build: Peter Muller, *The Complete Works*, Jacqueline C. Urford, Muller, 2012, p. 254.

The Matahari project on the stretch of beach: Darling, p. 34.

Muller said: 'We took out a fifteen-year lease: Interview with Peter and Carole Muller.

Peter Muller was not remotely interested in residential architecture: Interview with Peter and Carole Muller.

Peter Muller recalled: 'Charles kept wanting me to add more villas: ibid.

This was the Kayu Aya as I remember it from my second trip: 'Bali and the Kayu Aya', Tony Mathers, www.tonymathersblogspot.com.au, 10 April 2012.

When Terry Stanton died in 2010: 'Vale Terry Stanton', Made Wijaya, *Stranger in Paradise* blog, July 2010.

In early 1970 Zenik started selling soft drinks: Interview with Zenik and John, Poppies Cottages, Kuta, 2 October 2013.

Having moved rapidly from drink selling to warung *management*: ibid.

Five years younger than Zenik: Interview with Made Masih, Made's Warung, Seminyak, 17 October 2013.

Peter started filling the restaurant with Dutch colonial antiques: 'Why I Love Kuta', by Peter Steenbergen, from *Kuta and Kuta*, edited by Leonard Lueras, Bali Purnati Center For The Arts, 2005, pp. 137–39.

Endnotes

Chapter 12

We are the measure of all things: Underground filmmaker Jonas Mekas, quoted from a 1967 magazine in the introduction sequence of *Morning of the Earth*, Albert Falzon, 1972.

Never saw another white person: Interview with Richard E. Lewis, Café Kalimantan, Sanur, 14 May 2013.

June 1966. My family's red Jeep Wagoneer: Richard E. Lewis, www.balisurfstories.wordpress.com, 2010.

Wayan 'Bobby' Radiasa, also born in 1956: Interview with Bobby Radiasa, Café Batu Jimbar, Sanur, 6 June 2013.

By the late 1960s an emerging breed of surf adventurers: Interview with Geoff Watson and John Pratten, Avalon Beach, 26 November 2013.

Young Russ Hughes … was brought up tough: *More Stoked!*, Bob McTavish, Harper Collins, 2013, p. 9.

After the world titles, Hughes had made his way: Interview with Rusty Miller, Byron Bay, 12 July 2013.

Hughes spent a couple of months in Bali: Interview with Richard E. Lewis.

In that same dry season, Bobby Radiasa saw his first surfboard rider: Interview with Bobby Radiasa, Café Batu Jimbar, Sanur, 6 June 2013.

After endless months dodging bullets in the frontlines: Interview with Leonard Lueras, Taman Mertasari, Sanur, 4 June 2013.

Born Warren Anderson in Laguna Beach, California: Interview with Warren Anderson, Seaside Café, Legian, 9 October 2013.

There was a cool scene developing in Kuta: *Thai Stick: Surfers, Scammers, and the Untold Story of the Marijuana Trade*, Peter Maguire and Mike Ritter, Columbia University Press, 2013, p. 40.

California-born filmmaker Bill Leimbach met Boyum: Interview with Bill Leimbach, Avalon Beach, 24 March 2013.

You would have expected the two men to have an immediate bond: Interview with Warren Anderson.

Endnotes

Perhaps one of the reasons for Abdul's animosity: Maguire and Ritter, pp. 44–45.

Elfick came up with an idea: Email exchange with Lissa Coote, 22 November 2013.

'The last place I wanted to travel to was Asia': Interview with Albert Falzon, Noosa Heads, 20 August 2013.

When they paddled out to distant Kuta Reef one day: Interview with Rusty Miller.

And then the surf went flat: Interview with Albert Falzon.

Chapter 13

Kuta also serves as the home of a few score international hippies: Bali Chronicles, Willard A. Hanna, Periplus Editions, 2004 (1976), p. 128.

Around the middle of 1971 a lean, bearded American: Home page, www.GridleyWright.com, Chris Lorenz, 2002.

The London version of Oz, probably the most influential: 'Hippie Fingers in Bali Sugar', Jim Anderson, Oz, no. 43, July/August, 1972.

Sometimes the lines between surf adventurers and hippies: Slightly Dangerous, John Ogden, Cyclops Press, 2012, pp. 50–51.

Ogden later wrote: ibid.

Not all the Australian hippies arrived on the bemo *in the sky*: Interview with Mark Keatinge, Sanur, 23 May 2013.

A couple of months after the Kimbala *limped into Benoa Harbour*: Interview with Lawrence Blair, Kumala Pantai Hotel, Legian, 11 October 2013.

By the mid-1970s there were even more hippies in Bali: Interview with Vitek Czernuszyn, Point Piper, 26 November 2013.

The junkies gravitated to safely isolated outposts: Interview with Jean Lane, TJs Mexican Restaurant, 4 October 2013.

Chapter 14

The consistency and quality of Bali's waves amazed: 'A Place of Challenge', Bill Boyum, The Surfer's Journal, vol. 2, no. 1, 1993, pp. 108–25.

Endnotes

Laverty made a solo recon trip to Java: Thai Stick: Surfers, Scammers, and the Untold Story of the Marijuana Trade, Peter Maguire and Mike Ritter, Columbia University Press, 2014, p. 50.

Bill Boyum has about three or four different versions: Interview with Warren Anderson, Seaside Café, Legian, 9 October 2013.

Again, the circumstances surrounding Bob Laverty's death: Boyum, pp. 108–25.

Before departure, Ritchie and Chidgey had a blow-up: Interview with Mitchell Rae, Nusa Dua Beach Grill, Nusa Dua, 6 October 2013.

Falzon's Morning of the Earth *premiered*: Sydney Morning Herald, 27 February 1972, p. 85.

At the end of 1972, after yet another sell-out show: Interview with Dick Hoole, Byron Bay, 13 July 2013.

The 1966 world champion and then guru: Nat's Nat and That's That, Nat Young, Nymboida Press, 1998, pp. 257–67.

Before he had to leave, Lynch managed to spend: Young, pp. 257–67.

The Australian surfers stayed in losmens *along Jalan Pantai*: Interview with Dick Hoole.

On one of their first visits to the Summerhouse: Interview with Dick Hoole.

Lopez and Hakman soon fell into the web: Interview with Warren Anderson.

As a sideline to his photography, Hoole: Interview with Dick Hoole.

Mexican Sumpter recalls: 'It started out: Interview with David Mexican Sumpter, Byron Bay, 13 July 2013.

Hoole says: 'We began to get very close to the people: Interview with Dick Hoole.

Grajagan was back on the radar in 1974, with Abdul skippering: Interview with Warren Anderson.

Chapter 15

The expats who made their lives and businesses in Bali: Interview with Dick Hoole, Byron Bay, 13 July 2013.

Endnotes

Robert had left school in 1970 and apprenticed: Interview with Robert Wilson and Stephen Palmer, Bukit Peninsula, 2 May 2013.

Sydney surfer and advertising cadet Peter Neely: Email interview with Peter Neely, April 2013.

Here is a last-minute message that will help you on this tremendous adventure: Private correspondence of Robert Wilson.

In 1974 two surfing mates from the NSW Central Coast: Interview with David Thomas, Eungai Creek, NSW, 24 November 2013.

Young English businessman Richard Flax arrived in Bali: Interview with Richard Flax, Nakula Plaza, Legian, 21 May 2013.

Rex Patten, a young engineer from New Zealand: Interview with Rex Patten, Seminyak, 9 October 2013.

Tim Watts got the lowdown on Bali from a girl he'd dated: Interview with Tim Watts, Café Batu Jimbar, Sanur, 23 May 2013.

The sack was filled with 10,000 vanilla beans: 'Same Old Glimpse of Paradise', Leonard Lueras, *The Surfers Journal*, vol. 12, no. 4, 2003, pp. 66–83.

By the middle of the 1980s, Bali had become an epicentre of cool: Interview with Vitek Czernuszyn, Point Piper, Sydney, 26 November 2013.

Chapter 16

Some of the most precious memories of my life: Email interview with Peter Neely, April 2013.

In 1969 Australian publisher Kevin Weldon visited Bali: *Tandjung Sari, A Magical Door to Bali*, Diana Darling, Editions Didier Millet, 2012, p. 154.

When filmmaker Bill Leimbach arrived in Kuta: Interview with Bill Leimbach, Avalon, NSW, 24 March 2013.

Over those four years, Balinese surfing went ahead: 'Balinese Surfer', *Bali Echo*, April 1999.

Australian surfer Peter Neely arrived in 1975 and surfed: Email interview with Peter Neely.

Endnotes

It is difficult to imagine how much the rising tide: 'Tourism in a Balinese Village', Antonia Hussey, 1989, quoted in 'Learning to Surf in Kuta, Bali', Alex Leonard, ANU, 2006.

Despite his many flaws, Mike Boyum became: Interview with Bobby Radiasa, Café Batu Jimbar, Sanur, 6 June 2013.

When Bill Leimbach returned in 1976 to make: Interview with Bill Leimbach.

As well as Bobby Radiasa, the surfers included: Interview with Bobby Radiasa.

Tim Watts had been hired by Boyum: Interview with Tim Watts, Café Batu Jimbar, Sanur, 23 May 2013.

Despite the fact that he had 'a real job in a restaurant': Interview with Bobby Radiasa.

For its second season, Boyum had to compromise: Interview with Tim Watts.

By that time the other boys were having troubles: Interview with Bobby Radiasa.

Back in Bali, the idea of the Bali Surfing Club: Interview with Paul Anderson, Billabong, Kuta Central Plaza, 3 June 2013.

Bradley, like many surfers in Bali in the 1970s: 'Balinese Surfer', *Bali Echo*, April 1999.

In running the day-to-day affairs of the club: Interview with Paul Anderson.

Om Bali and its sister company, Firefly: Interview with Stephen Palmer, Bukit, 2 May 2013.

The Om Bali Pro Am 1980 was meant to be: Interview with Paul Anderson.

The view from the sponsor's tent, had there been one: Interview with Stephen Palmer.

Chapter 17

I mix special drink for you today, Rhonda: Australian television commercial for AAMI Insurance, 2013.

The wiry little man in the white singlet limped: Interview with Ketut Putrawan, Pererenan, 15 May 2013. This account also appeared in slightly different form in *Noosa Today*, 24 May 2013.

Endnotes

Soon after he met Made Ringan, Fly told his friends: Interview with Dick Hoole, Byron Bay, 13 July 2013.

Fly Bradley was a fearless charger in the biggest waves: Email interview with Peter Neely, April 2013.

Jero Asri Kerthyasa, the royal princess of Ubud, throws back her head: Interview with Jero Asri Kerthyasa, Biku, Petitenget, 15 May 2013.

According to Asri, the royal wedding at the Ubud palace: 'An Australian Girl married her prince', *The Australian Women's Weekly*, vol. 46, no. 6, 12 July 1978, pp. 4–5.

The writer, editor and former sculptor Diana Darling: Interview with Diana Darling, Warwick Ibah Villas, Campuhan, Ubud, 21 October 2013.

In my early years in Bali, I remember walking: Fragrant Rice, My Continuing Love Affair With Bali, Janet DeNeefe, HarperCollins, 2003, p. ix.

Born and raised in Melbourne, Janet came to Bali: Interview with Janet DeNeefe, Honeymoon Guesthouse, Ubud, 21 October 2013.

Janet returned to Melbourne after eight months: De Neefe, p. 40.

Chapter 18

Cokorda Nawang lived in the local palace: 'The Weight of Paradise', Diana Darling, Ubud Writers and Readers Festival, October 2012.

According to the Ram Dass website, Alpert's transformation: 'Kuta Is Kool', Kevin Lovett, *Kuta and Kuta*, Bali Purnati Center For The Arts, 2005, pp. 76–95.

I like anthropologist and author Fred Eiseman's: Bali: Sekala and Niskala, Essays on Religion, Ritual and Art, Fred B. Eiseman, Jr, Tuttle, 1990, p. xiii.

Filmmaker Albert Falzon had no idea what: Interview with Albert Falzon, Noosa Heads, 20 August 2013.

David Thomas was already a spiritualist when he arrived: Interview with David Thomas, Eungai Creek, 24 November 2013.

Richard Flax, now an insurance entrepreneur: Interview with Richard Flax, Nakula Plaza, Legian, 21 and 22 May 2013.

Endnotes

Mish Pulling (now Saraswati Mish: Interview with Sarawati Mish Pulling, Kerobokan, 3 June 2013.

One of a small number of Westerners who have: Interview with Mark Keatinge, Sanur, 23 May 2013.

The Balinese authorities had no problems with: Interview with Bill Leimbach, Avalon, NSW, 24 March 2013.

But Ubud had seen nothing yet: 'EPL Fever Hits Bali', Muhammad Cohen, *Asia Times Online*, 18 August 2010.

Ubud has become a haven for middle-aged, single Australian women: Interview with Rio Helmi, Warung Cambodia, Kerobokan, 7 June 2013.

Diana Darling told the Asia Times: 'EPL Fever Hits Bali', Muhammad Cohen, *Asia Times Online*, 18 August 2010.

Consider Morgana Rae, an American woman: www.morganarae.com.

So has modern materialism and Bali's phenomenal growth: Interview with Diana Darling, Ibah, Ubud, 21 October 2013.

David Thomas says: 'Bali is not what it was in: Interview with David Thomas.

Diana Darling has a more positive view: Interview with Diana Darling.

Chapter 19

Bali today is you buy the largest piece of land you can afford: Stuart Membrey, quoted by Vitek Czernuszyn, Interview Point Piper, 26 November 2013.

Expat businessman and mystic Stephen Palmer is showing us: Interview with Stephen Palmer, Padang Padang, Bukit, 11 October 2013.

The first expats of the modern (post-revolution) era were artists: *Tandjung Sari, A Magical Door to Bali*, Diana Darling, Editions Didier Millet, 2012, p. 52.

In 1971, in response to the 1969 opening of the Ngurah Rai: *Tourism in South-East Asia*, Michael Hitchcock, Victor T. King, and Michael J.G. Parnwell, eds., Routledge, 1993, p. 79.

Three years later the Indonesian Government sponsored: *Bali, A Paradise Created*, Adrian Vickers, Tuttle, 2012 (1989), p. 257.

Endnotes

And there was clear evidence that this was true: 'Tourism in a Balinese Village', Antonia Hussey, *Geographical Review*, no. 79, July 1989.

But New Zealander Rex Patten claims to have built: Interview with Rex Patten, Seminyak, 9 October 2013.

In 1978 Melbourne party boy and sometime rag-trade retailer: Interview with Malcolm Williams, Pererenan, 15 October 2013.

For a few years, Blue Ocean rocked: Phil Jarratt personal diary, 1983–86, entry 5 September 1984.

Vitek Czernuszyn recalls: 'There was a very strong bond: Interview with Vitek Czernuszyn, Point Piper, 26 November 2013.

Although German graphic designer Hans Hoefer: Interview with Sarita Newson, Kayu Api, Sanur, 26 May 2013.

The only problem was—and this became apparent: 'The smart money heads south', *Stranger in Paradise* blog, Made Wijaya, July 2008.

As Tommy Suharto and other unscrupulous developers: *The Cultural and Environmental Politics of Resort Development in Bali*, Carol Warren, Murdoch University, 1996, no page numbers.

Although they had their own minor league plans: Email interview with Peter Neely, April 2013.

The Bukit really came of age: Wijaya, 2008.

Chapter 20

I couldn't believe: Interviews with Wayan Agus Parwita, Umah Kembar, Pererenan, May/June 2013.

It was after midnight when Richard Flax drove home: Interview with Richard Flax, Nakula Plaza, Legian, 21 May 2013.

Unable to sleep, Alison Chester sat up through the early-morning: Interview with Alison Chester, Jodie O'Shea Orphanage, Benoa, 3 October 2013.

Saraswati Mish Pulling was woken with a start: Interview with Saraswati Mish Pulling, Kerobokan, 3 June 2013.

Endnotes

Hung-over and emotionally drained: Interview with Tony Eltherington, Padang Padang, 14 May 2013.

Within forty-eight hours of the Kuta bombings, Richard Flax's: Interview with Richard Flax.

Flax later wrote: 'Compassion blended with tragedy: 'Paradise Found', Richard Flax, *Kuta and Kuta*, Bali Purnati Center For the Arts, 2005, p. 48.

The bombings of October 2002, which ultimately claimed: Interview with Jero Asri Kerthyasa, Biku, Petitenget, 15 May 2013.

Businessman Stephen Palmer recalls: 'The entire island: Interview with Stephen Palmer, Bukit Peninsula, 2 May 2013.

Tourism and hotel management graduate Wayan: Interview with Wayan Agus Parwita.

While the bombings at Kuta Square and Jimbaran Bay: Interview with Jero Asri Kerthyasa.

Australian expat photographer Jason Childs: Interview with Jason Childs, Café Bali, Seminyak, 29 May 2013.

Paul 'Gringo' Anderson had a regular Saturday: Interview with Paul Anderson, Kuta Central Plaza, 3 June 2013.

Chapter 21

Police say the scant security measures put in place: www.balidiscovery.com, News Update no. 872, 20 May 2013.

First, the good news: 'Is Bali Doing as Well as it Should Be?', Lia Collinson, www.abc.net.au, 15 May 2012.

Now the bad news: Interview with Rio Helmi, Warung Cambodia, 7 June 2013.

Even some of the solutions are part of the problem: 'Benoa Environmental Threat', *Jakarta Post*, 7 May 2013.

The carrying capacity of the island has hit critical mass: 'Losing Paradise in Bali', Rio Helmi, *The Huffington Post*, September 2011.

Bali already has too much of just about everything: 'Bali ahead of tourism target', *Jakarta Post*, 27 August 2010.

Endnotes

One of the most astute explanations of the seriousness: *Vanishing Paradise: Planning and Conflict in Bali*, Gusti Ayu Made Suartika, University of NSW, 2005, p. 26.

Rio Helmi writes: 'The most bitter feuds in Bali: Helmi, *Huffington Post*.

In January 2013, a major feature in The Australian*'s*: 'Shadows over paradise', Deborah Cassrels, *The Australian*, 19 January 2013.

According to a report by the Japan International: Collinson.

Most of the hotel water comes from artesian wells and bores: 'Relentless tourism spawns trouble in paradise', Michael Bachelard, *The Age*, 5 May 2013.

So yes, it's a 'dysfunctional urban mess', as one former: Interview with Vitek Czernuszyn, Point Piper, NSW, 26 November 2013.

Chapter 22

Some of the footage is almost hard to believe: *TV Tonight* blog, David Knox, 5 April 2014.

The Bali exposé has been a hardy perennial: *The Dark Side of Paradise*, Denholm Hitchcock, Nine Network, July 2013.

Drawn together in sadness and comfort, the bombing volunteers: Interview with Alison Chester, Jodie O'Shea Orphanage, Benoa, 3 October, 2014.

In 2010 the Bali Advertiser *newspaper reported*: 'Bali's Orphanage Scams', *Bali Advertiser*, July 2010.

He recalls: 'It was a household of three women and me: Interview with John Fawcett, Sanur, 27 May 2013.

Matt George is pacing up and down in his shabby little office: Interview with Matt George, *Surf Time* offices, Kuta, 28 May 2013.

Half a dozen years ago, veteran Noosa (Queensland) waiter: Interview with Johnny Blundstone, Bali Eco Stay, 14 May 2011, published in part in *The Weekend Australian*, 'Travel and Indulgence', 6 September 2011.

Chapter 23

It should be clear by now that the oft-repeated question: 'Cultural Tourism in Bali', Michel Picard, *Indonesia*, no. 49 (April 1990), pp. 37–74.

Endnotes

Out in the line-up, my friend Monty: Interview with Jennine and Steve Montell, Canggu, 4 June 2013.

Humphrey, a photographer and filmmaker: Interview with Dustin Humphrey, Deus Temple of Enthusiasm, 19 October 2013.

Lorca Lueras was just four years old: Interview with Leonard Lueras, Mertasari, Sanur, 4 June 2013.

Lorca's earliest memories of life in Bali: Interview with Lorca Lueras, Blue Ocean, Seminyak, 5 June 2013.

Many of Bali's international children: Interview with Luca de Coney, Ombak Café, Pererenan, 19 October 2013.

Epilogue

In Indonesia, where Jokowi's reintroduction: 'Australia lacks cultural competence', Pierre Marthinus, *Jakarta Post*, 5 May 2015.

A few weeks before Jokowi took office: Indonesian foreign policy under President Jokowi, Aaron L Connelly, Lowy Institute, October 2014.

One thing that Western nations fail to understand: *Jakarta Post*, 6 May 2015.

While so far there has been no indication: Swellnet.com, 30 March 2015.

Trying to hose down the hysteria: www.Balidiscovery.com, 2 April 2015.

These are strange days in Bali: 'Bali Booms … Expat Residents Tremble', *Bali Advertiser*, 15–29 April 2015.

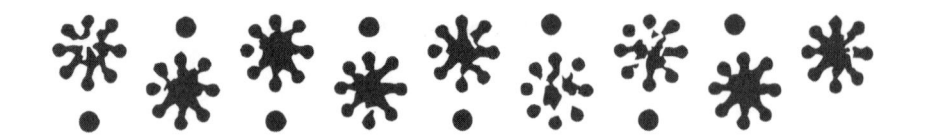

Acknowledgements

For this, my fifth book with Hardie Grant, I am again fortunate to have had the same winning team in my corner. Publisher Fran Berry has been my first point of contact, and is always ready to listen to an idea, and even more importantly, to guide it down the rocky road to publication, like some wonderful but wayward child. In addition, non-fiction editor Rose Michael and editor Alexandra Nahlous have again been firm but fair, allowing the writer the odd indulgent flourish, but reining him in where necessary.

For my part, I don't think I've ever enjoyed researching and writing a book as much as this one. After a forty-year love affair with the subject, I have had many months of pleasure tracking down the myths and legends of Bali, its fabulous cast of characters and its fascinating history. And for once in my life, I have been able to spend months and months in Bali without feeling guilty about it.

Most of the research and some of the writing of *Bali: Heaven and Hell* have been done in Bali, and our long stays there would not have been possible without the generosity of our dear friend Sue Cummings, who has made a room available in her villa in Pererenan whenever we have needed it. She has also shared in many of the joys of discovery as I have endeavoured to peel back a few layers of the Bali onion, always an enthusiastic sounding board. We have been enjoying Bali with Sue for more than thirty years, and hopefully we've got another thirty in us. Likewise, our Bali experiences with Pererenan neighbour and Sue's partner in Umah Kembar, Bliss Swift, go back a long way, her Indonesian is far superior to ours, and she made available her considerable library of Bali books. Thank you, Bliss.

Wayan Agus Parwita started out as my driver for this project, on loan from Sue Cummings. I already knew that he was a smart and savvy young man who would be a big help in translating and explaining cultural issues.

Acknowledgements

I had no idea how involved he would become in the research, sharing his own family story, suggesting many interview subjects, and helping fill in the gaps in my understanding of contemporary Balinese society. Wayan, his wife, Made, and small children, Putu and Kadek, are the future of Bali, and I am so grateful that they are part of this book.

The story of surf exploration in Bali and the surf colonisation of Kuta and the Bukit is told here through many voices, but I particularly want to thank Robert Wilson and Stephen Palmer for their strong support of this project, and my friend Norm Innis for bringing us together. In the 1980s I met a man called Richard Flax who let me leave a surfboard at his compound in Legian, saving me the effort of bringing one with me each trip. It was an important piece of Bali's surfing history, being the board on which Terry Fitzgerald won Bali's first professional surfing contest in 1980, but I left it at Richard's too long and it died of dings. Richard has made a career out of helping people in Bali and I am again indebted to him for giving generously of his time and his vast knowledge of the island.

Dustin Humphrey at Deus Ex Machina has also been generous in his support, providing everything from office backup at the Temple of Enthusiasm to surfboard loans. And on a final surfing note, my old friend Dick Hoole has been incredibly generous not only with his immense knowledge of early surf days in Bali, but in finding and scanning so many important images from his vast library.

My many secondary sources are credited elsewhere, but special mention here to a few people: Made Wijaya's *Stranger in Paradise* blog posts are frequently outrageously funny, but they also offer keen insight into the relationships between Balinese and *bule*s; Dick Lewis's balisurfstories.com has some lovely material about many aspects of Bali (not just surf) that you won't find anywhere else; Rio Helmi's blogs on *The Huffington Post* cut right to the chase on Bali's social issues in graceful, witty prose; and Diana Darling's *Painted Alphabet* is simply the best fiction I have read on Bali, while her more recent articles and lectures offer new insights delivered with great wit and charm.

Finally, my family has again been my rock. Special thanks to my wife, Jackie, who has been with me all the way on this project, read each chapter draft and made helpful suggestions. And a big hug to my daughters, Ellie, Sophie, and especially Sam, who often had to do my share of our surf festival business because I was having fun in Bali.

PJ

Index

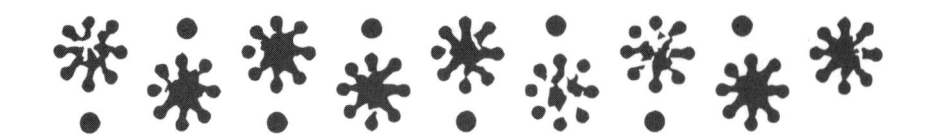

Abbott, Tony, 285–86
ABDA (American, British, Dutch and Australian forces command), 84–87
Abdul. *see* Anderson, Warren 'Abdul'
accommodation, tourist (in Bali)
  inns *(losmens)*, 140, 168–69, 209
  villas, 241, 257–62
  see also hotels (in Bali)
acid (drug), use of, 135, 148, 165, 217–18
adat (Balinese tradition). *see* Balinese tradition *(adat)*
agriculture (Balinese)
  disappearance of, 256–60, 263, 272–73
  exporting of, 187–88
air service to Bali, beginning of, 74
Allen, Belinda, 5–6
Alpert, Dr Richard (Ram Dass), 217–18
Anderson, Jim, 147–49
Anderson, Paul 'Gringo', 199–202, 254, 295
Anderson, Warren 'Abdul', 295
  background, 137
  on Bob Laverty, 138, 163–64
  expeditions to G-Land and, 160–62, 168, 172–73
  on Mike Boyum, 170
  residence built by, 140
Apple Films, 156
art exhibition on Bali (1917), 44
artists, Western (in Bali), 58–60, 64–66
  see also Puri Campuhan

Australia, relations between Bali and, 265–67, 285–88

Babington, Janice. *see* Mantjika, Jan
Badung Strait, battle of, 86
Baldan, Ferry Mursyidan, 292–93
Bali
  Christian missionaries in, 97–99
  communism in, 108–15
  Dutch control of (*see* Dutch)
  expats in (*see* expatriates [in Bali])
  independence movement in, 93–95
  Japanese invasion and occupation of, 85–93
  Majapahit Empire's influence on, 12–14
  monarchy in, 12–14
  relations between Australia and, 265–67, 285–88
  surf culture, development of, 131–40, 142–45, 159–73, 191–98, 200–202
  tourism in (*see* tourism [in Bali])
  trade in (*see* trade [in Bali])
Bali Aga villages, history of, 10–11
Bali and Angkor (Gorer), 70–71
Bali Beach Hotel, 115
Bali bombings (2002). *see* bombings, Bali (2002)
Bali Defence Force (Prajura Corps), 94
Bali Easy Rider Travel Service, 170, 194, 235

Index

Bali Echo, 237
Bali Eco Stay, 276–77
Bali en Lombok (Nieuwenkamp), 58
Bali Hotel, 45, 60–62
Bali Hyatt Hotel, 120
Bali Oberoi Hotel, 124
Bali Surfing Club, 198–200, 202
Balinese art, 65–66, 103
Balinese culture
    expat integration with, 171–72, 182, 277, 280
    spiritual beliefs in, 26, 191, 229, 264
    surf culture introduced to, 191–96, 200–202
    tourism's impact on, 220–21, 226, 255, 257–60, 263, 277
    Western appropriation of, 223–26
    Western depictions of, 17, 43–44, 65, 69–70, 148
Balinese dance, 52, 63, 66
Balinese lifeguards, 190
Balinese music, 59, 62–63, 66
Balinese Surfer (film), 191, 193–96
Balinese surfers, 191–96, 198
Balinese tradition *(adat)*, 256–60, 263, 272–73
banjars (village councils)
    death lists created by, 111
    expat involvement in, 182, 233
    Western influence on, 100–101, 221, 258
Barton, Ralph, 53
Batavia, 16, 18, 20, 33, 88
Bateson, Gregory, 66–67
batik, art of, 177–79, 183–84, 187
battles, 86, 94
Baum, Vicki, 66, 105
Belo, Jane, 62–64
Benoa Basin, pollution in, 256
Bishop, Julie, 285–86
Blair, Lawrence, 154–57, 224
Blair, Lorne, 156, 224
blindness programs (in Bali), 271–72

Blue Ocean Bar, 233–35
Blundstone, Johnny, 275–77
bombings, Bali (2002)
    accounts of, 1–9
    community responses to, 243–51, 254, 267
    economic impact of, 250–51, 253–54
    perpetrators of, 286
bombings, Bali (2005), 253–54
Bonnet, Rudolf, 59, 65–66, 120
Bonnet Studio, rebuilding of, 120–21
books
    on Bali, 49, 53, 66, 210, 213, 224
    on Indonesia, 156
Boxing Day tsunami (2004), 274
Boyum, Bill, 159–60, 163
Boyum, Mike, xiv–xv
    background, 138
    Bali life of, 139, 170
    expeditions to G-Land and, 161, 194–95
    impressions of, 139, 170
    role in community, 126, 190, 193, 198
    surf camp established by, 173, 195–97
Bradley, Kim 'Fly'
    death of, 295
    early surfing days, 166
    life in Bali, 171
    marriage of, 205–6
    as part of bombing relief effort, 248
    role in surf community, 198–200, 202
Bukit Badung Peninsula, 228–30, 232, 237–41
Bulelang, regency of (Bali), 20, 30, 32, 45, 60
bules. *see* expatriates
Bulgari Hotel, 240–41
burning of widows *(suttee)*, 17

Calon Arang (film), 51
Campbell, Shelley, 5–6
camps, surf, 195–98
Campuhan salon. *see* Puri Campuhan

* 325 *

Index

Canggu, 259, 261–62
capital punishment (in Indonesia), 285–89
Carlisle, Chris, 119–20
Chan, Andrew, 285–89
Chaplin, Charlie, 53–56
Chegaray, Jacques, 102–5
Chester, Alison, 5, 245–46, 267–69
Chidgey, David, 165–66
children of expats, 279, 281–84
Childs, Jason, 254
cholera (in Bali), 35
civil wars (in Bali), 33
cleft-lip-and-palate programs (in Bali), 271
clothing trade (in Bali), 177–79, 182–84, 186–89, 246
clubs, surfing (in Bali), 198–200, 202
Coen, Jan Pieterszoon, 16–17
colonialism, Dutch, 33–41
communism (in Bali), 108–15, 148
competitions, surf. *see* surf competitions
Coney, John de, 282–83
Coney, Ketut Luca de, 282–84
Cooney, Stephen, 140, 144
coup, attempted (1965), 110
    see also killings of 1965–1966
Covarrubias, Miguel, 12, 59–60, 62–63, 66
Covarrubias, Rose (Rose Rolanda), 59–60
Cowan, Rosemonde (Rose Rolanda), 59–60
Coward, Noel, 68
culture, Balinese. *see* Balinese culture
culture, surf. *see* surf culture
Czernuszyn, Vitek, 157, 188–89, 235, 237

Dance and Drama in Bali (Spies and Zoete), 66
Dalton, Bill, 236
Darling, Diana (born Pugh), 210–13, 216, 226–27, 295
Darling, John, 211–12, 224
Darsana, Joe, 192
death penalty (in Indonesia), 285–89

deaths, tourist (in Bali), 261, 266
DeNeefe, Janet, 213–15, 296
Denpasar, 37–38, 60–61, 149, 268
Deus Ex Machina Temple of Enthusiasm, 280
development, land (in Bali)
    of Bukit Badung Peninsula, 228–30, 232, 237–41
    lack of regulation in, 258, 259–60
    negative effects of, 255–64
    observations on, 293–94
    residential, 228–30, 232, 241–42, 257–62
Dewa Agung (title of ruler of Klungkung)
    1980 *puputan* and, 38
    cremation ceremony for, 110
    Dutch negotiations with, 18, 33
    greeting of Dutch fleet by, 15
    installment of, 12–14
    Mads Lange and, 12–15, 30–31
    resistance to Dutch rule by, 30, 33, 36–37
DJ Ketut Funky. *see* Putrawan, Ketut Gede
Doojiwaard, Willem, 59
Dora, Miki, 165
Drake, C.L., 59
Drake, Sir Francis, 14
drugs (in Bali)
    foreigners' use of, 147–50, 217–18
    legal consequences, 279, 286
    opium, 17, 27–28, 34–36, 38
    smuggling, 152–53, 160, 164–66, 290–93
    see also opium
Dutch
    as colonialists, 33–41
    first contact between Balinese and, 15–17, 19
    military interventions by, 30–31, 33, 37–38, 94–95
    and missionaries, 98–99

✳ 326 ✳

Index

negotiations between Balinese rajas and, 18, 20–21, 30
negotiations between Sukarno and, 95
opium trade and, 34–36
return to Bali in 1946 by, 93–95
sovereignty recognised by, 95
Dutch East India Company (VOC), 16–18
Dutch East Indies, tourism in, 42–57
Dutch Ethical Policy, 39–41
Dutch Royal Packet Navigation Company (KPM), 42–43, 45

Eat, Pray, Love (Gilbert), 224–25
Eck, Reverend R. van, 98
eco-tourism, 275–77
economic conditions (in Bali)
  impact of bombings on, 250–51, 253–54
  statistics, 193, 255
  under Sukarno's presidency, 102, 109–10
  tourism's impact on, 193, 255, 257, 260
Eisman, Fred, 218
Eka Dasa Rudra, 106–7
Elenberg, Joel, 210–11
Elfick, David, 140–42, 145
Ellis, Rennie, 241
Eloso, Marta, 282
Eltherington, Tony 'Doris', 4, 248, 296
energy consumption (in Bali), 264
Ennis, Reverend, 98
environment, natural (in Bali)
  attempts to protect, 275–77, 282
  tourism's impact on, 256, 263–64
executions (in Indonesia), 285–89
expatriates (in Bali)
  in the 1930s, 57–72
  children of, 279, 281–84
  contributions of, 243–51, 254, 267–69, 271–77
  cultural integration by, 171–72, 182, 277, 280
  export businesses of, 177–80, 182–84, 186–88
  Kuta community of, 136–40
  leaseholding laws and, 290–93
  in mixed marriages, 129–30, 204–206, 207–10, 212–15, 223
  publications for, 236–37
  residences built for, 140, 228–30, 232, 241–42, 257–62
  spiritual experiences of, 218–22
  see also hippies (in Bali)
expeditions, early European, 14–16
export businesses, 177–80, 182–84, 186–88

Falzon, Albert, xi–xiii, 296
  on Bali's spirituality, 218–19
  film career, 141–45
  on Kim Bradley, 166
  magazine work of, 140, 237
famines (in Indonesia), 110
fashion trends (in Bali), 188–89
Fawcett, John, 256, 269–73
films
  on Balinese spirituality, 224
  early depictions of Bali in, 50–54
  on surfing in Bali, 141–45, 166–67, 170, 191, 193–96
Flax, Richard, 296
  arrival and settlement in Bali by, 181–82
  background, 3
  on Balinese culture, 220–21
  as expat entrepreneur, 182–84
  on night of Bali bombings (2002), 2–4
  as part of bombing relief efforts, 243, 248–50
  production of *Balinese Surfer* and, 193–94
  as support for expatriates, 268
food stalls *(warungs)*, 125–26, 128–30
foreign residents (in Bali). *see* expatriates (in Bali)
Friend, Donald, 119–20, 231

Index

G-Land (surf spot)
  expeditions to, 159–62, 168, 172–73, 185–86, 194–96
  surf camp at, 195–98
Gama, Vasco da, 14
gamelan music, 59, 62–63
Gardner, Eddy (Big Eddy), 168, 169
Garland, Linda, 232, 235
Garrett, Louise. *see* Koke, Louise
Gelgel, 13
genocide
  of 1965–1966, 110–15, 148, 286
  of Bandanese islanders, 16–17
George, Matt, 272–73, 274–275
Gilbert, Elizabeth, 224
Gillespie, Jane. *see* Kerthyasa, Jero Asri (Jane Gillespie)
Goona-Goona, An Authentic Melodrama (film), 51–52
Gorer, Geoffrey, 69–71
Grajagan (surf spot). *see* G-Land (surf spot)
guidebooks on Bali, 235–36
Gunung Agung (volcano), 106–7

Hak Milik (leasehold), 291
Hak Pakai (leasehold), 291
Hak Sewa (leasehold), 291
Hakman, Jeff, 169–70, 173
Hatta, Mohammad, 92–93
health care (in Bali), observations of, 105–6
health programs, expat-founded, 271–72
Helmi, Rio, 119, 237, 255, 257–59, 262–63, 296
Helms, Ludvig Verner, 28–29
Hendriany, Rainy, 292
Hind, Majell, 288
Hindu Dharma, 11
Hinduism (in Bali), 11–13, 17, 218
hippies (in Bali), 136, 146–58
Hirschfeld, Al, 55
History of Java (Raffles), 19
Hoëvell, Wolter Robert van, 39–40

Hoff, Linda vant, 275–76
Hoff, Norm vant, 275–76
Hoole, Dick, xv, 167,168–72
hotels (in Bali)
  on Bukit peninsula, 237–38, 240–41
  early building of, 45, 73–83
  modern and Bali style fusion in, 118–24
  statistics on, 232, 256–57
  in Ubud, 209–10
  see also individual hotel names
Houtman, Cornelise de, 15–16
Hughes, Russell, 134–35
Humphrey, Dustin, 280

Ibah Hotel, 209–10
ikats (weavings), 179–80
independence movement (in Indonesian), 93–95
Indonesia
  communism in, 108–15
  famines in, 110
  revolution in, 93–95
Indonesia: A Traveler's Notes (Dalton), 236
Indonesian Communist Party (PKI), 108–15
Indonesian Democratic Party of Struggle (PDI-P), 288–89
Indonesian Handbook (Dalton), 236
Indonesian nationalism, 91–95
Indonesian Revolution, 93–95
inns *(losmens)*, 140, 168–69, 209
Insel Bali (Krause), 44
International Colonial Exposition (Paris), 63
Interplast, 271
interracial relationships, 68–69
  see also mixed marriages
inventory, land (in Bali), 290–93
investment, foreign (in Bali), 257, 290–93
  attempted regulation of, 290–93
  by the Chinese, 238
  negative effects of, 255–58

✳ 328 ✳

Index

irrigation system, traditional *(subak)*, 263
Islam, 12–13, 285
Island of Bali (Covarrubias), 66
Island of the Demons (Black Magic), 52

Jacobs, Julius, 40
Jaffray, Dr Robert A., 99
Jakarta, 16
   see also Batavia
Japan, occupation of Bali by, 88–93
Java, 85–89, 91, 93, 95
   see also Batavia; Jakarta
Javanese workers (in Bali), 262
Jennings, Dare, 279–80
jewelery trade (in Bali), 182–83
Jimbaran Bay, bombings at, 108–15
Jokowi, President (Joko Widodo), 286–89

K3ni (Kalompek Karja Krisis Nominee Indonesia), 293
Karangasem, Gusti Wayan Nuray (Nicodemus), 98
Karnanda, Rizani Ida, 198, 202
Kayu Aya Resort, 121–24
Keatinge, Mark, 151–54, 223
Kerthyasa, Jero Asri (Jane Gillespie), 206–10, 250–51, 253–54
Kerthyasa, Tjokorda Raka, 208–10
killings of 1965–1966, 110–15, 148, 286
King, George Peacock, 25, 30
Klungkung, regency of
   1965–1966 killings in, 111–13
   after eruption of Gnung Agung (1963), 106
   Christian missionary's accounts of, 99–101, 104
   civil wars involving, 33
   Dutch attacks of, 31
   puputan at, 38
   see also Dewa Agung (title of ruler of Klungkung)
Kodja Inn, 168–69
Koke, Bob, 75–79, 82, 95–96

Koke, Louise (born Garrett), 75–79, 82
Kol, Henri Hubert van, 36, 40–41
Kompiang, Ida Bagus, 118
Krakatoa Business Centre, 235
Krause, Gregor, 43–44
Kuba Krishna, 157–58
Kunst, Jaap, 59
Kuta (Bali)
   bombings in, 1–9, 243–51, 253–54, 267
   descriptions of, 26–27
   in the early 1970s, 149
   early expat community in, 136–40
   economic shift in, 193
   emergence of surf culture in, 131–40, 142–45, 191–96
   first hotels at, 73–83
   hippie communities in, 136, 157–58
   history of, 26
   Mads Lange in, 25–32
   touristic development of, 231–32
Kuta Beach Hotel, 76–79, 95
Kuta Carnival, 251
Kuta cowboys, 203–4

La Falaise, Henry de, 52, 292–93
land (in Bali)
   certificates for, 228, 238, 291
   laws on ownership of, 290–93
   loss of agricultural, 256–60, 263, 272–73
Lane, Jean, 129, 157–58, 205
Lange, Mads Johansen, 22–25, 26, 27–32
Laverty, Bob, 138, 159–64
Laverty II, Roger, 138
Laverty, Roger M., 138
Le Mayeur, Adrien-Jean, 65, 118
Leary, Timothy, 217
leaseholds (in Bali)
   examples of foreign, 140, 228–30, 232, 241–42
   government regulation of, 290–93
   types of, 291
Legian, 221, 232
Legong: Dance of the Virgins (film), 52–53

Index

Leimbach, Bill, 138, 191, 193–96, 224
Leimbach, Claire, 194
leprosy (in Bali), 105–6
Lewis, Dick, 104, 111–13, 131–32, 135, 296
Lewis, Leila, 296
    background, 100
    early years in Bali, 97, 100–101
    on Gunung Agung eruption (1963), 106–7
    health challenges, 106
    on killings of 1965–1966, 113
    on life under Sukarno presidency, 109
    missionary work of, 99, 104–5
Lewis, Richard (E.) *see* Dick Lewis
Lewis, Rodger, 100, 109, 111–13
Liefrinck, Frederick Albert, 40
lifeguards, Balinese, 190
Lombok, 24
Lombok Wars, 25
Lombok Strait, battle of, 86
Lopez, Gerry, 169–70
losmens (inns), 140, 168–69, 209
Love and Death in Bali (Baum), 66, 105
Lovett, Kevin, 183, 217–18
LSD. *see* acid (drug), use of
Lueras, Leonard, 136, 281, 296
Lueras, Lorca, 281–82
Lynch, Wayne, 167–68, 169

Made's Warung, 128–30
Magellan expedition, 14
Maguire, Peter, 160, 164
Majapahit Empire, 10, 12–14
Mantjika, Djati, 108–9, 115
Mantjika, Jan, 108–10, 115–16, 296
Mantra, Ida Bagus, 271
Marga, battle of, 94
Markandeya, Maharishi, 10
marriages, mixed, 129–30, 204–10, 212–15, 223
Martyn, Mick, 6–7
Masih, Made, 128–30
Maskell, Gary, 151, 153

Matahar Hotel, 119–20
Mataram Empire, 12–13
McCartney, Jason, 6–7
McCoy, Jack, 167, 169
McPhee, Colin, 60–64, 66
Mead, Margaret, 66–67
media portrayals (of Bali), 265–67
Megawati Sukarnoputri, President, 288–89
Mershon, Jack, 64
Mershon, Katharane, 64
military interventions, by the Dutch
    in Bali, 30–31, 33, 37–38, 94
    in Java, 95
Miller, Rusty, 142, 144–45
Minas, M.J., 46–47
missionaries (in Bali), 97–99
    see also Lewis, Leila
mixed marriages, 129–30, 204–10, 212–15, 223
    see also interracial relationships
Mona, Wayan Kaleanget, 153–54
monarchy, history of (in Bali), 12–14
Monroe, James Robert. *see* Anderson, Warren 'Abdul'
Montell, Jennine, 279
Montell, Steve 'Monty', 279–80
Mooi Indië school of painting, 59
Morning of the Earth (film), 141–45, 166–67, 170
Mourant, Frances, 204–5
movies. *see* films
Muller, Peter, 120–22, 124, 231
murders of Bali tourists, 261
Murphy, Heidi, 261
Music of Bali (McPhee), 66
Musik des Orients, 62

Narmada, Gde, 192
nationalism, Indonesian, 91–95
native rights (in Bali)
    European advocacy for, 39–41
Natour Beach Hotel, 132

Index

natural disasters (in Indonesia), 269, 274
Neely, Peter, 192–93
Negus, George, 265
New Order, 114–15, 117, 146
Ngurah Rai International Airport, 134, 231
Ni Polok, 65, 118
Nieuwenkamp, Wijnand Otto Jan, 44, 58
nominee crisis, 290–93
North, Denni, 261
Nusa Dua, development of, 232, 237–38
Nusakambangan Island, 285–86

Oberoi, Biki, 124
O'Donnell, Amber, 5–6
Ogden, John, 149–51
Om Bali Clothing Company, 178, 200–201
Om Bali Pro Am (1980), 200–202
opium
    Balinese use of, 17, 27–28, 34–36
    Dutch monopoly of, 27, 34–36, 38
opiumregie, 34–36
orphanages (in Bali), 268–69
Osborn, Charles, 121–22
O'Shea, Jodie, 246–47, 267
Our Hotel in Bali (Koke), 76
Oz (magazine), 147

Paddy's Pub, 6–7
pagi sore (dying technique), 183–84
painters, Western (in Bali), 58–59, 65
paintings of Bali, 58
Palmer, Stephen, 297
    Bali's spiritual influence on, 221–22
    business ventures of, 177–79
    development built by, 228–30
    early surfing days, 174–75
    response to Bali bombings (2002), 7–8, 251
    as sponsor of Om Bali Pro Am (1980), 200–201
Pandy, Jimmy, 118, 231
Partai Nasional Indonesia (PNI), 92

Parwita, Wayan Agus, 1, 251–53, 297
pasanggrahan (rest houses), 45
Patimah, Mah, 45–46
Patten, Rex, 184, 197, 232
PDI-P (Indonesian Democratic Party of Struggle), 288–89
Pearsen, Murial Stuart (K'tut Tantri). *see* Tantri, K'tut (Murial Stuart Pearsen)
Pendidikan Nasional Indonesia (PNI), 92
photographs of Bali, 43–45
PKI (Indonesian Communist Party), 108–15
political parties (Indonesian), 92
pollution (in Bali), 256, 275, 282
Poppies Restaurant (Bali), 127–28, 169
population, Bali, 26–27, 193, 256
Portuguese traders, history of, 14–15
Powell, Hickman, 47–49
Prajura Corps (Bali Defence Force), 94
Pratten, John, 132–34
prisons, Indonesian, 285–86
property ownership laws (in Bali), 290–93
prostitution (in Bali), 102
Pugh, Diana. *see* Darling, Diana (born Pugh)
Pulling, Saraswati Mish, 222, 247–48, 250
puputan (ritual suicide), 37–38, 58, 66, 105
Puri Campuhan
    decline of, 71, 83
    establishment of, 50
    life at, 67–68, 77
    sexual exploits at, 71
    visitors to, 52, 55–56, 67–68, 77
Putrawan, Ketut Gede, 203–5, 260

Quest for Healing (film), 224

Radiasa, Wayan 'Bobby', 132, 135, 193–98, 297
Rae, Mitchell, 164–66
Rae, Morgana, 225–26
Raffles, Thomas Stamford, 19
Rai, I Gusti Ngurah, 94

Index

rajas (Balinese rulers)
    claim to salvage rights, 36–37
    Dutch defeat of, 37–39
    European alliances with, 24, 25
    negotiations with Dutch, 18, 20–21, 30
    resistance to Dutch colonialism by, 30–31, 33–34, 36–38
    wars between, 25
Ram Dass, 217–18
Rasmussen, Ricky, 197, 201
real estate development (in Bali). *see* development, land (in Bali)
Reed, Spencer, 105–6
reef rights *(tawan karang)*, 29–30
religions, Eastern
    Western adoption of, 216–20, 223
religious beliefs (in Indonesia), 11–13, 17, 218, 285
rest houses *(pasanggrahan)*, 45
restaurants (in Bali), 124–30, 157–58, 169, 232–35
Revolt in Paradise (Tantri), 76
rice fields, 256–60, 263, 272–73
rice trade, history of, 24–25, 29
Ring of Fire (Blair), 156
Ringan, Made, 205–6, 295
Ritter, Mike, 160, 163–64, 173
ritual suicide *(puputan)*, 37–38, 58, 66, 105
Rolanda, Rose (Rosemonde Cowan), 59–60, 62
Roosevelt, Andre, 47, 49–52
Rose Rolanda (Covarrubias, Rose), 59–60
Royal Batavian Society for the Arts and Sciences, 39
Ruins of Den Pasar (Nieuwenkamp), 58
rulers, Balinese. *see* rajas (Balinese rulers)

salon, Campuhan. *see* Puri Campuhan
salvage rights, Bali's claim to, 36–37
Sanur, 64–65, 117–18, 231
Sari Club, 6
Sarinbuana Lodge, 275–76
Schwartz, H.J., 36

Scidmore, Eliza, 43, 57
Segara Beach Hotel, 118
Segara Village Hotel, 118
Sembiran (Bali), history of, 10–11
settee (widow burning), 34
settee (widow burning), 17
Sharp, Bill, 274
Shearer family, 183–84
Singer, Brian, xiii–xv
slave trade, 17–18
smallpox (in Bali), 34–35
smuggling, drug, 152–53, 160, 164–66, 290–93
Snitcherling, Tony Wayne. *see* Hughes, Russell
Soesetio, Oemaiati 'Tatie', 119
South East Asia on a Shoe String (Wheeler and Wheeler), 236
sovereignty contracts, 30
sovereignty, Indonesian (1949), 95
spice trade, Eastern, 14
Spies, Walter
    arrest of, 71
    early life, 49–50
    influence in Balinese art community, 50–52, 55, 58, 62–63, 65–66, 77
    internment and death of, 81–82
    see also Puri Campuhan
Sri Kumala (shipwreck), 37
Stanton, Terry, 123
Starr, Ringo, 156
Steenbergen, Peter, 129
Strasser, Rolland, 59
Suara Segara Hotel, 80–81, 83
subak (irrigation system), 263
Suharto, Hutomo Mandala Putra (Tommy), 238–40, 286
Suharto, President
    killings of 1965–1966 under, 110–15, 118, 286
    tourism and development under, 115, 117, 201, 231–32
suicide, ritual *(puputan)*, 37–38

Index

Sukarno, President
  arrests of, 92, 95
  as art aficionado, 120
  background, 91
  collaboration between Japan and, 92–93
  conditions in Bali under, 98–104, 108–10
  early political activity, 91–93
  Ganyang Malaysia (Crush Malaysia) campaign, 108–9
  independence movement led by, 93–95
  negotiations between Dutch and, 95
  ousting of, 114
Sukenny, Zenik, 125–28
Sukumaran, Myuran, 285–89
Sumpter, David 'Mexican', xii–xiii, 167, 170, 172
surf camp at G-Land, 195–98
surf competitions
  in Australia, 169
  in Bali, 192, 200–202
surf culture (in Bali), 131–40, 142–45, 159–73, 191–98, 200–202
  see also expatriates (in Bali); individual surfer names
surf spots, discoveries of, 143–44, 159–62
surfers, Balinese, 191–96, 198
surfing clubs (in Bali), 196, 198–200, 202
Suryakusuma, Julia, 289
sustainability, expat emphasis on (in Bali), 275–77, 282
suttee (burning of widows), 17
Suwita, I Nyoman, 251–53

Taffin, Fredo, 228
Tanah Lot, 133–34, 257
Tandjung Sari Hotel, 118–19, 190, 231
Tantri, K'tut (Murial Stuart Pearsen), 51–52, 73–81, 83
taxi business, establishment of (in Bali), 45–47
textile trade (in Bali), 178–80, 187

The Dark Side of Paradise (documentary), 266
The Kris (film), 51
The Last Paradise (Powell), 49, 53
The Painted Alphabet (Darling), 210, 213
Thomas, David, 297
  on Bali's spirituality, 219–20
  blacklisting of, 239
  business ventures of, 179–80
  on Western influence on Balinese culture, 227
Tjetjak Inn, 209
tourism (in Bali)
  in the 1930's, 73–80
  advent of, 42–57
  after anti-communist purges, 115–16, 117
  crime associated with, 262
  deaths associated with, 261, 266
  development related to, 231–32, 237–41, 255–60
  economic impact of, 193, 255, 257, 260
  environmental impacts of, 256, 263–64
  guidebooks for, 235–36
  impact of bombings on, 250–51, 253–54
  master plan for, 231–32
  observations on, 293–94
  spiritual tourism as part of, 216–18, 224–26
  statistics on, 57, 170, 232, 256–57
  sustainable approaches to, 275–77
  see also expatriates; hotels; restaurants
tourist agencies, advent of (in Bali), 115–16
tourist-development zones, 238, 240
Tracks (magazine), xi–xii, 140, 170
trade (in Bali)
  clothing, 177–79, 182–84, 186–89, 188–89, 246
  jewelery, 183
  opium, 34–36
  rice, 24–25, 29

Index

slave, 17–18
textiles, 178–80, 187
vanilla beans, 187–88
wood carving, 182–83, 252–53
traders, foreign
   in Bali, 14–17, 182–84, 186–89
   in Java, 16
tradition, Balinese *(adat)*. *see* Balinese tradition *(adat)*
Troet, Jan, 18
Tuban airfield, 74, 81, 85, 115, 134
Tuuk, Herman van der, 40

Ubud, 224–25
Uluwatu (surf spot)
   Bob Laverty's death at, 162–63
   development around, 201
   discovery of, 143–44
Untung, Lieutenant Colonel, 110

Van Imhoff (POW transport ship), 82
vanilla bean trade (in Bali), 187–88
villas (in Bali), 241, 257–62
violence against foreigners (in Bali), 261
volcanic eruptions (in Bali), 106–7
Vroom, Reverend J. de, 98

Waanders, Bloeman, 34
Wallace, Alfred Russel, 11
Wallace Line, 11
warungs (food stalls), 125–26, 128–30
water (in Bali)
   Balinese tradition and, 191, 263
   shortage of, 256, 263–64
Watson, Geoff, 132–34

Watts, Tim, 185–88, 195–97, 281
Wawo-Runtu, Judith, 104, 118–19
Wawo-Runtu, Wija, 118–20, 190
Weather Underground, 137
weavings, Balinese, 179–80
Weissenborn, Margarethe Mathilde, 44–45
Weldon, Kevin, 190, 231
westerners (in Bali). *see* expatriates (in Bali); tourism (in Bali)
What Really Happens in Bali (television series), 266–67
White, Ian, 233–35
White, Michael. *see* Wijaya, Made
widow burning *(settee)*, 17, 34
Wijaya, Made (Michael White), 151, 153–54, 236, 282, 297
Williams, Malcolm, 233–35
Wilson, Robert, 174–79, 297
Windro, 171–72
Wiranatha, Natalia, 5
Wirinatha, Kadek, 5, 228, 242, 297
Witzig, John, 140
women, Balinese
   restrictions on nudity of, 103
   Western depictions of, 17, 40, 43–44, 52, 65, 69–70
wood carving trade (in Bali), 182–83, 252–53
Wright, Gridley, 146–47
Wyllie, Dave, 179–80, 200, 202, 232

Young, Nat, 167–68

Zoete, Beryl de, 66